Arms, Politics, and the Economy

Arms, Politics, and the Economy

Historical and Contemporary Perspectives

Edited by
ROBERT HIGGS

Foreword by
WILLIAM A. NISKANEN

Independent Studies in Political Economy

HOLMES & MEIER
NEW YORK   LONDON

Published in the United States of America 1990 by
Holmes & Meier Publishers, Inc.
30 Irving Place
New York, NY 10003

The paper used in this publication meets the requirements of the American
National Standard for Permanence of Paper for Printed Library Materials,
Z39.48-1984

Library of Congress Cataloging-in-Publication Data

Arms, politics, and the economy : historical and contemporary
  perspectives / edited by Robert Higgs.
      p.   cm. — (Independent studies in political economy)
   A selection of revised papers originally presented at the Second
Conference on Political Economy, held Oct. 22-23, 1987, at Lafayette
College in Easton, Pa.
   Includes index.
   ISBN 0-8419-1231-9 (alk. paper)
   ISBN 0-8419-1283-1 (pbk., alk. paper)
   1. United States—Defenses—Economic aspects—Congresses.
2. United States—Armed forces—Appropriations and expenditures—
Congresses.   3. Defense contracts—United States—Congresses.
4. Government spending policy—United States—Congresses.   5. United
States. Dept. of Defense—Congresses.   I. Higgs, Robert
II. Conference on Political Economy (2nd : 1987 : Lafayette College)
III. Series.
HC110.D4A79   1990
338.4'76233'0973—dc20   89-32844
                                                                        CIP

Manufactured in the United States of America

The INDEPENDENT INSTITUTE

THE INDEPENDENT INSTITUTE is a tax-exempt, scholarly research and educational organization which sponsors comprehensive studies on the political economy of critical social and economic problems.

The politicization of decision-making in society has largely confined debate to the narrow reconsideration of existing policies, the prevailing influence of partisan interests, and a stagnation of social innovation. In order to understand both the nature of and possible solutions to major public issues, the Independent Institute's studies adhere to the highest standards of independent inquiry and are pursued regardless of prevailing political or social biases and conventions. The resulting studies are widely distributed as books and other publications, and are publicly debated through numerous conference and media programs.

Through this uncommon independence, depth, and clarity, the Independent Institute pushes at the frontiers of our knowledge, redefines the debate over public issues, and fosters new and effective directions for government reform.

Contents

Foreword: The Political Economy of U.S. Defense

WILLIAM A. NISKANEN

One of the most important roles of the federal government is to "provide for the common defense." Our current system of planning and organizing U.S. military forces, however, does not serve us very well. Over the past decade, for example, real defense expenditures increased about 60 percent. Several important elements of U.S. military forces, however, are now smaller or more vulnerable than at the beginning of this record peacetime increase in defense spending, and no dimension of military capability has increased in proportion to the increase in real defense spending. Moreover, the expensive new weapons now in the development and procurement pipeline will probably force a broad reduction in military forces. A huge increase in real defense expenditures, in summary, does not appear to have significantly increased U.S. military capability.[1]

Maybe this should not have been a surprise. The Department of Defense is the third largest planned economy in the world, led only by the total economies of the Soviet Union and the People's Republic of China. All planned economies are grossly inefficient, and Americans have no special advantage in managing a planned economy. Other sectors of the American economy that are primarily organized and/or financed by government have a similarly dismal record. Over the past decade, real expenditures also increased sharply for education and medical care. Real expenditures per student in public primary and secondary schools increased about 40 percent with no significant change in average student performance. Real expendi-

William A. Niskanen is chairman of the Cato Institute, a former member of the Council of Economic Advisers, and a former Director of Special Studies in the Office of the Secretary of Defense.

tures per person for medical care increased about 60 percent with no significant effect on average health status. In each of the defense, education, and medical sectors, a substantial part of the increase in real expenditures was reflected in higher relative prices for the inputs to these services and in expensive new technologies of questionable value. Total U.S. expenditures for defense, education, and medical care are now nearly 25 percent of GNP, and the performance of these sectors merits their description as the stagnant quarter of the American economy.

The specific problems of organizing U.S. defense are not new. Over the postwar years, several major "blue ribbon" commissions have addressed the problems of defense organization and weapons acquisition. The most disturbing observation about the reports of these commissions is that their recommendations are very similar, but each successive commission has not reflected on why the recommendations of the prior commissions were not implemented or were not effective. The most recent Packard Commission, for example, identified six characteristics of an effective weapons acquisition process: "clear command channels, stability, limited reporting requirements, small high-quality staffs, communications with users, [and] prototyping and testing" (from the Kovacic article in this volume). The many able businessmen who have served on these commissions, in effect, have recommended that the Department of Defense operate in ways similar to that of an efficient private firm, but they have not reflected on the conditions that make the "market" for defense lead to very different behavior than that of a private firm.

The primary problem of U.S. defense organizations is that there is no clear separation of the demanders and suppliers of military forces and weapons. Congress, the administration, and the several services jointly determine the demands for military forces. Budgets are then allocated directly to the services, which are responsible for training, equipping, and supplying the forces. An informal "cartel" among the services prevents each service from competing for missions assigned to the other services. The services and the defense contractors jointly determine the characteristics of new weapons. The services then contract with private defense contractors (usually on a negotiated basis subject to intermittent renegotiation) to develop and produce the weapons. The services then have the primary responsibility for testing and evaluating new weapons for which they have contracted. Congress also complicates this process by imposing many constraints on the allocation of spending by type of input and the location of subcontracts and bases.

One group that has almost no input to any stage of this process is the unified and specified commands (the "CINCS"), although they have the primary responsibility for maintaining the mission forces and the conduct of a war. These commands receive no direct budget allocation and have little voice in determining the forces allocated to these commands, the selection of new weapons, or the testing and evaluation of these weapons. In addition, promotions are primarily determined by each service, with little input from the commands. In summary, the commands have the major responsibility for maintaining military capability in each mission, but have very little voice in choosing their forces and weapons or in motivating their personnel.

The major opportunity for improving the performance of the Department of Defense is to change the relative roles of the commands and the services. Most of the defense budget, for example, could be allocated directly to the unified and specified commands. These commands, either separately or jointly, should have their own organizations for testing and evaluating new weapons. The four services would then compete to provide forces, weapons, and supplies to the commands. Most of the service budgets, then, would be channeled through the commands, in contrast with the current system in which budgets are allocated directly to the services and forces are assigned to the commands.

Two changes would be needed to make such a system effective. The "Key West agreement," in effect a cartel to divide missions among the services, should be terminated. Doing so would permit the Army to provide strategic missiles and fixed-wing combat aircraft, the Marine Corps to provide forces to the major regional commands, and the Air Force to compete for the sea-control mission. The promotion system for higher-grade officers should also be changed in order to reward superior performance among officers in the joint commands and to protect them when the priorities of their commands conflict with the interests of their respective services. The Department of Defense Reorganization Act of 1986 was a step in this direction, but its immediate effects are likely to be quite limited.

There is probably no way to make the Department of Defense as responsive and efficient as private firms in competitive markets. Americans, however, should organize defense in a way that they do best, not by trying to make a planned economy more efficient, but by separating the roles of buyers and sellers and increasing the competition among the sellers (both the services and the contractors) in supplying forces and weapons to the mission commands.

A major reorganization of the Department of Defense along the lines suggested deserves careful review, but such a review should not be delayed. A more efficient organization of U.S. defense and, possibly, our national security are at stake.

NOTE

1. For summary and evaluation of the major recent defense buildup, see William A. Niskanen, "More Defense Spending for Smaller Forces: What Hath DoD Wrought?" (Washington: The Cato Institute, Policy Analysis no. 110, July 29, 1988.)

Preface

In 1986 a group of distinguished scholars from across the country began participation in a research project to produce a volume on the political economy of U.S. military spending, procurement, and related activities. Their common interest lay in the complex of institutions, behaviors, and consequences associated with this important and volatile part of our polity and economy. The results of the work have now been completed for publication under the auspices of The Independent Institute and its president, David Theroux.

On October 22–23, 1987, the participating scholars assembled at Lafayette College in Easton, Pennsylvania, for the college's second Conference on Political Economy. Eight research papers (chapters 1, 2, 4, and 6–10 in the present volume) were presented. Each was criticized and discussed at length in sessions of unusual astuteness and camaraderie—surely nothing brings more joy to scholars than a genuinely constructive and cooperative exploration of ideas.

Along with the authors of the papers, many faculty members from Lafayette College—Mike Connell from the Department of Economics, Dick Welch from the Department of History, Jim Lennertz and Lisa Langenbach from the Department of Government and Law—made important contributions to the discussions. Other formal discussants included Dan Klein of New York University, Ted Galen Carpenter of the Cato Institute, and Vince Munley and Ted Morgan of Lehigh University. For financial support of the conference, the participants are grateful to the administration of Lafayette College, led by President David Ellis and Provost Sarah Blanshei.

After the intellectual dust of the conference had settled, the chapters were extensively revised and two additional chapters (3 and 5 in the present volume) were added, one by Jeffrey Hummel and Don Lavoie and another by William E. Kovacic. This volume now presents the completed results. The contributors hope that it will add substantially to greater understanding of that vitally important and devilishly complicated subject, the political economy of American defense.

Introduction: Fifty Years of Arms, Politics, and the Economy

ROBERT HIGGS

For half a century, Americans have devoted substantial political and economic resources to the planning, production, and deployment of military arms. We have maintained, some say, a warfare state alongside our welfare state. Doing so was a novel experience.

Consider the situation in 1939. Then, as always before, the national security of the United States rested primarily on the vast ocean barriers separating the country from any powerful potential adversary. (Neighboring countries in the Western Hemisphere posed little threat.) Given the military technology of the day, European or Asian enemies could scarcely bring much force to bear on Americans residing in the continental territory. To make sure that we would not inject ourselves into other people's quarrels, our foreign policy avoided entanglements. In accordance with this traditional position, membership in the League of Nations had been rejected after World War I. In 1935, 1936, 1937, and 1939, Congress passed neutrality laws to prohibit international transactions that might tend to drag Americans into foreign wars. We belonged to no military alliances; we maintained no military bases in other countries. Should war become unavoidable, America's enormous human, material, and technological resources could eventually be mobilized, as they had been during 1917–18. Barring an actual shooting war, most people viewed the maintenance of large armed forces as politically and economically unwise—a threat to democracy and an unnecessary drain on the taxpayers.

Not everyone agreed with these traditional policies. A few leaders of the armed forces and a few big businessmen, led by Bernard M. Baruch,

Thanks to Charlotte Twight, Ted Galen Carpenter, Dwight Lee, and Gordon Tullock for comments on a previous draft.

worked throughout the interwar years to create plans and institutions for military-industrial cooperation and mobilization. Baruch had headed the War Industries Board during World War I, and his experience as an economic "czar" left an indelible impression on his thinking. He gave encouragement and advice to the assistant secretary of war, who drew up mobilization plans in 1931, 1933, 1936, and 1939. But as Jordan Schwarz shows, the nationalistic planners in Baruch's circle had far more success in domestic policy than in military policy. (See Chapter 1.) As late as 1939, President Franklin D. Roosevelt reacted to the proposals of an ad hoc War Resources Board by disbanding the board and suppressing its report.

The armed forces themselves remained woefully short of men and material. In 1939 the U.S. Army had 190,000 officers and men, making it the world's sixteenth largest, ranking below the armies of Yugoslavia, Turkey, Spain, Romania, and Poland. The U.S. Navy, including the Marines, had a personnel strength of about 145,000.[1] Although both the Army and the Navy had aircraft, there was no separate Air Force. The American fleet was relatively formidable and certain units of the armed forces were in fair shape, but in general America's forces were not only small but ill-equipped and poorly supplied. Against any of the world's leading military powers, they could not have sustained much of a fight. Even had the armed forces themselves been enlarged—the nation did have a huge population to draw on in an emergency—they could scarcely have been equipped to fight in the short run. The nation possessed nothing even approximating an armaments industry. A few Army arsenals and Navy yards plus a handful of private contractors building airplanes on a craft-shop basis—that was about the extent of it. Only with difficulty could one imagine a great nation less prepared to win a world war, or less interested in doing so.

In retrospect it is astonishing how completely and how quickly the old regime disappeared, and how totally the new regime became entrenched and almost unquestioned, at least until the late 1960s. The turning point was 1940. After the breathtaking German victories of the spring offensive, culminating in the fall of France and the near-destruction of the British Army, the U.S. government suddenly decided that the country's defenses must be strengthened as quickly as possible. The first peacetime military conscription act was passed in September 1940. Congress opened the budgetary floodgates. New procedures for dealing with arms contractors were approved: negotiated, as opposed to competitively bid, contracts; cost-plus-fixed-fee compensation; advance and progress payments; tax breaks; government financing of plants and equipment. All these actions had the effect of shifting risk from the contractors to the government, that is, ultimately to the taxpayers. With less risk to bear and an enlarged military market assured, private firms had greater incentive to convert and enlarge their facilities for the production of armaments and related industrial materials. In addition, the War and Navy Departments and the Maritime Commission made major industrial investments on their own accounts, as did the Defense Plant Corporation and other subsidiaries of the depression-spawned Reconstruction Finance Corporation. Many of the government-financed plants were operated by private contractors holding options to purchase the properties on favorable terms after the war.[2]

The military buildup, already well under way when the Japanese attacked Pearl Harbor, accelerated rapidly in 1942 and 1943. The nation performed a series of amazing feats to reallocate the economy's resources to war production. (See table 1.) By the peak in 1944, more than 41 percent of the GNP went for military consumption. The armed forces employed 12 million uniformed personnel, 1.5 million civilians and, indirectly, about 13 million others in war-related industries—altogether more than 26 million workers in a country whose prewar labor force had been only about 56 million. The private share of GNP fell to 54 percent. Over the course of the mobilization and demobilization, 1939–47, military purchases of goods and services cumulated to $2,164 billion (1982 dollars) in an economy only about a third as large as today's. Never before or since has the United States built anything even approximating the awesome garrison economy of World War II.[3]

During 1945–47, as U.S. demobilization proceeded rapidly, the wartime Grand Alliance of nations opposing Nazi Germany was breaking down and the seeds of the Cold War were sprouting. Besides disagreeing over postwar arrangements for Eastern Europe and especially Germany, the former allies came into conflict over the Soviet occupation of northern Iran, the Soviet attempt to secure naval bases in Turkey, and the civil war between

Table 1. Indices of Mobilization, 1939–47

Year	Active Duty Military Personnel (millions)	Military Purchases (billions of 1982 $)	Military Share of GNP (percent)	Government Nonmilitary Share of GNP (percent)	Private Share of GNP (percent)
1939	0.3	10.2	1.4	13.5	85.1
1940	0.5	17.7	2.3	11.9	85.8
1941	1.8	100.0	11.0	8.9	80.1
1942	3.9	336.1	31.1	6.6	62.3
1943	9.0	528.5	41.4	4.7	53.9
1944	11.5	571.9	41.4	4.5	54.1
1945	12.1	469.4	34.5	4.4	61.1
1946	3.0	84.5	7.7	6.0	86.3
1947	1.6	45.3	4.3	7.0	88.7

Sources: Military personnel from U.S. Bureau of the Census, *Historical Statistics of the United States, Colonial Times to 1970* (Washington: Government Printing Office, 1975), p. 1141; other series calculated from data in U.S. Council of Economic Advisers, *Annual Report* (Washington: Government Printing Office, 1987), pp. 244–48.

Communists and anti-Communists in Greece. Emboldened by their sole possession of atomic weapons, American leaders pressured the Soviets to leave Iran and abandon the attempt to gain control of the Dardanelles. Aid was given to anti-Communist forces in Greece. In 1947 President Harry Truman declared what would become known as the Truman Doctrine, an open-ended pledge to assist virtually any government threatened by Communists, whether from within or without.

To secure its position in Europe, the United States devised the Marshall Plan and entered into the North Atlantic Treaty, America's first formal military alliance since the one with France during the War of Independence. In 1948 the Communist coup in Czechoslovakia prompted a brief but serious war scare, which the Truman administration used as a lever to pry enlarged military appropriations out of Congress. The Berlin crisis of 1948, the establishment of NATO in 1949, and the outbreak of the Korean War in 1950 tipped the balance permanently in favor of a policy of global containment and deterrence of the Soviet Union.

Henceforth there would be no distinct peacetime and wartime. The Soviets quickly developed nuclear weapons. Superpower hostility, probing, and confrontation, backed by long-range bombers, intercontinental ballistic missiles, and missile-carrying submarines, made instantaneous world war an ever-present possibility. American policy thereafter would be premised on the permanent maintenance of large military forces, constantly ready to deter or resist Soviet or Soviet-sponsored aggression wherever it might occur. After the Korean War ended in 1953, the United States continued to devote unprecedented "peacetime" resources to military purposes. Over the entire period 1948–86, real military purchases of currently produced goods and services cumulated to a total of $6,316 billion (1982 dollars), averaging about $162 billion per year or 7.6 percent of GNP. While real military outlays increased over the long run, the GNP increased somewhat faster, so the trend of the military share was downward. Substantial fluctuations occurred in military spending, as major buildups took place during 1950–53, 1965–68, and 1978–87. (See figure 1).[4] Cumulative military spending during 1987–89 alone came to more than $1 *trillion* (1982 dollars).

Such immense spending generated considerable employment, a matter of great concern to generations whose attitudes had been shaped by the mass unemployment of the Great Depression. Total defense employment (uniformed military personnel plus Department of Defense [DOD] civilian jobs plus defense-related jobs in industry) stood at about 3 million during the postwar trough of the late 1940s. The Korean War buildup pushed the total to 9.5 million, of which more than 4 million were in industry. Defense employment declined after the Korean War but remained in the range of about 6–8 million during 1954–71, with 2–3 million of the total in industry. Defense jobs hit their post–Korean War low during the 1970s, when they remained fairly steady at about 5 million total, with somewhat fewer than 2

million in industry. The defense buildup after 1978 pushed total employment to some 6.6 million in 1986, divided about equally between DOD
(uniformed personnel and civilians) and defense-related industry.[5]

From these data one may infer that defense spending now generates
fewer jobs per (real) dollar spent than it used to generate. This trend reflects
the changing character of defense purchases. Relatively less now goes for
ordinary support items (e.g., food, clothing, and housing for troops),
ammunition, and vehicles; relatively more goes for research, computers and
software, and high-tech weapons such as ballistic missiles, nuclear submarines, and high-performance aircraft. Defense employment has become
more the preserve of the upper middle class, including many scientists,
engineers, and technicians, and less the domain of mass-production
operatives and unskilled laborers.

One thing has remained the same: defense-related jobs have served
continually as a major determinant of congressional defense decisions.
(James Lindsay gives the arguments pro and con and provides a thorough
survey of the literature in chapter 8, below.) It is a rare member of Congress,

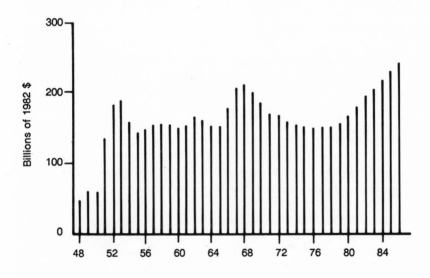

Figure 1. Real Military Purchases (billions of 1982 $), 1948–86

Source: Calculated from nominal-dollar purchases and GNP deflator in U.S. Council of Economic Advisers, *Annual Report* (Washington, D.C.: Government Printing
Office, 1987), pp. 249, 252.

whether liberal or conservative, who would forgo an opportunity to attract and keep defense-related employment in his or her district. Resistance to base closures, in particular, has prompted the most exquisite legislative maneuvers. So iron-clad did this legislative obstruction become that for more than a decade after 1977 the Department of Defense found it impossible to close any large U.S. base, no matter how obsolete or otherwise unwarranted. (See Charlotte Twight's analysis in chapter 10, below, and related discussion by James Lindsay and Kenneth Mayer in chapters 8 and 9.) Special legislation enacted late in 1988 promised to break this resistance, but the effectiveness of the new system for base closures remains to be established, and no one should be surprised if it is somehow sabotaged. The limited number of bases selected for closure during the next five years shows how strong the congressional urge to preserve existing jobs remains.

Although military base employment has been the most jealously guarded, the defense-related employment of private arms contractors has scarcely been neglected. Of course, more than jobs is at stake here. Billions of dollars of corporate profits, along with millions for congressional honoraria and campaign contributions, also enter the political calculus.

In fiscal year 1985, for example, DOD entered into prime contracts (counting only those over $25,000) with a total value of $150.7 billion. Eleven companies received prime contract awards of $2 billion or more, ranging from McDonnell Douglas with $8.9 billion to Martin Marietta with $2.7 billion. (See table 2.) These eleven firms accounted for a total of $55 billion, or more than 36 percent of the total value of prime contract awards in FY 1985.[6] This distribution is typical. Usually the top 100 prime contractors receive 65–75 percent of the total prime contract dollars; the top ten firms get about a third of the business. The distribution was almost identical during World War II and, despite minor fluctuations and yearly turnover among the constituent firms, has remained remarkably stable ever since.[7]

Scarcely a day passes that the big arms companies do not appear in the headlines. Often the news is bad.[8]

- General Dynamics Underestimated Cost of Submarines on Purpose, Report Says
- Rockwell Pleads Guilty to Charge of False Billing
- McDonnell Douglas to Pay $1.6 Million to Settle U.S. Case
- Northrop Corp. Faces New Accusations of Falsifying Tests of Missile Equipment
- Litton Pleads Guilty to Defrauding U.S. on Pentagon Work, Will Pay $15 Million
- TRW Says Its Overcharges to Pentagon Range from $10 Million to $23 Million

Table 2. Leading Prime Defense Contractors, Fiscal Year 1985

COMPANY	AWARDS ($ billions)	MAJOR PRODUCTS
1. McDonnell Douglas Corp.	8.9	F-18 Hornet, F-15 Eagle, AH-64 Apache, KC-10 Extender, and AV-8 Harrier aircraft, Tomahawk and Harpoon missile systems.
2. General Dynamics Corp.	7.4	F-16 Falcon fighter aircraft. Nuclear submarines. Tomahawk, Sparrow, Stinger and RIM-66 standard missile systems. M-1 and M-60 tanks. MK-15 close-in weapon system.
3. Rockwell International Corp.	6.3	B-1 bomber and M&R of C-130 Hercules aircraft. MX, Navstar, Hellfire, and Minuteman missile systems. Various electronics and communication equipment.
4. General Electric Co.	5.9	T-700, J-85, J-79, and TF-34 turbofan and turbojet engines. Nuclear reactors for submarines. Underwater sound equipment. Transmission components for M-2 infantry fighting vehicles. RDT&E for missile and space systems.
5. The Boeing Co., Inc.	5.5	Electronic countermeasures and aircraft accessories for B-1 bomber. M&R, miscellaneous equipment, management services, etc., for H-46 Sea Knight, B-52 Stratofortress, C-135 Stratolifter,

Table 2 *(continued)*

COMPANY	AWARDS ($ billions)	MAJOR PRODUCTS
		E-3A, and A-6 Intruder aircraft. CH-47 Chinook helicopter. MX missile. Miscellaneous electronics and communication equipment.
6. Lockheed Corp.	5.1	C-5 Galaxy, C-130 Hercules, and P-3 Orion aircraft. RDT&E for missile and space systems and electronics and communication equipment. Operation of government electronic and communications facility.
7. United Technologies Corp.	3.9	F-100 and TF-30 aircraft engines. UH-60 Blackhawk, CH-53 Sea Stallion and SH-60 Seahawk helicopters.
8. Howard Hughes Medical Institute	3.6	Maverick, Tow, Phoenix, and AMRAAM missile systems. Radar equipment and guided missile systems for F-14, F-15, F-18 and A-6 aircraft. Optical sighting and ranging equipment for M-1 tank. RDT&E for electronics and communication equipment and missile and space systems.
9. Raytheon Co.	3.0	Patriot, Sparrow, Hawk, Sidewinder, and Pershing missile systems. RDT&E electronics and communication equipment.

Table 2 *(continued)*

COMPANY	AWARDS ($ billions)	MAJOR PRODUCTS
10. Grumman Corp.	2.7	F-14 Tomcat, E-2 Hawkeye, EA-6B Prowler, A-6 Intruder, and C-2 Greyhound aircraft. RDT&E for weapons, aircraft, and electronics and communication equipment.
11. Martin Marietta Corp.	2.7	Pershing, Hellfire, and Patriot missile systems A-64 Apache aircraft. Guided missile launchers. RDT&E for MX and Titan missile systems and space transportation systems.

Source: U.S. Department of Defense, Directorate for Information Operations and Reports, *100 Companies Receiving the Largest Dollar Volume of Prime Contract Awards, Fiscal Year 1985* (Washington: Government Printing Office, 1985), pp. 4–6.

No wonder the public doubts the claim that the big weapons firms are managed by dedicated patriots. The spare-parts scandal of recent years, featuring stories of $2,043 paid for a 13-cent nut, $1,118 paid for a 31-cent stool cap, $696 paid for a $9 aircraft ashtray, and $670 paid for a $25 aircraft armrest, only added fuel to the fire of public indignation and outrage. (One ought to recognize, of course, that these whopping charges resulted largely from the application of bizarre but perfectly legal accounting rules.) In the summer of 1988 an even larger scandal arose as the press began to report on a Justice Department investigation focused on the use (and sale) of insider information by defense consultants, their clients, friends, and confederates.[9] The hackneyed phrase "waste, fraud, and mismanagement" comes easily to mind.

As William Kovacic makes clear in chapter 4 below, these problems—and many others—are not new. In addition to DOD's ongoing internal efforts and Congress's spasmodic actions to fix the defense procurement system, three major studies have been carried out during the post–World War II era by so-called Blue Ribbon Commissions. Oversimplifying just a little, one may say that each study turned up similar problems; each made similar recommendations; and each had little impact on the fundamental structure and functioning of the system. Why so little result? Kovacic argues that part of the problem arises from the failure of each study panel to consider seriously why similar recommendations have proven unavailing in the past and to reconsider its own recommendations accordingly. Moreover, administration officials face incentives that encourage them to opt for quick fixes and to reject solutions promising better results in the longer term— elections are always coming up soon. Hence, little effort goes into monitoring the procurement system to insure that recommended changes are properly implemented. Reforms are announced with a flourish, but too little follow-up occurs. The Pentagon bureaucracy hunkers down and waits for the storm to pass.

Dwight Lee, in chapter 2 below, presents a more abstract argument that may be viewed as extending to its logical limit the kind of argument advanced in Kovacic's case study. The root problem of the military-industrial-congressional complex (hereafter the MICC), Lee argues, is that the existing institutions, with their characteristic incentives and constraints, fail to create a complete correspondence between actions that are self-interested and actions that are in the public interest. Taking the public-choice theoretical view that all actions, whether in economic or political contexts, are narrowly self-interested, Lee supposes that members of the MICC always act accordingly: contractors seek profits; military officers seek rank, pay, and perquisites; members of Congress seek votes. But no one seeks to promote the public interest, because doing so would not make sense when the public's interest is in the creation of a public, or genuinely collective, good.

By the economist's definition, "public goods," if created for anyone, are created for all (within a specified domain); there is no rivalry for their consumption. Deterrence of attacks against the United States, one presumes, is a public good for all residents of the country. But even though every American wants it, no one has a private interest in doing what is required to create it, because whether or not any individual does so, the outcome will be the same. Even if I spend my entire income in attempting to deter my country's enemies, I will have no effect on deterrence; my efforts are infinitesimal. If I shirk my share of payment for the collective effort, holding onto my entire income, I will still have no effect on deterrence; my shirking is also too small to matter. The "rational" thing for me to do is to regard national security as I would regard a state of nature, as wholly beyond my control. I thereby minimize my personal cost/benefit ratio without noticeably affecting the amount of the public good provided, which will be whatever it will be no matter what I do.

According to this line of argument, the *only* economic incentive members of the MICC have to make a contribution to the national defense comes from the privately appropriable benefits—the corporate profits, union wages, military perks, congressional votes, scientific research grants, and so forth. We ought to be glad, Lee argues, that people seek such privately appropriable benefits by engaging in actions that have the *wholly incidental* effect of producing a contribution to the creation of national security.

Further—and here he is sure to ruffle some feathers—if members of the MICC were not doing what they are now doing, at public expense and with a full measure of waste, fraud, and mismanagement, then their portion of the public budget would surely be seized by other political factions whose actions would bring even less benefit to the public and might even harm the public on balance. So, somewhat astonishingly, Lee concludes that the MICC, for all its apparent faults, deserves at least two cheers. We get *some* national defense; it is the *most* we can get, given the existing political institutions; and reforms would only make matters *worse,* because the same argument that applies to members of the MICC applies equally to those who would presume to reform it.

Lee's argument, at the very least, should provoke a deeper analysis of long-standing but superficial criticisms of the MICC. Needless to say, not everyone will be persuaded, much less reassured, by the argument. Some readers may consider it outrageous because of its unrelenting economic reductionism. Whether one is persuaded or not, the argument deserves serious consideration. A compelling refutation, if one can be given, will require a subtle and sophisticated consideration of the role of institutions, information, and ideology in the operation of our political economy.

Chapter 3 by Jeffrey Hummel and Don Lavoie, though written independently, may be read as a response to the challenge posed by Lee's paper. Hummel and Lavoie offer a fundamental reassessment of national defense as the classic example of a public good. They question the presumption that the activities of the U.S. military establishment—or those of any country's military establishment—necessarily provide security for the lives, liberties, and property of the citizens as opposed to protection of the interests of the government in power. They argue that the government's military program may foster as many public-good problems (pro–free loaders) as it solves (contra–free riders). To get to the root of the issue, they step back from the defense question per se to examine how any society contains the potential tendencies of its members toward free-riding behavior of all kinds, from tax evasion to simple dishonesty and immorality. They maintain that the analysis of public-goods problems offered by current public choice theory misrepresents human nature. In particular, it exaggerates the importance of *narrow* self-interest and minimizes or dismisses entirely the importance of ideologically motivated action—that is, self-interest more broadly construed. Hummel and Lavoie conclude that the existing allocation of resources to military activities may be excessive rather than "efficient" (à la Lee) in the existing institutional circumstances.

No matter what one concludes with respect to the "efficiency" of the MICC, it is clear that the defense business is different from the typical commercial business, especially for the major prime contractors. Jacques Gansler and Murray Weidenbaum have catalogued the many unusual aspects of the defense "market," emphasizing the following.

1) The market is monopsonistic, as the government is the only buyer. (During the past twenty years, however, sales to foreign governments have become substantial, and in these transactions the Department of Defense acts only as a sort of broker. See Ilan Peleg's discussion in chapter 6.)

2) The market is oligopolistic, as usually only a few suppliers—sometimes only one—have the capability to supply the product.

3) Price is a relatively unimportant aspect of the sale, whereas technical attributes of the product are supremely important, almost regardless of cost.

4) Competition takes the form mainly of technical and political rivalry to receive the initial research and development contract. After the project begins, the initial supplier often becomes the sole source for the product *and* all subsequent spare parts, modifications, maintenance, and support. In this "follow-on" business, which is much larger than the general public appreciates and may last for decades, the supplier is a monopolist and therefore able to extract relatively favorable terms from the governmental purchaser.

5) Given the budget constraint and the huge size of the major weapons programs, only a few can be financed at once. Therefore, the defense business is somewhat erratic, having a feast-or-famine quality for individual firms. Failure to obtain a single major contract may jeopardize the ability of a producer to remain in the industry.

6) To insure that major arms producers do not leave the industry, dispersing their precious technical teams and draining their reservoir of experience, the government uses various devices to subsidize their continuance in the business: subsidies to keep facilities open and to finance ongoing research and development, plus loans and loan guarantees, government-supplied plants and equipment, tax breaks, and—some analysts believe—strategic placement of new contracts.

7) Hence, not surprisingly in view of its extensive commitments and guarantees to the contractors, the government plays a pervasive role in the industry, prescribing in great detail the specifications of the products and the conditions under which they must be produced. As William Kovacic makes clear in chapter 5, below, no industry is more heavily regulated.[10]

The defense business, notwithstanding the rhetoric of the corporate managers involved in it, is not private enterprise in anything like the classic sense. But it is not public enterprise either. It is *sui generis*. Therein lies much of the difficulty of rationalizing and reforming it, or even talking about it sensibly. Because so many distinct kinds of actors bear a degree of responsibility for its performance—the president and his aides, members of Congress, the armed forces and the Department of Defense, contractors, workers and labor unions, research and educational institutions, the electorate—it is difficult to place the blame for its shortcomings or allocate praise for its accomplishments.

Before World War II, arms procurement was usually (there were exceptions) simple and straightforward. The armed forces produced a substantial share of their arms in government arsenals and shipyards. When military officials needed to purchase an item from the private sector, ordinarily they drew up a detailed specification of the desired product and placed public advertisements inviting bids. Would-be contractors submitted sealed bids. At an appointed time, the bids were opened. The military purchaser then placed the contract with the lowest bidder. Period. In fiscal year 1940, the War department made 87 percent of its purchases from the private sector in this way.[11]

After the legislative changes in the procurement regulations enacted in mid-1940, the old system of open-access, sealed-bid competition became relatively unimportant. In the first eight months of fiscal year 1941, the War Department placed 74 percent of its contracts, by value, through negotiation.[12] Negotiated deals have predominated ever since. The Department of Defense seems always to be bragging about the increased emphasis it is placing on competition for its contracts, but over the long haul the importance of genuinely competitive contracting never changes much. In one way or another, sooner or later, the parties end up negotiating—then renegotiating, then renegotiating again and again, rendering the initial terms of the contract quite irrelevant. Along the way "competition," whatever it meant at the start, becomes transformed into something akin to mutual back-scratching.

Nor is the negotiation and renegotiation of contracts the only occasion for governmental officials and private parties to rub shoulders. As Bernard Udis and Murray Weidenbaum have observed, "the procurement of sophisticated weapons systems takes place in a rarified atmosphere in which the distinction between buyer and seller becomes blurred due to the interdependence of the organizations, the growing commonality of goals, and the daily intermingling of personnel from both groups over extended periods of time. . . . [This is] an environment far removed from the presumed 'arms length' dealings of the market." General James P. Mullins, former commander of the Air Force Logistics Command, has recently remarked that the defense business "is not business as usual among *independent* parties. This is a family affair among terribly *interdependent* parties. . . ." He also affirms that the contractors, far from awaiting the government's demands, actively generate and shape those demands. "The contractor validates the design [of a weapon system] through the process of marketing it to one of the services. If successful, the contractor gets the contract. Thus, to a substantial degree, the weapon capabilities devised by contractors create military requirements. In the defense business, then, the prime contractors are where the babies really come from."[13]

Again, World War II may be seen as the wellspring of modern practices. During the defense period before the Japanese attack on Pearl Harbor, many businessmen were reluctant to accept contracts for munitions. They did not trust the governmental officials with whom they would have to deal.

Gradually, however, especially after 1941, the relations of governmental buyers and private suppliers became more relaxed. By the end of the war, they were downright cordial. According to Elberton Smith, the official historian of Army mobilization, the nexus of the government and its military contractors became "an undefined but intimate relationship." In this cozy arrangement, contracts "ceased to be completely binding" and fixed prices "often became only tentative and provisional." Moreover, "potential losses resulting from many causes—including errors, poor judgment, and performance failures on the part of contractors—were averted by modification and amendment of contracts."[14] This description is as apt today as it was in 1944.

Aside from the serenity that attends the spending of other people's money, military-industrial dealings are smoothed by the personal passages back and forth across the border between the government and the contractors. A man sits on your side of the negotiating table today, on the opposite side tomorrow; and vice versa. Senator William Roth has complained that "one cannot do business in some Army procurements unless one is part of the 'old boy network,'" and Senator William Proxmire has pointed to "an active, ever-working, fast-moving, revolving door between the Pentagon and its big suppliers." Thousands of high-ranking military officers and civilian governmental officials retire and find immediate executive employment in the defense industry—not uncommonly on the same project—while industry officials routinely occupy high-ranking positions in the Pentagon bureaucracy while on leave from their firms.[15] In these circumstances one easily forgets who is working for whom, and where private interest ends and public responsibility begins. The natural tendency is to consider the whole enterprise to be, as General Mullins expressed it, a "family affair."

In our political system, anything involving so much money, so many jobs, and such vast power is bound to become completely politicized; certainly the MICC has become so. The political process in the arms field is extraordinarily complicated because so many powerful officials and institutions are involved. As a rule of thumb, one might venture to say that the national security elite, headed by the President and his National Security Council, play the leading role in setting the overall defense budget. Together, the armed forces and the contractors speak loudest about which specific weapon systems will be developed. For a long time, Congress brought up the rear, making marginal changes in the defense budget and validating the Pentagon's choices of specific weapons. Since the early 1970s, however, members of Congress have become more pervasively involved in the details of the defense program. Not that Congress ever stood completely aside; attention was always given, for example, to "real estate questions" involving the location of domestic bases and production facilities. But the congressional role clearly has become more important. The rise of congressional micromanagement has gone hand in hand with the emergence of political action committees (PACs), among which the defense industry is well represented. (See Frank Lichtenberg's essay below for a rigorous econometric assessment of the PACs.)

Congress now scrutinizes the defense budget line by line—there are some three thousand lines altogether—making hundreds of changes each year. As always, real estate matters receive prime attention. Base closures must be resisted at all costs, as Charlotte Twight explains in her essay below. But members of Congress hardly restrict themselves to such obvious vote-getting measures. They have at their disposal a great variety of subtle devices for diverting defense expenditures into channels of maximum political serviceability. Limitation riders, with which the defense authorization and appropriations acts are loaded down, make policy and enrich constituents and other friends under the guise of merely prohibiting or requiring particular expenditures. Much of this pork-barreling goes relatively unnoticed because it affects not the major weapon systems but the "soft underbelly" of the operations and maintenance accounts, where defense spending totalling tens of billions of dollars attracts little public attention or news media scrutiny.[16]

In addition, certain projects may gain congressional approval not because of who will be the prime contractor—procurement procedures and regulations make it difficult for members of Congress to dictate primes—but because of who will get the subcontracts. (Subcontracting is discussed by Kenneth Mayer in chapter 9.) Ordinarily, about 50 percent of the value of a prime contract for a major weapon system goes into subcontracts. As Ernest Fitzgerald, the Air Force's Management Systems Deputy, has said, when you see a military aircraft, you are looking at a huge collection of spare parts flying in close formation.[17] Parts contracts can be spread around; they can be, and ordinarily are, spread so as to create the maximum political appeal for a project in Congress. It is quite possible that the strict regulations that apply to the making of prime contracts have little effect because in practice the politicians can achieve their ends almost as readily via the placement of subcontracts.[18]

Perhaps in defense acquisition, too, as political scientists have argued with respect to economic regulation, Congress is more "the keystone of the Washington establishment" than most people suspect.[19] The essays below by Lindsay, Mayer, and Twight make major contributions to our knowledge of the congressional role in the defense economy (see chapters 8, 9, and 10).

The defense establishment is a huge political, economic, and bureaucratic apparatus staffed by millions of fallible men and women responsible for disposing of some $300 billion every year. It is entitled to its fair share of waste, fraud, and mismanagement, and one would be naive to suppose that it can be made perfect when everything else in the world is imperfect. Still, citizens may with justification demand that it adhere to a superior standard of performance. For the nation's security—indeed the fate of the earth—hinges on how the members of the MICC conduct America's defense business. It is chimerical to suppose that politics can be removed from the defense program. The nature of the political animal is hardly to shy away from money and power. But we may still ask: Are our political institutions constructed so as to create the maximum achievable correspondence between private interests and the public's interest in national security? Most of us, it seems to me, think they are not. But if better institutions— institutions whose incentives and constraints will entail a reduction of waste, fraud, and mismanagement—are to be created, they must be built on a solid foundation of knowledge and understanding. The essays in this volume are offered in the hope that they will help to lay that foundation.

NOTES

1. U.S. Bureau of the Census, *Historical Statistics of the United States, Colonial Times to 1970* (Washington: Government Printing Office, 1975), p. 1141; Lawrence J. Korb, *The Fall and Rise of the Pentagon: American Defense Policies in the 1970s* (Westport, Conn.: Greenwood Press, 1979), p. 5.

2. Robert Higgs, "Private Profit, Public Risk: Institutional Antecedents of the Modern Military Procurement System in the Rearmament Program of 1940–1941," in *The Sinews of War: Essays on the Economic History of World War II*, ed. Geofrey T. Mills and Hugh Rockoff (Ames: Iowa State University Press, in press).

3. War employment data from historical tables in Office of the Assistant Secretary of Defense (Comptroller), *National Defense Budget Estimates for FY 1988/1989* (May 1987), pp. 124, 126.

4. Data displayed in figure 1 go up to 1986. Using data for 1987 and preliminary data for the first three quarters of calendar year 1988, as reported in the CEA's *Annual Report* of 1989, pp. 309, 312, one finds that real defense purchases increased by 3.0 percent between 1986 and 1987. Thus, after two years, the much lamented post-1985 defense budgetary retrenchment still had not appeared in the real spending data. After several years of rapid increases in budgetary authority, several additional years are required before decreases in budgetary authority work their way through to the outlay amounts. Only in 1988 did real spending finally fall, by 2 percent (based on preliminary data for the first three quarters).

5. Office of the Assistant Secretary of Defense (Comptroller), *National Defense Budget Estimates*, pp. 124–25. Others have estimated much higher defense-related employment, partly by expanding the scope of what is defined as "defense-related." See Hugh G. Mosley, *The Arms Race: Economic and Social Consequences* (Lexington, Mass.: Lexington Books, 1985), pp. 89–111.

6. U.S. Department of Defense, Directorate for Information Operations and Reports, *100 Companies Receiving the Largest Dollar Volume of Prime Contract Awards, Fiscal Year 1985* (Washington, D.C.: Government Printing Office, 1985), pp. 1–4.

7. Smaller War Plants Corporation, *Economic Concentration and World War II* (Washington, D.C.: Government Printing Office, 1946), pp. 29–30, 32, 52–53; Murray L. Weidenbaum, *Business, Government, and the Public*, 3rd ed. (Englewood Cliffs, N.J.: Prentice-Hall, 1986), p. 348.

8. Headlines from *Wall Street Journal,* April 3, 1985; Oct. 31, 1985; Jan. 25, 1988; Dec. 21, 1987; July 16, 1986; March 6, 1987. For a recent, lengthy catalog of similar horrors, see J. Ronald Fox, *The Defense Management Challenge: Weapons Acquisition* (Boston, Mass.: Harvard Business School Press, 1988), pp. 327–40.

9. Spare parts prices as compiled in a fact sheet issued by the National Taxpayers Union, 325 Pennsylvania Avenue, S.E., Washington, DC 20003. Early reports on the 1988 scandal include Eileen White Read, "Bribery Scandal Puts Military Contractors on Defensive," *Wall Street Journal,* June 23, 1988; John H. Cushman, Jr., "Justice Dept. Under Pressure to Tell Pentagon of Inquiry," *New York Times,* June 26, 1988; Tim Carrington, "Defense-Contracting Scandal Takes Some Luster Off Carlucci, a Key Figure in Previous 'Reforms,'" *Wall Street Journal,* June 29, 1988; and David E. Rosenbaum, "Pentagon Fraud Inquiry: What Is Known to Date," *New York Times,* July 7, 1988.

10. Jacques S. Gansler, *The Defense Industry* (Cambridge, Mass.: MIT Press, 1982), pp. 30–31; Weidenbaum, *Business, Government, and the Public,* pp. 342–47. See also Richard A. Stubbing, *The Defense Game* (New York: Harper & Row, 1986), pp. 163–218; William J. Weida and Frank L. Gertcher, *The Political Economy of National Defense* (Boulder, Colo.: Westview Press, 1987), pp. 8–10, 24–25, 109–62; *Toward a More Effective Defense: Report of the Defense Organization Project,* ed. Barry M. Blechman and William J. Lynn (Cambridge, Mass.: Ballinger, 1985), pp. 31–37, 88–101, 146–49; Fox, *Defense Management Challenge,* pp. 11–51; and chapter 5, below.

11. A. Elberton Smith, *The Army and Economic Mobilization* (Washington: U.S. Army, 1959), pp. 72, 223, 243–47.

12. Ibid.

13. Bernard Udis and Murray L. Weidenbaum, "The Many Dimensions of the Military Effort," in *The Economic Consequences of Reduced Military Spending,* ed. Bernard Udis (Lexington, Mass.: Lexington Books, 1973), p. 33; James P. Mullins, *The Defense Matrix: National Preparedness and the Military-Industrial Complex* (San Diego, Calif.: Avant Books, 1986), pp. 113, 91 (emphasis in original). See also Gordon Adams, *The Politics of Defense Contracting: The Iron Triangle* (New Brunswick, N.J.: Transaction Books, 1982), pp. 21–54; Fox, *Defense Management Challenge,* pp. 27, 43, 163.

14. Smith, *The Army and Economic Mobilization,* p. 312.

15. Sen. Roth as quoted by Dina Rasor, *The Pentagon Underground* (New York: Times Books, 1985), p. 204; William Proxmire, *Report from Wasteland: America's Military-Industrial Complex* (New York: Praeger, 1970), p. 152. For recent data on the revolving door, see U.S. General Accounting Office, *DOD Revolving Door: Relationships Between Work at DOD and Post-DOD Employment,* GAO/NSIAD-86-180BR, July 1986. See also Fox, *Defense Management Challenge,* pp. 128–29, 142–46, 222, 233–39, 286–87, 302.

16. Robert Higgs, "Hard Coals Make Bad Law: Congressional Parochialism versus National Defense," *Cato Journal* 8 (Spring/Summer 1988): 79–106, and Robert Higgs, "Beware the Pork-Hawk," *Reason* 21 (June 1989): 28–34. On the "soft underbelly," see Stubbing, *The Defense Game,* esp. pp. 221–31. On the changing congressional role in general, see Robert J. Art, "Congress and the Defense Budget: New Procedures and Old Realities," in *Toward a More Effective Defense,* ed. Blechman and Lynn, pp. 125–67; James M. Lindsay, "Congress and Defense Policy: 1961 to 1986," *Armed Forces & Society* 13 (Spring 1987): 371–401; and chapter 8 below.

17. A. Ernest Fitzgerald, speech at Lafayette College, Oct. 22, 1987. Fitzgerald is the most famous Pentagon whistle-blower. See his *The High Priests of Waste* (New York: Norton, 1972); "Overspending to Weakness," in *More Bucks, Less Bang: How*

the *Pentagon Buys Ineffective Weapons,* ed. Dina Rasor (Washington: Fund for Constitutional Government, 1983), pp. 299–320; and *The Pentagonists* (Boston, Mass.:
Houghton Mifflin, 1989).

18. For well-documented case studies of the politics of subcontracting, see
(with regard to the C-5B cargo plane) Rasor, *Pentagon Underground,* pp. 232–53, and
(with regard to the B-1 bomber) Nick Kotz, *Wild Blue Yonder: Money, Politics, and the
B-1 Bomber* (New York: Pantheon, 1988), passim.

19. The "keystone" phrase comes from Morris P. Fiorina, *Congress: Keystone of
the Washington Establishment* (New Haven: Yale University Press, 1977).

1

Baruch, the New Deal and the Origins of the Military-Industrial Complex

JORDAN A. SCHWARZ

Dwight D. Eisenhower knew some history. His knowledge may have been the product more of his personal experience than of wide reading, but unlike his fact-mongering predecessor, Harry Truman, Eisenhower had a philosophy of history. He was a conservative. The general believed that wars were revolutionary in their impact upon societies. He had seen profound changes in his time. In his 1961 Farewell Address, which gave us the phrase, "military-industrial complex," Eisenhower noted that "Our military organization today bears little relation to that known by any of my predecessors in peacetime, or indeed by the fighting men of World War II or Korea. Until the latest of our world conflicts, the United States had no armaments industry. . . . This conjunction of an immense military establishment and a large arms industry is new in the American experience." A large arms industry was imperative to a soldier's livelihood, but a soldier's livelihood was not the livelihood of the nation. He believed that an economy of war transformed an economy of growth and development into an economy of waste. Thus, on April 16, 1953, he told the American Society of Newspaper Editors that he preferred plowshares to swords:

> Every gun that is made, every warship launched, every rocket fired signifies—in the final sense—a theft from those who hunger and are not fed, those who are cold and are not clothed.
> This world in arms is not spending money alone.
> It is spending the sweat of its laborers, the genius of its scientists, the hopes of its children.
> The cost of one heavy bomber is this: a modern brick school in more than thirty cities.
> It is: two electric power plants, each serving a town of 60,000 population.

It is: two fine, fully equipped hospitals.
It is some fifty miles of concrete highways.
We pay for a single fighter alone with half a million bushels of wheat.
We pay for a single destroyer with new homes that could have housed
more than 8,000 people.
This is not a way of life at all, in any true sense. Under the cloud of
threatening war, it is humanity dangling from a cross of iron.

As did many conservatives of his time, Eisenhower believed that capitalism's decline would occur when its military spending pauperized national treasuries and eroded standards of living through war-induced inflation. Yet other Americans of the time did not see the problem as an either/or
proposition: the public and its policymakers did not want to decide between
guns and butter. Prior to the modern epoch and America's world role as a
political and military leader, the United States had achieved power without
a military to assert it. The Spanish-American war did not make the U.S. a
world power; it merely confirmed the fact which had been created by
American industrial might. Nevertheless, many influential Americans still
eschewed an aggressive imperial posture abroad in favor of developing the
national political economy. They believed that neither the big stick nor
dollar diplomacy suited national interests. Rather, overseas interests would
be furthered by internal development. Capital would be better invested in
the south's colonial economy or the west's enormous economic potential.
For even as late as the period between the world wars, the United States was
a superpower with vast regions of undeveloped lands.

Military prowess needed economic development. Certain Westerners
and Southerners assumed a somewhat Whiggish view of history that argued
for a twentieth-century national economic policy to extend liberal currency
and credit arrangements beyond the Northeast and the Great Lakes regions,
along with fair transportation rates, equitable energy distribution, and
available federal funds for building roads and waterways. By using Washington to make Americans efficient producers at home and competitors
abroad in a liberal world order, progressives believed they could confront
European imperialism in its home and colonial markets. Armed with the
practical idealism of economic might and liberal ideals, asserting that
hegemonic colonialism was both anachronistic and evil, Americans challenged European imperialists for world economic leadership. Although
Royalists and Reds labelled this behavior economic imperialism, the United
States set its own terms for superpower status.

While Americans eschewed a military establishment as expensive and
inefficient, the United States was not a pacifistic power. Americans always
considered the likelihood of overseas interests involving them in a war.
Should war be necessary, internal economic reforms and improvements
undertaken prior to the emergency would enhance a call to arms later.
Thus, the perils posed by the strategic geopolitics of the twentieth century
reciprocally rationalized innovative national economic policies. Although

the military organization of 1961 bore no relationship to that of 1911, some Americans a half-century before, dreaming of national greatness, had imagined it.

Taxes ⟹ Defense industry

I

A military establishment is a public enterprise whose capital governments find in competitive capital markets and conscript in taxes. To parody Justice Oliver Wendell Holmes, Jr., taxes are what we pay for the uncivilized society of war. No military-industrial complex could exist without the willingness of a public to pay for it.

Like our military establishment, "The federal tax system as we know it today is of relatively recent origin."[1] Washington levied an income tax during the Civil War but it took the ideological conflicts of the 1890s to revive it and then motivate the Supreme Court to narrowly rule it unconstitutional in *Pollock* v. *Farmer's Loan and Trust* (1895).[2] Customs duties still paid for the war against Spain in 1898 and Washington's subsequent administration of territories in two hemispheres. At that time, the protectors of capitalism considered the income tax a threat; a little more than a decade later some would come to see it as a weapon for defense of the system.

In the twentieth century, the income tax is the price Americans pay for their world role. In 1909 Congress surprisingly passed both a tax on corporate incomes and an amendment to the Constitution which permitted the general income tax; the states ratified it within four years. Why? The reasons may have been as numerous as the states approving it. For one, many people blamed rising consumer prices on high tariffs, which could be replaced with an income tax. Also, midwestern agrarians wanted federal development of waterways to enhance exports of grain without inducing retaliatory foreign barriers to trade. And, significantly, Americans were mindful that war in Europe, motivated by imperial jealousies, was possible and would disrupt international trade, thereby reducing Washington's flow of revenues from imports.

A general European war could devastate the American marketplace and ultimately draw in the United States. Modern national economies called for big international, interdependent organizations. Modern war likewise called for an immense, comprehensive, national organization and the means to fund it. This point was made in 1910 when a leader of the fight for the income tax, congressman Cordell Hull of Tennessee, declared:

> During the great strain of national emergencies an income tax is absolutely without a rival as a relief measure. Many governments in time of war have invoked its prompt and certain aid. . . . We cannot expect always to be at peace. If this nation were tomorrow plunged into a war with a great commercial country from which we now receive a large portion of our imports, our

[handwritten annotations in margins: "Take the form of Income", "Taxes take"]

customs revenues would inevitably decline and we would be helpless to prosecute that war or any other war of great magnitude without taxing the wealth of this country in the forms of incomes.

Surveying the accomplishments of the income tax nearly four decades later, Secretary of State Hull was satisfied that it had played a vital role in twice mobilizing and stabilizing the national economy during an overseas war.[3]

Concomitant with the drive for an income tax was a movement to rationalize banking and currency. The bank panics of the first decade of the twentieth century called forth demands for monetary stabilization through the establishment of a public-sanctioned central banker to rival the power of J. P. Morgan & Company and to provide cheap credit to agrarian and manufacturing groups beyond New York's normal sphere of activity. The innovation of the Federal Reserve System in 1913 was intended to resolve these concerns. A central banker, it was felt, could mobilize money to ameliorate industrial crises or respond to international crises such as war.[4]

The United States in the early twentieth century was paradoxically a world power in international politics and a developing country in certain areas of its economy. Nowhere was the sense of American industrial inferiority felt more keenly than in the south. Southerners, aided by Westerners and sometimes by rural Midwesterners, spearheaded movements for nationalizing American industrial development. Senator Carter Glass of Virginia, "the Father of the Federal Reserve System," dominated banking regulation for nearly a quarter century. The Wilson administration's Treasury secretary was a Tennessean, William Gibbs McAdoo, a major spokesman and philosopher for governmentally aided national economic development.[5] A private promoter of transportation systems, McAdoo organized a generation of Southerners in Wall Street into a "Southern Society," a fraternity of maverick speculators outside of the big investment houses that included John Skelton Williams and Bernard Mannes Baruch. What distinguished them from the investment establishment of the time was their involvement in politics as Democrats. Asserting the need for efficient national transportation, equitable banking systems, and cheap public power, with federal leadership to foster the economic growth of the colonial South and the remote Far West, McAdoo and his cohorts attached themselves to the presidential ambitions of the Virginia-born Governor of New Jersey in 1912, Woodrow Wilson.[6]

The Wilsonians did not pursue a national economic policy because they anticipated American involvement in war, but they were not indifferent to the role Europe's wars might play in their designs. Thus when war erupted in Europe seventeen months after Wilson became President, the Southern Society ardently advocated American military preparedness and industrial mobilization. Baruch, in particular, made himself a zealous champion of preparedness, even though his opinions on foreign policy often verged upon isolationism. The administration created a cabinet-level Council of National Defense, and its Advisory Commission of civilians studied and discussed industrial requirements for war. Baruch was a member of the Advisory Commission. While McAdoo and Baruch sincerely deplored the war, they saw it realistically as a boon to their plans for development. They only worried that it might end before they could put their plans for economic mobilization and stabilization into effect. Baruch presciently tied the Federal Reserve Act to economic planning for war and forecast that if he could organize "an adequate defense, I believe this country would embark on one of the greatest eras of prosperity ever experienced." The war had made the United States a creditor nation, the principal banker for other nations. Wilson was not ignorant of his cabinet's ambitions for the economy, but in 1916 he ran for reelection as the president who "kept us out of the war."[7]

When the United States entered the war months later, it was not prepared. American troops did not reach Europe for several months following the declaration of war. Even then, they lacked the necessary ordnance; no industrial mobilization worthy of the name existed. Apprehensive that he would needlessly dislocate the economy and arouse further dissent, Wilson proceeded cautiously. Like Lincoln in search of a winning general, Wilson preferred failure before he turned the conduct of the war over to a leader who violated the rules of engagement and tested public morale. In this sense, the U. S. Grant of the Great War was B. M. Baruch.

It is pointless to dwell on the fact that Baruch was a Jewish Wall Street speculator and that his appointment in April 1918 as chairman of the War Industries Board was the near-equivalent of putting Ivan Boesky in charge of the Defense Department today. Baruch had made himself an expert of sorts on industrial preparedness and a staunch advocate of centralized planning for war. War spending, both from abroad and from Washington, had exacerbated demand for raw materials and credit, thereby making extreme medicine palatable. Inflation had been rampant since 1915. Baruch had shown some real administrative ability in coordinating Allied purchasing with American requirements, and when McAdoo insisted that Baruch be appointed to head the new War Finance Corporation, Wilson tabbed him to lead the WIB. Besides, the speculator astutely cultivated a new image as a business generalist—a broad-gauged fellow who understood how markets and governments influenced each other.

Only in war could Washington get away with what the war managers attempted in 1917–18. Not only were their economic innovations of dubious legality, they also could be invitations to political suicide for the emergency administrators. However, men like Baruch in the War Industries Board, McAdoo in the Treasury and the Railroad Administration, Harry Garfield in the Fuel Administration, Vance McCormick in the War Trade Board, Eugene Meyer in the War Finance Corporation, and Herbert Hoover in the Food Administration professed with varying degrees of disingenuousness to be above politics. They unabashedly appealed to patriotism in support of their truly unprecedented actions that demonstrated nothing less than an organizational and public-relations genius. In only months they built a government-business structure that has never been duplicated—partly because so many Americans resented its unvarnished regimentation. It was not "war socialism"; it was state capitalism. The economic conduct of the war did not give power to the workingmen of America, although it benefited them with wage and hour improvements in return for industrial peace. Significantly, Washington replaced Wall Street as the principal source of large capital for the conduct of the war; it could hardly expect J. P. Morgan to finance tanks instead of automobiles or finance shipbuilding and railroad repairs for the ephemeral purpose of war. War as an enterprise invited wasteful inefficiencies, albeit accompanied by swollen but brief profits. War was the business of government and it would have to pay for it alone through taxation or borrow mightily from banks and the public. In this manner, a precedent was set: Washington could augment private banks in order to generate industry in the national interest.

Ironically, Wilson wanted a mobilization that would disturb business as little as possible. Even when the war was over, the President insisted that no "reconversion" of the economy was necessary because the economy had never been converted to a real war footing. He maintained that a "readjustment" would suffice because markets had simply been adjusted for war output.[8] But what an adjustment!

While Washington did not abolish the marketplace during the war, it is not too much to say that it cartelized the American economy through the various temporary administrations. The WIB organized production industry by industry, effecting standardizations of products that could not have been achieved without challenging the antitrust laws. Likewise the Food and Fuel Administrations commanded greater output and restrained domestic consumption. Not content merely to manipulate supply and demand, the war agencies frequently resorted to outright price-fixing. For that matter, should a corporation balk at the government's orders, the WIB could threaten seizure of a factory if it decided such drastic action served a national need.[9] Washington seized the railroads in the name of efficiency when embarrassing bottlenecks threatened to prevent men and materials from reaching Europe, but the actual operation of the roads remained in management's hands. Management could hardly protest against the tremendous investment in road improvements and additional rolling stock that flowed in from the federal treasury.[10] In other ways, too, McAdoo made the war a promoter's dream. In the name of the national emergency, he pumped millions of federal dollars into shipbuilding. While the hundreds of new ships were not ready in time for war service, many were sold at bargain prices after the war. Because the country and its associates at war in Europe needed nitrates for fertilizer and explosives and nitrogen could be extracted from the air, the War Finance Corporation built a dam at Muscle Shoals, Alabama, on the Tennessee River to supply the necessary power. All of these wartime actions had postwar consequences. Most importantly, they established precedents for substantial investment by the U.S. Treasury that could benefit private investors.

The Wilsonians believed that wartime price stabilization would have profound postwar benefits. Almost from the very inception of the European war, America was hit by rising prices of raw materials. As European and American money chased a scarcer supply of commodities, an enormous inflation ensued. The prices of certain metals increased by as much as three hundred percent in one year. Prices already had a full head of steam when the government started spending for armaments.[11] After April 1917, when the Government joined the crowd of buyers, the Treasury sought to restrain its own costs by limiting the higher prices of metals needed in the war effort. The Wilsonians wanted full value for the federal dollar. By holding down the price of steel and metals widely used in industry, the Wilsonians hoped to save the government millions of dollars, as well as keeping the nation's prices low enough as to encourage a postwar private expansion of exports and domestic markets. Their ingenious price manipulations successfully limited some prices.[12]

The Wilsonians deserve credit for approaching war finance with ethical considerations in mind. They believed in paying for the war as much as possible out of current funds, lest it be left to a future generation to clean up their mess. Conscious that certain businessmen profited enormously from the war, they imposed a stiffly progressive income tax. Aware that business profiteering was as rampant as wartime dissent, they anticipated the Nye Committee's accusation in the 1930s that the war had been fought to benefit a few bankers and arms merchants. With lives on the line in Europe, there had to be fairness at home in war finance. Realistically, however, the Treasury incurred debts to be borne by future generations when it sold bonds to cover the inevitable budget deficit. To avoid a situation where a few rich corporations and banks would own a debt to be paid off by the mass of Americans, the Wilsonians made a conscientious effort to encourage mass savings and thereby broaden the debt's ownership.[13]

As a rule Wilsonians argued that future war-related social discord, debt and taxes would be lessened if wartime inflation were restrained. The Wilsonians avidly pursued low prices in the interests of labor peace and uninterrupted production. Savings and taxed incomes contributed to that effort. And when all else failed, imposed austerity was sold to the public as "simplification." Following the lead of Hoover's Food Administration— which took pride in practicing the "patriotism of the lean garbage pail" by restricting the American diet to substitutes for the beef, pork and wheat that it sent abroad—in the summer of 1918 Baruch's WIB endeavored to make American clothing "cheap but serviceable," by emphasizing a "Liberty

Shoe" that came in only three colors and only ten designs that used less material and needed no advertising to a captive public.[14]

The United States government's mobilization for war presented the world with a marvelous paradox which only a German general, Paul von Hindenburg, could adequately appreciate: "Her brilliant, if pitiless war industry had entered the service of patriotism and had not failed it. Under the compulsion of military necessity, a ruthless autocracy was at work and rightly in this land at the portals of which the Statue of Liberty flashes its blinding light across the seas. *They understood war.*"[15] And well might the Germans have envied the discipline obtained by the American administrators from the liberty-loving Americans. Although the Germans had planned for war, time and again during the unexpectedly protracted conflict Berlin failed to win the degree of cooperation from German industrialists that Washington extracted from American industrialists.[16]

How did the WIB do it? To hear its propagandists talk, the powers of persuasion and sweet reason prevailed. It had sold Americans on the glory of "voluntary cooperation." Cooperation had many symbols. The WIB seal, for instance, was a mishmash of eagle, stars, shield, ships, and soldiers; prominent in the foreground were two clasped hands, their sleeves representing capital and labor (labor on the right), under a pennant fluttering from the beak of an eagle bearing the inscription, "Together we will win." The WIB letterhead also contained a quotation from Woodrow Wilson: "The highest and best form of efficiency is the spontaneous cooperation of a free people."

The WIB won "spontaneous cooperation" by assuring a fair profit for the producer. Inevitably it walked a thin line between fair and exorbitant profits, but the WIB found ways of wringing "cooperation" from bullheaded manufacturers. If an incentive price for war services failed to induce cooperation, then it resorted to priorities, ratings of "essentiality" to the war whereby those who cooperated with the WIB won the highest rating and assured themselves of first crack at government-controlled raw materials, fuel and transportation. The businessmen who transformed the American economy into a war machine appreciated an incentive system. Baruch had a knack for recruiting up-and-coming executives to run his industrial committees with the same fervor for patriotism that they had shown for profits. However, when the automobile industry rejected a WIB request to convert 30 percent of its production from cars to tanks, the WIB threatened to cut off steel for slackers. Eventually the government demanded that 80 percent of the automobile industry's output be devoted to war, a test of wills which the Armistice averted. But the WIB's greatest enemy among corporate war resisters was the hoarder. Baruch treated them more roughly than other recalcitrant types—with confiscation and resale of hoarded materials.[17]

Without a war there was no patriotism, no cooperation, no price-fixing, and no legal status for government-inspired industrial organizations which openly flouted the antitrust laws. When the Armistice was signed, the WIB closed up shop, and the Food Administration lingered a while. Baruch and Hoover headed for fame in Paris as advisers to President Wilson at the Peace Conference. McAdoo had left the Treasury and the Railroad Administration before the Armistice in quest of the presidency itself. The war, as McAdoo and Baruch anticipated, made American industry boom by stimulating investment of public capital in transportation and industry. An expanded American merchant marine became the object of much British and French apprehension. American products and commodities flooded world markets. The war made Europeans more dependent upon American credit, manufactures, raw materials, and foodstuffs, temporarily in certain instances such as food, for the long term in others. And yet, to the consternation of European liberals like John Maynard Keynes, America was prepared to return home with its capital, a superpower intent upon its own internal investing.

II

For most people the war experience had been an expedient without any postwar lessons; for Baruch, however, it had two peacetime legacies. For one, cooperative organization, however obtained, could benefit American prosperity and development. For another, industrial planning for war was imperative to stabilize modern industrial economies (and Baruch was pessimistic enough about mankind to believe that American interests would be tested again by aggressors). But the lessons of cooperation and planning he drew from the experience of the war got a mixed response in the 1920s, notwithstanding certain advocates in the academic and business communities.[18] If Baruch and others had had their way, the blueprints for a military-industrial complex would have been in government files awaiting the time for execution.[19]

Cooperative organization, not "rugged individualism," was a major theme of the 1920s.[20] It stressed associationalism—the organization and expansion of trade associations[21]—promoted by government, especially by Secretary of Commerce Herbert Hoover.[22] However, Americans were not committed to economic planning. The abortive efforts of the Industrial Board of the Department of Commerce under George Peek, a WIB administrator and businessman, to stabilize prices in 1919 underlined the lack of popular support for an incomes policy in peacetime.[23] Americans did not want a permanent WIB.[24]

Nevertheless, Baruch kept the value of the WIB experience alive through reunions, press releases, magazine articles, and a history by its publicist. A talented publicist himself, Baruch espoused a "Supreme Court of Commerce," the economic equivalent of the United States Supreme

Court, a quest to take politics and Congress out of economics through a "properly constituted arbitral authority" over price disputes.[25]

While Baruch advocated a somewhat abstract ideal, Hoover advanced the mediator role of government through a myriad of government-fostered trade associations and regulatory bodies.[26] Hoover promoted cooperation in fiercely competitive industries such as bituminous coal. Informal cooperation already existed in a highly concentrated industry such as steel, where Judge Gary's cartel had been the object of widespread fear and loathing by the public and consumers of steel since early in the century. The real challenge and reward lay in organizing cooperation in agriculture. While its individualism and distrust of cooperation made agricultural marketing cooperation unlikely, if farmers could be made to cooperate, their example would make cartelization of any industry possible. No wonder Hoover and Baruch gave farm problems in the 1920s their attention and agricultural cooperatives their encouragement. While they disagreed on whether government should aid farmers in marketing their crops (Baruch endorsed the McNary-Haugen Plan for federal sales of surpluses abroad and Hoover opposed it), both hoped that agrarians could recapture their wartime prosperity through self-imposed production controls.[27]

But how could the lessons of the war be applicable to future wars if Americans believed it had been "the war to end all wars"? Besides, in a fiscally conservative era only radicals desired a military establishment that increased taxes. Although Baruch believed that industrial mobilization for war was too important to be left to the War Department, the National Defense Act of 1920 gave the assistant secretary of war broad discretion in planning for mobilization.[28] About all the Army did was to create an Industrial College, a think-tank for the study of military-industrial problems. None of this satisfied Baruch, not even the Army's first industrial mobilization plan—the "M-Day" scheme of 1930, which he helped Marshall, Eisenhower and MacArthur write.[29]

Politics in the 1920s had its paradoxes and contradictions. Thus the drive for frugal government ran counter to the drive for government-aided development—both of which thrived, sometimes in the same person. Baruch was both a fiscal conservative and an advocate of cooperative planning. Other promoters and planners espoused public works that had potential utility in peace and war. Western Republicans in the Senate such as Wesley Jones of Washington and Charles McNary of Oregon, or a Democrat such as Key Pittman of Nevada, yearned for federal investment in public power and land reclamation projects; to be a westerner then meant to put one's faith in the Treasury of the United States for his region's development. By the Great Depression they and their southern compatriots felt resentful of Eastern and Republican parsimony toward federal public works.[30] The ideal—economic planning for community development without abandoning capitalist individualism—had but one precedent: the themes and organizational strategies of 1918. Large-scale development required the analogue, if not the anticipation, of war. The historian William E. Leuchtenburg correctly observes, "When in 1933 a new government came to power in the midst of a major crisis, it would know no way to mobilize the country save by invoking the experience of World War I. . . . As a result, the early New Deal would draw [on the men] who had gained their first governmental experience in wartime Washington and cherished their memory of it through the 1920s."[31]

Leuchtenburg's theme[32] is so widely accepted that it is made treacherous by a narrow historical focus that explains only the early New Deal while hinting at a discontinuity between prewar progressivism and Eisenhower's military-industrial complex. Nevertheless, the New Deal is a bridge between the prewar business promoters who sought cheap transportation and energy for a nonindustrial America and those promoters who brought military contracts and bases to the South and West during and after World War II. Obviously the New Deal's National Recovery Administration (NRA) and the Agricultural Adjustment Administration (AAA) used experienced leadership—Hugh Johnson and George Peek—organization, methods, techniques and strategy gained from Baruch's War Industries Board.[33] But by 1936 both NRA and AAA had been done in by the Supreme Court, although New Dealers found other ways of sustaining cartelization in agriculture. The parts of the New Deal (deliberately leaving out amelioratives such as Social Security) whose impact transcended the Depression decade were the Public Works Administration (PWA), the Tennessee Valley Authority (TVA), the Rural Electrification Administration (REA), and the Reconstruction Finance Corporation (RFC), including its subsidiary, the Electric Home and Farm Authority (EHFA). These were the great and sometimes less-heralded projects of those who foresaw the need for government's visible hand participating in and enhancing American capitalism.

When it came to building a war machine in 1940–41 and thereafter, Roosevelt turned to the Southerners and Westerners who had dreamed of government-aided development. Many of them were either Wilsonians whom he had known during his own stint as assistant secretary of the navy in 1918 or during his pursuit of the presidency after 1920. The Democratic party was his vehicle to the White House and he appreciated that its best operatives owed much to those who came from the industrially underdeveloped South and West. Thus Cordell Hull was his 1932 campaign manager and helped Roosevelt sweep western and southern delegates and states. That Baruch was a latecomer to FDR's bandwagon was not allowed to detract from his contributions of money or that of Hugh Johnson to the brains trust—Roosevelt's academic advisors, Raymond Moley, Rexford Tugwell and Adolf Berle. The brains trust was dedicated to blending government's collectivist dollars with capitalism's individual initiative.[34] Thus a consensus for economic planning guided the early New Deal. And a mili-

tary-industrial complex would never exist without a commitment to planning and government-aided development.

III

The fullest expressions of "socialized investment" were the aforementioned PWA, REA, TVA and RFC. To run the PWA and enhance his
consensus for planning, Roosevelt wanted a western progressive Republican
senator, but settled for Harold Ickes when his two leading candidates,
Hiram Johnson of California and Bronson Cutting of New Mexico, recommended the Chicago Bull Moose lawyer. PWA tackled the great projects,
particularly the big dams of the west, the Grand Coulee and Bonneville
dams. In New York state Roosevelt had been one of the most dedicated
advocates of public power, in the St. Lawrence valley and elsewhere, to aid
the upstate rural areas.[35] Through public power the New Deal modernized
rural America and enhanced all sorts of commercial development. In 1935
one out of ten farms had electricity; in 1941 the figure was four of ten farms;
and in 1950 it was nine of ten farms.[36]

TVA owed its existence to Roosevelt's commitment to public power
and its World War I origins at Muscle Shoals. For a dozen years following
the war Republicans had debated what to do with the energy project: should
it be left to rot or sold off to private promoters such as Henry Ford? FDR
opted for federal development and expansion. David E. Lilienthal, a Har-
vard-trained Chicago labor lawyer experienced in Wisconsin public regulatory agencies and committed to what he and other New Dealers like Adolf
Berle and Jerome Frank called "state capitalism," was given TVA's leadership.

As Arthur Schlesinger, Jr., writes, under the leadership of Texas banker
Jesse Jones the RFC grew "into a powerful instrument of state capitalism."
Reluctantly begun by the Hoover administration to save the credit of failing
big banks and railroads, the RFC drew on the experience of the War Finance
Corporation and was initially presided over by WFC's former chairman,
Eugene Meyer. The New Dealers, however, expanded the RFC's role to
include financing of state and federal public works, as well as loans to
industry. RFC's New Deal leader, Jesse Jones, was a conservative and
promoter who had been introduced to public life in the Wilson administration. During the 1920s Jones and Cordell Hull had played important roles as
fund-raisers for the Democratic party.[37]

NRA and AAA upstaged RFC early in the New Deal, and its survival
was threatened by the prospect of economic recovery. However, RFC
figured more prominently in Roosevelt's second term, which otherwise was
only saved from political disaster by the outbreak of war in Europe. The
Roosevelt depression of 1937–38 expanded RFC's role to financing public

works that included defense projects. The link between energy for industry and the national defense was advanced by a young New Deal congressman from Texas, Lyndon B. Johnson. The war touched off a boom in 1940 and a race among New Dealers to become war managers.[38] Henry J. Kaiser, the industrialist who had spearheaded the construction of most of the great dams of the West with RFC financing, now shifted his attention to shipping and the war's need for steel, magnesium, and aluminum—all of which won the generous financing of RFC or its subsidiary, the Defense Plant Corporation, along with direct financing from the War and Navy departments.[39] Thus, RFC became the financier of the mobilization of 1940–41.

Financing government projects through the RFC was important in maintaining a broad consensus for public works and refuting the image of the New Deal as profligate. Actually, New Deal fiscal policy was usually conservative and even deflationary. Although a supporter of progressive taxation, FDR also called for balancing the budget with pay-as-you-go taxation.[40] Accordingly, Social Security was regressively financed in order to make its contributors its beneficiaries without affecting the public treasury. The most controversial revenue act of the New Deal was not the so-called "Wealth Tax Act" of 1935 (which could not match the tax law of 1932 for progressivity); the dread and hostility of business were aroused by the Brandeis-inspired undistributed profits tax in the 1936 law. Baruch and his friends in Congress won its repeal in 1938, thereby removing a disincentive to expansion at a time when compensatory public works spending was about to take on a strong defense component.[41]

Throughout the defense and war period Bernard Baruch was never far from the policymaking centers of power, although he seldom had an official role. A major financial angel for Democratic senatorial campaigns since 1920, Baruch heavily influenced Senators Joe Robinson of Arkansas, Pat Harrison of Mississippi, Jimmie Byrnes of South Carolina, and Key Pittman of Nevada—the most powerful Senate Democrats during the Hoover and New Deal years. Hoover consulted Baruch on the RFC, and Roosevelt had him coordinate strategy for the London Economic Conference of 1933. Otherwise, Baruch was an *eminence grise* during the New Deal until he emerged to oppose FDR's tax act, to mastermind economic warfare ("cash and carry"), and to promote industrial planning for war.

To nobody's surprise, Baruch wanted a revival of the WIB. He got a War Resources Board, but it lacked power and, even worse, it lacked Baruch. Its advisory board was chaired by Edward R. Stettinius, Jr., a big-business friend of the New Deal, and had friends of Baruch on it. An outpouring of criticism by New Dealers that the Board augured a big-business takeover moved FDR to dismiss it and lock up the WRB's report calling for a WIB-like agency to guide future mobilizations. The nonevent was significant: the president did not want a powerful mobilization agency outside of the regular departments; and he did not want Baruch. Indeed,

Baruch proved to be a touchstone during the war for military-industrial policies, with New Dealers depicting a big business conspiracy in anything espoused by him.[42]

To be sure, Baruch favored big business. He had nothing against small businesses, but in a crisis Baruch favored centralization of power. His long-time interest in the railroads and their successful coordination during World War I led him to conclude that the national interest was best served by mergers and concentration in a few hands—which is what he espoused in the National Transportation Committee of 1932, a private group in quest of a national transportation policy. But Baruch was up against eastern railroad interests that did not want to be subordinated to a national organization and automobile interests that did not want to see the rails strengthened as competitors. Likewise, Baruch's proposals for a superorganization to engage in national economic development and planning for war went against a president who did not want to share political power with economic administrators who were unaccountable to the electorate.[43]

Nevertheless, after Pearl Harbor Baruch's ideas tended to prevail. With an extraordinary appreciation of public relations and numerous influential friends in the Washington press corps, Baruch took to holding press conferences on a park bench in Lafayette Square, opposite the White House, to dramatize his differences with the President. Communicating a sense of trustworthiness, Baruch's demands for a centralized mobilization program increasingly made sense. Also, nobody was a stauncher advocate of inflation controls to accompany mobilization than Baruch. Price controls were no longer viewed as a big business plot to impose wage restraints or as necessarily antiprofit and regimenting of industry.[44] In 1942 Roosevelt, Congress and big business endorsed centralization of mobilization authority in one agency, the War Production Board under Sears executive Donald Nelson. In 1943 it was made subordinate to the Office of War Mobilization under Baruch's old friend, Jimmie Byrnes. As it had in 1918, American industrial output for war easily surpassed that of friend and foe. The history of industrial mobilization in other countries suggests that American war mobilization was more disciplined during World War II than that of Britain under Nazi bombs (the U.S. lost fewer hours of production to strikes) or Germany with its vaunted fascist efficiency (American production by the end of 1941 already surpassed that of Nazi Germany, which had developed the blitzkrieg partly to satisfy a German public that would not support a protracted war).[45]

IV

One of the lessons that Baruch drew from his World War I experience was that the economic management of war was too important to be left to generals or even their civilian superiors. Military men and their advocates thought only of their own needs and wants, disregarding the fact that military spending was apt to dislocate the entire economy unless Washington interceded in behalf of the public interest to supervise the marketplace. In other words, while a great power had geopolitical interests worth defending, war required industrial planning, lest, as a consequence of a military victory, the U.S. lose the economic peace. That had been Baruch's rule. Unfortunately, however, Baruch found that during the interwar period the only friends of industrial planning for war were military men. Few politicians and businessmen were enlightened on the likelihood and necessity of a planned war economy. Not even Pearl Harbor changed many minds and made advocates of planning. Surprisingly, during World War II Baruch found his most enthusiastic planners among the civilians of the War and Navy departments, the very agencies he had deplored in 1917. The under secretaries were the principal operatives in both departments: Robert Patterson and James Forrestal, a Republican Wall Street lawyer and a Democratic Wall Street investment banker, respectively, were no-nonsense types who harkened unto Baruch's wisdom as the gospel of mobilization. At the second level of the War Production Board was Wall Street broker Ferdinand Eberstadt, a powerful intellect and another Baruch acolyte. During the war Roosevelt tried to keep Baruch at arm's length, but he did not have arms long enough to keep Baruch and his kibitzing from the rest of the wartime bureaucracy.[46]

What made Baruch's arguments for wartime economic planning so powerful was the fearful anticipation of postwar inflation and/or unemployment.[47] Moreover, the Cold War did not allow Americans to be lulled by peace into forgetting how to make war. At the urging of Baruch's friend Eberstadt, Congress in 1947 created the National Security Resources Board (NSRB), "a considerable achievement" that gave the U.S. for the first time in its history "a peacetime agency devoted to assessing the nation's economic capacity for war."[48] In its planning NSRB built upon Eberstadt's "Controlled Materials Plan of 1942," but making that planning effective was something else. Congress barely tolerated NSRB through the Korean War and by 1953 it was reorganized out of existence. The long-range corporate schemes of a few businessmen seemed fatuous to politicians dealing with the immediate realities of an unpopular war. This is not to say that the experiences of the world wars were totally disregarded in the Cold War. At least the Pentagon adopted the principles of the Controlled Materials Plan as the basis of war procurement through the Korean and Vietnam wars. Moreover, Old Man Baruch was back at age 80 to campaign for a sweeping stabilization bill during the Korean War. There is a sizable file of spontaneous letters in President Truman's papers filled with the public's vivid memories of wartime shortages and inflation that testifies as to the wisdom and popularity of Baruch's message. A reluctant President Truman bowed to the clamor from Congress that echoed Baruch's admonition for combining mobilization with stabilization and agreed to standby price controls.[49]

Nevertheless, this may have been an exceptional instance in which generals, mobilizers and politicians learned from precedent. More usual is the observation of an economic historian: "Although the First World War had left massive files of invaluable administrative experience on the shelves of government, which in 1939 had often only to be reached for and dusted, the influence of wartime events on economic attitudes in the interwar period had been small."[50] World War II administrators treated the 1918 experience as something alien to them, preferring to benefit from New Deal developments. Thus, industrial mobilization during World War II owed much to the New Deal's state capitalism—which ironically owed something to the 1918 experience. The Korean War administrators tried to forget it all. Of course, that was not for lack of Baruch's efforts at influence. But without a war to panic the populace, Baruch's admonitions were apt to fall on deaf ears. Baruch feared that wars were pricing America's manufactures out of world markets. Although wartime inflation went hand in hand with a higher standard of living, it would be temporary. "What is going to happen when Japan and Germany and other economies we have helped get into full swing?" he asked rhetorically. "I have always figured on not only winning the war, but winning the peace."[51]

Even if the wartime experiences in stabilizing the economy were expediently forgotten, some continuity between war and peace was undeniable. Thus, two New Deal agencies which played a leading role in the war mobilization of 1942 were the RFC and TVA, both of which had their origins in the 1918 war experience. From his administrative base in the New Deal RFC, head Jesse Jones expanded his wartime capacities to include Federal Loan Administrator, Secretary of Commerce, and all the RFC subsidiaries such as the Defense Plant Corporation and the Rubber Reserve Corporation.[52] He was the Robert Moses of wartime Washington. Jones's power awed Baruch and others. Likewise, the men who promoted energy expansion during the 1930s played an enormous role in the war; TVA attained industrial maturity during the mobilization for war. War plants for the production of lightweight metals such as magnesium and aluminum, as well as other plants, required great quantities of energy, much of which was generated by dams in the Tennessee Valley or in the West. New Deal expansion of energy made possible expanded wartime manufacturing in the South and on the Pacific coast.[53] Cheap federally developed energy made possible the development of atomic energy for war and peace at Oak Ridge, Tennessee, and Hanford, Washington. Indeed, New Dealer David E. Lilienthal went from leading TVA to leading the atomic project.

Industrial preparedness for war was a spin-off from the dreams of New Deal promoters and developers. War itself, or the anticipation of it, had long been symbiotic with economic development, and together they go far to

Does war foster Economic Development?

explain the impetus for the military-industrial complex. World War II enhanced the relationship. Driven by the need for production uninterrupted by concerns of climate, Washington located defense plants and shipyards in warm areas of the country not hitherto known for heavy industry. For that matter, towns sitting amid cornfields, counting their populations in the hundreds, suddenly found themselves manufacturing war parts or assembling the craft themselves that would be used to storm the beaches of far-off Normandy or Iwo Jima. The New Deal had given those towns electricity, sidewalks and other community improvements, but the war brought them well-paying jobs, airstrips, and even homes for the thousands of war workers. In what would come to be called the Sunbelt, the war made the most profound demographic and developmental changes. Thousands of workers saw the Gulf of Mexico or the Pacific Ocean for the first time and decided to stay. Thousands of fliers saw the desert of Arizona during the war and considered its possibilities for postwar enterprises (powered by air-conditioning from electricity generated at Hoover Dam). Thus socialized investments such as Hoover Dam and TVA in the thirties lay the seeds for a great postwar migration of Americans to the South and West and development of the Sun Belt; World War II cultivated those seeds, and the military-industrial complex continues that cultivation.

Has the military-industrial complex become our only source of economic planning? Certainly that is not what was intended. Senator Walter F. George of Georgia expressed the trepidation of old conservatives when, confronted with the prospect of military aid for Europe in 1949, he declared that he could "visualize it as a mammoth pump-priming program, if you want to put it plainly."[54] But other politicians welcomed defense spending as the public works programs of a modern era—Georgia politicians not being exempt from such enthusiasms. It was this that made the Department of Defense the PWA of our times. Of course, reasons for defense against Communist threats are plentiful, and wars against Communists in Korea and Southeast Asia were real. Nevertheless, Americans now are less prone to treat military spending as a necessary evil.

Nor are politicians the only expedient souls to use defense spending as pump priming. Indeed, in the 1950s certain economists such as James Tobin depicted spending for defense as doubly wise and railed against the Eisenhower "new look" in defense for its foolish parsimony or antique dread of inflation.[55] The ascendant Keynesianism, characterized by Tobin-like cheers for fearless federal spending and daring to march to the brink of runaway inflation, marked the economists' contribution to the military-industrial complex. Nearly forgotten is the other side of Keynesianism that pointed to military spending as inherently unproductive and knowingly reminded us that "War and inflation are particularly old friends."[56]

Baruch and left-wing Keynesians had much in common when it came to favoring controls against inflation, a fact that discomforted the latter more than it bothered the old conservative: he had long since learned to value any allies. They agreed that military spending was inflationary and deplored its wanton spending as economically immoral. Good morals and sound economics went hand-in-hand. However, this advocacy alienated Baruch from both old conservatives (the *Chicago Tribune* accused Baruch of trying to impose socialism upon America) and Keynesians such as Galbraith and Schlesinger who lampooned him in their writings. Baruch welcomed the military-industrial complex, and he had fathered it by his advocacy of industrial preparedness for war for half a century.

However, the other side of the coin was that Baruch called for restraints upon inflation and for sound economic management. He was not a supply-side economist. A peacetime military establishment, he believed, could not be built upon a debt to be shifted to successor generations. A rickety economic policy could not shield the country militarily. Strength came from within; a society believing in the obligation of national service for youth had to be morally courageous enough to obligate its wealth currently without passing the burden along to the children of those who wore the uniform—no draft-dodging and no tax-dodging! But the politicians, generals, businessmen, and economists who also promoted the military-industrial complex ignored Baruch's point because they preferred ad hoc responses that fulfilled specific needs for development instead of the social discipline demanded by Baruch's total planning. The Old Man did not want to see the American military establishment turned into a pork-barrel. In his eyes, a military-industrial complex, for practical plus ethical reasons called for equality of individual sacrifice—and that required economic planning that employed taxes, priorities and perhaps even price controls.

Eisenhower understood Baruch's point, but he was unwilling to be a general who would regiment the American economy as much as Baruch wanted. Not wanting a military establishment of the magnitude that brought inflation, Eisenhower hoped to restrain the former in order to limit the latter. He hoped to restrain the very pluralism that Baruch feared.[57]

In principle, Baruch too espoused "organized self-restraint," but he knew that powerful incentives existed for limitless freedom. Was free enterprise synonymous with "freebooting," whereby a willful and greedy gang of businessmen promoted military projects for the sake of profits rather than the national interest? Could the military be trusted to let contracts which were cost-efficient? Was the national welfare hidden behind the military establishment while selfish businessmen in collusion with generals and labor unions indiscriminately boosted the cost of government which the public paid in higher taxes and/or inflation? Would Congress use military spending to boost local economic development? Freedom and military establishments were attainable together only at the cost of principles, ethics, and morality. Baruch wanted the military-industrial complex, but he knew that he, and others like him, could not have it unless the American people were willing to sacrifice certain freedoms of the marketplace. Without those sacrifices, Baruch sincerely doubted that other values and freedoms could be preserved from the ravages of inflation and debt. Always, as had been the case in 1918, circumstances have called for priorities. He believed that if Americans gave the highest priority to the military marketplace, they would have to give their next highest priorities to paying for their defense with taxes while controlling deficits, profits and prices. To the Old Man, this was common sense. Yet he knew that he asked too much.[58]

NOTES

1. Joseph A. Pechman, *Federal Tax Policy* (Washington: The Brookings Institution, 1971), p. 247.

2. Robert Higgs, *Crisis and Leviathan* (New York: Oxford University Press, 1987), pp. 97–105.

3. Lawrence M. Friedman, *A History of American Law* (New York: Simon and Schuster, 1973), pp. 496–97; Roy G. and Gladys C. Blakey, *The Federal Income Tax* (New York: Longman, Green, 1940), pp. 22–68; Cordell Hull, *Memoirs* (New York: Macmillan, 1948), pp. 48–61, quote on p. 61.

4. Robert Wiebe, *Businessmen and Reform* (Cambridge, Mass.: Harvard Univeristy Press, 1962), pp. 127–45; Elmus R. Wicker, *Federal Reserve Monetary Policy 1917–1933* (New York: Random House, 1966); Donald F. Kettl, *Leadership at the Fed* (New Haven, Conn.: Yale University Press, 1986), pp. 18–27.

5. John J. Broesamle, *William Gibbs McAdoo: A Passion for Change 1863–1917* (Port Washington, N.Y.: Kennikat Press, 1971), pp. 3–75.

6. Dale Norman Shook, "William G. McAdoo and the Development of National Economic Policy, 1913–1918," unpublished doctoral dissertation, University of Cincinnati, 1975, pp. 46–79.

7. Jordan A. Schwarz, *The Speculator: Bernard M. Baruch in Washington, 1917–1965* (Chapel Hill: University of North Carolina Press, 1981), pp. 41–43.

8. Burl Noggle, *Into the Twenties: The United States from Armistice to Normalcy* (Urbana: University of Illinois Press, 1974), pp. 42–83.

9. On the WIB, see Robert D. Cuff, *The War Industries Board: Business-Government Relations during World War I* (Baltimore: Johns Hopkins University Press, 1973).

10. On the Railroad Administration, see K. Austin Kerr, *American Railroad Politics, 1914–1920: Rates, Wages and Efficiency* (Pittsburgh: University of Pittsburgh Press, 1968).

11. David M. Kennedy, *Over Here: The First World War and American Society* (New York: Oxford University Press, 1980), pp. 101–5; Charles Gilbert, *American Financing of World War I* (Westport, Conn.: Greenwood Press, 1970), pp. 177–99.

12. Hugh Rockoff, *Drastic Measures: A History of Wage and Price Controls in the United States* (New York: Cambridge University Press, 1984), pp. 43–84.

13. Alexander D. Noyes, *The War Period of American Finance, 1908–1925* (New York: Putnam, 1926).

14. Schwarz, *The Speculator*, pp. 194–96; on Food, see Kennedy, *Over Here*, pp. 117–23.

15. Von Hindenburg quoted in Hugh Johnson, *The Blue Eagle from Egg to Earth* (Garden City, N.Y.: Doubleday, Doran, 1935), p. 88.

16. On the German war effort, see Gerd Hardach, *The First World War, 1914–*

1918 (Berkeley: University of California Press, 1977), pp. 55–73.

17. Schwarz, *The Speculator,* pp. 79–88; Cuff, *War Industries Board,* pp. 193–219.

18. Guy Alchon, *The Invisible Hand of Planning: Capitalism, Social Science, and the State in the 1920s* (Princeton: Princeton University Press, 1985).

19. Ellis W. Hawley, *The Great War and the Search for a Modern Order: A History of the American People and their Institutions, 1917–1933* (New York: St. Martin's Press, 1979), pp. 80–104.

20. Robert F. Himmelberg, *The Origins of the National Recovery Administration: Business, Government and the Trade Association Issue, 1921–1933* (New York: Fordham University Press, 1976).

21. Louis C. Galambos, *Competition and Cooperation: The Emergence of a National Trade Association* (Baltimore: Johns Hopkins University Press, 1966).

22. Ellis Wayne Hawley, "Herbert Hoover, the Commerce Secretariat, and the Vision of an 'Associate State,' 1921–1928," *Journal of American History* 61 (June 1974): 116–40.

23. Robert F. Himmelberg, "Business, Antitrust Policy and the Industrial Board of the Department of Commerce, 1919," *Business History Review* 42 (Spring 1968): 1–23.

24. E. Jay Howenstine, Jr., "The Industrial Board, Precursor to the N.R.A.: The Price Reduction Movement after World War I," *Journal of Political Economy* 51 (June 1943): 235–50; Schwarz, *The Speculator,* pp. 207–12.

25. Grosvenor B. Clarkson, *Industrial America in the World War* (Boston: Houghton Mifflin, 1923); Bernard Baruch, "The Consequences of the War to Industry," *Current History* 29 (November 1928): 189–96; Schwarz, *The Speculator,* pp. 212–19.

26. Ellis Wayne Hawley, "Three Facets of Hooverian Associationalism: Lumber, Aviation, and Movies, 1921–1930," in *Regulation in Perspective: Historical Essays,* ed. Thomas K. McCraw (Cambridge, Mass.: Harvard University Press, 1981), pp. 95–123.

27. Schwarz, *The Speculator,* pp. 227–41; James H. Shideler, *Farm Crisis, 1919–1923* (Berkeley: University of California Press, 1957); Gilbert C. Fite, *George N. Peek and the Fight for Farm Parity* (Norman: University of Oklahoma Press, 1954).

28. Robert D. Ward, "Against the Tide: The Preparedness Movement of 1923–1924," *Military Affairs* 38 (April 1974): 59–61; Albert A. Blum, "Birth and Death of the M–Day Plan," *American Civil-Military Decisions,* ed. Harold Stein (Tuscaloosa: University of Alabama Press, 1963), pp. 65–67.

29. Harry B. Yoshpe, "Bernard M. Baruch: Civilian Godfather of the Military M–Day Plan," *Military Affairs* 29 (Spring 1965): 1–15; Paul A. C. Koistinen, "The 'Industrial-Military Complex' in Historical Perspective: The Interwar Years," *Journal of American History* 56 (March 1970): 819–39.

30. Jordan A. Schwarz, *The Interregnum of Despair: Hoover, Congress and the Depression* (Urbana: University of Illinois Press, 1970), passim.

31. William E. Leuchtenburg, *The Perils of Prosperity, 1914–1932* (Chicago: University of Chicago Press, 1959), pp. 41–42.

32. Also, see William E. Leuchtenburg, "The New Deal and the Analogue of War," in *Change and Continuity in Twentieth-Century America,* ed. John Braeman et al. (Columbus: Ohio State University Press, 1964), pp. 81–143.

33. Ellis W. Hawley, *The New Deal and the Problem of Monopoly* (Princeton: Princeton University Press, 1966); Theda Skocpol and Kenneth Finegold, "State Capacity and Economic Intervention and the Early New Deal," *Political Science Quarterly* 97 (Summer 1982): 255–79.

34. Elliot A. Rosen, *Hoover, Roosevelt, and the Brains Trust* (New York: Colum-

bia University Press, 1977); Rexford Tugwell, *The Brains Trust* (New York: Viking Press, 1968).

35. Roosevelt was the chief proponent of power from the St. Lawrence seaway in 1939–1940, mostly for reasons of continental defense. Jordan A. Schwarz, *Liberal: Adolf A. Berle and the Vision of an American Era* (New York: Free Press, 1987).

36. William E. Leuchtenburg, *Franklin D. Roosevelt and the New Deal* (New York: Harper & Row, 1963), pp. 157–58.

37. Arthur Schlesinger, Jr., *The Coming of the New Deal* (Boston: Houghton Mifflin, 1958), p. 433; Jesse H. Jones, *Fifty Billion Dollars: My Thirteen Years with the RFC* (New York: Macmillan, 1951); Bascom N. Timmons, *Jesse H. Jones* (New York: Henry Holt, 1956).

38. James Stuart Olson, *Herbert Hoover and the Reconstruction Finance Corporation, 1931–1933* (Ames: Iowa State University Press, 1977) and Olson's *Saving Capitalism* (Princeton, N.J.: Princeton University Press, 1988).

39. See the forthcoming biography of Henry J. Kaiser by Mark Foster.

40. Schwarz, *Interregnum of Despair*, pp. 212–15.

41. Mark Leff, *The Limits of Symbolic Reform: The New Deal and Taxation, 1933–1939* (Baltimore: Johns Hopkins University Press, 1984); Schwarz, *The Speculator*, pp. 314–28.

42. Koistinen, "The 'Industrial-Military Complex': The Interwar Years," p. 839; Albert A. Blum, "Roosevelt, The M-Day Plans, and the Military-Industrial Complex," *Military Affairs* 36 (April 1972): 46; Schwarz, *The Speculator*, pp. 356–63.

43. Schwarz, *The Speculator*, pp. 264–66.

44. Ibid., pp. 401–15.

45. Alan S. Milward, *War, Economy and Society, 1939–1945* (Berkeley: University of California Press, 1977), pp. 23–30, 113–117.

46. Schwarz, *The Speculator*, pp. 415–33.

47. Ibid., pp. 458–66.

48. Robert Cuff, "Ferdinand Eberstadt, the National Security Resources Board, and the Search for Integrated Mobilization Planning, 1947–1948," *Public Historian* 7 (Fall 1985): 37–52.

49. Higgs, *Crisis and Leviathan*, pp. 244–45; Schwarz, *The Speculator*, pp. 528–34; Robert D. Cuff, "From the Controlled Materials Plan to the Defense Materials System, 1942–1953," *Military Affairs* 51 (January 1987): 1–6.

50. Milward, p. 17.

51. Schwarz, *The Speculator*, p. 534.

52. See Timmons, *Jesse H. Jones*, pp. 281–82.

53. George B. Tindall, *The Emergence of the New South, 1913–1945* (Baton Rouge: Louisiana State University Press, 1967), pp. 694–701; Gerald D. Nash, *The American West Transformed: The Impact of the Second World War* (Bloomington: Indiana University Press, 1985), pp. 17–36.

54. George quoted in Lloyd C. Gardner, *A Covenant with Power: America and World Order from Wilson to Reagan* (New York: Oxford University Press, 1984), p. 81.

55. James Tobin, "Defense, Dollars, and Doctrines," *Yale Review* 47 (Spring 1958): 321–34.

56. Robert Lekachman, *Inflation: The Permanent Problem of Boom and Bust* (New York: Random House, 1973), p. 3; also, see Lekachman, *The Age of Keynes,* (New York: Random House, 1964), p. 66, and John Kenneth Galbraith, *A Theory of Price Control* (Cambridge, Mass.: Harvard University Press, 1952).

57. Richard A. Aliano, *American Defense Policy from Eisenhower to Kennedy: The Politics of Changing Military Requirements, 1957–1961* (Athens: Ohio University Press, 1975).

58. Schwarz, *The Speculator*, pp. 575–80.

2

Public Goods, Politics, and Two Cheers for the Military-Industrial Complex

DWIGHT R. LEE

INTRODUCTION

David Stockman was correct when he told Congress in 1985 that military personnel were more interested in protecting their pensions than in protecting the country.[1] More generally, it is safe to say that those who are professionally connected to that amalgam of interests known as the military-industrial complex (MIC) are motivated more by their paychecks and profits than by the desire to maintain our military strength. This desire for private gain, even if it comes at the expense of our national defense, goes a long way in explaining why there is so much waste in military spending and why there is such widespread sentiment for diminishing, or better yet eliminating, the political influence of the military-industrial complex.[2]

The purpose of this paper is to argue that diminishing the political influence of the MIC is likely to be both inefficient and dangerous. The argument makes no attempt to deny that narrow self-interest motivates the political activity of the MIC or to downplay the waste that results when narrow self-interest is coupled with political influence. To the contrary, these two political facts of life form the basis for our case in favor of applauding the political power of the MIC.

The analytical approach of the paper is that of public choice. In a nutshell, public choice is the application of economic analysis to an understanding of the political process. The distinguishing feature of public choice as an approach to studying political behavior is its willingness to assume

The author would like to thank the Earhart Foundation for support in the preparation of this paper. Comments by Robert Higgs and Daniel Klein have been helpful, although it should be emphasized that these two individuals want no credit, and deserve no blame, for the conclusion of the paper.

that political decisions, like market decisions, are motivated by the desire to advance private interests. This imposes a methodological consistency on the analysis of private and public sector activity that disciplines the widespread, but simplistic, tendency to see market failure as a priori justification for government remediation. Market failure is pervasive, but government failure is equally pervasive for exactly the same reason: the failure of self-interest to unerringly motivate behavior that produces public-interest outcomes in a world of imperfect institutional incentives. Determining the appropriate mix of private and public activity requires comparing failure against failure, not naively opting for the one with every failure of the other.

The only complaint public choice economists have against Stockman's comment on the motivation of military personnel is that he did not keep going. Those who work for the Environmental Protection Agency are surely more interested in protecting their pay than they are in protecting the environment; those who work for public welfare agencies are more interested in helping themselves than they are in helping the poor; those who work for the Department of Agriculture are more interested in protecting their perks and paychecks than they are in protecting the family farm; those who work for the Federal Reserve System are more interested in their careers than they are in monetary stability. This listing could continue indefinitely to include employees of other government agencies, the politicians who fund the agencies, and those who seek influence over the policies of the agencies.

The purpose here is not to be critical of those who attempt to promote their private advantages through political activity. Who among us is sufficiently unblemished by self-interest to throw the first stone? We have no basis for criticizing those who pursue their self-interest through the political process even though we are convinced that this pursuit generates unfortunate social outcomes. The criticism should be directed at the incentive structure that shapes the actions of political decision-makers, not at the motivation behind these actions. When public choice economists advocate reforms for improving political outcomes, it is reform of the political institutions that they have in mind, not moral reform of people who lack enthusiasm for putting the interests of others ahead of their own.

Appropriately reforming political institutions is no easy task, however. First, there is the question of who has the motivation to work for the type of reform that genuinely promotes the public interest. There will be no shortage of suggested reforms, but the self-interest motive is just as robust when people are acting to reform political institutions as when they are acting within existing institutions. Most recommended political reforms would have the effect of promoting selective private interest at the larger sacrifice of the public interest.

Second, and quite apart from the motivation individuals have to work for political reform that is socially beneficial, is the difficulty of knowing if a given reform is genuinely beneficial or not. Altering political incentives, like altering market incentives, generates a wide range of direct and indirect effects, the aggregate effect of which is hard to evaluate. Economists have always been quick to point out to those who want to reform the market with government interventions that you cannot do only one thing. Even when the direct effects of a government reform of the market place is desirable, the reform is commonly ill-advised because of indirect and long-run effects that are harmful. The same problem exists with attempts to reform the political process. The beneficial direct effect of a political reform may be swamped by unfortunate indirect effects.

With this in mind, it may be that attempts to reduce government waste and improve efficiency in military spending by imposing restrictions on the political influence of the military-industrial complex will be no more successful than, for example, attempts to reduce poverty by increasing the minimum wage. This paper discusses in detail the problems that are likely to arise from attempts to diminish the influence of the MIC. The standard argument for relying on the government to provide national defense is presented, and then qualified from a public choice perspective. The qualification serves not as an argument against government provision of national defense, but as background for explaining the waste that is found in military spending. Some particular examples of military waste are presented and discussed, and arguments are presented in defense of the military-industrial complex's political influence, the proximate cause of military waste. Finally, these arguments are set in the context of public choice theory, as applied to an area where collective action has the advantage over private action.

PUBLIC GOODS AND POLITICS

National defense belongs to a special class of goods which economists refer to as public goods. Unlike the benefits of most goods, the benefits one individual receives from a public good in no way reduce the benefits others can receive. National defense has the additional characteristic, one common to many public goods, that it is difficult to deny to some the benefits provided once they are made available to others. If my neighbor benefits from national defense, it is difficult to prevent me from benefiting as well. The result is that no one has an incentive to reveal his demand for public goods through a willingness to pay for them. If others contribute to national defense, I can benefit as a free-rider; and if others do not contribute, my contribution will be useless. Consequently, voluntary purchases in the market place cannot be relied upon to accurately transmit the demand for public goods to potential suppliers. This market failure provides the rationale for government provision of national defense, as well as other public goods. The advantage government has over the market is derived from its power to force people to contribute to public goods. But if the coercive power of government is to be the means of efficiently providing public goods, it has to be responsive to the preferences of the public.

The primary objective of democratic political institutions is to make the exercise of political power accountable to the public. By allowing citizens to vote, it is hoped that political representatives will receive accurate information on citizen preferences and be motivated to respond appropriately to the information. As opposed to a decision to contribute to a public good in the market place, a decision to contribute to a public good in the voting booth will result in no cost to the voter unless the vote obligates everyone to contribute. There is no fear of a useless sacrifice, or hope of free-riding off the sacrifices of others, to distort the transmission of preferences. And politicians, ever anxious for reelection, are supposedly motivated to put forth public-good proposals that benefit as many as possible, which means providing those public goods that generate benefits in excess of costs and providing them efficiently.

This is, of course, a very idealized and misleading vision of how the democratic process works, but it forms the basis for much of the criticism directed at the military-industrial complex. If consumer preferences for national defense could be communicated through the political process with the same accuracy and effectiveness as are consumer preferences for private goods through the market process, then the special-interest waste created by the MIC would be intolerable. But preferences for national defense, or any other public good, simply cannot be communicated through the political process with anything close to the same effectiveness that preferences for private goods can be communicated through the market.

The demands for public goods are difficult to transmit through the political process for much the same reason that they are difficult to transmit through the market. An individual's motivation to sacrifice for a public good is not increased by giving government responsibility to provide it. Without doubt, a cost-effective national defense proposal, for example, with costs distributed over taxpayers in proportion to benefits and clearly presented to the public, would receive an overwhelmingly, if not a unanimously, favorable vote. What is the motivation, however, for an individual to incur the costs of becoming informed as to what constitutes a cost-effective national defense proposal, organizing such a proposal, getting it on the ballot, and working for its efficient implementation when approved? Each individual can free-ride on the political efforts of others in the provision of public goods just as he can free ride on the market contributions of others.

But what about the motivations of elected representatives? Are not politicians anxious to put together public-good packages that mobilize constituent support? Of course. But politicians realize that the biggest political payoff is in providing programs that concentrate private benefits on organized groups within their political districts, not in providing public goods that spread general benefits over many political districts. As with market decisions, the dominant motivational force behind political decisions is the desire to promote private, not public, purposes. The controlling influence behind military programs will not be the preferences of citizens as consumers of national defense. Consumer preferences for national defense cannot be transmitted effectively through market institutions, nor can they be transmitted effectively through political institutions. The public's desire for national security will provide a necessary justification for military expenditures. But it is the organized interests of the suppliers of national defense, the interests that comprise the military-industrial complex, that generate the political influence that shapes the details of particular military programs.

AN AROUSED PUBLIC VS. AN APATHETIC PUBLIC

While it is common to overstate the influence the general public has on political decisions such as military spending, it is important not to understate its influence. Indeed it is impossible to appreciate fully the power of special-interest control over the details of military spending without understanding why it is that the public demand for national defense will tend to be exaggerated by the political process.[3]

In discussing the public's demand for national defense, it first needs to be recognized that national defense is not something that can be easily evaluated in terms of quantity or quality. In the absence of actual wartime conditions, it is almost impossible to know whether a given military spending program increases or decreases the security of the country. An additional Trident submarine may increase our security under one set of foreign policy decisions and decrease it under another, and the interactions between weapons systems, foreign policy decisions, other relevant political decisions, and national security are so complicated that no one, no matter how well informed, can be sure that any particular decision increases our peacetime security.

This is not to deny, however, that people form strong subjective feelings about whether national security has been increased or decreased. It is obvious that international incidents have powerful effects on the public's perception of national security. Acts by foreign powers that may pose minimal, even nonexistent, risks to the American public will often be seen as major threats to our security and major affronts to the nationalistic pride that most of us possess. And because of the aforementioned complexities and ambiguities in what may be loosely termed the national defense production function, spending programs and political rhetoric can often go a long way in satisfying the public's desire that something be done about perceived threats to the nation's security.

It is one thing, however, to have aggressive feelings of nationalism and another thing to be willing to act on these feelings in response to rather slight provocation. Most people would find their aggressive urges moderated by a clear sense of accountability if they personally had their finger on the button, so to speak. But because of the simple arithmetic of majority voting, individuals, when expressing their demand for national prestige and security at the polls, will have little sense of accountability for their decisions. In all elections that influence decisions of the federal government the number of voters is sufficiently large that the probability of any one voter determining the outcome is vanishingly small. And because each voter is aware, at least at the subliminal level, that his vote will not be decisive, voting offers the opportunity to express feelings about political outcomes without costs, without any sense of responsibility for those outcomes.

When applied to nationalistic feelings, the phenomenon here is not unlike the expressions of hostility often heard at well-attended sporting events. It is obvious that few people would personally injure an official who calls a crucial penalty against the home team if given the opportunity to do so. Personal accountability would serve as a powerful restraint. But it is not uncommon for individuals, caught up in the emotions of a sporting contest and knowing that their expressive "vote" will not be decisive, to yell out in genuine anger, "kill the umpire." If "majority rule" were given free rein at sporting events there is no doubt that atrocities would be committed by fans; atrocities that no one fan would ever dream of committing as an individual. Crowd control is a well-advised means of suppressing "majority rule" wherever large numbers of people gather.

The constitutional checks and balances constraining the operation of our democratic system can be justified as a form of crowd control. But the fact remains that candidates for political office can capture political support by appealing to the nationalistic feeling of constituents who experience little sense of individual responsibility when expressing themselves at the polls. Promises to "stand tall" with military force will generate far more enthusiasm than will a careful explanation of foreign policy complexities. And these political promises, backed by the voter support they generate, translate into larger military appropriations than would be possible if political decision makers at every level experienced full accountability for their decisions.

It is to be expected, however, that military appropriations will experience significant fluctuations. Politicians may seize upon international incidents as excuses to increase political support by expanding military spending. But while politicians have some ability to create international incidents of the type that will fan nationalistic feelings at home, this ability is limited. There will typically be significant periods of time when the international scene is relatively calm and politicians will find it easier to build political support by appealing to the desire for peace that prevails in the absence of international turmoil. During such periods military spending will decline as a percentage of government spending and may drift down absolutely. But as soon as a few foreign provocations occur, such as the Soviet invasion of Afghanistan and the capture and public humiliation of U.S. embassy personnel in Iran, the result will be another upswing in military spending.

The greater the military spending the greater the potential for waste in military spending. But it is not necessarily the case that military waste will increase as military spending increases. A crucial consideration is the motivation the public has to monitor military spending. What motivation does an individual have to monitor military programs and engage in political activities aimed at increasing the effectiveness of these programs? In general, the answer is very little. The individual who went to the considerable time, effort, and expense necessary for such an undertaking would be contributing to the provision of a public good, since improved efficiency in military spending would provide nonexcludable benefits to everyone in the country. As noted in the previous section, individuals have little motivation to make personal sacrifices in efforts to provide public goods.

During periods of perceived national emergency and genuinely felt patriotism, however, the standard economic model of public goods and free-riding becomes less applicable. Some people, indeed large numbers of people, can be moved to work for the "good of the country." In the context of the present discussion, this will translate into powerful political pressure to employ military resources effectively and to avoid the type of waste that generally goes unnoticed during periods of tranquility. Furthermore, in wartime conditions, it becomes much easier to monitor the effectiveness of military activities. Battles are being won or lost; troops are either advancing or retreating; we are destroying more of the enemy's ships and planes than he is destroying of ours, or vice versa. These are not perfect measures of military effectiveness, and the data will often be distorted, but clearly evidence of military waste and incompetence is far easier to come by during wartime than during peacetime.

It is quite possible, then, that the ratio of military meat to military fat will increase as military spending increases during wartime. During periods of peace the public turns its attention to nonmilitary matters with the result that military spending will typically decline, but so will monitoring of this spending. Therefore, it is likely that the ratio of military meat to military fat will decline along with military spending.

Public apathy with regard to the details of military spending will never reach the point where waste consumes the entire budget. Before that point is reached the evidence would become overwhelmingly obvious even during peacetime. But during normal peacetime conditions public apathy, coupled with the difficulty of assessing the effectiveness of military programs, will give the military–industrial complex ample latitude to dominate the details of military spending.

SOME SPECIFICS BEHIND MILITARY WASTE

Because the political influence of the military–industrial complex dominates that of the general public on the details of military spending, the procedures and programs that generate the most political support per dollar spent will not generate the most defense per dollar spent. Relying more on open bidding in awarding defense contracts would reduce defense costs, but would also reduce the profits of politically influential defense contractors. Defense costs could be reduced by closing many of the military bases scattered around the country, but such closures would also reduce the reelection prospects of many incumbent politicians. Procurement policies that currently emphasize limited numbers of extremely expensive, overly complicated, and operationally questionable weapons at the sacrifice of a larger number of less exotic but more reliable weapons generate less defense per dollar spent, but more profit per dollar spent for politically organized interests.

Consider some specifics. Approximately 60 percent, in dollar terms, of all defense contracts is awarded noncompetitively. An additional 30 percent is awarded under exceptions to the "normal" procedure of open competitive bidding.[4] Even with competitively awarded contracts, price increases resulting from changes in the original specifications are determined by sole-source negotiations, typically on a cost-plus basis. It should come as no surprise that changes are frequent and expensive. The problem of cost escalation in defense contracts is intensified by the temptation for contractors to "buy in" to a contract by intentionally understating the expected cost of performance. The Department of Defense (DOD) is often a willing partner in the underbidding practice since a weapon system, once begun, is seldom terminated and the DOD budget can expand with cost overrides. According to a 1979 GAO report, "Since 1969 the initial (planning) estimate (submitted by the DOD) has turned out to be approximately [50] percent below the actual costs of major systems. . . . The review . . . failed to find one example where the Department of Defense accurately estimated or overestimated the cost of any major weapon system."[5]

In addition to biased cost estimates, the cost-plus approach to defense contracting also encourages criminal abuse. Prime defense contractors typically have both cost-plus and fixed-cost contracts. The temptation is to shift cost overruns occurring on fixed-cost contracts, which should be paid by the company, to cost-plus contracts, which will be paid by the taxpayer. General Dynamics and General Electric recently yielded to this temptation, as was brought to light in 1985. But these cases are only recent examples of a practice that has a long history. For example, an audit in the late 1970s revealed that Rockwell International's cost-plus contracts had cost overruns of up to 400 percent while their fixed-cost contracts had none.[6]

Unfortunately, the government's dependence on a few contractors for crucial weapons serves to protect major contractors against serious penalty even when caught defrauding the public. Though General Dynamics was reprimanded in 1985 for fraudulent billings, and temporarily denied new government contracts, by 1986 DOD had increased orders for General Dynamics submarines, tanks, and jet fighters, and General Dynamics led its closest rivals in the defense contracting business by over $1.5 billion in awarded contracts through April 1986.[7]

Political pressure results not only in less efficiently produced and excessively priced weapons systems, it also results in inefficiencies in the mix of weapons. The Joint Chiefs of Staff have called for a substantial buildup in conventional forces, which are said to be dangerously thin given U.S. military commitments. What is needed is a capacity for limited but rapid intervention in trouble spots. Despite this, military budgets emphasize the buildup of small quantities of high-tech, high-cost weapon systems that, even when performance is as advertised, are unsuited for the type of military action with which the Joint Chiefs are most concerned. Retired Admiral Noel Gaylor, former director of the National Security Agency, writes, "We can cut the defense budget significantly and improve our security [by cutting] out useless, dangerous and inordinately expensive new . . . weapons programs."[8]

It is important to emphasize that politicians are no more reluctant to exploit the taxpaying public with wasteful military spending than are defense contractors. Military waste is commonly the direct result of politicians' mandating it. Congress commonly requires expensive alterations in weapons that have more to do with spreading profits and employment over particular congressional districts, and making sure that one weapon system is not unacceptably competitive with other congressionally favored systems, than with how much the alterations add to our national security. In reviewing the 1985 defense budget, for example, Congress required changes in over 1,800 separate defense programs.[9] Congressional regulations on procurement details require over 16,000 pages of text and hundreds of additional pages of appendices, and cover such things as whether specific products can be imported, the type of industrial engineering and planning system to utilize, acceptable minimum and average rates of pay, and the amount of overtime that can be authorized.[10] Only the most naive can believe that most, or even many, of the detailed restrictions Congress imposes on defense contracting are motivated by an informed concern for efficiency in military spending.

Congress's urge to micromanage defense spending is not indifferent to

Sq weed

the trivial. It is well known that Congress overrides Pentagon decisions to close inefficient military bases. But Congress also involves itself in decisions on whether or not lamb is sold in commissaries; whether officers clubs serve margarine, butter, or both; and the ingredients that go into the preparation of sugar cookies consumed by military personnel.[11]

The reason for Congress's urge to micromanage military spending is the same regardless of the size or importance of the affected program, i.e., to capture as much political advantage as possible from the military budget. Although we will continue referring to the military-industrial complex out of respect for tradition, it would be more accurate to refer to the military-industrial-congressional complex.

POLITICAL REALISM AS A DEFENSE FOR THE MILITARY–INDUSTRIAL COMPLEX

While it is easy to find fault with the MIC as the source of military waste, to do so can deflect our attention from the fundamental cause of military waste. It is the difficulty citizens have transmitting effectively their desire for the efficient provision of national defense that explains military waste. If the demand for national defense could be communicated to suppliers in the same accurate and compelling way that the demands for private goods are communicated in the market, then the level of military waste that exists currently would be impossible. But the demand for national defense cannot be so accurately and compellingly communicated, and for this reason a significant level of military waste is inevitable. Given the latitude afforded by a rationally ignorant and apathetic public, the MIC will continue to do what all special interests do when given the opportunity, i.e., capture private advantage by imposing generalized cost in the form of waste and inefficiency.

The tendency is strong to depict the military-industrial complex as a destructive force, a malignancy that is exploiting the public for private gain and weakening our nation's defense in the bargain. If only the political influence of the MIC were brought to heel, according to this depiction, then national defense would be produced adequately and efficiently. Convenient though this view may be, it is based on a grossly distorted perception of political reality. Given the realities of the political process, the influence of the MIC, though undeniably a force for military waste, is at the same time essential to the defense of our nation and likely reduces the general level of waste in government.

In order to present the argument as vividly as possible, consider the political incentives in a democracy with no MIC.[12] As always, political representatives would be motivated to provide their constituents that combination of government services that generates the greatest political support. Each congressional representative would realize, for example, that his constituents place a positive value on national defense and, if need be, would be willing to sacrifice alternative government services for that defense. Each representative, however, would realize also that this sacrifice could be mitigated for his constituency by free-riding on the sacrifices of other constituencies. Residents in Florida, for example, receive as much military protection from an atomic submarine patrolling the oceans as do the residents of Washington state, regardless of whether the sub is paid for by taxes on those in Florida or those in Washington. A congressional representative from Florida, therefore, has a strong motivation to lighten the defense burden on his constituents by diverting funds out of the military budget in order to finance programs that provide local benefits. Most of the benefits from such a diversion go to those whose support is needed for reelection, and the costs in terms of reduced national defense are spread over the entire country. In the absence of organized special interests in Florida benefiting directly from military expenditures, there would be little political opposition to reductions in the military budget.

What is true of congressional districts in Florida would be equally true of congressional districts in all other states. The most effective political pressure comes from groups organized around special-interest and constituent-specific benefits, not from groups motivated by the desire to advance broad social objectives. In a political setting lacking special-interest groups organized around military expenditures, the military budget would be largely defenseless against the demands of other special interests.[13]

This is not to argue that there would be no effective political pressure to defend the country in the absence of the MIC. The general public demand for national security would not be completely ignored by politicians. Certainly the public demand for military protection would motivate a profusion of political rhetoric in favor of a strong defense. The situation with defense would be much like the existing situation with budget deficits. It is clear that the public is concerned about chronic budget deficits, but without a politically organized group in a position to capture special-interest benefits from a balanced budget the political response to this public concern is lots of rhetoric in support of fiscal responsibility but little action to back up that rhetoric. Could we survive as a nation if our politicians were no more concerned with protecting our borders than they are with balancing the budget?

Imposing restrictions aimed only at the political activity of the MIC would surely reduce the security of our country in our hostile world. We should consider ourselves fortunate that the MIC exists and has the political influence that it does. Without the special-interest benefits the MIC is able to capture and the political incentives they generate, there would be little hope that the broadly based public demand for national defense could be transmitted through democratic political institutions except during periods of patriotic fervor.

The standard argument for caution in attempts to cut the waste, or fat, out of the military budget is that such attempts will never be surgically precise; meat as well as fat will be removed. There is no quarrel with this argument here, except to point out that it does not go far enough. There is a potentially serious problem with attempts to cut fat out of the military budget even if it were known than only fat would be eliminated. Cutting fat from the military budget reduces the incentive for politically organized groups to exert influence in favor of military spending. The incentive to engage in political combat rather than leave the field to special interests organized around nonmilitary spending would be reduced, and the result would be less spending on both military fat and military meat.

Not only would attempts aimed specifically at reducing military waste run the risk of weakening our country's security, such attempts would in all probability increase the overall level of government inefficiency. Any attempt to reduce inefficiencies in military spending runs immediately into the problem of the theory of second best.[14] If there were no inefficiencies elsewhere in the political process (or more generally, the entire political economy), then reducing military inefficiencies would represent an unequivocal gain. But because inefficiencies are pervasive, an improvement in military efficiency may result in a reduction in efficiency generally. The problem here goes beyond that of vague theoretical generalities. There are very specific flaws in the political process, flaws that have already been discussed at length, which suggest that reducing inefficiencies in military spending may be inefficient.

Controls on the MIC designed to curb military waste would reduce the amount of spending going into military programs by reducing the ability and incentive for the MIC to exert political influence. This reduction in political influence would result in a net gain to society if the resources diverted out of the military were reallocated in accordance with the preferences of the general public. But this is surely not what would happen. The influence vacuum created by controls on the MIC would be quickly filled by the influence of other special-interest groups and they would gain control of most, if not all, of the resources diverted away from the military.[15]

The diversion of resources out of the military and into domestic special interest programs would with high probability reduce overall government efficiency. Additional military strength does increase the security of our borders, thereby having a positive social value. Many of the special-interest programs into which military savings would be diverted impose decisively negative consequences on society. Would we really be better off to reduce military spending in order to fund larger farm programs, more public housing projects, more generous export subsidies, bigger bailouts and subsidies, a larger Department of Energy, more extensive welfare programs, an expansion of the World Bank, and the expansion and creation of a host of additional transfer programs? In the second-best political world in which we live, the opportunity cost of military spending may well be negative.

CONCLUSION

A primary purpose of social institutions is to channel private-interest behavior into public-interest outcomes. No set of institutions succeeds in achieving this goal with anything near perfection. Economists have long employed their theoretical rigor to establish the shortcomings of market institutions. More recently, public choice economists have used the same theoretical approach used to establish market failure to establish the pervasiveness of government failure.

The emergence of public choice as a respected subdiscipline of economics has provided a healthy intellectual balance to the market failure emphasis that had dominated economic thought. Public choice forced economists to accept the obvious fact that market failure is an insufficient justification for turning to government for solutions. Public choice provides a consistent analytical framework for realistically comparing the market process with the political process, and an intellectually respectable argument for less reliance on government to correct market imperfections. And indeed, the side of the public choice coin that gets the most attention is the side that criticizes government.

But it is the other side of the public choice coin that this paper has focused on; the side that provides an argument for being less critical of government failure in the pursuit of those objectives where collective action has the advantage over private action. Just because the political process fails is no reason to believe that the failures are easily corrected. Because frictions, transactions costs, and externalities are so pervasive in the political process, it is advisable to be cautious when attempting to reform that process. This general point has been illustrated in this paper with a defense of the military-industrial complex.

There is no denying that the private interests of those who comprise the MIC are poorly connected to actions that respond efficiently to the national defense concerns of the general public. And certainly, no reasonable person would oppose institutional reform that improved the connection between the self-interest of all political actors, including those who are members of the MIC, and actions that advance the public interest. It should be kept in mind, however, that the public-good nature of national defense makes it difficult to connect producer and consumer interests through the political process for the same reasons it is difficult to do so through the market process. That this connection is made as well as it is, is due in large measure to the activities of the military-industrial complex.

The military-industrial complex may not deserve three cheers, but surely it deserves two.

NOTES

1. *Washington Post,* February 6, 1985.

2. When Americans were asked to rank a list of national problems in order of seriousness, "waste and fraud in federal spending for national defense" was second only to the budget deficit. The list included unemployment, inflation, the nuclear arms race, the fairness of the federal income tax, the effectiveness of the U.S. military as a fighting force, and waste and fraud in federal spending for domestic programs. On average, it is believed that nearly half of federal expenditures on the military is wasted. The most important cause of military waste is thought to be "fraud and overpricing by defense contractors." See the President's Blue Ribbon Commission on Defense Management, *A Quest for Excellence: Final Report* (Washington, D.C.: U.S. Government Printing Office, 1986), p. 190.

3. It may seem that this statement contradicts the earlier statement that consumer preferences for national defense cannot be effectively transmitted through political institutions. It will become clear, however, that by exaggerating the public's demand for national defense the political process is less likely to respond appropriately (i.e., effectively) to this demand.

4. See Jacques S. Gansler, *The Defense Industry* (Cambridge, Mass.: MIT Press, 1980), p. 76.

5. Quoted ibid., p. 91. The source says "100 percent below," obviously an impossibility. I assume that the writer meant that the actual cost was 100 percent greater than the initial estimates, which makes the latter 50 percent less than the former.

6. John Hanrahan, "Whistleblower," *Common Cause Magazine* (March/April, 1983): 17–23.

7. John Koten and Tim Carrington, "Beating the Rap: For General Dynamics Scandal over Billings Hasn't Hurt Business," *Wall Street Journal,* April 29, 1986.

As serious a problem as cost overruns and fraudulent pricing are in military spending, this problem is not as serious as recent stories about exorbitantly priced coffeepots, toilet seats and screwdrivers indicate. The extraordinary prices that the military is reported to pay for seemingly commonplace items often reflect the unusual features of the items being purchased or misleading accounting practices. See Steven Kelman, "The Grace Commission: How Much Waste in Government?" *The Public Interest* (Winter 1985): 62–82.

8. Noel Gaylor, "OK, Mr. President, Here Are Some Big Military Cuts," *Wall Street Journal,* March 7, 1984.

9. Commission on Defense Management, *A Quest for Excellence,* p. 21.

10. Gansler, *The Defense Industry,* pp. 73, 295–96.

11. Gregory A. Fossedal, "The Military-Congressional Complex," *Wall Street Journal,* August 8, 1985.

12. More precisely, there are no economic rents associated with the supply of national defense either marginally or inframarginally. That this situation is impossible to arrange is obvious and no attempt is made here to argue otherwise. It is useful

to consider such an extreme situation, however, for the purpose of understanding the consequences of moving toward it.

13. Congressional representatives who favor social programs and oppose military spending, as reflected by their rating by the Americans for Democratic Action (ADA), still demonstrate a strong tendency to vote for military spending programs when these programs concentrate spending in their district or state. See Douglas Nelson and Eugene Silberberg, "Ideology and Legislative Shirking," *Economic Inquiry* (January 1987): 15–25.

14. Richard G. Lipsey and Kelvin Lancaster, "The General Theory of Second Best," *Review of Economic Studies* 26, no. 1 (1956): 11–32.

15. That people are constantly calling for reductions in military spending in order to provide more funding for a host of domestic programs is obvious to all who follow politics. Even supposedly conservative economists get caught up in the desire to fund domestic programs at the expense of the military budget. For example, consider the statement by the late Arthur Burns: "For example, if the resources devoted to military and space activities during the past decade had been put instead to civilian uses, we could surely have eliminated urban slums. . . ." See A. Burns, "The Defense Sector: An Evaluation of Its Economic and Social Consequences," in J. Javits, C. Hitch, and A. Burns, *The Defense Sector and the American Economy* (New York: New York University Press, 1968).

3

National Defense and the Public-Goods Problem

JEFFREY ROGERS HUMMEL AND DON LAVOIE

$\mathbf{N}$ational defense, according to the popular ideal, is a service provided by the state to its citizens.[1] It entails protection from aggressors outside the state's jurisdiction, usually foreign states. The most sophisticated theoretical justification for government provision of this service is the public-goods argument. Roughly stated, this argument claims that the incentive to free-ride inhibits people from providing enough protection from foreign aggression voluntarily. Thus, it is in people's best interests to coerce themselves. Taxation is necessary to ensure sufficient military expenditures.

Many opponents of arms control treat the public-goods problem as if it alone were sufficient to discredit any radical reduction in military spending. We, however, will challenge this presumption. This chapter will not question the validity, realism, or relevance of the public-goods concept.[2] Indeed, we think that the core service within national defense—safety from violence and aggression—captures the essence of a public good more fully than economists have appreciated. But this essential feature, rather than providing a solid justification for heavy military expenditures, offers one of the most powerful objections to such a government policy.

We wish to acknowledge the invaluable assistance of Williamson M. Evers and Joe Fuhrig in working out the themes of this paper. Tyler Cowen, David Friedman, Marshall Fritz, M. L. Rantala, David Ramsay Steele, Richard H. Timberlake, Jr., David J. Theroux, and Lawrence H. White all gave us helpful comments upon earlier drafts. They do not necessarily share our conclusions, however, and we alone are responsible for any remaining errors.

We will first reexamine the nature of national defense in order to clarify the underlying goal of military spending. The presumption that the state's military establishment automatically provides safety from aggression needs careful scrutiny. The taxation necessary to fuel military expansion often generates more public-goods problems than it circumvents. This leads us to the more general question of how the free-rider incentive is ever overcome, despite theoretical predictions to the contrary. Public-goods theory seems to misunderstand human nature, by exaggerating the importance of narrow self-interest and confining attention to artificially static Prisoners' Dilemmas. A more social and dynamic model of human action is better able to account for the observed fact that free-rider problems are overcome in the real world all the time.

WHAT IS A PUBLIC GOOD?

Economists have called many things public goods and then endlessly debated whether the label really applies, but national defense has remained the quintessential public good. Although rarely discussed in detail, it is universally invoked as the classic representative of the public-goods category.[3]

Two characteristics distinguish a pure public good from a private good, and both are exhibited by the case of national defense. The first is *nonrival consumption*. One customer's consumption of a marginal unit of the good or service does not preclude another's consumption of the same unit. For example, in an uncrowded theater, two patrons' enjoyment of the same movie is nonrival. The second characteristic is *nonexcludability*. The good or service cannot be provided to an individual customer without simultaneously providing it to others. The owner of a dam, for example, cannot provide flood control separately to the individual farmers residing downstream.[4]

Although these two characteristics frequently come in conjunction with each other, they do not necessarily have to. Nonexcludability from the dam's flood-control services is accompanied by nonrival consumption of the services among the various farmers, but the owner of a nearly empty theater can still exclude additional patrons. Yet, according to the public-goods argument, either characteristic alone causes "market failure"—that is, an allocation of resources that is less than Pareto optimal. Thus, either can be sufficient to justify state intervention.[5]

Even national defense is not a pure public good. Americans in Alaska and Hawaii could very easily be excluded from the U.S. government's defense perimeter, and doing so might enhance the military value of at least conventional U.S. forces to Americans in the other forty-eight states. But in general, an additional ICBM in the U.S. arsenal can simultaneously protect everyone within the country without diminishing its services. In that respect, consumption of national defense is nonrival. Moreover, a technique that defends just a single American from the Soviet state without necessarily defending his or her entire community and perhaps the entire nation is difficult to visualize. That makes national defense nonexcludable as well.

We are going to focus, however, only upon nonexcludability. If consumption of a service is nonrival, but businessmen and entrepreneurs can exclude those who do not pay for it, then they still have strong incentives to provide the service. The most serious "market failure" that is alleged to result is underutilization of the service. Some people will be prevented from benefiting from the quantity of the service that has been produced, even though permitting them to do so costs nothing. Furthermore, even this imperfection will dissipate if the market permits discriminatory pricing.[6]

On the other hand, nonexcludability creates opportunities for free riders, who will pay for the service only if doing so is absolutely necessary to receive it. From the perspective of economic self-interest, every potential customer has an incentive to try to be a free rider. If enough of them act on this incentive, the service will not be produced at all, or at least not enough of it.

Another way to think about nonexcludability is as a positive externality in its purest form. Many goods and services generate additional benefits for people other than those who directly consume and pay for them. There is often no way for the producers of these goods to charge those who receive these external benefits. A nonexcludable good or service is one where the positive externalities are not just an incidental by-product but rather constitute the major benefit of the good or service.[7]

Clearly, the justification for the state's provision of national defense does not stem from any major concern that in its absence protection services would be produced but underutilized. Rather, it stems from the assumption that, unless taxation or some other coercive levy forces people to contribute, national defense will be inadequately funded and therefore its core service of safety from aggression will be underproduced. It is this widely held but rarely examined assumption that we wish to question.

WHAT IS NATIONAL DEFENSE?

Before we can explore the free-rider dynamics of the state's military establishment, we must clarify the meaning of the term "national defense." The public-goods justification for military expenditures rests upon a fundamental equivocation over exactly what service national defense entails. When economists discuss national defense, the core service they usually have in mind, explicitly or implicitly, is protection of people's lives, property, and liberty from foreign aggressors. This also appears to be what people have in mind when they fear foreign conquest, particularly in the case of the American fear of Soviet conquest. People throughout the world believe that their own government, no matter how disagreeable, defends them from foreign governments, which they think would be even more oppressive.

This defense of the people is not synonymous with another service that goes under the same "national defense" label: protection of the state itself and its territorial integrity. Historically, the state has often embarked on military adventures unrelated to the defense of its subjects. If this were not the case, people would require no protection from foreign states in the first place. Many Americans seriously doubt that the U.S. bombing of North Vietnam and Cambodia had very much to do with protecting their liberty. One defense-budget analyst, Earl Ravenal, contends that nearly two-thirds of U.S. military expenditures goes toward the defense of wealthy allied nations in Europe and Asia and has little value for the defense of Americans.[8]

The distinction between the two meanings of national defense does not apply only when the state engages in foreign intervention or conquest. Even during unambiguously defensive wars, the state often systematically sacrifices the defense of its subjects to the defense of itself. Such universal war measures as conscription, confiscatory taxation, rigid economic regulation, and suppression of dissent aggress against the very citizens whom the state is presumably protecting. People believe the state defends their liberty; in fact, many end up surrendering much of their liberty to defend the state.

People of course may consider some trade-off worth it. They may accept the costs and risks of the state's protection in order to reduce the risks and costs of foreign conquest. But in most discussions of national defense, the aggressive acts taken by the government against its own subjects are arbitrarily excluded from the discussion. It is this frequently overlooked cost which is suggested in Randolph Bourne's famous observation: "War is the health of the State."[9]

In other words, the national interest and the public good do not automatically coincide. We do not deny the possibility of an incidental relationship between the defense of the state and the defense of the people. But in the next section, we will present general reasons why we think this relationship is not as strong as usually supposed. Before we can do that, we must fully expose the conceptual gulf between the two meanings of national defense.

The pervasive doctrine of nationalism obscures this fundamental distinction. Nationalism treats nations as collective entities, applying principles drawn from the analysis of individual interaction to the international level. In a war between two nations, the nationalist model focuses on essentially two parties: nation A and nation B. As in fights between individuals, one of these two nations is the aggressor, whereas the other is the defender. As a result, the model axiomatically equates protecting the state with protecting its subjects.

The basic flaw in the nationalist model is its collectivist premise. Although the model informs many of the formal economic analyses of international relations, it represents a glaring example of the fallacy of composition. The state simply is not the same thing as its subjects. Democracies are sometimes referred to as "governments of the people," but this is, at best, rhetorical sloppiness. The state and the people interpenetrate one another and in complex ways, but they clearly do not have exactly the same purposes or interests.

Consequently, any conflict between two nations involves not just two parties, but at least four: the state governing nation A, the state governing nation B, the people with the (mis)fortune to live under state A, and the people with the (mis)fortune to live under state B. Whatever the merits of a dispute between states A and B, the dispute need not divide a significant portion of people A from people B.[10]

Abandoning this collectivist identification of the State with its subjects exposes *the* critical insight about the national-defense service. If one is truly concerned about defense of peoples' lives, property, and liberty, then the transfer of their capital city from one location to another is not intrinsically significant. In some cases it might even be thought an improvement. Many Americans are convinced that the territory constituting Russia is in a very real sense already conquered—by the Soviet government. Some even believe that the Soviet people would fare better with Washington, D.C., as their capital city. What ultimately matters is whether transferring the capital city brings the citizens a net loss or gain.

The danger therefore is not foreign conquest per se, but the amount of power the conquering government can successfully wield. In the final analysis, protection from foreign states is not a unique service. It is a subset of a more general service: protection from aggression by anyone—or any state. Whether we formally label an oppressive state "foreign" or "domestic" becomes a secondary consideration.

People admittedly may highly value their own state's preservation and glorification, in and of itself. Their government's military establishment may directly enter their utility functions, the same way their favorite baseball or football team does. But nationalism is not just a subjective preference. It is also a positive social theory, as legitimately subject to criticism for its policy recommendations as any other. The military's coercive funding unfortunately prevents people from revealing their true preferences about national defense directly and unambiguously. Some citizens may still want a huge and expensive military establishment even if they discover that it gives them less protection than they thought. But meanwhile, an examination of whether military expansion truly does defend people's lives, property, and liberty is still in order.[11]

THE FREE-RIDER DYNAMICS OF GOVERNMENT INTERVENTION

When Paul Samuelson first formalized public-goods theory, many economists unreflectively subscribed to what Harold Demsetz has called the nirvana approach to public policy. Demonstrating some "market failure" with respect to an abstract optimum was considered sufficient to justify state action. Economists assumed that the costless, all-knowing, and benevolent state could simply and easily correct any failure.

Since then, economists have become far more realistic. Public-goods theory has advanced to the point where it is now an exercise in comparative institutions. Demonstrating "market failure" is no longer sufficient. One must compare the market with the state, not as one wishes the state would behave in some ideal realm, but as it must behave in the real world. To justify state action, one must show that the agents of government have the capacity and the incentive to do a better job than participants in the market. Can the state provide the public good without costs that exceed the benefits? And is there some incentive structure that would conceivably ensure that it do so?[12]

Economists within the field of public choice have done some of the most important work on the comparative capabilities of the state—by applying public-goods insights to political action itself. They have come to the realization that the free-rider incentive does not only arise for market enterprises. As Mancur Olson has demonstrated, the free-rider incentive can arise for any group, especially political groups wanting to influence state policy. This imparts an inherent public-goods character to all political decisions.[13]

Assume that one of us wishes to change some state policy that we personally find particularly onerous—for instance, to repeal a tax. We are members of a fairly large group that will benefit if the tax is repealed. If enough of us contribute money, time, or other resources to bringing about the tax's repeal, we will succeed and all be better off. The money we save in taxes will more than reimburse us for our effort. Once the tax is repealed, however, even those who did not join our campaign will no longer have to pay it. We cannot exclude them from the benefits of the tax's repeal. They will be free-riders on our political efforts.

Just as in the case of a nonexcludable good in the market, every potential beneficiary of the tax repeal has an incentive, from the perspective of economic self-interest, to try to be a free-rider. If enough of them act according to this incentive, the tax will never be repealed. Public choice economists call this result "government failure," completely analogous to the "market failure" caused by nonexcludability.

Of course, this example grossly oversimplifies the problem. Under a democratic state, people do not directly purchase changes in state policy; they vote for them. Or more precisely, some of them vote for representatives who then vote on and bargain over state policy. If the tax repeal example were completely accurate, nearly every intentional benefit provided by the state would be a pure private good, similar to the current salaries of politicians and bureaucrats. With voting, political entrepreneurs and vote maximizing firms (which are called political parties) have some incentive to provide us with our tax repeal, even if we do not politically organize, in order to entice us to vote for them.[14]

This incentive, however, is not very great. First of all, voting itself gives rise to a public good. An individual must expend time and other resources to vote, but he or she can avoid these expenditures by free-riding on the voting of others. Only in the very remote case where the voter anticipates that a single vote will decide the election's outcome does this incentive to free-ride disappear. Consequently, the political entrepreneur must have some reason to expect that we will vote at all. And if we do in fact vote, he must in addition have some reason to expect that the tax repeal, among all the other competing issues, will affect how we vote. Our forming a political organization to repeal the tax gives him reason to believe both these things.[15]

In short, unorganized groups have some influence upon the policies of a democratic state. But other things being equal, groups that organize and campaign for policies have a significant advantage. That is presumably why they organize and campaign. It strains credulity to suppose that all the people who pour vast sums of money into political lobbying are utterly mistaken in the belief that they thereby gain some leverage on policy. The common observation that special interests have inordinate influence upon a democratic state is without doubt empirically well founded.

Two variables affect the likelihood that a group will overcome the free-rider problem and successfully organize. These variables operate whether the group is trying to attain nonexcludable benefits on the market or from the state. The first is the size of the group. The smaller the group, *ceteris paribus,* the more likely the members are to organize successfully. The larger the group, the more difficult it is to involve enough of them to secure the public good.

The second variable is the difference between the value of the public good to the members of the group and the cost to them. The greater this difference, *ceteris paribus,* the more likely they are to organize successfully. Indeed, if this difference is great enough, one single member might benefit enough to be willing to pay the entire cost and let all the other members of the group free-ride. The smaller this difference, on the other hand, the more essential becomes the contribution of each potential member.[16]

The democratic state therefore makes it much easier to enact policies that funnel great benefits to small groups than to enact policies that shower small benefits on large groups. Because of this free-rider–induced "government failure," the state has the same problem in providing nonexcludable goods and services as the market—with one crucial difference. When a group successfully provides itself a public good through the market, the resources it expends pay directly for the good. In contrast, when a group successfully provides itself a public good through the state, the resources it expends pay only the overhead cost of influencing state policy. The state then finances the public good through taxation or some coercive substitute.

Moreover, the group that campaigned for the state-provided public good will *not* in all likelihood bear very much of the coerced cost of the good. Otherwise, they would have had no incentive to go through the state, because doing so then costs more in total than simply providing themselves the good voluntarily. Instead, the costs will be widely distributed among the poorly organized large group, who may not benefit at all from the public good.

This makes it possible for organized groups to get the state to provide bogus public goods, goods and services which in fact cost much more than the beneficiaries would be willing to pay even if exclusion were possible and they could not free-ride. In this manner, the state generates externalities, and ones that are negative. Rather than overcoming the free-rider problem, the state benefits free-loaders, who receive bogus public goods at the expense of the taxpayers. Provision of these goods and services moves the economy away from, not toward, Pareto optimality. When the bogusness of such public goods is obvious enough, economists call them transfers.

What is the upshot of this "government failure" for national defense? In the case of defending the state itself, we are dealing quite clearly with a service that the state has enormous incentives to provide. If this is a nonexcludable good or service at all, then it is a public good that benefits small groups very highly. But in the case of defending the people, we are talking about, in the words of David Friedman, "a public good . . . with a very large public." The benefits, although potentially great, are dispersed very broadly.[17]

Thus, to the extent that the free-rider obstacle inhibits market protection of liberty, it raises an even more difficult obstacle to the state's ever undertaking that vital service. The state has strong incentives to provide national defense that protects itself and its prerogatives, but it has very weak incentives to provide national defense that protects its subjects' lives, property, and liberty. This explains the common historical divergence between defending the state and defending the people.

Furthermore, there is a perverse inverse relationship between the people's belief that the state defends them and the reality. To the extent that they accept this nationalistic conclusion, their political resistance against the domestic state's aggression, however weak because of the public-goods problem to begin with, decreases further. This is most noticeable during periods of actual warfare. The belief of the state's subjects that it provides protection actually reduces the amount of protection they enjoy, at least against the domestic state.

Nationalism thus results in an ironic paradox. It views the state as a protection agency, but this very view contributes to the possibility that the state will take on the literal role of a protection racket. Those who decline to pay for the state's protection become its victims. This in turn gives the state an added incentive to find foreign enemies. For without a foreign threat, the justification for the state's protection becomes far less persuasive.[18]

Our remarks have thus far been confined to the democratic state. They apply, however, even more strikingly to the undemocratic state, insofar as there is any significant difference between the political dynamics of the two types. We believe that many economists have overemphasized the operative significance of formal voting. Both types of states are subject to the influence of groups that marshal resources in order to affect policy. Formal voting only makes it possible for some changes to manifest themselves faster and less painfully.

Our argument does not rule out the possibility that the state might actually defend its subjects. Whereas the difference between the political dynamics of democratic and undemocratic states is overdrawn, states do differ markedly in the amount of aggression they commit against their own subjects. If we automatically assume that a conquering government can wield as much power over foreign populations as it does over its domestic subjects, then a relatively less oppressive government will, in the process of defending itself, provide some protection for its subjects. But this is often only an unintended positive externality.

Moreover, a military policy designed primarily to defend the state's prerogatives will generally differ from what would be sufficient for the protection of its subjects. This difference may unnecessarily involve the people in dangerous military commitments and adventures. Their lives, liberty, and property, beyond being sacrificed to the interests of the domestic state, will then be at greater risk from foreign governments as well. Even when countering oppressive governments, national defense therefore generates negative externalities that may more than offset the possible positive externality.

Above all, the value of this defense hinges entirely upon the assumption that conquering governments can oppress a foreign population more fully and easily than can that population's domestic government. But this assumption is highly simplistic. It treats the power of the state as exogenously determined. Yet, if our concern is for the protection of people's lives, property, and liberty from *any* state, then a state's oppressiveness becomes the most critical variable of all. One state's military policy might not only directly affect the liberty of its own subjects, but it might also indirectly influence the power of opposing states. Only a more sophisticated understanding of oppression's fundamental determinants can tell us how best to ward off foreign aggression.

THE FREE-RIDER DYNAMICS OF SOCIAL CONSENSUS

To this point, our conclusions have been somewhat pessimistic, justifying Earl Brubaker's observation that the free-rider assumption *makes* economics a dismal science.[19] Based on that assumption, neither the market nor the state has much incentive to provide any direct protection of peoples' lives, property, and liberty. To the extent that historical accident has resulted in marked differences in the power of various states over their own subjects, some such protection might be produced as an unintended externality of the state's effort to protect its own territorial integrity. But that very effort at self-protection will also have a significant countervailing negative impact on the degree to which the state aggresses against its own subjects.

Attributing a difference to historical accident, however, is simply another way of saying that the difference is unexplained. Not until we explain the marked differences in domestic power of the world's states will we fully comprehend the relationship between protecting the state and protecting the people.

One naive explanation common among economists is the public-goods theory of the state. This theory often rests upon a sharp dichotomy between two types of states, usually democratic and undemocratic. Undemocratic states according to this theory are little better than criminal gangs, run by single despots or small groups of oligarchs essentially for their own personal ends. The subjects of these states suffer under their rulers but can do very little about their plight. Any effort on their part to change the situation, whether through violent revolution or other means, produces an outcome that is a public good; again, we are caught in the free-rider trap.[20]

Democratic states, in contrast, are the result of social contracts. According to the public-goods theory of the state, people create democratic states to solve the free-rider problem. At some obscure moment in the past, they drew up constitutional rules in which they agreed to be coerced in order to provide public goods for themselves. Over time, because the free-rider problem generates "government failure," democratic states have a tendency to fall under the influence of special interests. Perhaps better constitutional decision rules could alleviate this decay. Nonetheless, democratic states always retain vestiges of their public-goods origin. That is why they aggress against their own subjects far less than do undemocratic states.[21]

We do not have to turn to the readily accessible historical evidence to refute this naive theory about the origin of democratic states. The theory's proponents quite often do not literally believe it. Instead, they view the theory as merely explaining the conceptual nature rather than the concrete origin of the democratic state. Either way, however, the theory has an inner contradiction. Creating a democratic state of this nature is a public good itself. A very large group must in some manner have produced it. Because of the free-rider problem, they have no more incentive to do that than to revolt against an undemocratic state or to provide themselves any other nonexcludable benefit.[22]

A more realistic alternative to the public-goods theory of the state is what we can call the social-consensus theory of the state. All states are legitimized monopolies on coercion. The crucial word is "legitimized." This legitimization is what differentiates states from mere criminal gangs. Any society in which people refrain from regularly killing each other enjoys some kind of social consensus. No government rules through brute force alone, no matter how undemocratic. Enough of its subjects must accept it as necessary or desirable for its rule to be widely enforced and observed. But the very consensus which legitimizes the state also binds it.[23]

The social consensus bears little resemblance to the mythical social contract of public-goods theory. Whereas the social contract is generally conceived of as an *intentional* political agreement, agreed upon explicitly at some specific moment, the social consensus is an *unintended* societal institution, like language, evolving implicitly over time. Sometimes, the evolution of the social consensus can be very violent. Often, particular individuals or even fairly large groups will strongly disagree with certain features of their society's consensus. But at all times, members of society are socialized into the consensus in ways that they only dimly grasp, if at all.[24]

Consider a classroom filled with average American citizens. Ask for a show of hands on the following question: how many would pay their taxes in full if no penalties resulted from nonpayment? Very few would raise their hands. This shows that taxation is involuntary. Then ask the group a second question: how many think taxes are necessary or just? This time, nearly every hand would go up. This shows that taxation is legitimized.[25]

Of course, one of the reasons Americans generally view taxation as legitimate is because they think it is necessary in order to provide public goods. All this proves, however, is that, although the public-goods theory of the state is utterly worthless as an objective description of the state's origin or nature, it is very valuable as an ideological rationalization for the state's legitimization. It performs a function analogous to that performed by the divine right of kings under monarchical states or by Marxist dogma under Communist states.

The social-consensus theory of the state suggests that if you conducted the same survey about taxation upon a group of average Russians living within the Soviet Union, or a group of average Iranians living under the Ayatollah (and you could guarantee them complete immunity regardless of how they answered), you would get similar results. These foreign and "evil" undemocratic states are not exogenous and alien institutions imposed on their subjects by sheer terror. They are complex products of the culture, attitudes, preferences, and ideas, whether explicit or implicit, that prevail within their societies.[26]

The vast ideological and cultural differences among the peoples of the world are what explain the marked differences in the domestic power of their states. The consensual constraints upon states differ in content, but all states face them. The Soviet leaders fully realize this, which is why they devote so many resources to domestic and foreign propaganda. The shifting social consensus also explains the many changes in the form and power of the state over time. Although professional economists tend to ignore the ideological and cultural components of social dynamics, professional historians give these factors the bulk of their attention.

History records that in the not-so-distant past the world was entirely in the grip of undemocratic states, which permitted their subjects very little liberty. Democratic states evolved from undemocratic states. States that now must tolerate a large degree of liberty emerged from states that did not have to do so. Public-goods theory is in the awkward position of theoretically denying that this could have happened. It raises an across-the-board theoretical obstacle to every conceivable reduction in state power that benefits more than a small group of individuals.[27] The social-consensus theory, in contrast, attributes this slow progress, sometimes punctuated with violent revolutions and wars, to ideological changes within the social consensus.

Thus, history is littered with drastic changes in state power and policy that resulted from successful ideological surmountings of the free-rider obstacle. The Minutemen volunteers who fought at Concord Bridge could not even come close to charging all the beneficiaries of their action. They produced tremendous externalities from which Americans are still benefiting today. The Abolitionist movement produced such a cascade of positive externalities that chattel slavery—a labor system that was one of the world's mainstays no less than two hundred years ago, and had been so for millennia—has been rooted out everywhere across the entire globe. We could multiply the examples endlessly.[28]

Indeed, the existence of any voluntary ethical behavior at all faces a free-rider obstacle. Society is much more prosperous if we all cease to steal and cheat, but the single individual is better off still if everyone else behaves ethically while he or she steals and cheats whenever able to get away with it. Thus, everyone has a powerful personal incentive to free-ride on other people's ethical behavior. If we all succumbed to that incentive, society would not be possible at all.

We must avoid the mistaken impression that the government's police forces and courts are what prevents most stealing and cheating. To begin with, the initial creation of such a police and court system (at least under government auspices) is another public good. But far more important, the police and courts are only capable of handling the recalcitrant minority, who refuse voluntarily to obey society's norms. A cursory glance at varying crime rates, over time and across locations, clearly indicates that the total stealing and cheating in society is far from solely a function of the resources devoted to the police and the courts. Certain neighborhoods are less safe, making an equal unit of police protection less effective, because they contain more aspiring ethical free-riders. If all members of society or even a substantial fraction became ethical free-riders, always stealing and cheating whenever they thought they could get away with it, the police and court system would collapse under the load.[29]

In short, every humanitarian crusade, every broad-based ideological movement, every widely practiced ethical system, religious and non-religious, is a defiant challenge hurled at the neoclassical economist's justification for state provision of public goods. The steady advance of the human race over the centuries is a series of successful surmountings of the free-rider obstacle. Civilization itself would be totally impossible unless people had somehow circumvented the public-goods problem.[30]

BEYOND THE FREE-RIDER INCENTIVE

If what we have been saying so far is even partly correct, there must be a serious flaw in public-goods theory. Howard Margolis points out that "no society we know could function" if all its members actually behaved as the free-rider assumption predicts they will. He calls this theoretical failure free-rider "overkill."[31]

Despite this flaw, public-goods theory explains a great deal, which is why it remains so popular among economists. It explains why so many eligible voters do not waste their time going to the polls. But it fails to explain why so many of them still do go. (We think an interesting empirical study would be to determine what percentage of economists who accept public-goods theory violate their theoretical assumptions about human behavior by voting.) It explains why the progress of civilization has been so painfully slow. But it fails to explain why we observe any progress at all.

Before we work out the implications of this theoretical flaw for the issue of national defense, let us digress briefly and try to identify it. It must involve some weakness in the theory's assumption about human behavior. We make no pretensions, however, to being able fully to resolve the weakness. Because this very issue sits at the conjunction of public-goods theory and game theory, it has become one of the most fertile areas of inquiry within economics and political science over the last decade. All we can do is modestly offer some tentative thoughts about the sources of the weakness.

Two possibilities suggest themselves. Either people do not consistently pursue the ends that the free-rider assumption predicts they will pursue, or they pursue those ends but using means inconsistent with the assumption. We will take up both of these possibilities in order:

1. Do people consistently pursue their self-interest, as the free-rider assumption defines self-interest? Public-goods theorists have offered not one but two motives that should cause a person to behave in accordance with the free-rider assumption. The most obvious is narrow economic self-interest. This end does provide a sufficient reason to free-ride, but visualizing someone choosing a different end is quite easy. Simple altruism is not the only alternative that will violate this narrow assumption. People may desire social improvements—liberty, justice, peace, etc.—not simply for their material benefits, but as ends in and of themselves, independently present within their utility functions. Patrick Henry may have been engaging in political hyperbole when he exclaimed "Give me liberty or give me death!", but he was still expressing a willingness to pay more for attaining liberty than its narrow economic returns would cover. Perhaps this willingness should be called ideological; no matter what we call it, it appears to be quite common in human history.[32]

Mancur Olson is the most prominent public-goods theorist to argue that a second motive beyond narrow economic self-interest justifies the free-rider assumption. This second motive applies even to the individual with ideological ends—*if* the group is large enough. He contends that only rationality in the pursuit of whatever end the individual chooses is strictly necessary. The individual will still choose to free-ride, because for a public good requiring a large group his meager contribution will have no perceptible effect on attaining the end.[33]

We could object that an individual's contribution to a cause is often not contingent in any way upon the cause's overall success. Consequently, how much the individual thinks his action will affect the probability of success is often irrelevant. Some people refuse to litter, for instance, fully aware that their refusal will have no perceptible impact on the quantity of litter. Such individuals gain satisfaction from doing what they believe is proper, regardless of its macro-impact. In addition to a sense of righteousness, ideological movements can offer their participants a sense of solidarity, of companionship in a cause, that keeps many loyal no matter how hopeless the cause.[34]

But this objection concedes far too much to Olson. As philosopher Richard Tuck has cogently pointed out, Olson's notion of "rationality" if consistently obeyed precludes some everyday activities. It does not just apply to an individual's contribution to the effort of a large group; it applies just as forcefully to the cumulative actions of a single person on a large individual project. Olson's "rationality" is simply a modern variant of the ancient philosophical paradox of the Sorites. In one version, the paradox argues that there can never be a heap of stones. One stone does not constitute a heap, nor does the addition of one stone to something that is not already a heap. Therefore, no matter how many stones are added, they will never constitute a heap. (Of course, in the other direction, this paradox argues that there can never be anything but a heap of stones.)

One more dollar will not make a perceptible difference in a person's life savings. One day's exercise will not make a perceptible difference in a person's health. If the fact that the individual's imperceptible contribution goes toward a group rather than an individual effort is what is decisive, then we are simply back again at the motive of narrow self-interest. No doubt, this type of "rationality" does influence some people not to undertake some actions under some circumstances. But just how compelling people find it is demonstrated by the millions who vote in presidential elections, despite the near certainty that the outcome will never be decided by one person's vote.[35]

2. Do people pursue their self-interest but in a manner inconsistent with the free-rider assumption? Olson, again, has suggested one way that individuals might effectively organize despite the free-rider obstacle. Groups can link their efforts at achieving nonexcludable benefits with excludable by-products. Such by-products include low group-rate insurance and professional journals. The incentive provided by these by-products helps counteract the incentive to be a free rider.[36]

One intriguing aspect of the by-product theory is the easy method it seems to offer for providing national defense without a state. Why couldn't the purchase of national defense be linked to some excludable by-product that everyone wants, such as protection insurance or contract enforcement? Indeed, most of those advocating voluntary funding of national defense have hit upon some such scheme.[37]

But this solution is too easy. If the excludable by-product is really what people want, then a competitor who does not link it with the nonexcludable good or service can sell it at a lower price. Only if the group has a legal monopoly on marketing its by-product can it really counteract the free-rider incentive. Every really successful example of groups relying upon by-products that Olson discusses involves some sort of legal monopoly. But the group's initial attainment of this legal monopoly remains an unexplained surmounting of the public-goods problem.[38]

Far more promising than the by-product theory for explaining the empirical weakness of the free-rider assumption is some of the recent dynamic analysis being done in game theory. As many scholars have pointed out, the free-rider problem in public-goods theory is identical to the famous Prisoner's Dilemma in game theory.[39]

The Prisoner's Dilemma derives its name from an archetypal situation where two prisoners are being held for some crime. The prosecutor separately proposes the same deal to both prisoners, because he only has sufficient evidence to convict them of a minor crime with a light sentence. Each is told that if he confesses, but the other does not, he will get off free, while the other will suffer the full penalty, unless the other also confesses. If they both confess, they both will be convicted of the more serious crime, although they both will receive some small leniency for confessing. This deal gives each prisoner an incentive independently to confess, because by doing so he individually will be better off regardless of what the other does. Consequently, they both confess, despite the fact that they both collectively would have had much lighter sentences if they both refused to confess.

The public-goods problem is essentially a Prisoner's Dilemma with many prisoners. We cannot delve into the details here of the recent work, both theoretical and empirical, of such game theorists as Michael Taylor, Russell Hardin, and Robert Axelrod, but essentially they have explored the Prisoner's Dilemma within a dynamic rather than static setting. Their conclusion: whereas in a static single Prisoner's Dilemma, cooperation is never rational; in dynamic iterated Prisoner's Dilemmas, with two or more people, cooperation frequently becomes rational for even the most narrowly self-interested individual. What this work implies is that in many real-world dynamic contexts, ideological altruism or some similar motive beyond narrow self-interest may not be necessary at all to counterbalance the free-rider incentive.[40]

CONCLUSION

We have seen that putting domestic limitations upon the power of the state is a public-goods problem, but nonetheless one that in many historical instances for whatever reason has been solved. We have also seen that national defense, in the sense of protecting the people from a foreign state, is a subset of the general problem of protecting them from any state, domestic or foreign.

Because of "government failure," the domestic military establishment itself can become the greatest threat to the lives, property, and liberty of the state's subjects. The danger from military expansion, moreover, is not confined to its domestic impact. By threatening the opposing nation, it cannot even unambiguously guarantee greater international safety. The same threat that deters can also provoke the opposing side's military expansion.

Perhaps the factors that already provide protection from the domestic state are the very factors to which we should turn for protection from foreign states. The same social consensus that has voluntarily overcome the free-rider obstacle to make the United States one of the freest, if not the freest, nation may be able to overcome the free-rider obstacle to protect American freedom from foreign states.

Nearly all of us desire a world in which all states have been disarmed.

Of course, most of the formal economic models of international relations are not very sanguine about this eventuality. Yet our analysis points to two possible shortcomings in such models and suggests at least a glimmer of hope. First, they are generally built upon a static formulation of the Prisoner's Dilemma, whereas dynamic formulations are more realistic and more likely to yield cooperative outcomes. Second, they generally commit the nationalistic fallacy of composition, ignoring the interactions of the state with its own and foreign populations. Like the public-goods theory they emulate, these models are very good at explaining the cases where disarmament fails. They do not do so well at explaining the cases where it succeeds—as for instance, along the U.S.-Canada border since 1871.[41]

The domestic production of disarmament is itself a public good, confronting the same free-rider obstacle that confronts every nonexcludable good and service. Should a majority in any one nation come to endorse this policy, the narrow—or not so narrow—special interests who benefit from an armed state would undoubtedly be willing to commit vast resources to keeping a huge military establishment. Thus, like all significant gains in the history of civilization, the disarming of the state could only be accomplished by a massive ideological surge that surmounts the free-rider obstacle.

NOTES

1. By "the state" we mean government. We use the two terms interchangeably, unlike many political scientists, who use the term the "state" either for what we are calling the "nation," i.e., the government plus its subjects, or for some vague intermediate entity which is less than the entire nation but more than just the government. We recognize that the state and its subjects can often be intricately interwoven into a complex web of mixed institutions, but the distinction is still fundamental.

2. Although we will not take up these issues here, some economists suggest that the characteristics that make something a public good are almost never physically inherent in the good or service but are rather nearly always a consequence of choosing one out of many feasible methods for producing the good or service. See Tyler Cowen, "Public Goods Definitions and Their Institutional Context: A Critique of Public Goods Theory," *Review of Social Economy* 43 (April 1985): 53–63; Tom G. Palmer, "Infrastructure: Public or Private?" *Policy Report* 5 (May 1983): 1–5, 11; Walter Block, "Public Goods and Externalities: The Case of Roads," *Journal of Libertarian Studies* 7 (Spring 1983): 1–34; Murray Rothbard, "The Myth of Neutral Taxation," *Cato Journal* 1 (Fall 1981): 532–46; Kenneth D. Goldin, "Equal Access vs. Selective Access: A Critique of Public Goods Theory," *Public Choice* 29 (Spring 1977): 53–71; and Earl Brubaker, "Free Ride, Free Revelation, or Golden Rule," *Journal of Law and Economics* 18 (April 1975): 147–61.

3. Examples of economists treating national defense as the quintessential public good include Paul A. Samuelson, *Economics,* 10th ed. (with Peter Temin), (New York: McGraw-Hill, 1976), p. 159; James M. Buchanan and Marilyn R. Flowers, *The Public Finances: An Introductory Textbook,* 4th ed. (Homewood, Ill.:

Richard D. Irwin, 1975), p. 27; and John G. Head and Carl S. Shoup, "Public Goods, Private Goods, and Ambiguous Goods," *Economic Journal* 79 (September 1969): 567.

Among the few attempts of economists to look in any detail at national defense as a public good are Earl A. Thompson, "Taxation and National Defense," *Journal of Political Economy* 82 (July/August 1974): 755–82; and R. Harrison Wagner, "National Defense as a Collective Good," in *Comparative Public Policy: Issues, Theories, and Methods,* eds. Craig Liske, William Loehr, and John McCamant (New York: John Wiley & Sons, 1975), pp. 199–221.

4. Paul A. Samuelson's two classic articles, "The Pure Theory of Public Expenditure," *Review of Economics and Statistics* 36 (November 1954): 387–89, and "Diagrammatic Exposition of a Theory of Public Expenditure," ibid. 37 (November 1955): 350–56, are generally credited as being the first formal statements of modern public-goods theory.

Important further developments in public-goods theory include Paul A. Samuelson, "Aspects of Public Expenditure Theories," *Review of Economics and Statistics* 40 (November 1958): 332–38; Richard A. Musgrave, *The Theory of Public Finance: A Study in Public Economy* (New York: McGraw-Hill, 1959); James M. Buchanan and M. Z. Kafoglis, "A Note on Public Good Supply," *American Economic Review* 53 (January 1963): 403–14; Harold Demsetz, "The Exchange and Enforcement of Property Rights," *Journal of Law and Economics* 7 (October 1964): 11–26; Jora R. Minasian, "Television Pricing and the Theory of Public Goods," ibid., 71–80; William J. Baumol, *Welfare Economics and the Theory of the State,* 2nd ed. (Cambridge, Mass.: Harvard University Press, 1965); R. N. McKean and Jora R. Minasian, "On Achieving Pareto Optimality—Regardless of Cost," *Western Economic Journal* 5 (December 1966): 14–23; Otto Davis and Andrew Winston, "On the Distinction Between Public and Private Goods," *American Economic Review* 57 (May 1967): 360–73; James M. Buchanan, *The Demand and Supply of Public Goods* (Chicago: Rand McNally, 1968); E. J. Mishan, "The Relationship Between Joint Products, Collective Goods, and External Effects," *Journal of Political Economy* 77 (May/June 1969): 329–48; Head and Shoup, "Public Goods, Private Goods, and Ambiguous Goods"; John G. Head, *Public Goods and Public Welfare* (Durham, N.C.: Duke University Press, 1974); and Duncan Snidal, "Public Goods, Propery Rights, and Political Organizations," *International Studies Quarterly* 23 (December 1979): 532–66.

5. Much of the literature has conceded that, strictly speaking, very few actual goods or services exhibit either of the public-good characteristics in its polar form. Instead, in the real world we encounter a range of goods and services for which the potential capacity and quality of nonrival consumption is increasing or for which the costs of exclusion are increasing.

6. We have slightly understated the supposed "market failure" from nonrival consumption with excludability. The quantity of the public good could also be nonoptimal. There is a vast economic literature debating the intricacies of nonrival consumption. Some of the highlights include Paul A. Samuelson, "Contrast Between Welfare Conditions for Joint Supply and for Public Goods," *Review of Economics and Statistics* 51 (February 1969): 26–30; Harold Demsetz, "The Private Production of Public Goods," *Journal of Law and Economics* 13 (October 1970): 293–306; Earl A. Thompson, "The Perfectly Competitive Production of Collective Goods," *Review of Economics and Statistics* 50 (February 1968): 1–12; Robert B. Ekelund and Joe R. Hulett, "Joint Supply, the Taussig-Pigou Controversy, and the Competitive Provision of Public Goods," *Journal of Law and Economics* 16 (October 1973): 369–87; Harold Demsetz, "Joint Supply and Price Discrimination," ibid., 389–405; William H. Oakland, "Public Goods, Perfect Competition and Underproduction," *Journal of Political Economy* 82 (September/October 1974): 927–39; Dwight R. Lee, "Discrimination and Efficiency in the Pricing of Public Goods,"

Journal of Law and Economics 20 (October 1977): 403–20; Thomas Borcherding, "Competition, Exclusion, and the Optimal Supply of Public Goods," ibid. 21 (April 1978): 111–32; and Michael E. Burns and Cliff Walsh, "Market Provision of Price-Excludable Public Goods: A General Analysis," *Journal of Political Economy* 89 (February 1981): 166–91.

7. On the relationship of public goods and externalities, see Paul Samuelson, "Pure Theory of Public Expenditure and Taxation," in *Public Economics: An Analysis of Public Production and Consumption and their Relations to the Private Sectors,* ed. J. Margolis and H. Guitton (London: Macmillan, 1969), pp. 98–123; Buchanan, *Demand and Supply of Public Goods,* p. 75; John G. Head, "Externality and Public Policy," in *Public Goods and Public Welfare,* pp. 184–213; and Mishan, "The Relationship Between Joint Products, Collective Goods, and External Effects."

8. Earl C. Ravenal, *Defining Defense: The 1985 Military Budget* (Washington: Cato Institute, 1984). See also Bruce M. Russett, *What Price Vigilance? The Burdens of National Defense* (New Haven: Yale University Press, 1970), pp. 91–126.

9. Randolph Bourne, "The State," in *War and the Intellectuals: Essays by Randolph Bourne, 1915–1919,* ed. Carl Resek (New York: Harper & Row, 1964), pp. 65–104. A general substantiation (or refutation) of Bourne's observation has so far not attracted the professional energies of any historian, perhaps because they feel no need to belabor the obvious. There are lots of studies showing the growth of state power in particular countries during particular wars, but very few that even treat a single country during more than one war, or more than a single country during one war. A few exceptions that have come to our attention include: Clinton Rossiter, *Constitutional Dictatorship: Crisis Government in the Modern Democracies* (Princeton: Princeton University Press, 1948); Arthur A. Ekirch, Jr., *The Civilian and the Military: A History of the American Antimilitarist Tradition* (New York: Oxford University Press, 1956); Robert Higgs, *Crisis and Leviathan: Critical Episodes in the Growth of American Government* (New York: Oxford University Press, 1987); Charles Tilly, ed., *The Formation of National States in Western Europe* (Princeton: Princeton University Press, 1975); Tilly, "War Making and State Making as Organized Crime," in *Bringing the State Back In,* ed. Peter B. Evans, Dietrich Rueschemeyer, and Theda Skocpol (Cambridge: Cambridge University Press, 1985); and J. R. Hale, *War and Society in Renaissance Europe, 1450–1620* (New York: St. Martin's Press, 1985).

10. We cite examples of economic models exhibiting the nationalistic fallacy of composition below. One of the very few written challenges to the nationalistic model is Murray N. Rothbard, "War, Peace and the State," in Rothbard, *Egalitarianism as a Revolt Against Nature: And Other Essays* (Washington: Libertarian Review Press, 1974), pp. 70–80. We have profited greatly from this pathbreaking essay.

11. For a purely formal approach to people's utility functions with regard to national defense, see Wagner, "National Defense as a Collective Good."

12. Demsetz makes the comparison between the "nirvana" and "comparative institutions" approaches in "Information and Efficiency: Another Viewpoint," *Journal of Law and Economics* 12 (April 1969): 1–3. See also Ronald Coase, "The Problem of Social Cost," ibid. 3 (October 1960): 1–44; James M. Buchanan, "Politics, Policy, and the Pigovian Margins," *Economica,* 2nd ser., 29 (February 1962): 17–28; and Ralph Turvey, "On the Divergences between Social Cost and Private Cost," ibid. 30 (August 1963): 309–13.

13. Anthony Downs, *An Economic Theory of Democracy* (New York: Harper & Row, 1957); James M. Buchanan and Gordon Tullock, *The Calculus of Consent: Logical Foundations of Constitutional Democracy* (Ann Arbor: University of Michigan Press, 1962); Mancur Olson, *The Logic of Collective Action: Public Goods and the*

Theory of Groups, 2nd ed. (Cambridge, Mass.: Harvard University Press, 1971); William A. Niskanen, Jr., *Bureaucracy and Representative Government* (Chicago: Aldine-Atherton, 1971); Gordon Tullock, *Toward a Mathematics of Politics* (Ann Arbor: University of Michigan Press, 1967); Albert Breton, *The Economic Theory of Representative Government* (Chicago: Aldine, 1974); and Gary Becker, "A Theory of Competition among Pressure Groups for Political Influence," *Quarterly Journal of Economics* 98 (August 1983): 372–80.

14. Richard E. Wagner, "Pressure Groups and Political Entrepreneurs: A Review Article," *Papers on Non-Market Decision Making* 1 (1966): 161–70; and Norman Frohlich, Joe A. Oppenheimer, and Oran R. Young, *Political Leadership and Collective Goods* (Princeton: Princeton University Press, 1971), stress the political-entrepreneur thesis. Olson responds briefly in the second edition of *The Logic of Collective Action,* pp. 174–75. Brian Barry, *Sociologists, Economists and Democracy* (Chicago: University of Chicago Press, 1978) pp. 37–40, and Russell Hardin, *Collective Action* (Baltimore: Johns Hopkins University Press, 1982), pp. 35–37, go into the weakness of this thesis in greater detail.

15. Extended discussions of the outcome of voting as a public good include Yoram Barzel and Eugene Silberberg, "Is the Act of Voting Rational?" *Public Choice* 16 (Fall 1973): 51–58; Paul E. Meehl, "The Selfish Voter Paradox and the Throw-Away Vote Argument," *American Political Science Review* 71 (March 1977): 11–30; James M. Buchanan and G. Brennan, "Voter Choice: Evaluating Political Alternatives," *American Behavioral Scientist* 29 (November/December 1984): 185–201; and Barry, *Sociologists, Economists and Democracy,* pp. 13–19.

16. One of the clearest expositions of these factors appears in David Friedman's neglected *The Machinery of Freedom: Guide to a Radical Capitalism* (New York: Harper & Row, 1973), pp. 185–88. See also his *Price Theory: An Intermediate Text* (Cincinnati: South-Western, 1986), pp. 440–47. Olson's taxonomy of groups—privileged (small), intermediate, and latent (large)—in *The Logic of Collective Action* treats the two factors—group size and relative cost of the public good—simultaneously and thereby slightly confuses the issue. Hardin, *Collective Action,* pp. 38–42, clarifies Olson's taxonomy, correctly pointing out that a privileged group (one in which a single member values the public good enough to pay its entire cost) could theoretically be quite large.

Admittedly, there is some ambiguity about which *cetera* remain *pares* when group size is varied. Some scholars have consequently challenged the claim that larger groups have greater difficulty overcoming the free-rider incentive. See Norman Frohlich and Joe A. Oppenheimer, "I Get By with a Little Help from My Friends," *World Politics* 23 (October 1970): 104–20; John Chamberlin, "Provision of Public Goods as a Function of Group Size," *American Political Science Review* 68 (June 1974): 707–16; and Martin C. McGuire, "Group Size, Homogeneity, and the Aggregate Provision of a Pure Public Good under Cournot Behavior," *Public Choice* 18 (Summer 1974): 107–26. The best resolution of these questions is Hardin, *Collective Action,* pp. 42–49, 125–37.

17. Friedman, *The Machinery of Freedom,* p. 189. Dwight R. Lee, "The Soviet Economy and the Arms Control Delusion," *Journal of Contemporary Studies* 8 (Winter/Spring 1985): 46, makes the same observation about the political production of national defense, but because he does not recognize the distinction between defending the state and defending the people, he arrives at a much different conclusion: viz., democratic states will underproduce military defense relative to undemocratic states.

18. A similar point is made by Kenneth E. Boulding, "The World War Industry as an Economic Problem," in the collection he coedited with Emile Benoit, *Disarmament and the Economy* (New York: Harper & Row, 1963), pp. 3–27. He refers

to the world's competing military organizations as "milorgs" and insists that, in contrast to any other social enterprise (including police protection), military organizations generate their own demand. "The only justification for the existence of a milorg is the existence of another milorg in some other place. . . . A police force is not justified by the existence of a police force in another town, that is, by another institution of the same kind" (p. 10).

19. Brubaker, "Free Ride, Free Revelation, or Golden Rule," p. 153.

20. For the argument that revolution is a public good, see Gordon Tullock, "The Paradox of Revolution," *Public Choice* 9 (Fall 1971): 89–99, which became with minor alterations one of the chapters of his book, *The Social Dilemma: The Economics of War and Revolution* (Blacksburg, Va.: University Publications, 1974). Tullock distinguishes between what he calls "exploitative" and "cooperative" governments, rather than democratic and undemocratic, but the two classifications are almost identical.

21. The public-goods theory of the democratic state is still stated best in Baumol, *Welfare Economics and the Theory of the State*, p. 57.

22. Joseph P. Kalt, "Public Goods and the Theory of Government," *Cato Journal* 1 (Fall 1981): 565–84, pinpoints the contradiction in the public-goods theory of the state. The still devastating, classic, point-by-point refutation of the social contract remains Lysander Spooner, *No Treason: The Constitution of No Authority* (1870; reprint ed., Larkspur, Colo.: Pine Tree Press, 1966). See also Williamson M. Evers, "Social Contract: A Critique," *Journal of Libertarian Studies* 1 (Summer 1977): 185–94, which traces the literal notion of a social contract all the way back to Socrates.

23. Since the definition of the state (or government) is something political scientists cannot even agree upon, ours will obviously be controversial. By "legitimized" (a positive adjective), we of course do not mean "legitimate" (a normative adjective). Most economists should have no difficulty conceiving of the state as a monopolistic coercive institution, but noneconomists might balk. Members of the general public appear to have a bifurcated definition of the state, depending on whether it is domestic or foreign. They view hostile foreign states as simply monopolies on coercion, just like criminal gangs, which is why they fear foreign conquest. They overlook the legitimization of these states. On the other hand, that is the only element they seem to recognize about the domestic state, overlooking or at least deemphasizing the coercive element. This dichotomy is only a cruder version of the distinction made by public-goods theory between democratic and undemocratic states. For an extended defense of the implications of our universal definition, see Murray N. Rothbard, "The Anatomy of the State," in *Egalitarianism as a Revolt Against Nature*, pp. 34–53.

24. One of the earliest observations that a social consensus *always* legitimizes the state is Etienne de la Boëtie, *The Politics of Obedience: The Discourse of Voluntary Servitude* (1574; reprint ed., New York: Free Life Editions, 1975). Other writers who have since put forward a social-consensus theory of the state include David Hume, "Of the First Principles of Government," in *Essays, Moral, Political, and Literary* (1741–42; reprint ed. London: Oxford University Press, 1963), pp. 29–34; Ludwig von Mises, *Human Action: A Treatise on Economics,* 3rd rev. ed. (Chicago: Henry Regnery, 1966), pp. 177–90; and Gene Sharp, *The Politics of Nonviolent Action* (Boston: Porter Sargent, 1973).

25. We are confident about the empirical results, having conducted the test ourselves many times.

26. Victor Zaslavsky, *The Neo-Stalinist State* (New York: Oxford University Press, 1983), has actually conducted fairly reliable surveys among Soviet subjects, which indicate quite unambiguously that the Soviet state is legitimized. Good

single-volume histories that impart an appreciation for the domestic sources of the Soviet state are Robert V. Daniels, *Russia: The Roots of Confrontation* (Cambridge: Harvard University Press, 1985), and Geoffrey Hosking, *The First Socialist Society: A History of the Soviet Union from Within* (Cambridge: Harvard University Press, 1985). An introduction to the various interpretations of Soviet history by American scholars, written from a revisionist slant, is Stephen F. Cohen, *Rethinking the Soviet Experience: Politics and History since 1917* (New York: Oxford University Press, 1985).

27. This awkward position is clearest in Tullock's *Social Dilemma*. The new Society for Interpretive Economics, codirected by Don Lavoie and Arjo Klamer (Economics Department, George Mason University) is a welcome exception to the general neglect among economists of cultural and ideological dynamics. We also cite some specific exceptions below.

28. The premier work on the role of ideas in the American Revolution is Bernard Bailyn, *Ideological Origins of the American Revolution* (Cambridge: Harvard University Press, 1967), while a work that explores the international repercussions of the revolution is Robert R. Palmer, *The Age of Democratic Revolution: A Political History of Europe and America, 1760–1899*, 2 vols. (Princeton: Princeton University Press, 1959–64). A magisterial survey of the international history of chattel slavery is David Brion Davis, *Slavery and Human Progress* (New York: Oxford University Press, 1984). On the emergence of the international abolitionist movement, see his *The Problem of Slavery in the Age of Revolution, 1770–1823* (Ithaca: Cornell University Press, 1975).

29. Among the economists who recognize the public-goods nature of ethical behavior are James M, Buchanan, in "Ethical Rules, Expected Values, and Large Numbers," *Ethics* 76 (October 1965): 1–13, and *The Limits of Liberty: Between Anarchy and Leviathan* (Chicago: University of Chicago Press, 1975), pp. 123–29; Richard B. McKenzie, in "The Economic Dimensions of Ethical Behavior," *Ethics* 87 (April 1977): 208–21; and Douglass C. North, in *Structure and Change in Economic History* (New York: W. W. Norton, 1981), pp. 11–12, 18–19, 45–46. See also Dereck Parfit, *Reasons and Persons* (Oxford: Clarendon Press, 1984).

30. Rothbard, "The Myth of Neutral Taxation," 545, makes a similar observation: "Thus the free-rider argument proves far too much. After all, civilization itself is a process of all of us 'free-riding' on the achievements of others. We all free-ride, every day, on the achievements of Edison, Beethoven, or Vermeer."

31. Howard Margolis, *Selfishness, Altruism, and Rationality: A Theory of Social Choice* (Cambridge: Cambridge University Press, 1982), p. 6. See also John McMillan, "The Free Rider Problem: A Survey," *The Economic Record* 55 (June 1979): 95–107; Vernon L. Smith, "Experiments with a Decentralized Mechanism for Public Good Decisions," *American Economic Review* 70 (September 1980): 584–99; and Friedrich Schneider and Werner W. Pommerehne, "Free Riding and Collective Action: An Experiment in Public Microeconomics," *Quarterly Journal of Economics* 91 (November 1981): 689–704.

32. Several scholars are moving in this direction. For instance, Robyn M. Dawes, "Social Dilemmas," *Annual Review of Psychology* 31 (1980): 169–93; Earl R. Brubaker, "Demand Disclosures and Conditions on Exclusion," *Economic Journal* 94 (September 1984): 536–53; Barry, *Sociologists, Economists, and Democracy;* Higgs, *Crisis and Leviathan,* chapter 3; and North, *Structure and Change in Economic History,* chapter 5. Even Mancur Olson suggests this approach in "Economics, Sociology, and the Best of All Possible Worlds," *Public Interest* 12 (Summer 1968): 96–118, which contrasts economics, the study of rational action, with sociology, the study of socialization. But the most ambitious effort along these lines is Margolis's *Selfishness,*

Altruism, and Rationality, which is summarized in his journal article, "A New Model of Rational Choice," *Ethics* 91 (January 1981): 265–79.

We should note that we attach the adjective "narrow" to the term "self-interest" to indicate the usage that involves seeking particular, usually selfish, goals. This is to distinguish it from the broader usage of the term, which can encompass any goal, including altruism. Whether individuals do in fact pursue their narrow self-interest is a question subject to empirical verification or falsification, but individuals by definition always pursue their broad self-interest.

33. Olson, *The Logic of Collective Action,* pp. 64–65.

34. Higgs, *Crisis and Leviathan,* chapter 3, heavily emphasizes the role of ideological solidarity. James S. Coleman, "Individual Interests and Collective Action," *Papers on Non-Market Decision Making* 1 (1966): 49–62, postulates an individual's psychic investment in collective entities. Buchanan and Brennan, "Voter Choice: Evaluating Political Alternatives," think that this symbolic identification is the major motivation behind voting.

35. Richard Tuck, "Is There a Free-Rider Problem, and if so, What Is It?" in *Rational Action: Studies in Philosophy and Social Science,* ed. Ross Harrison (Cambridge: Cambridge University Press, 1979), pp. 147–56.

We can salvage Olsonian "rationality" under two strict conditions. When (1) a threshold level of resources is necessary before any of the public good becomes available whatsoever, *and* (2) people end up paying whatever resources they contribute, irrespective of whether they reach the threshold or not, it becomes rational not to contribute *if* a person predicts that the threshold will not be reached. In that special case, he or she would simply be throwing away resources for nothing. Notice that these two conditions apply more frequently to obtaining public goods through politics—which is often a win-or-lose, all-or-nothing, situation—than to obtaining public goods on the market. In particular, it applies to voting. Hardin, *Collective Action,* pp. 55–61, analyzes the first of these conditions, for which he employs the term "step goods."

36. Olson, *The Logic of Collective Action,* pp. 132–68. Olson also refers to excludable "by-products" as "selective incentives." Looked at another way. the by-product theory converts a full public good into a positive externality of a private good.

37. Those advocating voluntary funding of national defense through the sale of excludable by-products include Ayn Rand, "Government Financing in a Free Society," in *The Virtue of Selfishness: A New Concept of Egoism* (New York: New American Library, 1964), pp. 157–63; Jarret B. Wollstein, *Society without Coercion: A New Concept of Social Organization* (Silver Springs, Md.: Society for Individual Liberty, 1969), pp. 35–38; Morris and Linda Tannehill, *The Market for Liberty* (Lansing: Tannehill, 1970), pp. 126–35; and Tibor R. Machan, "Dissolving the Problem of Public Goods," in *The Libertarian Reader* (Totowa, N.J.: Rowman and Littlefield, 1982), pp. 201–8. For a telling critique of the by-product theory as applied to national defense, see Friedman, *The Machinery of Freedom,* pp. 192–93.

38. Hardin, *Collective Action,* pp. 31–34, criticizes the by-product theory.

39. The book that launched mathematical game theory was John von Neumann and Oskar Morgenstern, *The Theory of Games and Economic Behavior,* 3rd ed. (Princeton: Princeton University Press, 1953), the first edition of which appeared in 1944. According to Hardin, *Collective Action,* p. 24, the Prisoner's Dilemma itself was first discovered in 1950 by Merril Flood and Melvin Dresher. A. W. Tucker, a game theorist at Princeton University, later gave the Prisoner's Dilemma its name. For the personal reminiscences of one of the early researchers who worked on the Prisoner's Dilemma, coupled with a survey of the studies of the dilemma up to the

mid-seventies, see Anatol Rapoport, "Prisoner's Dilemma—Recollections and Observations," in *Game Theory as a Theory of Conflict Resolution* (Dordrecht: D. Reidel, 1974), pp. 17–34.

40. R. Hardin, "Collective Action as an Agreeable *n*-Prisoners' Dilemma," *Behavioral Science* 16 (September 1971): 472–81; Michael Taylor, *Anarchy and Cooperation* (London: John Wiley & Sons, 1976); Hardin, *Collective Action;* and Robert Axelrod, *The Evolution of Cooperation* (New York: Basic Books, 1984). Axelrod confines himself to two-person dynamic Prisoner's Dilemmas, while both Taylor and Hardin consider *n*-person iterated games. For a good review of the growing literature on *n*-person games, see Dawes, "Social Dilemmas."

41. Britain and the United States demilitarized the Great Lakes in the Rush-Bagot Treaty of 1817. The process of disarming the entire border was not complete until 1871, however. Both Philip Noel-Baker, *The Arms Race: A Programme for World Disarmament* (London: Atlantic Books, 1958), and Boulding, "The World War Industry as an Economic Problem," appreciate the significance of this example.

Economic studies of international relations that share these weaknesses include Lee, "The Soviet Economy and the Arms Control Delusion" and Tullock, *The Social Dilemma*. Most of the economic work in these areas has focused upon alliances. See for instance Mancur Olsen, Jr., and Richard Zeckhauser, "An Economic Theory of Alliances," *Review of Economics and Statistics* 48 (August 1966): 266–79; Olson and Zeckhauser, "Collective Goods, Comparative Advantage, and Alliance Efficiency," in *Issues in Defense Economics,* ed. Roland N. McKean (New York: National Bureau of Economic Research, 1967), pp. 25–63; Todd Sandler, "The Economic Theory of Alliances: Realigned," in *Comparative Public Policy,* ed. Liske, Loehr, and McCamant, pp. 223–39; and Todd M. Sandler, William Loehr, and John T. Cauley, *The Political Economy of Public Goods and International Cooperation* (Denver: University of Denver Press, 1978).

4

Blue Ribbon Defense Commissions: The Acquisition of Major Weapon Systems

WILLIAM E. KOVACIC

W hen his presidency ended in January 1989, Ronald Reagan left at least two distinctive imprints on United States defense policy. First and most evident, he had accomplished the largest program of peacetime expenditures for defense in the nation's history.[1] Out of these funds—over $2.02 trillion from fiscal years 1981 through 1988—the Department of Defense (DOD) has purchased or ordered weapon systems that will determine many of the country's defense capabilities for the next quarter-century.[2]

Beyond the roster of recently acquired and currently planned armaments, the Reagan administration's defense outlays yielded considerably more than military hardware.[3] As an unintended yet important consequence, the absolute volume of expenditures focused unequalled peacetime attention upon the adequacy of DOD acquisition policies. Pervasive concerns that increased funding would not provide corresponding enhancements in defense capability moved Congress and the Reagan administration to adopt or consider a broad collection of measures to reform the weapons acquisition process.[4]

The ongoing and contemplated procurement reforms have roots in the work of many institutions and individuals.[5] Since 1980, however, no single event or force has commanded greater attention in the procurement reform

The author wishes to thank William B. Burnett, Ted Galen Carpenter, Kathryn M. Fenton, J. Ronald Fox, Jerome F. Heavey, Robert Higgs, Dwight R. Lee, Jim Lennertz, Frank Lichtenberg, James M. Lindsay, Thomas J. Madden, Kenneth R. Mayer, Ilan Peleg, William Rogerson, Jordan A. Schwarz, and Charlotte Twight for their many useful comments and suggestions.

debate than the President's Blue Ribbon Commission on Defense Management.[6] Chaired by former DOD Deputy Secretary David Packard, the commission in 1986 proposed sweeping changes in the weapons acquisition process. President Reagan and the Congress enthusiastically embraced the commission's study as a sensible reform blueprint, and the president and many Congressional leaders pledged themselves to carry out its recommendations.[7]

This study examines the role that the Packard Commission and other "blue ribbon" panels have played in evaluating and reforming the weapons acquisition process in the United States since World War II.[8] More specifically, the ways in which these panels have evaluated and influenced the government's methods for buying major weapon systems are considered in detail.[9] By examination of their causes, proposals, and effects, the impact of blue ribbon panels upon the effectiveness with which public institutions form, execute, and evaluate weapons procurement policy is assessed. The national experience with blue ribbon commissions is used, among other purposes, to suggest why deficiencies in the process of major weapons procurement persist.

To begin with, the role of blue ribbon commissions in forming public policy in the United States is briefly described. Three preeminent post-war panels—the 1955 Hoover Commission Task Force, the 1970 Fitzhugh Commission, and the 1986 Packard Commission—that have considered issues involving the purchase of major weapon systems are then discussed. Finally, the significance of special commissions for the creation and review of weapons acquisition policy is assessed.[10]

ROLE OF THE BLUE RIBBON COMMISSION

The blue ribbon commission is a familiar instrument of American policymaking. On many occasions presidents or legislators have created special advisory bodies to consider matters of pressing public concern. For example, a partial list of special bodies convened by President Reagan in the second term of his administration alone includes commissions to study the Challenger space shuttle disaster, the spread of AIDS, the Iran-contra affair, privatization of government functions, the stock market collapse of October 1987, and defense procurement. Extensive modern experience with this policy tool makes it possible to identify generic analytical functions and political needs that special commissions fulfill.

Analytical Functions

Blue ribbon commissions ordinarily perform one or more discrete analytical functions. The completed work of most special panels usually contains some or all of the following elements.

The most basic commission function is to collect facts and determine the immediate cause of a specific event. The Warren Commission, for example, was formed "to uncover all the facts concerning the assassination of President Kennedy" and "to identify the person or persons responsible for both the assassination of President Kennedy and the killing of [Lee Harvey] Oswald."[11]

A second function is the extension of the factfinding task from the narrow focus causation inquiry into immediate causes to a broader focus on more basic causes. In this type of inquiry, the panel also identifies the immediate cause of a specific event. The "broad focus" panel then determines underlying conditions that allowed the immediate cause to occur and ordinarily proposes steps for adjusting the underlying conditions and correcting the immediate cause. The Rogers Commission, for example, pinpointed the immediate cause of the space shuttle Challenger's destruction (a failure of the solid rocket booster O-ring seals); identified the conditions that led NASA to launch the Challenger notwithstanding known flaws in the O-ring design and unfavorable weather conditions (a collection of NASA and Morton Thiokol management failures); and proposed changes in NASA's management processes and the shuttle's design.[12]

Besides these event-oriented panels, commissions are sometimes formed to propose solutions to problems whose existence has been recognized previously but whose seriousness is perceived to be growing dangerously. The decision to form such panels typically does not stem from a single catastrophic event, such as President Kennedy's assassination or the Challenger accident. Rather, the formation of these commissions usually follows a series of less dramatic events or developments that underscore the increasing seriousness of a known problem.[13]

Political Roles

In addition to performing the analytical functions outlined above, blue ribbon commissions serve important political purposes as a means of securing consensus and overcoming opposition. This often happens in cases where widely acknowledged public policy problems worsen because conventional policymaking institutions fail to create a consensus among affected groups and interests about the problem's scope and appropriate remedies. Blue ribbon panels sometimes assist in overcoming policymaking paralysis by providing a forum in which experts of divergent views and constituencies can "negotiate" acceptable consensus solutions. The National Commission on Social Security Reform in 1981 and 1983 played such a role in dealing with the threatened insolvency of the government's old age and survivor's insurance fund.[14]

In addition, the blue ribbon panel sometimes serves as a shield with which presidents and legislators can deflect criticism. In particular, the existence of a special commission enables its sponsor to "take action" with respect to a problem without firmly committing the sponsor to specific remedies. For example, President Reagan's creation of the Tower Commission served, among other ends, to dampen criticism of his conduct in the Iran-contra matter.[15]

Further, a special commission is one approach to solving problems whose resolution appears to demand a degree of objectivity or nonpartisanship that conventional policymaking forums seem unable to ensure. Matters deemed too important to be entrusted to overtly political institutions are occasionally submitted to blue ribbon panels whose objectivity, credibility, and expertise are presumed to be stronger.[16]

Besides these functions, the special commission affords the president a means for redirecting agencies to pursue the president's preferred policy aims. Left to their own devices, agencies might refuse to assist the president in developing plans or proposals to carry out his agenda. The blue ribbon panel provides an instrument beyond the agencies' control for evaluating the agencies' performance and suggesting methods for achieving the President's broad policy goals.

Strengths and Weaknesses

Experience with special commissions offers some basis for predicting when blue ribbon panels will induce formal policymaking institutions—notably, executive agencies and Congress—to adopt and implement reforms. Blue ribbon commissions typically do best in treating "discrete, well-defined, and relatively short-term controversies."[17] Blue ribbon panels have the greatest chance to succeed when solving the problem at hand essentially requires one-time intervention—a new regulation or statute, for example—by the formal policymaking body.[18]

By contrast, commissions that have tackled longer-term, open-ended policy controversies have enjoyed considerably less success.[19] Blue ribbon panels tend to make the smallest dent in problems whose solution requires not only changes in statutes, regulations, or organization charts, but also sustained, ongoing efforts to implement new commands and assess their effect. The problems of weapons procurement are decidedly long-term and open-ended, and these characteristics have much to do with the impact of the blue ribbon defense panels to which we now turn.

THE MAJOR POSTWAR DEFENSE COMMISSIONS

In the past forty years, a broad collection of private institutions and individuals have had a hand in shaping, monitoring, and evaluating the weapons acquisition process.[20] The roster of formal and informal participants is well known: Congress and its supporting research bodies; the Office of the President, the Office of Management and Budget, DOD, and other executive branch entities; the contractor community; private research institutions and defense consulting firms; academics; and citizens' groups. Since 1981 these organizations and individuals have generated a large literature that assesses the wisdom of prevailing weapons acquisition methods.[21]

Since World War II, Congress and the president have periodically supplemented this collection of actors with special commissions to examine the weapons procurement process and propose change. On three occasions—in 1955, 1970, and 1986—Congress or the president has formed blue ribbon panels that have devoted significant attention to problems in the acquisition of armaments, particularly for major systems.[22] The discussion below reviews the work of the three panels, focusing on the cause of each commission's formation, its findings, and its impact.

1955 Hoover Commission Task Force

In the decade after World War II, American policymakers confronted two basic questions arising from the country's wartime experience and postwar defense needs. The first was how to organize the nation's peacetime defense management. The war effort had demonstrated the vital importance of coordinated defense management within the executive branch and among the armed services. For this reason, one central object of defense reform legislation immediately after the war was to improve the armed services' organization and strengthen executive branch defense planning.[23]

The second fundamental policy question was how to procure weapons for postwar defense. By the time of Japan's surrender, several features of the likely peacetime procurement environment were becoming clear. First, America's peacetime defense establishment would be comparatively large and permanent.[24] Second, it was evident that future weaponry would grow swiftly and immensely in capability and sophistication. The coming generations of aircraft, missiles, ships, and tanks would be "weapon systems" that sought to incorporate state-of-the-art advances in several fast-moving technical disciplines simultaneously.[25]

Soon after the war Congress began considering new legislation that would facilitate comparatively large-scale peacetime production of complex weapon systems. The first and most significant result of this effort, the Armed Services Procurement Act of 1947, borrowed heavily from purchasing approaches used under emergency legislation during the war.[26] Built on the assumption that private firms almost exclusively would supply future weapons needs, the 1947 statute created a two-track acquisition process.

The first, and preferred, track established procedures for formal advertising by which defense buyers would issue specifications and solicit bids from suppliers. The second path permitted agencies to use "negotiated procurement" upon showing that the advertising approach was impractical.

Under the negotiation method, firms would submit proposals and negotiate final performance requirements and prices with the purchasing agency. Negotiation, which typically relied upon cost-reimbursement contracts early in the procurement cycle, soon accounted for the vast bulk of DOD contracts for major systems.[27]

The Hoover Commission: Formation

The first comprehensive evaluation of the new postwar defense acquisition process took place in 1955 as a study by the Commission on Organization of the Executive Branch of the Government. Created by Congress in 1947 and chaired by former President Herbert Hoover, the commission was to examine the massive growth of the executive branch since the late 1920's.[28] "As a result of depression, war, new needs for defense, and our greater responsibilities in the foreign field," the commission explained in its first report to Congress in 1949, "the Federal government has become the most gigantic business on earth. In less than 20 years the number of its civil employees has risen from 570,000 to over 2,100,000. The number of bureaus, sections, services, and units has increased fourfold to over 1,800. Annual expenditures have increased from about $3,600,000,000 to over $42,000,000,000."[29]

In the commission's view, the proliferation of government functions and entities had occurred with "a lack of order, a lack of clear lines of authority and responsibility, and a lack of effective organization in the executive branch."[30] Accordingly, the commission's principal aim was to propose how the instrumentalities of the executive branch could be reorganized to improve their efficiency and reduce their cost. Thus the commission considered the effectiveness of the country's weapons procurement system within the context of a wide-ranging evaluation of all federal organization.

The commission conducted its review of executive branch defense purchasing in two stages. The "First Hoover Commission" (1947–49) gave only limited attention to weapon system acquisition methods. Rather, in treating defense issues, the first commission's investigation dealt mainly with the overall organization and coordination of defense policymaking groups under executive control.[31] The first commission touched briefly upon the organization of military acquisition bodies but did not specifically analyze weapon systems procurement.[32]

Responsibility for evaluating the weapons acquisition process in detail fell to the "Second Hoover Commission" (1953–55) and its Task Force on Procurement. Headed by Lukens Steel Company Chairman Robert W. Wolcott, the Procurement Task Force consisted of fifteen members, including twelve corporate executives, many of whom worked for major defense suppliers; one corporate consultant; one attorney from a prominent law firm; and one trade association executive.[33] Supporting the task force was a seven-member advisory committee and a staff of 39 individuals.[34]

The Hoover Commission: Findings

Among other issues, the Hoover Task Force identified four reform priorities particularly significant for buying major systems once DOD had determined its specific arms needs. The basic content of and rationale for each reform is discussed in turn below.

Legal Encumbrances

The task force concluded that the legal framework for defense procurement was "out of step with contracting realities" and "needlessly cluttered with legalities which might generally be classified as costly nuisances."[35] Accordingly, the panel called for the secretary of defense to "take steps to remove needless legal and administrative encumbrances upon the placement of military contracts."[36]

To the Hoover panel, two features of the existing legal framework seemed to require change. First, the 1947 Armed Services Procurement Act had failed to recognize that negotiation was "generally a more efficient tool of purchasing than advertising in contracting for aircraft, ships, tanks, electronic gear, missiles and proprietary items."[37] The 1947 act allowed negotiated procurement, but only as an exception to formal advertising. The statute's requirement that DOD justify exceptions placed "considerable administrative burdens upon the contracting agency" and denied purchasing authorities valuable "latitude of judgment in developing suppliers of military products."[38] The imperatives of large systems purchasing and the 1947 statute's competition goals could best be reconciled by placing negotiation on a more equal footing with advertising and by using competition-oriented acquisition strategies as part of the negotiation process.[39] With or without competition, the Hoover panel added, the principal means by which military departments could insure themselves "fair and reasonable prices" were "skillful negotiation, sound cost analysis and repricing techniques."[40]

The second legal impediment to efficient purchasing consisted of "efforts to enforce social, economic and political objectives through the use of procurement dollars."[41] The Hoover Task Force questioned the desirability of using defense procurement to aid small business, strengthen distressed labor areas, and assist faltering domestic producers. The panel proposed that "when legal requirements are tied to social, economic or political objectives, examination should be made to ascertain their effectiveness in relation to their burden upon the contracting process."[42]

Contract Pricing Policy

In reviewing DOD pricing policies, the task force found that purchasing authorities "have not made the most of industry incentives to stimulate greater efficiency in contract performance."[43] The panel recommended that the secretary of defense "take steps to establish an effective contract pricing policy on a Department of Defense–wide basis and to see to it that pricing techniques and procedures directly support such policy."[44]

Beyond its general proposal, the Hoover panel suggested several specific ways for DOD to elicit better contractor performance through its pricing policies. One was to emphasize competition as a tool for obtaining lower prices in negotiated procurements. The task force believed that DOD had wisely concluded that formal advertising was unsuitable for major systems procurement. Nonetheless, DOD had often overlooked the benefits that competitive techniques could yield in negotiating contract prices.[45]

The task force also perceived that DOD had focused myopically upon reducing contractor profit rates rather than creating downward pressure on all elements of contract price. A misguided preoccupation with profit rates and amounts had deflected DOD's attention from the equally if not more important task of depressing costs. DOD pricing policies instead "should be directed toward contract cost reduction with emphasis upon full utilization of industry incentives for increasing production efficiency and lowering contract rates."[46] As one example, DOD might allow contractors to retain a portion of amounts saved owing to successful efforts to reduce costs.[47]

Contract Administration

The task force proposed that the secretary of defense "direct the establishment of a Department-of-Defense–wide program for streamlining the complex routine of contract administration to the fullest extent practicable."[48] The panel divided contract administration into "production" and "nonproduction" phases and suggested changes for each. Among its chief production phase proposals, the task force suggested that DOD "avoid major commitments under volume production contracts until designs and specifications are proven firm."[49] Particularly in the "highly technical fields of electronics and aeronautics," adequate laboratory and field testing before full-scale production would help detect problems that frequently delay delivery of acceptable hardware and substantially increase rework and maintenance costs.[50]

To improve DOD's performance of nonproduction administrative tasks, the Hoover panel recommended that the department simplify and reduce its suppliers' record retention requirements and improve its procedures for resolving disputes and developing procurement regulations.[51] In the panel's view, the latter of these reforms should entail more unified administration of the Armed Services Board of Contract Appeals, general publication of the board's decisions, and expansion of DOD's Armed Services Procurement Regulations to create a comprehensive set of procedures applying to all of the services.

Authority and Qualifications of DOD Contract Personnel

Fundamental to the success of the Hoover panel's reforms—indeed, to the reforms of any postwar blue ribbon defense commission—are the powers and competence of the personnel who represent the government in devising and administering its contracts. To the Hoover Task Force, DOD's procurement and personnel policies seriously impeded the ability of its contracting authorities to function effectively.

The most important handicap consisted of statutes and internal DOD policies that limited the authority of military buyers. By inhibiting "the proper exercise of a contracting officer's free judgment," these limitations caused delay, overstaffing, and uncertainty in the procurement process.[52] The Hoover panel's report thus described the restrictions' logic and effect: "The justification of legal and administrative safeguards is stated in terms of protecting public funds. The emphasis is upon avoiding bad deals, rather than making good ones. Good judgment is impaired and pride of job accomplishment is limited. Second guessing is invited."[53] To correct this deficiency, the task force urged that DOD "establish . . . policies to strengthen the role of contracting officers in the interest of more expeditious and effective buying."[54]

Expanding the authority of DOD's contract personnel would not by itself ensure that such officials performed well. The Hoover panel identified several DOD personnel policies that hindered the development of an expert procurement corps. Chief among the obstacles were practices that (1) discouraged capable military officers from accepting and retaining procurement assignments; (2) transferred acquisition managers after comparatively short tenure in any one position; and (3) assigned individuals with little training or experience to positions of significant contracting responsibility.[55]

To correct personnel policy flaws, the Hoover panel proposed that DOD "establish a policy requiring each military department to develop and assign career-trained personnel to technical and executive posts throughout the field of procurement management."[56] More specifically, the task force stressed the need to train career procurement employees and to fill contracting positions with individuals whose qualifications were equal to the task.

The Hoover Commission: Impact

Change in the weapons acquisition process can be measured on two levels. The first and most readily observable level consists of statutes, regulations, and other formal adjustment in official policy. Blue ribbon defense commissions generally fare relatively well in eliciting this type of formal, nominal reform. More significant and harder to monitor, however, is the extent to which formal commands reshape the practices of public and private officials responsible for major systems acquisition. On this second, substantive level, blue ribbon panels such as the Hoover Task Force have less to show for their efforts.

Judged by the formal reaction to its proposals, the Hoover panel could point to several reforms that directly or indirectly flowed from its study. DOD subsequently began initiatives to strengthen its contract administration process, including the creation of a new department (the Defense Contract Administrative Service) to perform administrative functions.[57] DOD also conducted a comprehensive review of its pricing policies and took steps to promote career development for its contracting officers.[58] Finally, the Hoover panel's proposals helped establish the foundation for legislation in 1962 that directed DOD to rely more heavily on competitive strategies in conducting negotiated procurements.[59]

Despite these traceable nominal changes, the Hoover panel's contribution to enduring substantive change in the weapons acquisition process was slight. Some comparatively limited technical changes—for example, unifying the operations of the Armed Services Board of Contract Appeals, and streamlining the procedures for adopting and disseminating new procurement regulations—yielded permanent improvements in the procurement process. Nonetheless, the anticipated substantial redirection of DOD contract formulation, pricing, administration, and personnel management practices did not occur. As one authoritative account observed in 1972:

> Since the Second Hoover Commission's recommendations on procurement, there have been many directives issued, organizational arrangements revised, and changes in procedures made. At the start of this study [1970], however, many of the problems identified by the Second Hoover Commission were still persisting in varying degrees.[60]

One can propose several hypotheses to account for the limited lasting effect of the Hoover recommendations. To the extent that the panel's persuasiveness and credibility would have hinged upon achieving broad representation on the task force, the Hoover study suffered. Most of the task force members were industry executives or members of institutions with close industry ties. The perception of "neutrality" that can increase the impact of a special commission's recommendations derives not from the apolitical character of each commission member, but from the political balance of a panel as a whole. Successful blue ribbon panels have gained a stamp of legitimacy for their work when the panels' proposals have emerged from the give and take of specialists of diverse viewpoints. With its overwhelming industry representation, the Hoover Task Force may have been seen as lacking the breadth of perspective to ensure that balanced proposals would flow from its deliberations.

A second limiting factor is suggested more directly in the task force report itself. The report fails to identify the political preconditions for successful implementation of its recommendations. Little account is taken of the institutions, public and private, whose political energies would need to be galvanized to mount and sustain a meaningful reform effort, or of how those energies would have to be applied to obtain enduring improvements. Although they are often designed to function as neutral, expert bodies, blue ribbon panels do not operate in a political vacuum. Accordingly, to succeed in stimulating desired change, the panel must confront implementation issues and suggest how such issues will be resolved. The Hoover Task Force slighted these implementation concerns. Notwithstanding the various formal initiatives that followed the 1955 study, many of the Hoover Commission's concerns remained active problems for consideration when the Fitzhugh Commission convened in 1969.

1970 Fitzhugh Commission

In the most immediate sense, the Fitzhugh Commission originated as a campaign promise. In the fall of 1968, presidential candidate Richard Nixon said his administration would undertake a major review of defense organization and management. By forming the Fitzhugh Commission the following year, the new President fulfilled his campaign commitment.[61] More broadly considered, President Nixon's decision to establish the Fitzhugh panel occurred at a time of considerable ferment in the weapons acquisition process. A sequence of three related developments set the context from which the Fitzhugh study emerged.

The sequence began in the early 1960's with the appearance of Merton Peck's and F. M. Scherer's exhaustive studies of weapons acquisition management.[62] Published as two volumes (one coauthored and one written by Scherer alone), the Peck and Scherer studies quickly became, and remain today, the preeminent works in the field. From their review of many major weapon systems acquisition programs, the two economists identified and examined four persistent management problems: (1) cost growth, (2) schedule delays, (3) inadequate means for estimating likely costs, and (4) flawed personnel policies that yielded insufficient numbers of qualified DOD contracting personnel and encouraged rapid turnover in critical management positions.

The Peck and Scherer volumes imparted substantial analytical force to the work of a new collection of DOD economic and management specialists seeking to correct chronic deficiencies in DOD major weapons procurement.[63] Drawn to the Pentagon by DOD Secretary Robert McNamara, the reform-minded officials experimented with a variety of techniques to improve contract formation and management.[64] Major contract management innovations included expanded use of incentive contracts, the development of total package procurement, and the establishment of program managers to oversee the purchase of major systems.[65]

By the end of the 1960's, there were few signs of success from reform efforts begun earlier in the decade. Instead, as one leading authority has explained, "serious cost, schedule, and technical performance problems continued to disrupt the acquisition process."[66] Moreover, several acquisition programs structured to apply innovative procurement techniques were encountering severe difficulties. The F-111, which McNamara unsuccessfully championed as single design that could serve the needs of the Air Force and the Navy, and the C-5A, which the Air Force purchased under a "total package procurement" contract, faced enormous cost growth.[67] To procurement officials and legislators, experience with these and other programs suggested a system largely out of control.[68] Speaking in 1970 at the annual meeting of the Armed Forces Management Association, Deputy Secretary of Defense David Packard commented: "Frankly, gentlemen, in defense procurement, we have a real mess on our hands, and the question you and I have to face up to is what we are going to do to clean it up."[69]

President Nixon and Defense Secretary Melvin Laird appointed the Fitzhugh Commission in July 1969.[70] To chair the panel, the president chose Gilbert W. Fitzhugh, chairman of the board of the Metropolitan Life Insurance Company. The sixteen-member commission included, among others, a future justice of the Supreme Court (Lewis Powell) and a future Nobel laureate in economics (George Stigler).[71] The panel's final report explained that "in order to get a fresh look" at DOD's operations, President Nixon had "selected members for the panel who were generally unfamiliar with the operations of the Department."[72] Supporting the commission's work was a research and administrative staff of forty-seven individuals.[73]

The Fitzhugh Commission: Findings

The Fitzhugh Commission devoted roughly half of its study to issues closely related to the acquisition of major weapon systems. The panel acknowledged that technological uncertainty associated with major systems procurement inevitably would cause some cost growth, schedule slippage, and performance shortfalls. Nonetheless, the panel observed, "the frequency and magnitude of such problems . . . surpass significantly those which can be attributable to unavoidable causes. It is clear that a substantial portion of the acquisition problems must be attributed to management deficiencies."[74]

Program Management

The Fitzhugh panel concluded that program managers frequently lacked authority to execute acquisition projects effectively. Program managers assigned to oversee specific procurement projects typically shared substantial authority with contract officers and auditors, with a consequent loss in needed control. At the same time, numerous layers of review separated program managers from DOD officials responsible for making important acquisition decisions. Both conditions severely reduced the program manager's ability to make timely decisions and execute them effectively.[75] The panel proposed that DOD increase the program manager's authority and establish shorter, more direct lines of communication between program managers and senior DOD procurement officials.[76]

Source Selection

The panel criticized several aspects of DOD source selection methods. First, it recommended that DOD simplify its selection process by reducing the number of technical criteria its evaluation teams must consider and by focusing attention upon "the more fundamental considerations."[77] DOD's "requests for proposals" should elicit leaner contractor responses that dealt with the most important criteria for evaluation. Simplification along these lines also would tend to curb "gold-plating" of major systems.

A second matter of concern was the tendency for source selection to proceed with comparatively little demonstration or testing of hardware. "Repeated experiences," the commission wrote, "demonstrate that technical uncertainty is inherent in the Engineering Development process and that paper studies alone cannot enable government or industry to forecast all of the problems that will arise."[78] Accordingly, the Fitzhugh panel recommended "more use of competitive prototypes and less reliance on paper studies" in selecting production designs.[79] As a further means for reducing technical risk, the panel urged that DOD adopt "a general rule against concurrent development and production, with the production decision deferred until successful demonstration of developmental prototypes."[80]

Contract Estimating and Pricing

Simplifying technical requirements and prototyping would serve to reduce uncertainty and to increase DOD's ability to make (and adhere to) realistic cost predictions. The Fitzhugh panel suggested additional measures for improving DOD's ability to predict program costs accurately. One suggested approach was to reevaluate program cost estimates at each milestone of a weapon system's development. The panel also urged DOD to rely more heavily on parametric cost estimating techniques. By using historical cost data to predict future costs, the parametric methodology would "help offset the difficulties of estimating the cost of unknowns."[81]

In turning to DOD's contract pricing policies, the Fitzhugh panel criticized the Department's "heavy emphasis" on fixed-price type contracts.

With the C-5A program's worsening cost problems fresh in mind, the panel warned:

> Fixed-price type contracts have been equated, in effect, with competition. The competitive pricing during Contract Definition has led to significant underpricing in numerous development contracts. As a result, cost overruns have been frequent and substantial. The concentration of risks in a single contractor is often out of proportion to the contractor's financial structure and capability, and can result in the Department of Defense being faced with either permitting a default on a critical program, or of salvaging the particular company with payments not clearly required under the terms of the contract.[82]

To the panel, DOD's most misguided use of fixed-price contracting was "total package procurement" through which contractors (such as Lockheed on the C-5A) were required to submit a fixed-cost bid covering all phases, from development through production, of a weapon system's acquisition.[83] Thus, the panel proposed that new DOD procurement policies include "a prohibition of total package procurement."[84]

Regulatory Structure

As the Hoover Commission had fifteen years before, the Fitzhugh panel criticized the failure of the Armed Services Procurement Act to give proper recognition to the negotiated procurement method. Despite amendments in 1962 that partly responded to the Hoover Commission's concerns, the Fitzhugh panel said "the priorities established by this statute do not reflect the realities of Defense procurement."[85] With its strong preference for formal advertising, the statute required elaborate justification before DOD officials could conduct a negotiated procurement—the dominant means for buying major systems. Consequently, the Fitzhugh report urged the secretary of defense to ask Congress to reduce substantially the burden of justifying departures from formal advertising.[86]

The Fitzhugh panel also took issue with the form and organization of DOD's procurement regulations and guidelines. The Department's Armed Services Procurement Regulations (ASPR) contained "a mixture of procurement policies, practices and procedures which obscures procurement policy, making it difficult to identify, interpret and to comply with."[87] Similarly, the panel added, "the Department of Defense directive and guidance system results in an avalanche of paper instructions which are duplicative, overlapping and sometimes contradictory. There is no evidence of a concentrated attempt to reduce the number and scope of directives and guidance, or to make these documents consistent and harmonious."[88]

To correct these conditions, the Fitzhugh panel recommended that DOD review its procurement regulations and its ASPR Committee to formulate a more efficient means for incorporating changes into the ASPR and to reduce ASPR's size and complexity.[89] As for the welter of other DOD guidance documents, the panel said "the need for assessment and review is conspicuous."[90]

Personnel

The Fitzhugh panel painted a dismal picture of procurement-related personnel policies. Government contract negotiators typically lagged well behind their industry counterparts in pay and experience. "The Defense Negotiator," the panel concluded, "is at a disadvantage, to say the least."[91] The lot of career military officers in procurement billets was no better. Promotion criteria gave little weight to procurement assignments, and frequent rotation guaranteed that officers in acquisition posts either would never master relevant skills or would leave their assignments at some critical juncture of the procurement life-cycle.[92]

The needed solutions were self-evident. "There is a particular urgency," the Fitzhugh report stated, "in the matter of upgrading personnel involved in contract negotiation and in the system of promotions and reward for the negotiators."[93] By the same token, it was necessary to increase the duration of procurement assignments for career officers. The panel said DOD's leadership must ensure that career officers who excel in acquisition posts receive promotions commensurate with their accomplishments.[94]

The Fitzhugh Commission: Impact

The Fitzhugh panel provoked positive developments in some programs after the publication of its 1970 report. Indeed, the path of some development efforts in the 1970's offered an appealing view of what broad application of the Fitzhugh reforms might yield. In the F-16 program, for example, the Air Force applied many of the Blue Ribbon panel's preferred acquisition techniques—simplified requirements, lean program organization, clear lines of authority, and prototyping—to build an airplane that most observers regard (with some reservations) as genuinely successful.[95] Judged by the benchmarks of acceptable cost, superior performance, and timely delivery, the F-16 program suggested that the process could produce satisfactory results.[96]

Though impressive as models of what can be achieved, these successes were comparatively few and idiosyncratic, stemming more from the inventiveness and risk-taking of a small number of DOD and industry officials than from fundamental, underlying change in DOD acquisition policy and practice. On the issue of the Fitzhugh panel's lasting effect, Ronald Fox seems closest to the mark:

> In 1970 the President's Blue Ribbon Panel made a number of recommendations to improve the acquisition process. . . . While the panel successfully identified

several problem areas in the procurement process, their report did not explain why previous recommendations along the same lines have never been successfully implemented. Many procurement officials in the Defense Department are, after all, aware that the present system has faults. But despite a steady succession of studies and recommendations, the procurement process has remained impervious to structural reform.[97]

Fox's evaluation is telling not simply for his conclusion that the Fitzhugh study had failed to stimulate basic reform. It identifies an important omission in the Fitzhugh panel's analysis and the methodology of blue ribbon commissions generally. The Fitzhugh report mentioned that the panel's "members and staff carefully reviewed many earlier reports of studies of the Department of Defense."[98] Yet, as Fox points out, the Fitzhugh panel did not attempt to explain why the earlier studies' proposed reforms had not taken hold.

One might have expected the Fitzhugh panel to suggest why its recommendations would have lasting effect although earlier studies had had little enduring impact. As was the case with the Hoover Task Force, the Fitzhugh panel seems to have neglected the issue of how its reforms would be carried out. DOD's apparent imperviousness to earlier reform efforts arguably should have led the Fitzhugh panel to assess and discuss the institutional obstacles to change and means for overcoming them.

1986 Packard Commission

As the introduction to this paper indicates, the substantial increase in defense spending in the early 1980's provoked greater scrutiny of the defense acquisition process and of the specific programs to which additional funds flowed. Although the build-up began in the Carter administration's final two years, the greater size of President Reagan's defense requests, coupled with his administration's efforts to cut growth in social program costs, made defense acquisition activities unusually visible.

Amid heightened sensitivity to defense procurement performance emerged a series of scandals concerning DOD's practices for buying spare parts. Following the first disclosures in 1983, news accounts and Congressional hearings soon featured a torrent of stories about exorbitantly priced hammers, coffeepots, and stool caps.[99] The spare parts revelations soon were joined by accounts of performance failures and cost overruns, leading an increasing number of legislators to challenge plans for continuing the spending build-up.[100] To restore public confidence in the effectiveness of the defense acquisition process, in July 1985 President Reagan created the President's Blue Ribbon Commission on Defense Management.[101]

To lead the blue ribbon commission, President Reagan chose David Packard, the chairman of the board of the Hewlett-Packard Company. Packard came to the task with exceptional qualifications. Not only had he founded and built a highly successful computer company, but he also had served as deputy secretary of defense from 1969 to 1971. As deputy secretary, Packard had championed defense management reform and in particular had become well known as an advocate for prototyping major systems before committing the government to full-scale production.[102] Moreover, he had observed at close range the work of the last major blue ribbon panel, the Fitzhugh Commission, and he was well aware of the limits of DOD's amenability to reform. As one commentator has described Packard's tenure as deputy secretary, "After three years of sustained effort to reform the procurement system, he left the Pentagon in 1972—disappointed at the bureaucracy's successful resistance to change."[103]

In addition to Packard, the new commission had fifteen members, including several former civilian and military officials at DOD, a former head of the President's Council of Economic Advisors, a former congressman, and two former cabinet officers.[104] Assisting the commission was a staff of forty-two individuals, including a number of experienced students of the weapons acquisition process.[105] The commission published preliminary recommendations in an interim report in February 1986, released an expanded version of its acquisition proposals in April, and issued its final study in June.[106]

The Packard Commission: Findings

In examining DOD's procurement activities, the Packard Commission "focused on the acquisition of major weapon systems, because improved efficiency there can lead to cost savings greater by orders of magnitude."[107] The commission's general assessment was discouraging, yet consistent with the conclusions of earlier blue ribbon groups:

> All of our analysis leads us unequivocally to the conclusion that the defense acquisition system has basic problems that must be corrected. These problems are deeply entrenched and have developed over several decades from an increasingly bureaucratic and overregulated process. As a result, all too many of our weapon systems cost too much, take too long to develop, and, by the time they are fielded, incorporate obsolete technology.[108]

Poor performance, the commission added, was "seldom the result of fraud or dishonesty" but instead was "symptomatic of other underlying problems that affect the entire acquisition system."[109]

As the basis for developing its reform proposals, the Packard Commission reviewed several successful commercial acquisition projects roughly comparable in size and complexity to major DOD programs. From this review the commission identified six characteristics—clear command channels, stability, limited reporting requirements, small high-quality staffs, communications with users, prototyping and testing—that collectively formed a model acquisition process that DOD should emulate.[110] The Packard group's specific recommendations proposed steps by which DOD could adopt the preferred model.

Acquisition Organization and Procedures

As a starting-point, the commission said it was necessary for Congress and DOD to "establish unambiguous authority for overall acquisition policy, clear accountability for acquisition execution, and plain lines of command for those with program management responsibilities."[111] It was likewise "imperative" that acquisition procedures be streamlined.[112]

The foundation for improved organization would be the creation of the new position of "Under Secretary of Defense (Acquisition)." The new under secretary would be DOD's "Defense Acquisition Executive" and would "supervise the performance of the entire acquisition system and set overall policy for R & D, procurement, logistics, and testing."[113] Each of the armed services, in turn, should establish a senior acquisition executive who would "be responsible for administering Service acquisition programs under policy guidance from the Defense Acquisition Executive."[114] Finally, each senior acquisition executive "should appoint a number of Program Executive Officers . . . who, like group general managers in industry, should be responsible for a reasonable and defined number of acquisition programs."[115] The Packard panel admonished the Defense Acquisition Executive to ensure that no additional layers were inserted into a chain of command that would run from individual program managers to program executive officers to service acquisition executives to the defense acquisition executive.

The panel proposed two further changes to supplement the realignment of management channels. One was to simplify the law and regulations governing the procurement process. Congressional and DOD efforts "to dictate management improvements in the form of ever more detailed and extensive law or regulations" had rendered the procurement system's legal framework "impossibly cumbersome."[116] An unrelenting stream of new requirements had made it "virtually impossible" for DOD's operating units "to assimilate new legislative or regulatory refinements promptly or effectively."[117] To help correct this condition, the Packard Commission recommended that "Congress work with the Administration to recodify federal law governing procurement in a single, consistent, and greatly simplified procurement statute."[118] Streamlining the management structure and regulatory framework would enable DOD to take the further step of substantially reducing the total number of personnel in the defense acquisition system. In short, the new system would employ fewer people operating with fewer distractions, more authority, and more accountability.[119]

Prototyping and Testing

The Packard Commission recommended that DOD place "a high priority on building and testing prototype systems to demonstrate that new technology can substantially improve military capability, and to provide a basis for realistic cost estimates prior to a full-scale development decision."[120] Early stages of research and development should use streamlined procedures that largely dispensed with detailed specifications common to approved production programs. Instead the R & D phase should emphasize "an informal competition of ideas and technologies, rather than a formal competition of cost."[121] By subjecting prototype hardware to developmental and operational testing, DOD would greatly increase its ability to make reliable judgments about the risks and benefits of incorporating state-of-the-art technology into new weapon system designs.[122]

Balancing Cost and Performance

The Packard panel saw a need for strengthening DOD's methods for deciding whether and how to undertake full-scale development of a new weapon system. DOD's existing mechanism, in the commission's view, had proven inadequate in assessing whether suggested improvements in capability justified their cost and in deciding whether to satisfy service requirements by either developing a new system or adapting an existing system.[123] The Packard panel proposed that DOD's Joint Requirements and Management Board (JRMB) be restructured to make cost/performance trade-offs and decide whether to proceed with a new system's full-scale development.[124] The new arrangement would force DOD to consider the "affordability" of new systems more rigorously and would correct DOD's tendency to forgo "many valid opportunities for adapting existing systems" to fulfill the services' needs.[125]

Program Stability

The commission suggested two ways to increase the stability (and thereby the efficiency) of major acquisition programs. First, at the time of DOD's decision to begin a new system's full-scale development, the system's program manager "should prepare a brief baseline agreement describing functional specifications, cost, schedule, and other factors critical to the program's success."[126] Within the bounds of the agreement, the program manager would have broad authority to execute the program. At certain major milestones of the program's life-cycle, the Service Acquisition Executive and JRMB would review the program and decide whether to proceed to low-rate or full-rate production. Developmental and operational testing would be prerequisites for any decision to begin full-rate production.[127]

A second stability-enhancing measure would be for Congress to approve multiyear funding for (a) the development and low-rate production of all major systems the JRMB has chosen for full-scale development, and (b) the full-rate production of major systems that have completed the required testing cycles.[128] The multiyear funding recommendation dovetailed with separate Packard proposals that Congress adopt a biennial budget process for defense and authorize and appropriate funds for major systems only at the key milestones of full-scale development and full-rate production.[129] Collectively these measures would increase the program manager's ability to plan and control the project effectively and would cut the time and cost to complete each program.

Commercial Products

The Packard Commission urged DOD purchasing authorities to make greater use of "off-the-shelf" components, systems, and services.[130] Because the quality of many commercially available components, such as microchips, often meets military standards, DOD could forgo the substantially greater expense of developing goods uniquely for military use. When commercially available items did not suit military needs, the panel recommended that DOD streamline its military specifications, tailoring military standards to track commercial specifications as much as possible. As a general rule, when program managers faced a choice between making a new component to meet military standards or buying an acceptable commercial counterpart, the Packard panel concluded "the presumption should be to buy."[131]

Competition

The commission proposed that DOD continue and expand its existing efforts to use competitive purchasing strategies.[132] Two principles were suggested to guide DOD efforts to use rivalry among suppliers for major systems. First, DOD should consider factors other than price in awarding contracts among competing bidders. Technical expertise, product quality, and reliability all warranted close consideration. Second, by giving more emphasis to nonprice criteria, DOD could dispense with writing detailed military specifications in favor of functional product descriptions. "Procurement officers," the Packard panel wrote, "must be allowed and encouraged to solicit bids through purchase descriptions stated as functional performance characteristics rather than through detailed design and 'how-to' specifications."[133]

Acquisition Personnel

Despite some recent improvements, the Packard Commission found DOD's acquisition corps and personnel policies to be little improved beyond conditions the Hoover and Fitzhugh panels had criticized harshly. "Our study convinces us," the Packard report stated, "that lasting progress in the performance of the acquisition system demands dramatic improvements in our management of acquisition personnel at all levels within the DOD."[134] To start at the top of the chain, the Packard study urged that Congress change a number of "disincentives to entering public service" that obstructed the recruitment of capable executives to fill high-level positions in the commission's suggested acquisition hierarchy.[135]

The Packard panel also said it was "vitally important to improve the quality" of DOD's procurement middle managers and line personnel.[136] "Each year billions of dollars are spent more or less efficiently, based on the competence and experience of these personnel," the Packard report observed. "Yet, compared to its industry counterparts, this workforce is undertrained, underpaid, and inexperienced."[137] As remedies, the commission proposed stronger training programs, continuation of ongoing DOD reforms to give military officers longer tenure as program managers, and more flexible management policies concerning the status, pay, and qualifications of civilian employees.[138]

Government-Industry Accountability

Allegations of pervasive contractor misconduct played a major role in the Packard Commission's formation. The commission's inquiry nonetheless looked well beyond episodes of spare parts overcharging to examine the procurement process comprehensively. From its assessment of the process as a whole, the panel concluded that fraud, though not a trivial concern, was not the acquisition system's most serious flaw:

> Widely publicized investigations and prosecutions of large defense contractors have fostered an impression of widespread lawlessness, fueling popular mistrust of the integrity of defense industry. . . . The public is almost certainly mistaken about the extent of corruption in industry. . . . While fraud constitutes a serious problem, it is not as extensive or costly as many Americans believe.[139]

"The nation's defense programs," the Packard group concluded, "lose far more to inefficiency than to dishonesty."[140]

Although it believed "fraud, waste, and abuse" to be second-order problems, the commission feared that a public perception of pervasive misconduct could hamper efforts to deal with the more serious matter of inefficiency. Specifically, a "popular impression of runaway fraud and waste" could undermine support for needed efficiency-related reforms and for important defense programs generally.[141] To restore public confidence in the acquisition process, the Packard report said "defense contractors must promulgate and enforce codes of conduct that address their unique problems."[142] To give such codes practical effect, defense firms should also develop and apply internal controls to ensure compliance with their conduct guidelines and government procurement standards. At the same time, the panel urged DOD to establish a coordinated audit policy that avoided duplication of effort by the department's audit units.[143]

The Packard Commission: Impact

Announcement of the Packard Commission's findings triggered a large array of formal efforts to apply the panel's proposals. At a White House ceremony in which he accepted the commission's acquisition recommendations, President Reagan promised to execute the panel's reform proposals "even if they run counter to the will of the entrenched bureaucracies and special interests."[144] By the end of 1986, the executive branch and the Congress had taken a number of formal steps to follow the Packard reform blueprint.

Legislative Initiatives

Congress built major elements of the Packard panel's acquisition recommendations directly into the National Defense Authorization Act for Fiscal Year 1987.[145] As approved by Congress and signed by President Reagan, the 1987 DOD Authorization Statute incorporated the following measures.

First, to strengthen acquisition management the 1987 Act created the position of Under Secretary of Defense for Acquisition.[146] Coinstent with the Packard Commission's conception of the new position's role, the acquisition under secretary would supervise DOD procurement activities and establish acquisition policies for the entire department.[147]

Second, to enhance program stability, the statute required DOD to establish a baseline description for each of DOD's major acquisition programs.[148] For each system, the baseline must identify technical characteristics, performance goals, anticipated costs, testing plans, and timetables for full-scale development and full-rate production. Program managers must inform the secretary of the purchasing service of expected cost, schedule, or performance deviations from the established baseline.[149]

Third, as a further stability initiative, the 1987 Act directed the Secretary of Defense to "take appropriate measures to ensure that the Department of Defense increases the use of multiyear contracting authority in fiscal year

1988."[150] The statute also authorized the three services to enter multiyear contracts for selected ongoing weapons programs.[151]

Fourth, the statute authorized the DOD Secretary to designate acquisition projects as "defense enterprise zones."[152] The enterprise zone programs would feature simple, clear lines of communication and would increase the program manager's authority to manage his program with limited reliance on outside review. As a companion measure, the 1987 Act committed Congress, for selected enterprise zone programs, to authorize funds for, respectively, full-scale development and full-rate production when the enterprise program approached those "milestones" in the program's baseline plan.[153]

Fifth, the statute compelled the secretary of defense to "require the use of a competitive prototype program strategy" to develop major weapons systems.[154] With limited exceptions, the acquisition plan for forthcoming major systems must provide for "a comparative side-by-side test" between two or more rival prototypes in conditions that mirror combat circumstances "to the extent practicable."[155] In a separate provision that reflects the Packard panel's emphasis on prototyping and operational testing, the 1987 Act directed the secretary of defense to require operational tests to assess survivability and lethality for certain categories of weapon systems and munitions.[156]

Finally, in addition to its generic mandate for competitive prototyping, the 1987 Act contained another specific provision intended to press DOD to draw more heavily upon rivalry-based strategies to elicit better performance from contractors on major systems. The act directed DOD to give Congress a report containing the department's acquisition strategy for the Air Force Advanced Technology ("Stealth") Bomber.[157] The report must discuss the possibility of using rival sources for the bomber's major systems and subsystems, as well as using competition during the bomber's integration and assembly. Consistent with the Packard panel's competition recommendations, this provision manifested Congress' preexisting preference that DOD employ contractor rivalry more broadly in buying major systems.[158]

Defense Department Initiatives

At President Reagan's direction, DOD began developing plans to implement Packard proposals that did not require Congressional action. DOD Secretary Weinberger outwardly embraced the Packard study as "extremely helpful" and committed the department to carrying out the panel's recommendations.[159] In January 1987 Secretary Weinberger informed Congress that DOD had distilled the Packard findings into "18 major action items." Of these, Weinberger wrote, "15 have been completed to date, while the remaining three are progressing satisfactorily and should be completed within the near future."[160]

DOD's principal stated accomplishment was the reorganization of its acquisition management process. In the fall of 1986, President Reagan appointed Richard Godwin to the new post of Under Secretary for Acquisition.[161] Godwin thus assumed responsibility for overseeing all of DOD's acquisition activities. Beneath Godwin DOD also established senior acquisition executives in each of the services to oversee the services' acquisition work.[162] Other completed tasks included restructuring of the Joint Requirements and Management Board to play a greater role in reviewing the progress of major programs.

The Packard Commission's recommendations also appeared to stimulate new or reinforce existing DOD efforts to use prototyping and contractor rivalry in new weapons programs. For example, by the end of 1986, the Air Force, Army, and Navy were each pursuing a major new aircraft program that would require the production of prototype aircraft followed by a competitive fly-off.[163] More generally, the services' reports to Congress suggested an expanded emphasis upon management strategies the Packard panel had identified as ingredients of successful major product development programs in the commercial sector.[164]

Lasting Effects

Notwithstanding many formal changes in the organization and procedure of weapons acquisition, subsequent events have raised growing doubts about the Packard Commission's effect upon the procurement process. The bases for current skepticism are several.

The first ground for disquiet is the Packard panel's apparent conviction that DOD thus far has moved too slowly to make needed changes. Barely one year after they issued their final report, Packard and his fellow commissioners sent President Reagan a letter complaining about DOD's lack of progress to date.[165] Explaining the group's dissatisfaction, panel member James Woolsey said that without further DOD action, "you are likely to get the form and structure, but not a great deal of the substance, of many of the acquisition reforms."[166] Panel Chairman David Packard was said to be particularly concerned that DOD's bureaucracy had failed to yield necessary authority to Richard Godwin, the under secretary for acquisition whose appointment was a direct consequence of the commission's work.[167]

Packard's fears soon received vivid reinforcement. The Packard Commission had said that its call for the creation of an under secretary for acquisition was a "pivotal recommendation,"[168] and Packard's own remarks in the months after the group's final report had indicated that the new office (and the new management system it foreshadowed) constituted the foundation of the commission's proposed acquisition reforms.[169] No sooner had Richard Godwin taken the new acquisition post, however, than signs appeared that DOD's existing procurement apparatus would willingly cede Godwin little of its power.

When Godwin made his first appearance before the House Armed Services Committee in March 1987, committee members expressed concern that DOD's bureaucracy was successfully resisting Godwin's efforts to set and execute acquisition policy.[170] When committee members told Godwin that the committee was considering legislation to expand the powers of his office, the under secretary responded, "Personally, I think that would be helpful."[171] Soon afterwards the House committee's chairman, Les Aspin, and its ranking Republican, William Dickinson, announced that they had written Secretary Weinberger to criticize a Pentagon directive that allowed service secretaries to appeal Godwin's decisions to Weinberger or his deputy. "A czar without authority is a eunuch," Aspin commented.[172]

In the months following the House hearings, Washington abounded with accounts of Godwin's failed efforts to gain the cooperation of the Pentagon's procurement hierarchy and the backing of other executive branch bodies involved in acquisition policy.[173] Citing frustration with the Pentagon's resistance to change, Godwin quit his position in mid–September 1987.[174] "My decision to resign," he later told the House Armed Services Committee, "rested simply upon my judgment that the Pentagon was not prepared to move ahead vigorously with the implementation of reforms and that the institution was not prepared to change the status quo."[175] He warned the committee that the armed services' leadership would continue to ignore or oppose DOD's under secretary for acquisition unless Congress bolstered the authority of the new office.[176]

Pentagon officials rejected Godwin's claim that the Department's leadership had hindered the under secretary. DOD spokesman Robert Sims said the department's chief officials had backed "all of the substantive Packard commission recommendations" and had "supported Mr. Godwin in the setting up of the acquisition office."[177] Other DOD officials said Godwin's discontent stemmed from his unrealistic view of his office's role. "Godwin was misled about the nature and duties of his authority before he came," stated William H. Taft IV, the deputy secretary of defense. "He came with a promise that he would be a czar . . . one shouldn't be told that. There aren't any czars in Washington."[178] Some detractors attributed Godwin's departure to his unwarranted impatience with the pace at which the services were undertaking complex, fundamental change, and to his intemperate "desire to win all battles" within the Pentagon.[179]

Some commentators have taken Godwin's experience as proof that the Packard Commission's management reforms, if not its entire acquisition agenda, are doomed to neglect.[180] Godwin's early departure is significant, but arguably a better test of the Packard panel's impact will come during the tenure of Godwin's successors. To fill Godwin's post, President Reagan selected Robert Costello, a former senior purchasing executive at General Motors who had served for six months as a Pentagon assistant secretary. Knowledgeable students of DOD noted that Costello possessed advantages as under secretary for acquisition that Godwin lacked.[181] Costello benefitted not only from his own experience in procurement at General Motors, but also from a close view of the events that undid Godwin. More important, Costello enjoyed—at least initially—strong support from a Congress that saw Godwin as a victim of Pentagon intransigence.[182] The prospect of close scrutiny from the Armed Services committees or passage of new legislation made DOD's acquisition leadership somewhat more responsive to Costello's commands.

A final factor that perhaps lent additional force to Costello's efforts was a change of command at DOD. In November 1987 Caspar Weinberger retired after nearly seven years as the secretary of defense. To replace Weinberger, President Reagan selected Frank Carlucci, who had served as a member of the Packard Commission. Like David Packard, Carlucci was an astute, experienced student of the acquisition process and a veteran of previous procurement reform efforts. Some observers have suggested that Weinberger, notwithstanding his public support for the Packard Commission's work, resented the blue ribbon inquiry and had little enthusiasm for seeing its management proposals executed. Carlucci, by contrast, was less disposed to obstruct the implementation of proposals he helped to devise.

Until leaving the Pentagon in May 1989, Costello appears to have made greater headway than his predecessors in using the new under secretary position as a platform for improving DOD acquisition policy. Among other accomplishments, Costello succeeded in focusing attention upon the need to upgrade contractor manufacturing facilities and to encourage defense suppliers to adopt quality-conscious design and assembly practices that characterize successful commercial goods firms.[183] On the whole, however, Costello made little progress toward establishing the under secretary for acquisition and the new defense acquisition executives as the engines for managerial reform that the 1987 enabling legislation envisioned. Observed a study prepared in November 1988 by the Johns Hopkins Foreign Policy Institute and the Center for Strategic and International Studies (CSIS):

> Our sense is that the new positions were simply superimposed on top of the existing system. There are new service executives and an under secretary, but they do not have the requisite authority to carry out their jobs. Intervening layers of bureaucracy between the executives and the program managers have not been dismantled. Moreover, each service accomplished this organizational directive in a different way, causing confusion and some question as to whether the intent of the legislation has been met.[184]

It remains to be seen how much effort Secretary of Defense Richard Cheney, Congress, and the Bush administration will devote to seeing that the unfinished business associated with the Packard management proposals and other acquisition reforms will be carried out. For reasons discussed immediately below, the history of blue ribbon defense panels gives few grounds for expecting these groups to ensure that the Packard recommendations have a substantial, enduring effect.

THE FAILURE OF BLUE RIBBON DEFENSE COMMISSIONS

As judged by most who have studied postwar movements to reform the weapons acquisition process, blue ribbon commissions have elicited little basic change in the way the United States buys armaments.[185] With some qualification, this view seems correct. Even though blue ribbon panels have periodically moved presidents, legislators, and defense secretaries to amend policy as a matter of form, few special commission recommendations have become so engrained in the procurement process that they reshaped the substance of weapons acquisition in practice. Why, then, do blue commissions come into being, and what accounts for their limited effect?

Two theories explain why presidents and legislators establish blue ribbon defense panels. One is that the commissions' creators neither expect nor desire that the panels effect change. Rather, the blue ribbon commissions offer an illusion of activity sufficient to permit the attainment of other goals. At least in part, the Packard Commission's creation enabled President Reagan to deflect Congressional attention away from stories of contractor misconduct and DOD mismanagement and to sustain support for requested defense appropriations. Special commissions may be seen as especially attractive political tools if one is confident (and history justifies such confidence) that the defense panels will issue reports, that nominal policy changes will take place, but that business will proceed essentially as usual.

A second theory is that special defense commissions arise from the inability of conventional policymaking institutions to achieve consensus about the causes of defense acquisition failure and the appropriate path for reform. Presumed to be largely free of the taint of self-aggrandizement and parochial interest, the special commission often functions with a measure of perceived credibility and objectivity that Congress and the executive branch find wanting in each other on defense matters. Thus, the nonpartisan, expert commission is deemed better suited to overcome policy deadlocks by identifying deficiencies and drafting reforms that Congress and the executive branch will endorse.

If the first of the two theories is the driving force behind the formation of special commissions, one need not search far to see why the panels have produced few enduring results. The commissions have no lasting effect because they are not intended to do so. Despite the availability of some

supporting evidence, this explanation is only partly satisfying. To a substantial degree, policymakers form special commissions because such panels seem to provide a means to attain better acquisition results. Experience with the Commission on Base Realignment and Closure provides evidence that the establishment of blue-ribbon panels is not invariably a cynical gesture. In establishing a new base closure procedure in 1988, Congress curbed its ability to interfere with facilities cuts and placed the choice of bases in the hands of an independent commission that lacked the motives for opportunism that many legislators had attributed to the executive branch in previous base closing episodes.[186]

The base closing commission subsequently identified 91 facilities to be closed entirely or in part.[187] The 1988 statute required Congress to accept or reject the list in its entirety, and Congress did not overturn the panel's recommendations by the April 15, 1989 deadline.[188] Though a clear sign of progress, the base closing process has not been an unqualified success. Some observers have noted that the commission targeted a relatively modest list of facilities, and it is not yet certain that Congress will appropriate the funds needed to execute the specified changes.[189] Nonetheless, it is doubtful that Congress would have passed the legislation in the first place if it had catered completely to the rent-seeking instincts of its members. Rather, it seems more appropriate to characterize the base closing measure as an exercise in legislative self-denial, "an example of legislation by which Congress, in order to promote public policy that is good for the nation as a whole, voluntarily deprives itself of the ability to take credit for standing up for constituents.[190]

To the extent that a genuine concern for the efficiency of the procurement process motivates the panels' creation, the question remains as to why reform proposals go unfulfilled. One cause of failure could be shortcomings in the work of the commissions themselves. But judged by the substantive merit of their specific reform proposals, the defense commissions generally have suggested sensible measures. Indeed, the accumulated logic and experience of the postwar era certify the soundness of many Hoover, Fitzhugh, and Packard recommendations. For example, acquisition management structures should be lean and unencumbered by endless layers of review. Cadres of capable, well-paid, and experienced acquisition personnel are likely to accomplish more than legions of less talented, undercompensated, and undertrained employees. Program managers should have freedom and responsibility to guide their projects in the knowledge that they will be rewarded handsomely for success and held strictly to account for failure. Prototyping, though it entails larger initial expenditures, tends to offer corresponding returns in reduced uncertainty and enlightened source selection. Competitive strategies can enable the services to obtain better supplier performances and discourage supplier opportunism. In these and other proposals, the blue ribbon panels have written wisely.

In a broader sense, however, there is a serious flaw in the panels' work. Their reports typically spend little, if any, time discussing why the often similar recommendations of earlier studies have failed to produce needed change. This omission is significant, because the inquiry it would entail would confront the special commissions with a problem whose solution is essential to the success of weapons acquisition reform.

Blocking the path to effective reform is a fundamental failure in public policymaking. Formal changes in policy—new statutes, regulations, and directives—do no more than begin the weapons acquisition reform process. To achieve needed effect, most suggested defense procurement remedies require sustained, long-term implementation and monitoring. Effective monitoring and oversight demand, among other tasks, continuing scrutiny of how the services have translated nominal policy changes into practice; ongoing assessment of the effects of changed practices; and adjustments in formal policies and practice in the light of experience. To do any of this well, the monitoring institutions must invest substantial resources in training personnel to learn the modern history of weapons procurement, the intricacies of the regulatory framework, and the culture and conduct of DOD and the defense industry.

Our conventional policymaking institutions usually disdain these types of necessary follow-up. The requisite monitoring requires long-term investments whose returns often accrue largely beyond the short-term horizons within which elected and appointed officials ordinarily plan and operate. Sustained monitoring is likely to yield returns that come after a specific official's tenure ends; such returns may not be readily traceable to the official's acts. In short, effective monitoring creates benefits that are often difficult for public officials who might invest in monitoring to claim as flowing from their own efforts. In defense reform, public officials have weak incentives to invest in monitoring, and consequently they do too little of it.

By the same token, the imperative to make one's investments pay a full, appropriable return within a short time (often two to four years) accounts for much of what passes under the name of weapons acquisition reform. The standard output is largely a mix of wholly symbolic gestures, long-term solutions truncated into disappointing half-measures, and formal policy adjustments that eventually falter for want of sustained implementation. The Justice Department's efforts in this decade to use criminal sanctions expansively to attack contractor misconduct reveals the incentives at their worst. Pressed by Congress in the mid-1980s to get instant results, the department launched a substantial antifraud program without, it appears, first investing the resources necessary to secure a sophisticated understanding of the defense procurement process—an effort that would require a significant period of preliminary analysis. The early campaign yielded many investigations and indictments, but relatively few convictions. It also produced a stunning embarrassment attributable to the department's poor comprehension of DOD's procurement regulations and practice.[191]

The latest and most visible criminal enforcement chapter opened in June 1988 with the disclosure of the Justice Department's "Operation Ill Wind" inquiry.[192] The Ill Wind investigation has focused chiefly upon the use by contractors of consultants to gather inside information about DOD's purchasing intentions. Congressional reaction to the initial Ill Wind revelations was characteristically exaggerated. "It is the most serious case in the history of the Department of Defense," declared Senator John Warner soon after the inquiry's existence was disclosed.[193] "It goes beyond our wildest imagination," said Senator Charles Grassley.[194] "I want to see somebody go to jail," added Senator James Exon.[195] In the following twelve months, the Ill Wind prosecutors achieved some substantial victories, but the results to date have failed to support the sweeping predictions that flowed from Capitol Hill and the U.S. Attorney's Office when the inquiry was revealed.[196] Notwithstanding the merits of specific cases, the preoccupation with the criminal inquiry and the predictable outburst of new proposals for a quick fix have diverted attention from the less glamorous but ultimately more important business of seeing that structural causes of weapons acquisition mismanagement and inefficiency are addressed.[197]

The costs of attempting defense procurement reform without the commitment to see changes through to fruition are formidable. Most obvious is the expense associated with ultimately barren and distracting rituals of reorganization, recodification, and public relations. Less quantifiable but more serious is the comfort that a predictable failure in implementation and monitoring gives those with a stake in things as they are. Despite Congress's strong displeasure with Richard Godwin's resignation and its promise to scrutinize Godwin's successors closely, DOD's existing acquisition leadership and their supporting constituencies outside the Pentagon have almost every reason to expect that they can wait out Congress's interest in the Packard proposals and allow recent statutory reforms to sink of their own weight.

Although the special commissions' studies generally fail to confront this issue, some blue ribbon panelists have recognized the problem created by the mismatch between the commissions' short-lived existence and the long-term nature of their assignment. In a speech several months after his commission completed its work, David Packard warned that executing the Packard panel's reforms required persistence. After applauding Richard Godwin's appointment as under secretary, Packard said:

> This is good progress in improving defense management, but it is only a small beginning on the job that needs to be done. Further progress will depend on continuing involvement on the part of those people and those organizations actively interested in improving defense management. . . . I am sure the rec-

ommendations we have made are not the optimum. Some probably should be modified, some may be wrong. For this reason, continued public discussion is important.[198]

To see that "continued public discussion" and other needed monitoring take place, some observers have suggested that blue ribbon defense panels be given longer lives and larger roles. The Center for Strategic and International Studies, for example, has proposed that Congress "create a mechanism, such as a General Advisory Board on Defense Acquisition, which would monitor progress of the intended reforms and provide an annual report to the President and Congress."[199] The advisory board would have a charter for no more than five years and would consist of representatives from the executive and legislative branches and the private sector. One immediately fears that Congress and the executive branch would simply shrug off the board's report. Nonetheless, the CSIS proposal seems a useful experiment. The board potentially would provide a means for attaining the continuity and depth of monitoring that the executive and legislative branches seem unable to provide and that remains beyond the reach of interested outsiders.

Whether or not improved monitoring mechanisms are forthcoming, there is a second approach that special commissions can pursue to increase the impact of their work. George Stigler's concurring statement to the Fitzhugh panel's study sets out the essential content and logic of an alternative technique:

> No organization can achieve or maintain efficiency in structure or operation by having a critical review made by expert outsiders once each five or ten years— even if, contrary to the experience of previous surveys of the Department of Defense, the recommendations of the review panel are unfailingly adopted. A good organization must have built into its very structure the incentives to its personnel to do the right things.[200]

As Stigler suggests, the special commission's surest means to obtain lasting change is to conceive structural reforms that (a) can be put in place through one-time intervention, probably in the months immediately following the release of the commission's study, and (b) create powerful incentives for acquisition officials to use the commission's preferred procurement methods.

Building a machine that can be installed quickly and will run properly on its own is hardly a simple task. The Packard Commission may have seen itself as seeking precisely such a result through its suggested management reforms, particularly the creation of the position of under secretary for acquisition and a simplified acquisition hierarchy. A good deal of implementation and monitoring are essential to the success of the structural, incentive-shaping change that Stigler endorses. Continuing oversight is necessary to see that the incentives have been installed and to evaluate the altered incentives' effect. One can reduce, but not eliminate, the need for ongoing monitoring.

Experience with the postwar blue ribbon commissions demonstrates that the inspiration to reform without the commitment to persevere yields little change. That Congress or the executive branch can or will improve the monitoring of reform initiatives is uncertain, but the consequences of relying upon the occasional blue ribbon panel to achieve fundamental reform are unmistakable. To do no more than wait fifteen years to empanel the next commission ensures that existing flaws in the country's weapons acquisition process will continue unrepaired into the next century.

NOTES

1. Recent treatments that place the Reagan defense spending program in its historical context include William W. Kaufmann and Lawrence J. Korb, *The 1990 Defense Budget* (Washington, D.C.: Brookings Institution, 1989), pp. 8–19; William W. Kaufmann, *A Reasonable Defense* (Washington, D.C.: Brookings Institution, 1986), pp. 18–30; Tim Carrington, "The Pentagon, Seeking Modest Rise in Budget, Is Trying Conciliation," *Wall Street Journal,* January 6, 1987, p. 1.

2. For data on expenditures, see United States Department of Defense, *Annual Report to the Congress, Fiscal Year 1989* (Washington, D.C.: U.S. Government Printing Office, 1988), p. 297; United States Department of Defense, *Annual Report to the Congress, Fiscal Year 1988* (Washington, D.C.: U.S. Government Printing Office, 1987), p. 325; United States Department of Defense, *Annual Report to the Congress, Fiscal Year 1987* (Washington, D.C.: U.S. Government Printing Office, 1986), p. 313. On the effects of ongoing and planned weapons purchases on future United States defense policy, see George C. Wilson, "600-Ship Navy Is Sailing Toward Rough Fiscal Seas," *Washington Post,* March 16, 1987, p. A1; David C. Morrison, "Downhill Slide," *National Journal,* February 21, 1987, p. 412; George C. Wilson, "Defense: Even with Crackdown, Spending Will Crest for Years," *Washington Post,* January 9, 1987, p. A21; Tim Carrington, "Star Wars Program Encounters Terrestrial Woes: It Might Cost More Than Budget Can Deliver," *Wall Street Journal,* March 18, 1986, p. 62.

3. Included among the major new systems accounted for in recent DOD expenditures and appropriations requests are next-generation fighter aircraft for the Air Force and Navy, respectively; a new Army attack helicopter; the Stealth bomber; a new attack submarine; two new nuclear-powered aircraft carriers; and elements of the Strategic Defense Initiative. See George C. Wilson, "Fine Print of Budget Comprises Catalog of Costly New Weapons," *Washington Post,* February 19, 1986, p. A4.

4. See pp. 82–84.

5. For example, current DOD efforts to rely more heavily upon competition-oriented purchasing techniques to buy major weapon systems have built upon the analysis and policy guidance of numerous public and private institutions and individuals. See William B. Burnett and William E. Kovacic, "Reform of United States Weapons Acquisition Policy: Competition, Teaming Agreements, and Dual-Sourcing," *Yale Journal on Regulation* 6 (Summer 1989):249–317.

6. President's Blue Ribbon Commission on Defense Management, *A Quest*

for Excellence—Final Report to the President (Washington, D.C.: U.S. Government Printing Office, June 1986) (known as the Packard Commission Report).

7. See, for example, President Reagan, "Message to Congress Outlining Proposals for Improvement to the Defense Establishment, April 24, 1986," reprinted in President's Blue Ribbon Commission on Defense Management, *A Quest for Excellence—Appendix* (Washington, D.C.: U.S. Government Printing Office, June 1986), pp. 43–50 (endorsing Packard Commission's initial recommendations); David Hoffman, "Pentagon Revamp Supported," *Washington Post,* April 2, 1986, p. A10 (discussing legislative support for Packard reforms).

8. The American mobilization program during World War II established the essential processes and institutional arrangements through which weapons acquisition takes place in the United States today. Selecting the postwar period for study is somewhat arbitrary, as one can trace important elements of the modern weapons acquisition process back to the turn of the century. See, for example, Benjamin Franklin Cooling, *Gray Steel and Blue Water Navy—The Formative Years of America's Military Industrial Complex, 1881–1917* (Hamden, Conn.: Archon Books, 1979). To most observers, however, World War II marks the full emergence of public and private institutions through which the country buys arms today. See Robert Higgs, "Private Profit, Public Risk: Institutional Antecedents of the Modern Military Procurement System in the Rearmament Program of 1940–41," in *The Sinews of War: Essays on the Economic History of World War II,* ed. Geofrey T. Mills and Hugh Rockoff (Ames: Iowa State University Press, forthcoming); Robert Higgs, *Crisis and Leviathan* (New York: Oxford University Press, 1987), pp. 211–15, 230–33.

9. By addressing the commissions' review of major weapons systems, the paper focuses upon the "big-ticket" programs (missiles, ships, tanks, aircraft) that account for the bulk of DOD's annual research and development and procurement outlays. The relative importance of such weaponry has inclined modern, comprehensive studies of defense procurement to focus primarily or exclusively upon major systems. See, for example, Jacques S. Gansler, *The Defense Industry* (Cambridge, Mass.: MIT Press, 1980); J. Ronald Fox, *Arming America: How the U.S. Buys Weapons* (Cambridge, Mass.: Harvard University Press, 1974); Murray L. Weidenbaum, *The Economics of Peacetime Defense* (New York: Praeger, 1974); William L. Baldwin, *The Structure of the Defense Market 1955–1964* (Durham: Duke University Press, 1967); F. M. Scherer, *The Weapons Acquisition Process: Economic Incentives* (Boston: Harvard University Press, 1964); Merton J. Peck and F. M. Scherer, *The Weapons Acquisition Process: An Economic Analysis* (Cambridge: Harvard University Press, 1962).

10. An additional definitional note is in order at the outset. Broadly defined, the "weapons acquisition process" encompasses a number of discrete activities. In rough chronological order, these are (1) identifying the country's security goals worldwide, (2) conceiving a military strategy to attain these goals, (3) determining the weapons needed to execute the strategy, (4) procuring the needed weapons, and (5) maintaining the weapons throughout their operating lives. This study focuses principally upon the analysis blue ribbon panels have brought to bear on the fourth of these steps, the procurement stage. "Procurement" itself is a shorthand term that embraces the techniques and procedures through which DOD and its suppliers perform research and development, build and test prototypes, and carry out full-scale production. In discussing the procurement stage, I do not treat the blue ribbon panels' analyses of DOD policies that define contractors' property rights in data created wholly or partly with DOD funds.

11. *Report of the President's Commission on the Assassination of President John F. Kennedy* (Washington, D.C.: U.S. Government Printing Office, 1964), p. xiv.

12. *Report of the Presidential Commission on the Space Shuttle Challenger Accident* (Washington, D.C.: U.S. Government Printing Office, 1986).

13. The circumstances surrounding President Nixon's decision in 1969 to create the American Bar Association Commission to Study the Federal Trade Commission illustrate this model. In 1969 a Ralph Nader–sponsored group published an unflattering critique of the FTC. The study focused widespread attention upon the agency, whose performance many commentators and task forces had rated poorly at various times since the FTC's creation in 1914. To many of the agency's Congressional overseers, the Nader study proved that an already quiescent agency had virtually abandoned efforts to deal with what Congress believed to be serious and growing consumer protection and antitrust problems. The resulting Congressional and public criticism of the agency moved President Nixon to establish the ABA Commission to evaluate the FTC. See William E. Kovacic, "The Federal Trade Commission and Congressional Oversight of Antitrust Enforcement: An Historical Perspective," in *Public Choice and Regulation: A View from Inside the Federal Trade Commission,* ed. Robert J. MacKay, James C. Miller III, and Bruce Yandle (Stanford: Hoover Institution Press, 1987), pp. 63–120; *Report of the American Bar Association Commission to Study the Federal Trade Commission* (Chicago: American Bar Association, 1969).

14. See Richard E. Neustadt and Ernest R. May, *Thinking in Time: The Uses of History for Decision-Makers* (New York: Free Press, 1986), pp. 17–33; *Report of the National Commission on Social Security Reform* (Washington, D.C.: U.S. Government Printing Office, 1983).

15. *Report of the President's Special Review Board* (Washington, D.C.: U.S. Government Printing Office, February 26, 1987).

16. This objectivity criterion arguably played a role in the establishment of a special commission to investigate President Kennedy's assassination. The selection of a prominent jurist—Supreme Court Chief Justice Earl Warren—to head the inquiry symbolized and reinforced the panel's nonpartisan character. Ironically, the Warren Commission's findings generated a degree of public skepticism or outright disbelief that few special panels have encountered.

17. James C. Miller III, Thomas F. Walton, William E. Kovacic, and Jeremy A. Rabkin, "Industrial Policy: Reindustrialization Through Competition or Coordinated Action?," *Yale Journal on Regulation* 2 (1984): 34–35.

18. See, for example, Neustadt and May, *Thinking in Time,* pp. 22–31 (discussing the work of the National Commission on Social Security Reform).

19. See William E. Kovacic, "The Federal Trade Commission and Congressional Oversight of Antitrust Enforcement," *University of Tulsa Law Journal* 17 (1982): 592–602 (discussing work of special panels formed to evaluate the work of the Federal Trade Commission).

20. By "monitoring" and "evaluation" I have in mind the public policy counterparts to the metering, policing, and observation functions economists have identified as elements of firm organization and performance. See Henry G. Manne, "Our Two Corporation Systems: Law and Economics," *Virginia Law Review* 53 (1967): 259; Armen A. Alchian and Harold Demsetz, "Production, Information Costs, and Economic Organization," *American Economic Review* 62 (1972): 777.

21. The critical literature that these groups have generated since 1980 is immense. Useful single-volume evaluations of weapons acquisition policy in this period include Thomas L. McNaugher, *New Weapons, Old Politics—America's Military Procurement Muddle* (Washington, D.C.: Brookings Institution, 1989); J. Ronald Fox, *The Defense Management Challenge: Managing Weapons Acquisition* (Boston: Harvard Business School Press, 1988); Andrew Cox and Stephen Kirby, *Congress,*

Parliament and Defense: The Impact of Legislative Reform on Defense Accountability in Britain and America (New York: Macmillan, 1986); Richard A. Stubbing, *The Defense Game* (New York: Harper and Row, 1986); Patrick Tyler, *Running Critical: The Silent War, Rickover, and General Dynamics* (New York: Harper and Row, 1986); Edward N. Luttwak, *The Pentagon and the Art of War* (New York: Simon and Schuster, 1985); Robert J. Art, Vincent Davis, and Samuel P. Huntington, eds., *Reorganizing America's Defense* (Washington, D.C.: Pergamon-Brassey's, 1985); Asa A. Clark IV, Peter W. Chiarelli, Jeffrey S. McKitrick, and James W. Reed, eds., *The Defense Reform Debate* (Baltimore: Johns Hopkins University Press, 1984); James Fallows, *National Defense* (New York: Random House, 1981); Jacques S. Gansler, *Affording Defense* (Cambridge, Mass.: MIT Press, 1989).

22. In concentrating on panels created by presidential or Congressional order and supported by public funds, this study does not discuss in detail the work of other commission-type bodies that have lacked "official" status but have nonetheless conducted significant investigations relating to weapons acquisition. Examples of the latter include Center for Strategic and International Studies, *U.S. Defense Acquisition: A Process in Trouble* (Washington, D.C.: Center for Strategic and International Studies, 1987); President's Private Sector Survey on Cost Control, *Report on the Office of the Secretary of Defense* (Washington, D.C.: U.S. Government Printing Office, 1983) (the Grace Commission). Also excluded from full treatment here are official commissions that have analyzed the practices of public authorities generally. See, for example, Commission on Government Procurement, *Report of the Commission on Government Procurement* (Washington, D.C.: U.S. Government Printing Office, 1972). Although it does not review the commissions mentioned in this note in detail, this study refers to selected aspects of their work.

23. The first and most important postwar organizational reform measures were the National Security Act of 1947 and the National Security Act Amendments of 1949. Together these statutes created the Department of Defense and its component Departments of the Air Force, Army, and Navy; designated the Joint Chiefs of Staff as the principal military advisors to the President and the Secretary of Defense; and established the National Security Council. See James K. Gruetzner and William D. Caldwell, "DOD Reorganization," *U.S. Naval Institute Proceedings,* May 1987, p. 136; C. W. Borkland, *The Department of Defense* (New York: Praeger, 1968), pp. 1–56.

24. By contrast, after World War I the United States substantially disbanded its armed forces, ceased most new weapons development, and largely liquidated its existing weapons inventories. Despite modest rearmament efforts after 1936, the country's weapons were—with some exceptions such as fleet submarines—relatively few in number and poor in quality when America entered World War II. See Ronald H. Spector, *Eagle Against the Sun* (New York: Free Press, 1985), pp. 9–32.

25. The World War II program that most clearly foreshadowed the features of postwar American weapons development efforts was the B-29 bomber. Incorporating large advances in aerodynamics, propulsion, and electronics, the B-29 dramatically surpassed the performance (and cost) of its predecessor system, the B-17. As one observer has noted, the B-29 was "the greatest gamble of the war—greater even than the atom bomb ($3 billion invested, as opposed to $2 billion for the bomb, on a similar absence of hard evidence)." Eric Larrabee, *Commander in Chief: Franklin Delano Roosevelt, His Lieutenants, and Their War* (New York: Harper and Row, 1987), p. 580. See also Richard Rhodes, *The Making of the Atomic Bomb* (New York: Simon and Schuster, 1986), pp. 584–85; Ray Wagner, *American Combat Planes* (Garden City: Doubleday, 1968), pp. 134–37.

26. Commission on Government Procurement, "Historical Development of

the Procurement Process," *Report of the Commission on Government Procurement, vol. 1,* Appendix G (Washington, D.C.: U.S. Government Printing Office, 1972), pp. 171–72.

27. William S. Cohen, "Competition in Contracting Act," *Public Contract Law Journal* 14 (1983): 6–7.

28. *The Hoover Commission Report on Organization of the Executive Branch of the Government* (New York: McGraw-Hill, 1949). The commission's authorizing statute provided that the panel would have twelve members, six from each party. President Truman, the president of the Senate, and the speaker of the House each were to choose four members.

29. Ibid., p. xiv. See also Higgs, *Crisis and Leviathan,* pp. 159–236 (documenting the expansion of federal government institutions during the Depression and World War II).

30. *1949 Hoover Commission Report,* p. xiv.

31. Ibid., pp. 185–97.

32. Ibid., p. 104. The First Hoover Commission made exceedingly general recommendations that defense acquisition management be improved. For example, the first commission urged Congress to "strengthen the Authority of the Secretary of Defense so that he may provide the leadership necessary for improving the supply operations of the National Military Establishment."

33. Commission on Organization of the Executive Branch of the Government—Task Force on Procurement, *Report on Military Procurement* (Washington, D.C.: U.S. Government Printing Office, 1955), pp. iii–iv. Defense suppliers represented on the panel included Lukens Steel, Borg-Warner, RCA, Chicago Bridge and Iron, U.S. Steel, Bell Laboratories, Republic Aviation, and Warner & Swasey.

34. Ibid., pp. iv, 85–87. The advisory committee consisted of four corporate executives, one attorney from a major law firm, and two industrial consultants. The task force's professional staff consisted of attorneys in private practice, military officers, management and industrial consultants, industry officials, and government career civil servants.

35. Ibid., p. 23.

36. Ibid., p. 27.

37. Ibid., pp. 23–24. The Hoover panel noted that the negotiation method had accounted for 85 percent of military contract dollars committed in the three years preceding its study.

38. Ibid.

39. Ibid., p. 24.

40. Ibid.

41. Ibid.

42. Ibid., p. 27.

43. Ibid., p. 28.

44. Ibid., p. 32.

45. Ibid., pp. 28–29.

46. Ibid., p. 32.

47. This possibility is suggested indirectly in the task force study. Ibid., p. 28.

48. Ibid., p. 39.

49. Ibid., p. 40.

50. Ibid., p. 35. Other production phase administration reforms included (a) the establishment of production scheduling controls to insure realism in planning deliveries and (b) exploring practices that might give prime contractors more responsibility for overseeing their subcontractors.

51. Ibid., pp. 40–41.

52. Ibid., p. 67.

53. Ibid.

54. Ibid.

55. Ibid., pp. 67–68.

56. Ibid., p. 68.

57. Commission on Government Procurement, "Historical Development of the Procurement Process," pp. 173–74.

58. Ibid., p. 174.

59. The 1962 Amendments to the Armed Services Procurement Act sought, among other ends, to obtain more competition when DOD resorted to negotiation rather than formal advertising. The 1962 statute also contained a provision, known as the Truth in Negotiations Act, that compelled suppliers to give DOD all "current, complete, and accurate" cost or pricing data on which the supplier based its proposals in a negotiated procurement. See Cohen, "Competition in Contracting Act," p. 8.

60. Commission on Government Procurement, "Historical Development of the Procurement Process," p. 174.

61. William J. Lynn, "The Wars Within: The Joint Military Structure," in Art et al., *Reorganizing America's Defense,* p. 203, n. 28.

62. Peck and Scherer's *The Weapons Acquisition Process: An Economic Analysis* appeared in 1962. Scherer's *The Weapons Acquisition Process: Economic Incentives* appeared in 1964.

63. The Peck and Scherer volumes complemented and extended the work of other specialists, many in think-tanks such as the RAND Corporation, who had devoted considerable attention to weapons acquisitions management in the late 1950s and early 1960s. Much of this work is discussed in Charles J. Hitch and Roland N. McKean, *The Economics of Defense in the Nuclear Age* (Cambridge: Harvard University Press, 1960; Atheneum Edition, 1966).

64. William W. Kaufmann, *The McNamara Strategy* (New York: Harper and Row, 1964), pp. 168–203.

65. Fox, *Arming America,* p. 2; Commission on Government Procurement, "Historical Development of the Procurement Process," p. 178.

66. Fox, *Arming America,* p. 2.

67. On the F-111, see Robert F. Coulam, *Illusions of Choice: The F-111 and the Problem of Weapons Acquisition Reform* (Princeton: Princeton University Press, 1977). On the C-5A, see Anthony Sampson, *The Arms Bazaar* (New York: Viking Press, 1977), pp. 218–19; A. Ernest Fitzgerald, *The High Priests of Waste* (New York: Norton, 1972).

68. Fox, *Arming America,* pp. 4–7.

69. Ibid., p. 7.

70. Blue Ribbon Defense Panel, *Report to The President and the Secretary of Defense on the Department of Defense* (Washington, D.C.: U.S. Government Printing Office, 1970), p. v. The preface to the Fitzhugh Commission's study noted: "We are told that this is the first broad-scale study of the Department of Defense in many years—in fact since the two Commissions on Organization of the Executive Department of the Government chaired by former President Herbert Hoover." Ibid.

71. Ibid., p. iii.

72. Ibid., p. i.

73. Ibid., p. iv.

74. Ibid., p. 63.

75. Ibid., pp. 79–81.

76. Ibid., p. 81.

77. Ibid., pp. 70–75.

78. Ibid., p. 73.

79. Ibid., p. 74.

80. Ibid. Related to the panel's emphasis upon preproduction prototyping was its separate recommendation that DOD strengthen its Operational Test and Evaluation program for systems accepted into the inventory. The panel believed that more rigorous, systematic testing was essential to determine whether new systems could meet their operational requirements. Ibid., pp. 88–91.

81. Ibid., p. 84.

82. Ibid., p. 73.

83. As conceived in the mid-1960s the chief goal of total package procurement was "to reduce the likelihood of competing contractors underestimating costs and attempting to 'buy in' to a major program during the development phase." Commission on Government Procurement, "Historical Development of the Procurement Process," p. 178. In practice, contractors still tended to underestimate costs and underbid. As a contractor overran its fixed-price total package contract and faced financial collapse, DOD ordinarily declined to insist that the firm adhere to its "fixed-price" commitment.

84. Blue Ribbon Defense Panel, *Report to The President and the Secretary of Defense on the Defense Department*, p. 74.

85. Ibid., p. 92.

86. Ibid., p. 95.

87. Ibid., p. 93.

88. Ibid., p. 94.

89. Ibid., p. 95.

90. Ibid., p. 94.

91. Ibid., p. 95.

92. Ibid., pp. 137–41.

93. Ibid., p. 95.

94. Ibid., pp. 138–41.

95. The Air Force Request for Proposals in the light-weight fighter program (from which the F-16 emerged) was twenty-one pages long. The Air Force limited each bidder's response to sixty pages—fifty for technical considerations and ten to discuss the bidder's management plan. The Air Force selected General Dynamics' F-16 design for full production after an intensive fly-off against a rival prototype. Program teams for the Air Force and General Dynamics were comparatively small and highly capable. See Jacob Goodwin, *Brotherhood of Arms—General Dynamics and the Business of Defending America* (New York: Times Books, 1985), pp. 203–37; Lyman C. Josephs III, "The Team Leader's Role in 'Design to Cost' Preliminary Design" (Paper presented at the AGARD Lecture Series No. 65 on Preliminary Aircraft Design, Brunswick, West Germany, May 6–7, 1974).

96. Although they regard the F-16 as a successful acquisition episode overall, some observers believe the program has suffered nonetheless from the services' proclivity to "goldplate" comparatively simple designs with exceedingly expensive technical refinements. See Luttwak, *The Pentagon and the Art of War*, pp. 90–91; Fallows, *National Defense*, pp. 95–106.

97. Fox, *Arming America*, p. 457.

98. Blue Ribbon Defense Panel, *Report to The President and the Secretary of Defense on the Department of Defense*, p. vi.

99. The spare parts scandals are recounted in Halloran, *To Arm a Nation*, pp. 198–202; James Coates and Michael Kilian, *Heavy Losses: The Dangerous Decline of American Defense* (New York: Viking, 1985), pp. 159–60.

100. See, for example, Jeffrey H. Birnbaum, "House Panel Jurisdiction Over Economy, Business Could Increase Rep. John Dingell's Political Clout," *Wall Street*

Journal, February 23, 1987, p. 50 (discussing Rep. Dingell's 1985 oversight hearings on defense procurement).

101. President's Blue Ribbon Commission on Defense Management, *A Quest for Excellence,* p. 41 (discussing the role of the procurement scandals in the commission's formation).

102. Goodwin, *Brotherhood of Arms,* pp. 209–12.

103. Fox, *Arming America,* p. 478.

104. President's Blue Ribbon Commission on Defense Management, *A Quest for Excellence,* p. 113.

105. Ibid., p. 115.

106. Ibid., p. 2.

107. Ibid., p. 44.

108. Ibid.

109. Ibid.

110. Ibid., pp. 49–51.

111. Ibid., p. 53. An early, unreleased draft report prepared by the Packard panel made the case for sweeping management reform through a biting description of existing DOD acquisition management policies. In one passage, the unreleased draft likened Pentagon procurement management to the story of the "Sorcerer's Apprentice," the master magician's young assistant who begins magical events but cannot stop them, sending everything out of control. The panel deleted this characterization and toned down its report, apparently due to some panelists' concern that the sharp commentary might focus attention exclusively upon the stewardship of DOD Secretary Caspar Weinberger and diminish support for fundamental, underlying change. See Michael Weisskopf, "Defense Report's Tone Divides Panel," *Washington Post,* February 19, 1986, p. A1.

112. President's Blue Ribbon Commission on Defense Management, *A Quest for Excellence,* p. 53.

113. Ibid. As described in a separate Packard Commission recommendation, the new under secretary also would be responsible for seeing that DOD acquisition programs incorporate industrial surge and mobilization considerations. Ibid., pp. 70–71.

114. Ibid., p. 54.

115. Ibid.

116. Ibid., p. 55.

117. Ibid.

118. Ibid.

119. Ibid.

120. Ibid., pp. 55–57.

121. Ibid., p. 56.

122. As a related measure, the Packard panel proposed that DOD's Defense Advanced Research Projects Agency conduct prototyping projects incorporating technology that might be used in joint service programs or by a single service. Ibid., p. 57.

123. Ibid., pp. 57–58. At the time of the Packard study, such decisions were made by the Secretary of Defense, acting on advice from the Defense Systems Acquisition Review Council.

124. Ibid.

125. Ibid., pp. 58–59.

126. Ibid., p. 59.

127. Ibid., pp. 59–60.

128. Ibid.

129. Ibid., pp. 21–30.

130. Ibid., p. 60.

131. Ibid., p. 61.

132. Ibid., pp. 62–64. In 1981, under the guidance of DOD Deputy Secretary Frank Carlucci (later to become a Packard Commission member), DOD had begun relying more extensively upon rivalry-based purchasing techniques to buy major systems. Congress soon accelerated this movement by enacting the Competition in Contracting Act of 1984, which required DOD to seek "full and open" competition through the use of competitive procedures. See Burnett and Kovacic, "Reform of United States Weapons Acquisition Policy: Competition, Teaming Agreements, and Dual-Sourcing." The 1984 Competition Act sought to give negotiated procurement a status equal to that of the formal advertising/sealed bid method and to establish procedures for obtaining competition through the negotiation process. To a large extent, therefore, the 1984 statute implemented the long-standing recommendation of several procurement-related special commissions (including Hoover and Fitzhugh) that the DOD acquisition statutes establish competitive negotiated pro-curement as a purchasing method no less acceptable than formal advertising. See above, pp. 51 and 74, and notes 37–39 and 85–86; see also *Report of the Commission on Government Procurement,* Appendix H.

133. President's Blue Ribbon Commission on Defense Management, *A Quest for Excellence,* p. 63.

134. Ibid., p. 66.

135. Ibid. To the Packard Commission, desirable adjustments would include "simplifying financial disclosures" and "allowing presidential appointees to defer capital gains taxes incurred by divesting assets to comply with conflict-of-interest provisions."

136. Ibid.

137. Ibid.

138. Ibid., pp. 67–70.

139. Ibid., pp. 76–77.

140. Ibid., p. 77.

141. Ibid.

142. Ibid., p. 81.

143. Ibid., pp. 90–94.

144. Hoffman, "Pentagon Revamp Supported," p. A10. See also "Defense Department Reforms: Statement of April 2, 1986 by the Principal Deputy Press Secretary to the President," reprinted in President's Blue Ribbon Commission on Defense Management, *A Quest for Excellence* (Washington, D.C.: U.S. Government Printing Office, June 1986), Appendix p. 33 (stating that President Reagan had signed "a directive to implement virtually all of the recommendations" presented to him in the Packard Commission's interim report).

145. P.L. 99–661. On the Packard Commission's pervasive influence upon the content of the 1987 Act, see *Senate Report No. 99–331,* 99th Congress, 2d Session (July 8, 1986), pp. 253–67.

146. P.L. 99–661, Section 901.

147. Ibid.

148. Ibid., Section 904.

149. One year earlier, in the Defense Authorization Act of 1986, Congress also had approved biennial budgeting to increase program stability. The 1986 Act di-rected the president to submit, for Fiscal Year 1988, a single DOD budget for Fiscal Years 1988 and 1989. The statute also mandated a two-year budget cycle for all years following Fiscal Year 1988. P.L. 99–145, Section 1405. For an insightful critique of the usefulness of this device, see James M. Lindsay, "Congress and the Defense Budget," *Washington Quarterly* (Winter 1988): 57.

150. P.L. 99–661, Section 911.

151. Ibid., Sections 107–8.

152. Ibid., Section 905.

153. Ibid., Section 906.

154. Ibid., Section 909.

155. Ibid. The 1987 Act allows the Secretary of Defense to dispense with competitive prototyping upon giving Congress a written report that explains why such an approach is not "practicable."

156. Ibid., Section 910. Beyond this more general section, the 1987 Act also required DOD to conduct operational tests (including live-fire tests) of the Army's Bradley Fighting Vehicle. Subsequent training exercises revealed flaws in the Bradley's design. See "Sinking Leads Army to Curb Water Use of Troop Vehicle," *New York Times,* April 14, 1987, p. A19; Molly Moore, "Soldier Drowns in Troop Carrier," *Washington Post,* April 8, 1987, p. A9.

157. P.L. 99–661, Section 141.

158. In the Defense Authorization Act of 1986, Congress prohibited DOD from starting full-scale development for major weapons systems until the DOD Secretary has given Congress an "acquisition strategy" that provides for competing alternative sources from full-scale development through the end of production. P.L. 99-145, Section 912. The acquisition strategy may waive competitive approaches upon showing that competition would increase total program costs, cause unacceptable delays, or "would be adverse to the national security interests of the United States." Ibid.

159. See United States Department of Defense, *Annual Report to the Congress, Fiscal Year 1988,* pp. 113–14.

160. Ibid., p. 114.

161. "Insult and Injury as 'Weapons Czar' Assumes New Post," *Washington Post,* October 6, 1986, p. A13.

162. United States Department of Defense, *Annual Report to the Congress, Fiscal Year 1988,* p. 114.

163. Burnett and Kovacic, "Reform of United States Weapons Acquisition Policy: Competition, Teaming Agreements, and Dual Sourcing."

164. See, for example, United States Department of Defense, *Annual Report to the Congress, Fiscal Year 1988,* pp. 99–119 (discussing recent management reforms in ongoing programs).

165. John H. Cushman, Jr., "Pentagon Seen Changing Little in Arms Buying," *New York Times,* July 15, 1987, p. A1.

166. Ibid. The Pentagon's chief public affairs official, Robert Sims, rejected Woolsey's and the panel's criticism. "There is no desire to fail to do what this Presidential commission has recommended," Sims said. "In fact, I think we've done a very good job of doing exactly what they did ask for." Ibid.

167. Ibid.

168. President's Blue Ribbon Commission on Defense Management, *A Quest for Excellence,* p. 66.

169. See, for example, David Packard, *Management of America's National Defense* (Washington, D.C.: American Enterprise Institute, 1987) (presenting Packard's Francis Boyer Lecture for the Fall of 1986).

170. "Acquisition Czar as Figurehead," *National Journal,* April 11, 1987, p. 906.

171. Ibid.

172. Ibid.

173. See, for example, John H. Cushman, Jr., "Arms-Buying Revisions Imperiled," *New York Times,* September 17, 1987, p. D6; Tim Carrington, "Weapons

Procurement Chief Godwin May Quit Pentagon Because of Disputes," *Wall Street Journal,* September 9, 1987, p. 8.

174. R. Jeffrey Smith and Molly Moore, "Pentagon's Purchasing Chief to Quit," *Washington Post,* September 14, 1987, p. A1; "Godwin Resigns Pentagon 'Acquisition Czar' Position," *Wall Street Journal,* September 14, 1987, p. 50.

175. Sarah Helm, " 'Resistance,' Not Reform, At Pentagon," *Washington Post,* September 23, 1987, p. A19.

176. John H. Cushman, Jr., "Pentagon Efficiency Criticized," *New York Times,* September 23, 1987, p. D9.

177. Ibid.

178. Molly Moore, "Godwin Was Misled About Authority, Hill Told," *Washington Post,* September 18, 1987, p. A25.

179. Smith and Moore, "Pentagon's Purchasing Chief to Quit," p. A1.

180. See, for example, Jeff Bingaman, "They're Just Not Serious About Cutting Costs," *Washington Post,* September 27, 1987, p. D7 (Senator Bingaman is Chairman of the Senate Armed Services Subcommittee on Defense Industry and Technology); "Another Failure to Fix the Pentagon," *New York Times,* September 21, 1987, p. A18 (editorial).

181. See Tim Carrington, ". . . Meanwhile, Back at the Pentagon, Nominee to Top Weapons Job Sets Sights," *Wall Street Journal,* September 25, 1987, p. 31.

182. Ibid. see also Bingaman, "They're Just Not Serious About Cutting Costs," p. D7.

183. See, for example, John H. Cushman, Jr., "Cost-Cutter's Target: Secret Bomber," *New York Times,* January 22, 1988, p. A24.

184. Johns Hopkins Foreign Policy Institute and Center for Strategic and International Studies, *Making Defense Reform Work* (Washington, D.C.: Johns Hopkins Foreign Policy Institute and Center for Strategic and International Studies, November 1988), p. 50.

185. See, for example, William J. Weida and Frank L. Gertcher, *The Political Economy of National Defense* (Boulder, Colo.: Westview Press, 1987), p. 160; see also J. Ronald Fox, "Revamping the Business of National Defense," *Harvard Business Review,* September–October 1984, pp. 63–70 (discussing the failure of postwar defense acquisition reform movements generally).

186. The discouraging history of past base closing efforts is analyzed in Charlotte Twight, "Department of Defense Attempts to Close Military Bases: The Political Economy of Congressional Resistance" (in this volume). The importance of an independent, nonpartisan commission to the operation of the 1988 legislation is suggested in Molly Moore, "The 'How-to' on Closing Surplus Bases," *Washington Post,* November 21, 1988, p. A11; Susan F Rasky, "Congress Agrees on Closing Bases But Leaves the Choices to a Panel," *New York Times,* October 13, 1988, p. A1; John H. Cushman, Jr., "An Impossible Dream May Soon Be Possible," *New York Times,* May 3, 1988, p. A32.

187. See Molly Moore, "91 Bases Face Cuts or Closing," *Washington Post,* December 30, 1988, p. A1.

188. See Don Phillips, "86 Military Facilities to Be Shut," *Washington Post,* April 19, 1989, p. A1.

189. See David C. Morrison, "Caught Off Base," *National Journal,* April 1, 1989, p. 801.

190. Steven Kelman, "Public Spirit Lives, Even in Congress," *Wall Street Journal,* September 13, 1988, p. 36.

191. The low conviction rate from the Justice Department's antifraud campaign against defense contractors through the mid-1980s is reported in "Pentagon Fraud Unit Marches Slowly," *Washington Post,* February 10, 1987, p. A19. The most

noteworthy failure of the government's antifraud criminal prosecution efforts has been the Justice Department's decision to seek dismissal of the indictment against General Dynamics and several of the company's former officials for the firm's conduct in producing the Divad antiaircraft gun. The government's original decision to prosecute rested upon a faulty understanding of the contract in question. See Judith Valente and John Koten, "General Dynamics Case Haunts Losers," *Wall Street Journal,* August 13, 1987, p. 6; Ruth Marcus, "Case Against General Dynamics Tripped Over Two Little Words," *Washington Post,* July 30, 1987, p. A17; Howard Kurtz, "Prosecuting General Dynamics was 'Wrong,' Justice Aide Says," ibid., June 23, 1987, p. A1. One General Dynamics executive has estimated that the cost to the company of defending the Divad lawsuit was $29 million. See Frederick S. Wood, Executive Vice President, General Dynamics Corporation, "Luncheon Address" (Tempe, Arizona: May 22, 1989) (Presentation at the American Bar Association/National Contract Management Association program on "Teaming Agreements and International Joint Ventures—Marriages of Convenience").

192. The origins of the Ill Wind inquiry are described in David E. Rosenbaum, "Pentagon Fraud Inquiry: What Is Known to Date," *New York Times* (National edition), July 7, 1988, p. A1.

193. Helen Dewar and George C. Wilson, "Hill Leaders Demand Swift Justice," *Washington Post,* June 18, 1988, p. A1.

194. Ibid.

195. Ibid.

196. See Caryle Murphy and Ruth Marcus, "Convictions, Guilty Pleas Rise As Pentagon Probe Continues," *Washington Post,* May 10, 1989, p. A1.

197. The tendency of recent criminal enforcement initiatives to dilute efforts to cure fundamental structural flaws in the weapons acquisition process is discussed in William E. Kovacic, "The Sorcerer's Apprentice: Public Regulation of the Weapons Acquisition Process" (in this volume).

198. David Packard, *Management of America's National Defense,* pp. 1–2.

199. Center for Strategic and International Studies, *U.S. Defense Acquisition: A Process in Trouble,* p. 50. Compare President's Private Sector Survey on Cost Control, *Report on the Office of the Secretary of Defense,* p. 28 (suggesting, in 1983, the desirability of forming a new Hoover Commission–type study of DOD organization and procedure).

200. Blue Ribbon Defense Panel, *Report to the President and the Secretary of Defense,* p. 198.

5

The Sorcerer's Apprentice: Public Regulation of the Weapons Acquisition Process

WILLIAM E. KOVACIC

Modern studies of economic regulation and regulatory reform have left few industries, public institutions or policy developments unexamined. The fruits of this exacting inquiry are now familiar features of the regulatory landscape. Industries once subject to extensive regulation have been transformed by the abandonment or weakening of limits upon entry and pricing.[1] Traditional forms of rate regulation have been displaced in part by the application of economically based incentives such as price caps to spur regulated firms to reduce costs and raise productivity.[2] Public regulatory bodies have shown a greater inclination to acknowledge their institutional limitations and to take fuller account of the costs associated with public control of business conduct.[3]

Scholarly treatments of these and other features of economic regulation are comprehensive except in one remarkable respect: the mainstream literature on regulation typically omits consideration of the regulatory processes the United States uses to buy arms for national defense. Evaluations of the

This article is a revised and expanded version of a paper entitled "The Expanded Use of Competition Strategies in the Acquisition of Major Weapon Systems" presented at the Rutgers University Graduate School of Management Advanced Workshop in Regulation and Public Utility Economics, Monterey, California, July 8, 1988. The author wishes to thank William B. Burnett, Michael A. Crew, Kathryn M. Fenton, Robert J. MacKay, David E. Morse, James F Nagle, Thomas L. Patten, Fereidoon P. Sioshansi, and William Wiginton for many useful comments and discussions. The author also is grateful to the Sarah Scaife Foundation for its support in the preparation of this article.

federal government's choice and application of regulatory reform approaches in the 1970s and 1980s rarely discuss or mention the country's most heavily regulated industry, defense, or the government's most powerful regulatory agency, the Department of Defense (DOD).[4] The leading prescriptive treatises on economic regulation seldom contain more than a passing reference to the government's role in regulating the conduct of weapons suppliers.[5] Similarly, the preeminent texts used to instruct law school students in the legal framework that governs regulated industries usually bypass the regulatory regime that controls defense contractors.[6]

The omission of weapons procurement from the mainstream regulation literature is striking for at least four reasons. The first is that private firms in the American defense industry are subject to public controls of unequalled scope and complexity.[7] The magnitude of the regulatory system is suggested by the Federal Acquisition Regulations (FAR) and the DOD FAR Supplement, two of the principal repositories of regulatory guidance for weapons acquisition.[8] These documents consist of over eighteen hundred pages of rules governing profit policy, accounting standards, ethical requirements, bidding, competition, warranties, and a host of other matters. Daunting in their own right, the FAR and the DOD FAR Supplement are but two elements of a massive body of regulatory commands that includes statutes, decisions by courts and administrative tribunals, directives, and interpretations. "By actual measurement in 1985," writes former Navy Secretary John Lehman, Jr., "existing legislation and case law governing navy procurement alone had grown to 1,152 linear feet of shelf space in the library."[9] Short of outright public ownership, no industry operates within a more detailed and pervasive regulatory system.

A second noteworthy feature of this regulatory regime is its instability. Over the past decade, defense procurement regulatory controls have changed and expanded in breathtaking fashion. Fundamental adjustments in most industry-specific regulatory systems—for example, financial services, transportation, communications, and electric utilities—occur infrequently. In the 1980s, the defense industry has witnessed far-reaching alterations to the regulatory scheme annually.[10] In 1988 alone, Congress passed eight statutes embodying roughly sixty separate provisions affecting the weapons acquisition process.[11] Each of these enactments will send waves of change throughout the purchasing agencies and the contractor community as implementing regulations are drafted, disseminated, and absorbed by management and the operating levels. Moreover, there are few signs that the recent pace of Congressional activity will abate significantly. The Department of Justice's ongoing investigation into corruption in weapons procurement— aptly named "Operation Ill Wind,"[12]—promises to set in motion substantial additional legislation in the coming years.[13]

The third noteworthy feature of the defense regulatory environment is the virtually universal assessment that most adjustments in the regulatory structure for weapons procurement in this decade have yielded decidedly unsatisfactory results.[14] To many thoughtful observers, a crippling flaw of defense acquisition reform in the 1980s has been the tendency to add layer upon layer of regulatory requirements in the misguided expectation that more expansive controls would elicit better performance.[15] In 1986, the Packard Commission on Defense Procurement observed that "[o]ver the years, Congress and DOD have tried to dictate management improvements in the form of ever more detailed and extensive laws or regulations."[16] The panel warned that "[t]he sheer weight of such requirements often makes well-conceived reform efforts unavailing. At operating levels within DOD, it is now virtually impossible to assimilate new legislative or regulatory refinements promptly or effectively."[17] In short, the Packard Commission concluded, "the legal regime for defense acquisition is today impossibly cumbersome."[18] What was "impossibly cumbersome" in 1986 has become ever more labyrinthine and intractable following the legislative spate of 1988.

The fourth remarkable aspect of the omission of defense procurement from mainstream regulation scholarship is the singular national importance of annual defense outlays. "The U.S. Department of Defense . . . is by far the largest and most complex business organization in the world," states Ronald Fox. "It operates more than fifty-four hundred installations world-wide and executes more than fifteen million contracts per year (more than sixty thousand per day)."[19] To fund these activities in Fiscal Years 1981 through 1988, Congress appropriated $2.02 trillion for defense—the largest program of peacetime expenditures for defense in the country's history.[20] In that period an average of over $100 billion per year was allocated to weapons research and development and procurement. Not only do these expenditures determine the nation's military capability, but they frequently influence the rate and direction of inventive activity in the economy as a whole.

This article describes and analyzes the regulatory framework through which the United States buys weapons. It first identifies the underlying forces that shape defense acquisition regulation. The basic governance structures the country has used to motivate contractors to supply weapons of reasonable price, acceptable quality, and timely delivery are then described. The third section identifies problems arising from recent Congressional and Department of Defense regulatory initiatives. Finally, suggestions are offered as to how the content and development of defense procurement regulation might usefully be changed.

In an unreleased draft report prepared early in 1986, the Packard Commission said that the condition of the weapons procurement process resembled the work of the Sorcerer's Apprentice, who used his incomplete grasp of the master magician's skills to unleash potent forces but could not harness them, sending everything out of control.[21] Defense acquisition regulation today is similarly chaotic. The following discussion considers the sources of turmoil and the possibilities for their control, and indicates above all the need for regulatory stability and simplification.

WEAPONS PROCUREMENT REGULATION: FORMATIVE INFLUENCES

The essential processes and institutions through which the United States buys arms have taken shape within the past fifty years. Antecedents of the modern American defense establishment date back to the turn of this century,[22] but the mobilization program immediately before and during World War II marked the emergence of the public and private institutions through which the government purchases weapons today.[23] Several features of that evolution have shaped the content of the defense procurement regulatory process.

Reliance on Private Enterprise

In the late nineteenth and early twentieth centuries, the paramount issue of public procurement was the conversion of the Navy's dilapidated fleet of Civil War–vintage wooden vessels into one of the world's most formidable naval forces. Following the Civil War, the fighting ability of the United States Navy declined dramatically while foreign governments accumulated large inventories of modern oceangoing warships. "At the present moment it must be conceded that we have nothing which deserves to be called a navy," wrote Navy Secretary William C. Whitney in 1885. "[I]t is questionable whether we have a single naval vessel finished and afloat at the present time that could be trusted to encounter ships of any important power."[24]

To amend this condition, Congress authorized an unprecedented program of peacetime defense expenditures to construct a modern fleet of steel-hulled, steam-powered warships.[25] The naval construction effort required the development of new domestic steelmaking capability to cast armor plate and forge large-diameter guns. With the buildup came a heated debate about the proper role of privately owned firms in supplying the government's defense needs. From the start, the shipbuilding program was beset by allegations of fraud on the part of private companies hired to supply steel plate and construct the vessels. Contractors were claimed to have fraudulently concealed defective armor plate, used retired naval officers to influence Navy Department officials improperly, and rigged bids on armor plate and explosives to extract inflated prices from the government.[26]

To critics of the contractors, the appropriate path for public policy seemed clear: The government should create publicly owned factories for manufacturing materials essential to its defense plans. As construction accelerated before World War I, Congressman Augustus Stanley of Kentucky said that "it is time this Government, who can make its own armor plate and who should make it, if necessary, shall say that it will not become . . . the maintainer of an illicit, illegal, and lawless combination in restraint of trade."[27] Stanley and like-minded legislators ultimately prevailed upon Congress to build and operate an armor and projectile factory.[28]

In the years between World War I and World War II, the government depended mainly on a mixture of public arsenals and ad hoc private efforts (particularly by aircraft suppliers) for its weapons needs. During World War II, however, the country turned decisively to private firms to meet most of its armaments requirements.[29] Soon after the war's end, Congress decided that with limited exceptions, private firms would be the principal means of arms production in peacetime as well.[30] The turn toward private industry rested substantially upon the belief that placing production in private hands would yield greater efficiency and swifter adaptation to changing weapons needs. Among other virtues, private firms enjoyed greater flexibility in providing salaries and fringe benefits needed to recruit and retain capable technical personnel whose skills would be essential to developing successful weapon systems in the nuclear age.

This delegation of authority posed an unprecedented and difficult regulatory challenge to policymakers. Dwight Eisenhower's famous Farewell Address in 1961 framed the dilemma. On the one hand, the advent of nuclear weapons and the country's assumption of global responsibilities meant that the postwar armaments supply sector necessarily would be large and enduring. "Until the latest of our world conflicts," Eisenhower observed, "the United States had no armaments industry. American makers of plowshares could, with time and as required, make swords as well. But now we can no longer risk emergency improvisation of national defense; we have been compelled to create a permanent armaments industry of vast proportions."[31]

On the other hand, the emergence of a substantial, permanent military supply sector required the development of governance structures that would both ensure efficiency and preserve individual liberty. "In the councils of government," Eisenhower warned, "we must guard against the acquisition of unwarranted influence, whether sought or unsought, by the military-industrial complex. The potential for the disastrous rise of misplaced power exists and will persist."[32] The president added that "[o]nly an alert and knowledgeable citizenry can compel the proper meshing of the huge industrial and military machinery of defense with our peaceful methods and goals, so that security and liberty may prosper together."[33]

The effort to reconcile the tension Eisenhower identified has accounted for several features of the postwar regulatory framework. The establishment of profit policy provides a major illustration. A powerful social aversion to the prospect of "profiteering" by arms manufacturers dictated that considerable attention be given to controlling nominal contractor profit rates. Strict

only Private Sector will be capable to provide skilled labour with the reward desired, but are bound by Parliament/Congress.

profit controls were deemed essential lest contractors benefit unduly from (or have unseemly motives to promote) expenditures for national defense. The consequent fixation upon nominal profit rates meant that far less concern would be focused on giving contractors sufficient incentives to reduce contractor costs, including by allowing contractors to retain a portion of savings realized by productivity increases.

More generally, solving Eisenhower's dilemma placed a premium upon the ability of public bodies, notably DOD and the Congress, to oversee contractors successfully and guarantee that private firms served public ends. Among other factors, the quality of DOD's efforts to oversee contractors would depend upon its success in recruiting and retaining skilled acquisition personnel to manage research, development, and production programs of unmatched difficulty. The effect of Congressional oversight would hinge crucially upon the willingness of legislators to invest their time in appropriate forms of monitoring and oversight.

Technological Dynamism and Complexity

The World War II mobilization experience showed that future armaments would grow quickly and enormously in capability and sophistication. The wartime weapons development programs foreshadowed forthcoming generations of "weapon systems" that would incorporate state-of-the-art advances in several swiftly changing technical disciplines.[34] Defense suppliers frequently would be unable to rely on modified versions of commercially available products to meet DOD weapons requirements. Instead, to build new generations of increasingly sophisticated missiles, aircraft, and ships, suppliers would be required to invest in facilities and equipment dedicated exclusively to weapons development and production.

This trend has had three major regulatory implications. First, in most instances, DOD is the sole purchaser for the output of privately owned defense-specific assets.[35] To establish and maintain an acceptable supplier base, DOD (and Congress) must give contractors adequate incentives to invest in these assets. In determining profit policy and choosing particular contractual forms, this requires difficult judgments about the appropriate allocation of risk between DOD and its contractors on individual projects. More recently, the perceived need to sustain domestic capability in certain technical disciplines has led DOD to consider playing a broader role in sponsoring collaborative efforts by private firms to pursue research, development, and production ventures in specific areas.[36]

Second, many firms that make investments in defense-specific assets also participate extensively in markets for commercial goods and services. The mixed military and commercial character of these contractors calls for the establishment of accounting conventions that ensure that DOD pays only for activities properly attributable to defense (and not for commercial) contracts. Among other issues, devising such conventions entails decisions about whether certain categories of expense (for example, advertising, marketing, entertainment) routinely incurred in ordinary commercial practice would be chargeable to DOD where such costs arguably were connected with defense contracts.

Third, the fact of rapid technological change has shaped the structure of the supply sector and the nature of competition for new programs. Aggressively pursuing state-of-the-art gains in several technological disciplines on a single program usually leads to high development and unit-production costs.[37] These cost trends have meant that the military services start fewer new programs over time and produce fewer units of each weapon system annually.[38] The decline in the number of new programs has resulted in a gradual shrinking of the pool of firms able to seek new weapon system contracts, thereby limiting the field of competitors from which DOD can draw. In addition, low annual production rates often have made it infeasible for DOD to have more than a single supplier for major systems in production.

The foregoing considerations underscore an important respect in which the "market" for weapon systems differs from ordinary commercial markets. Competition in the conventional sense of ongoing rivalry among numerous suppliers to serve the needs of numerous purchasers rarely exists in defense supply markets.[39] In the most extreme cases, DOD relies upon a single contractor to supply a major weapon system.[40] In many others, following a period of vigorous rivalry among contractors for initial design awards, DOD enters into sole-source supply contracts for the full production phase of the procurement cycle. These structural features of the defense industry—a small number of active suppliers, high barriers to entry, and a declining number of major new programs—have forced the development of regulatory mechanisms to act as surrogates for the market-based competitive forces that ordinarily drive firms to improve performance in commercial markets.

Multiplicity and Inconsistency of Goals

The most obvious purpose of weapons procurement is the maintenance of defense capability. This capability has both short-term and long-term dimensions. The short-term aspect of this goal is the production of military hardware to enable the country to defend its borders and to pursue its national interests overseas. The long-term dimension is the preservation of industry design and manufacturing capability. Sustaining industry design expertise affords DOD an array of possible contractors to provide alternative technical approaches for future programs. Maintaining industry manufacturing capability permits expanded production in times of conflict.

Achieving these objectives accounts for substantial elements, but hardly all, of the regulatory system that governs defense procurement. The capability goal coexists with a variety of other aims that Congress pursues through the defense acquisition process. Among other ends, the weapons procurement system enables legislators to achieve interrelated patronage and wealth redistribution goals. Annual appropriations and authorization measures routinely contain provisions designed to channel benefits to specific legislative districts.[41] Generic procurement legislation and specific funding measures likewise require DOD to allocate contract dollars to a variety of broader interest groups, including small business, minority-owned enterprises, and organized labor.[42] Still other Congressional commands discourage recourse to foreign suppliers.[43]

Though sometimes coincident, the goals of enhancing military capability, dispensing patronage, and redistributing wealth often collide. The regulatory regime for defense procurement nonetheless embodies all three. The natural consequence of using the weapons acquisition process to achieve often inconsistent ends is that each weapon system costs more than it would if the efficient realization of military capability were the sole purpose of defense expenditures. In sum, to a large extent, the weapons acquisition process operates "inefficiently" because efficiency is not the system's only (or even paramount) goal. The country and its legislators look to defense expenditures to achieve social and reelection goals, and doing so has a price.

Institutional Incentives of Individual Legislators

The incentives facing members of Congress influence the regulatory system in an important respect beyond the enactment of provisions designed to dispense patronage and redistribute wealth.[44] Legislators generally invest their resources in activities that will yield appropriable returns within a comparatively short time horizon. Individual members prefer to devote their time to projects that will yield tangible "accomplishments" for which the member can persuasively claim credit in the relatively short term. By contrast, projects whose benefits become apparent over the long term or are largely untraceable to an individual's efforts are disfavored.

In the defense regulation arena, this creates a strong bias in favor of enacting new regulatory requirements rather than investing resources in seeing that existing requirements take root and are refined appropriately. A characteristic Congressional response to procurement scandal is to propose and pass "tough" remedial legislation to fix the problem at hand. The sponsors of such enactments can stand before the public and point to the newly adopted measure as proof of their willingness to crack down on corrupt contractors or slothful, inattentive DOD bureaucrats.

The credit-claiming impulse does not manifest itself solely in the passage of new legislation. Its other principal outlet is the "ready, fire, aim" demand for swift, sweeping administrative action in response to each reported episode of DOD or contractor misconduct. The pattern of legislative response is familiar: individual legislators are quick to overstate the significance of each revelation, and commands for instant cures—the standard proposals involve either criminal prosecution or new regulatory controls—are issued.[45]

At the same time, legislators devote far too little attention to carefully evaluating the causes of the immediate scandal, to assessing the adequacy of existing regulations, to evaluating the costs associated with applying proposed additional requirements, or to monitoring the implementation of new remedial measures. All of the foregoing are activities for which credit-claiming is difficult because their benefits often are not readily appropriable. Thus, Congress overinvests in passing new legislation and demanding immediate administrative correctives, and it chronically underinvests in seeing that forthcoming or existing regulatory requirements are sound in theory or effective in practice. After each "reform" outburst, the long-lived structural sources of managerial and regulatory failure remain largely undisturbed or grow worse.

Adequacy of DOD Personnel

Throughout the postwar period, a succession of blue ribbon commissions and individual commentators have concluded that significant improvements in defense procurement will not occur without sustained efforts to increase the skills and experience of individuals who represent DOD in the contracting process.[46] These insistent warnings have largely been ignored. Rather, the public and its elected officials have clung to the illusion that DOD can attract and retain the services of highly skilled and capable program managers and contracting officials on the cheap. Consequently, the personnel of private contractors generally are brighter, better paid, more experienced, and more highly motivated than their government counterparts.

The asymmetries in human capital between DOD and its suppliers help explain the size and content of the defense procurement regime. Extensive regulatory controls are partly a second-best solution to compensate for weaknesses in DOD's procurement corps. Because DOD's contracting personnel are overmatched by their industry counterparts, Congress and DOD have sought to rebalance the playing field by mandating layers of procedural "safeguards" and intricate internal review processes. By having a large number of less talented eyes look long enough at a given problem, it is assumed that the government can prevent contractors from picking its pocket.

This strategy has enormous costs. Programs proceed at a glacial pace as contractors and government purchasing personnel carry out required review and auditing procedures. Authority is dispersed so widely among a large collection of program managers, contract officers, senior DOD executives, auditors, and inspectors that accountability vanishes. Government payrolls expand, and contractors hire legions of contract administrators to respond to the requirements of enlarged, multitiered DOD procurement organizations. All the while, the procurement system drifts further away from the management approach that appears to be the key to success in technically complex projects of the type that make up the weapons acquisition agenda: entrust each project to a small number of highly capable people, give them freedom to manage the project, and hold them to account for the results.[47]

THE GOVERNANCE STRATEGIES OF WEAPONS PROCUREMENT

It is under the influence of these basic environmental and institutional forces that the specific governance structures embodied in the system of defense industry regulation have evolved.[48] Since 1945 Congress and DOD have used six governance strategies to ensure that private firms perform defense contracts at acceptable cost, in a timely manner, and with suitable quality.[49] The following discussion deals with each of these strategies individually.[50] In general, the nature and mix of strategies have reflected a fundamental ambivalence about the correct approach for controlling the conduct of arms suppliers. In particular, the means chosen to motivate private contractors to achieve productive and managerial efficiency in the postwar era have displayed a basic tension between comprehensive public utility regulation on the one hand and market-driven rivalry on the other.[51]

Competition

Using competition to improve performance in the production of major weapon systems has been a stated aim of United States procurement policy since passage of the Armed Services Procurement Act of 1947, the principal legal foundation for postwar weapons acquisition policy.[52] For most of the postwar era, this goal has rarely been attained in practice. Contractors often have competed intensely for initial design and development awards, but until recently sole-source supply agreements usually formed the basis for full-scale production of most major weapon systems.

A distinctive feature of procurement reform in the 1980s is how extensively Congress has mandated, and DOD has embraced, competition as the means for governing the performance of defense suppliers.[53] Since 1984 Congress has enacted three measures that compel greater attention to competitive procurement techniques. The Competition in Contracting Act of

1984 (CICA) requires DOD to use "full and open competition" through the use of competitive acquisition procedures.[54] The Defense Authorization Act of 1986 bars DOD from beginning full-scale development for major weapon systems[55] until the Secretary of Defense has submitted to Congress an "acquisition strategy" that provides for the maintenance of competitive alternative sources from full-scale development through the end of production.[56] The Department of Defense Appropriations Act of 1987 directs the Secretary of Defense to use a competitive prototype program strategy in developing major weapon systems.[57]

Collectively, these measures create a rebuttable presumption that competition shall serve as the primary acquisition strategy throughout the procurement life cycle. All three measures allow DOD to waive the competition requirements under limited circumstances.[58] Congress has established several devices to ensure that DOD does not inappropriately dispense with its competition commands. Waivers of specific requirements often must be made in writing and reported to Congress. DOD and each of its principal purchasing subunits also are required to establish a "competition advocate" to promote rivalry-based procurement methods.[59] In addition, CICA strengthened the ability of disappointed contract-seekers to file bid protests with the General Accounting Office (GAO) to challenge contract awards that fail to conform to competition requirements.[60]

These legislative enactments have complemented and codified parallel executive-branch initiatives to use rivalry more extensively in weapons procurement. DOD's recent efforts to use competition more fully began in 1981 with a department study (headed by then–Deputy Secretary Frank Carlucci) that urged defense purchasers to establish plans for increasing competition among suppliers.[61] These proposals received additional impetus in 1982 when President Reagan issued an executive order requiring executive departments to "[e]stablish criteria for enhancing competition and limiting noncompetitive actions."[62] Similarly, the Packard Commission recommended in 1986 that "[f]ederal and DOD regulations should provide for substantially increased use of commercial-style competition, relying on inherent market forces instead of governmental intervention."[63]

The combination of external and internal policy guidance has led the armed services to make rivalry a major ingredient of many major acquisition programs.[64] DOD's preferred competition strategy has been dual-sourcing—the maintenance of two or more competitors into the production phase of the procurement life cycle. Though dual-sourcing is not a new acquisition technique, DOD has significantly increased the use of this method since 1980.[65] Noteworthy subjects of dual-sourcing programs in this decade have been expensive systems such as fighter aircraft, helicopters, attack submarines, cruise missiles, combat surface vessels, and aircraft engines.[66]

Disclosure and Cost Observation

The defense regulatory scheme contains a number of provisions that require DOD's suppliers to provide cost, pricing, quality control, and other information to the government. The most important of these measures is the Truth in Negotiations Act.[67] Passed in 1962, the statute compels contractors to submit certain cost data to DOD negotiators before the parties agree upon the contract price.[68] This measure seeks to give DOD better means to observe contractor costs and to evaluate the reasonableness of pricing proposals from suppliers unconstrained by normal market forces.[69] To monitor compliance with the statute's disclosure requirements, DOD enjoys broad access to contractor records.[70] As indicated below, failure to satisfy the disclosure obligations can expose the contractor to civil and criminal sanctions.

The Defense Contract Audit Agency (DCAA) is the principal organization through which DOD exercises its rights to observe contractor cost and other data. Established in 1965, DCAA today has over six thousand professional auditors located in offices throughout the United States and resident in the facilities of major defense suppliers.[71] Each year DCAA auditors conduct roughly sixty thousand audits and reviews involving more than thirteen thousand contractors and subcontractors.[72] In 1982 Congress created an Office of the Inspector General within DOD to increase the department's efforts to detect and prevent contractor fraud. The DOD Inspector General enjoys access to contractor records that exceeds the reach of DCAA's expansive power to gather and review data.[73] Finally, GAO possesses broad authority to audit government contracts, including defense procurement agreements.[74]

Profit Controls

Congress and DOD have established profit ceilings for many types of defense contracts.[75] Within these ceilings the nominal profit allowed in a weapons acquisition contract is set through negotiations between DOD and the supplier. Extensive auditing powers enable DOD to monitor the impact of DOD profit policies on overall contractor profitability.[76] As indicated above, DOD's contracting personnel have tended to focus inordinately on holding nominal profit rates in check and have devoted inadequate attention to eliciting reductions in contractor costs—by far the greatest element of the overall contract price. As one commentator has observed, DOD's negotiators "should be attempting to reduce the total price of the equipment, of which profit is only a small percentage."[77] Many observers have suggested that DOD, private contractors, and the public would benefit from policies that allowed higher profit rates but encouraged more determined efforts to cut costs by raising productivity.[78]

Contractual Incentives

Over the past half-century, the government has used a variety of contract pricing formulas and incentives to acquire major weapon systems. Throughout World War II and well into the 1950s, DOD relied heavily on "cost-plus-fixed-fee" contracts for the development and initial production phases of major system programs.[79] Such arrangements paid contractors their actual performance costs and set a "fee" calculated as a percentage of initially estimated total costs. Concern that such formulas encouraged firms to use resources inefficiently led DOD to introduce incentive provisions in the 1960s that made the size of the fee depend upon the contractor's success in reducing performance costs.[80]

Late in the 1960s, DOD introduced "total package procurement" to discourage contractors from submitting unrealistically low bids to win new development contracts ("buying-in") and then seeking increased payments during the course of full production. Under total package procurement, firms committed themselves to a single, fixed price for the development and production phases of the acquisition life cycle. Grumman and Lockheed signed total package procurement contracts to build, respectively, the F-14 fighter and the C-5A cargo plane. As full-scale development began, both firms discovered that they had seriously underestimated their likely costs and incurred massive overruns. The two companies reached the brink of bankruptcy before DOD agreed to renegotiate the contracts and raise the firms' compensation.[81]

The 1970s also yielded a distinctive contractual innovation. DOD began using incentive clauses that gave contractors bonuses for meeting designated schedule and quality targets.[82] Known as "award fees," the bonuses are given periodically during the life of the contract on the basis of performance evaluations conducted by the purchasing agency. The evaluation process confers substantial discretion upon the government's contracting officer in setting the fee, again underscoring the importance of personnel selection and training to successful contract administration.

In the 1980s, DOD has emphasized the use of fixed price contracting formulas for the development and production of several major weapon systems. For example, the contract for the Navy's Advanced Tactical Attack aircraft reportedly requires the team of McDonnell Douglas and General Dynamics to complete early production under a fixed price contract formula.[83] The use of fixed price terms at comparatively early points of the acquisition life cycle does increase contractor incentives to reduce costs.[84] If applied too aggressively, however, using fixed price formulas for development and early production contracts can have at least two adverse consequences. First, the contractor may forgo desirable research and development outlays out of concern that such expenditures will result in large overruns that the company will absorb as losses. Second, contractors may adhere strictly to the original contract specifications and may insist upon treating all apparent deviations as contract changes for which additional compensation is required. This phenomenon can introduce rigidity and delay into the program as attorneys and contracting personnel squabble continually over the meaning and interpretation of the contract's specifications.

Cost Structure Evaluations

DOD cost oversight and disclosure systems have focused chiefly upon whether the contractor has in fact incurred certain costs and properly allocated them to its government contracts.[85] In the 1970s DOD began reviewing contractor operations periodically to assess supplier efficiency by means of "should-cost" and "design-to-cost"[86] studies to identify inefficient production and management practices. DOD has used such cost evaluations to set negotiation cost targets based upon what a hypothetical efficient contractor would require to accomplish specific tasks. DOD prefers that its contractors enhance productivity by investing in new plant and equipment. This aim, however, is unlikely to be attained unless greater program funding stability is attained and financial incentives (including profit policy) are adjusted to encourage investments in capital assets.[87]

Enhanced Compliance Mechanisms

The combination of sharply increased defense outlays and recurring procurement scandals in the 1980s has generated significant adjustments in the regulatory mechanisms by which DOD seeks to elicit compliance with Congressional and executive-branch mandates.[88] The most important change has taken the form of a substantially greater emphasis upon criminal prosecution as a sanction against departures from regulatory requirements.[89] In a related development, DOD has shown a greater willingness to suspend or debar contractors indicted or convicted for procurement-related misconduct.[90] From calendar year 1980 through 1987, the total number of DOD suspension and debarment actions rose from 78 to 934.[91] A growing number of these actions has involved DOD's larger suppliers.[92]

To detect and deter contractor misconduct, both DOD and the Department of Justice have increased the number of personnel assigned to procurement fraud investigations.[93] Congress has supplemented this public detection and deterrence machinery by giving private citizens (specifically, contractor employees) powerful incentives to bring lawsuits on behalf of the United States to redress contractor procurement misconduct.[94] In 1986, Congress amended the "qui tam" mechanism of the False Claims Act to provide a substantial bounty to individuals who are the source of evidence of false claims by contractors against the government.[95] The statute also allows successful qui tam plaintiffs to recover their attorney's fees—a provision that has created a flourishing qui tam practice in the private bar.[96] Since 1986, the prospect of massive recoveries and the availability of attorney's fees have combined to generate over 140 qui tam lawsuits against major defense contractors such as General Electric, Northrop, McDonnell Douglas, Raytheon, Hughes, Singer, and TRW.[97] Indeed, it is a rare major defense contractor today that is not the subject of a qui tam action.

Recurring Regulatory Failures

Consideration of the enhanced compliance systems strategy provides an introduction to recurring problems that have characterized defense procurement regulation in the postwar era, particularly in this decade. Various commentators and legislators have applauded the recently adopted compliance strategies and have called for more expansive recourse to criminal sanctions and whistle-blower bounty measures.[98] It is apparent that the criminal enforcement effort has targeted some unambiguous instances of outright corruption.[99] This hardly means, however, that the existing emphasis upon criminal prosecution and private enforcement tools such as qui tam bounties has been entirely, or even in the main, well-conceived.

Three problems deserve fuller consideration by government policymakers. The first is the danger that indiscriminate application of criminal sanctions will greatly increase the costs of transacting defense contracts. Since 1981, Congress and DOD have relied increasingly on procedures by which high-level contractor personnel certify that various acts (most commonly, information disclosures) have been performed. In today's procurement environment, the signing of each such certificate can have criminal implications if the representations prove to be erroneous.[100] Awareness that a faulty certificate can become grist for a grand jury necessarily delays the contracting process as supplier personnel seek certainty that all representations to DOD officials are correct.

The second danger is that the qui tam whistle-blower mechanism will elicit numerous baseless lawsuits for each action that contains genuine merit. The qui tam machinery offers employees a formidable tool for extracting more favorable contractual terms from employers or for discouraging legitimate managerial activities, including discipline. The attorney's fees provision also gives the private bar strong inducements to bring qui tam suits, and the new qui tam mechanism contains relatively weak disincentives to pursue unmeritorious actions.[101] It remains to be seen whether the principal effect of this mechanism will be to deter and punish fraud, or merely to improve the bargaining position of contractor employees or increase the wealth of the private bar.

The third and most serious hazard is that the preoccupation with contractor fraud will deflect needed attention from more important institutional and structural causes of poor performance in weapons acquisition. The Packard Commission correctly said that "[t]he nation's defense programs lose far more to inefficiency than to dishonesty. . . . Though government is critically important to the acquisition process, no conceivable number of additional federal auditors, inspectors, investigators, and prosecutors can police it fully, much less make it work more effectively."[102] The inefficiency to which the Packard Commission refers flows substantially from the extraordinary complexity of the defense procurement regulatory system, the weaknesses of the government personnel to whom the system's operation is entrusted, and the often perverse incentives the regulatory process creates.

At best, a massive, highly publicized campaign against fraud will cure only a comparatively small part of the procurement problem. Yet the single-minded emphasis on expanded sanctions and fraud detection schemes is altogether representative of the path of much defense regulation reform in the 1980s. In this and in many other reform initiatives of this decade, Congress and DOD have violated several fundamental preconditions for the development of a regulatory scheme that will ensure superior weapons acquisition results. Each of these failures is treated separately below.

Regulatory Instability

Certainty and predictability are crucial ingredients of successful regulatory systems. Sensible business planning requires that executives be able to make reliable judgments about future regulatory requirements and to order their firms' affairs accordingly. Even substantively flawed rules frequently are tolerable if they are relatively clear and stationary. It is not unusual to hear contractor officials state that they can live with imperfect rules so long as the rules are plainly stated and left in place.

Defense regulatory policy in the 1980s has thumbed its nose at the stability axiom. Viewed in isolation, the annual authorization and appropriations bills have injected destabilizing change into the regulatory process, yet these measures have been dwarfed almost annually by separate enactments that accomplish dramatic adjustments in the regulatory process. As suggested above, a peak of turbulence was achieved in 1988 with the passage of eight pieces of legislation affecting weapons procurement. It is difficult to conceive of a more effective strategy for defeating the type of middle- and longer-term planning that is essential to sound business administration.

Regulatory Overload

An annual cascade of new regulatory requirements is not only destabilizing but also indigestible. Institutions of all kinds have a finite ability to absorb and implement changes in the rules that govern their behavior.

New legislation must be interpreted, implementing regulations must be devised, new requirements must be distributed and explained to managers and operating personnel, and compliance with new commands must be monitored. To be done well, this process takes time. The blinding rate of change in defense regulatory requirements since 1980 ensures that the new commands will not be absorbed properly.

Both DOD and its suppliers can respond to the regulatory avalanche in essentially two ways. One is to mount diligent (and frantic) efforts to implement new requirements as they emerge. This approach commits the purchasing agencies and their suppliers to spend large resources on ensuring that managers and operating personnel stay atop the regulatory pyramid. Such an approach becomes extremely expensive as each regulation is displaced in short order by another command. The futility and cost of this path suggests a second strategy—to ignore the new requirements in the expectation that a forthcoming round of directives will render the existing edicts unimportant. A regulatory process that frequently changes course undermines respect for the law and the lawmaker. In doing so, it creates a powerful, corrupting inducement for affected parties to simply ignore or slight nominal requirements in order to get things done.

Implementation Costs

New regulatory requirements generate a collection of significant implementation costs, several of which are suggested above. The affected agency must interpret each new statute and develop implementing regulations or policy guides. The affected companies in turn must analyze the regulatory requirements, communicate them to their employees, and establish procedures for ensuring that employees comply. Each step of this process consumes the time of top management and operating personnel within the purchasing authority and the supplier industry. The cost of ongoing compliance can be especially high when the regulation imposes affirmative obligations such as assembling and supplying information on a routine basis to government officials.

Several statutes enacted in 1988, notably the Drug-Free Workplace Act and the ethics provisions of the Office of Federal Procurement Policy Authorization Act, impose ambiguous, far-reaching obligations in sensitive areas upon DOD and its suppliers. One can search fruitlessly in the legislative histories of these measures for any sign that Congress seriously considered what it would cost to put them into effect. Implementation, it would appear, was assumed to be automatic and costless. Of course, carrying out these and other statutes will consume time and resources that are real costs of building new weapon systems. DOD and its suppliers will increase the size of their overhead organizations by hiring specialists to implement the new rules, and skilled technicians and program managers will spend hours each week seeing that another regulatory command is fulfilled. All the while, a declining percentage of the resources of buyer and seller alike will be applied directly to the business of designing and building armaments.

This is not to say that the existence of implementation costs should bar the adoption of new regulations. It does underscore, however, the desirability of meaningful efforts to identify and assess these costs before embracing a new regulatory requirement. The necessity of such a calculation for responsible policymaking is basic and self-evident if net anticipated regulatory benefits are to be measured correctly. In defense procurement regulation, this elementary lesson from other fields of regulatory experience is routinely ignored.

Inadequate Evaluation

The development of sound regulatory policies requires ongoing efforts to assess the impact of existing statutes and related regulations. To make sensible judgments about the correct approach for future policymaking, Congress and DOD should systematically evaluate the effects of each regulatory initiative.[103] In many instances, the path of regulatory change in defense procurement in the 1980s renders the process of evaluation almost impossible. Specifically, the annual cycle of extensive statutory change seriously impedes efforts to determine which results have flowed from individual reforms.

Underinvestment in Monitoring

A fundamental flaw of defense procurement reform since World War II has been the failure to follow through. The studies of blue ribbon commissions and distinguished students of the procurement process have demonstrated that hit-and-run solutions have little positive effect.[104] Rather, it is the credible commitment to provide long-term scrutiny to the implementation of a given reform that generates genuine change. Because the problems are long-term and persistent, so too must be the solutions.[105]

The need for a long-term orientation in defense regulation goes chronically unattended in the short-term policymaking environment of the nation's Capitol. Guided by a political calculus that demands payouts in two years or less, most members of Congress ordinarily prefer to invest their time in launching new initiatives than in seeing that existing requirements are implemented. Eye-catching new enactments provide richer credit-claiming opportunities than careful, sustained efforts to determine whether DOD and its suppliers have abided by previous legislative guidance. Not surprisingly, Congressional intervention in the name of regulatory "reform" in defense acquisition usually has taken the form of the ineffective and often counterproductive quick fix.

CONCLUSION

Recent experience with defense procurement regulation makes it easy to envision a cycle of doom. Despite repeated calls for simplification and stability, the past decade has offered uninterrupted doses of complexity and turbulence, and there is no end in sight. Indeed, the Justice Department's Ill Wind inquiry has unleashed pressure for Congress to add another layer of controls. Despite the seemingly relentless trends to the contrary, it is useful to consider what genuine regulatory reform would involve.

It would begin with a moratorium on the imposition of new regulatory controls. Specifically, Congress would serve the procurement system well if it enacted no significant adjustments to the existing regulatory scheme for the next two years. A moratorium would afford a much-needed period for DOD and its suppliers to assimilate the statutory avalanche of 1988.

The moratorium would not be a time of inactivity. A major priority would be for Congress and DOD to formulate a plan for improving the quality of the government's acquisition personnel. The sheer mass and complexity of the defense procurement system are dismal concessions to the limitations of the personnel who buy the systems for the government. For over a decade the inadequacies of procurement personnel have been finessed by adding layer upon layer of procedural and regulatory "safeguards" to ensure that contractors perform their tasks properly.

A second priority during the legislative hiatus would be to undertake a serious evaluation of the effects of regulatory initiatives adopted in the 1980s. Such an evaluation process would have several elements. A major ingredient would be to examine the costs of implementing and complying with existing regulatory requirements. Determining the costs associated with individual regulatory controls is an essential first step toward assessing the relative merits of continuing the existing regulatory regime.

The examination of recent regulatory reforms will not invariably point to the abandonment of experiments Congress and DOD have pursued since 1980. Current defense acquisition policies that emphasize competition in the procurement of major weapon systems have the desirable goal of using rivalry to elicit better supplier performance and preserve an essential level of industry design and manufacturing capability to meet future defense needs. These policies also have important institutional implications, for they offer a basis for substantially reducing the transaction costs associated with regulating the conduct of defense contractors on some programs. The competition-oriented procurement reforms establish grounds for deemphasizing disclosure and auditing controls and simplifying program management structures.

There are several preconditions for success in implementing these competition reforms. DOD must choose wisely in selecting the optimal competition strategy for its major acquisition programs. As it applies competition strategies, DOD must relax regulatory controls that assume the discipline of rivalry is nonexistent.[106] The department must establish lean program management structures that give a smaller number of talented procurement professionals more responsibility to direct major acquisition programs.

None of this will happen without a sustained commitment from Congress to see that the legislative competition reforms of the 1980s take hold. One would hesitate to say that the likelihood of sustained, effective Congressional monitoring is strong, as legislators have weak incentives to devote their scarce resources to pursuits whose success demands long-term effort and whose returns are not readily appropriable to legislators who invest in monitoring.[107] One can only hope that the perceived urgency of limiting federal expenditures while maintaining an adequate defense may gradually convince congressmen that the effort is worth their attention.

There is a final respect in which efforts to reduce regulatory complexity are important. As the defense procurement regulatory process becomes less transparent, it grows progressively less amenable to effective monitoring by outside groups seeking to evaluate the performance of the procurement system.[108] By creating and expanding regulatory structures that are seemingly incomprehensible and beyond mortal control, Congress ultimately will make DOD and its suppliers less accountable for their conduct and less prone to efforts to discourage behavior that denies the country full value for its defense outlays.

NOTES

1. The weakening of limits on entry and pricing in the transportation sector is treated in Thomas G. Moore, "Rail and Trucking Deregulation," in *Regulatory Reform: What Actually Happened,* ed. Leonard W. Weiss and Michael W. Klass (Boston: Little, Brown, 1986), p. 14; and Elizabeth E. Bailey, David R. Graham, and Daniel P. Kaplan, *Deregulating the Airlines* (Cambridge, Mass.: MIT Press, 1985). Regulatory change in the telecommunications industry is analyzed in Peter Temin, *The Fall of the Bell System* (Cambridge: Cambridge University Press, 1987). The realignment of the electric utility industry is considered in Paul L. Joskow and Richard Schmalensee, *Markets for Power: An Analysis of Electric Utility Deregulation* (Cambridge, Mass.: MIT Press, 1983).

2. On the application of price caps in the telecommunications field, see Bellcore, "The Impact of Federal Price Cap Regulation on Interstate Toll Customers" (March 17, 1988) (mimeo); Calvin Sims, "AT&T Is Granted Greater Freedom to Set Its Prices," *New York Times,* March 17, 1989, p. A1. Other recently developed incentive tools include the use of total factor productivity benchmarks to assess the performance of public utilities. See Michael A. Crew and Paul R. Kleindorfer,

"Productivity Incentives and Rate-of-Return Regulation," in *Regulating Utilities in an Era of Deregulation*, ed. Michael A. Crew (New York: St. Martin's Press, 1987), p. 7.

3. For example, these adjustments were pronounced during the Reagan administration in agencies such as the Federal Trade Commission that possess broad economic regulation authority. See *Public Choice and Regulation: A View from Inside the Federal Trade Commission*, ed. Robert J. MacKay, James C. Miller III, and Bruce Yandle (Stanford: Hoover Institution Press, 1987); William E. Kovacic, "Public Choice and the Public Interest: Federal Trade Commission Antitrust Enforcement During the Reagan Administration," *Antitrust Bulletin* 33 (Fall 1988): 467.

4. See, e.g., Martha Derthick and Paul J. Quirk, *The Politics of Deregulation* (Washington, D.C.: Brookings Institution, 1985); George C. Eads and Michael Fix, *Relief or Reform? Reagan's Regulatory Dilemma* (Washington, D.C.: Urban Institute Press, 1984); Robert E. Litan and William D. Nordhaus, *Reforming Federal Regulation* (New Haven: Yale University Press, 1983); Barry M. Mitnick, *The Political Economy of Regulation* (New York: Columbia University Press, 1980); Roger C. Noll and Bruce M. Owen, *The Political Economy of Deregulation: Interest Groups in the Regulatory Process* (Washington, D.C.: American Enterprise Institute, 1983); *The Politics of Regulation*, ed. James Q. Wilson (New York: Basic Books, 1980); *Promoting Competition in Regulated Markets*, ed. Almarin Phillips (Washington, D.C.: Brookings Institution, 1975); *Public Regulation: New Perspectives on Institutions and Policies*, ed. Elizabeth E. Bailey (Cambridge, Mass.: MIT Press, 1987); *Reforming Regulation*, ed. Timothy B. Clark, Marvin H. Kosters, and James C. Miller III (Washington, D.C.: American Enterprise Institute, 1980).

5. See, e.g., Stephen Breyer, *Regulation and its Reform* (Cambridge, Mass.: Harvard University Press, 1982); Alfred E. Kahn, *The Economics of Regulation: Principles and Institutions* (Cambridge, Mass.: MIT Press, 1988); Michael A. Crew and Paul R. Kleindorfer, *The Economics of Public Utility Regulation* (Cambridge, Mass.: MIT Press, 1986).

6. See, e.g., William K. Jones, *Cases and Materials on Regulated Industries*, 2d ed. (Mineola, N.Y.: Foundation Press, 1976); Thomas D. Morgan, *Cases and Materials on Economic Regulation of Business* (St. Paul: West Publishing, 1976).

7. See Jacques S. Gansler, *Affording Defense* (Cambridge, Mass.: MIT Press, 1989), pp. 150–54; Norman R. Augustine, "Defense: A Case of Too Many Cooks," *Fortune*, December 15, 1988, p. 219; Center for Strategic and International Studies, *U.S. Defense Acquisition: A Process in Trouble* (Washington, D.C.: Center for Strategic and International Studies, 1987), pp. 29–30.

8. The origin and content of the Federal Acquisition Regulations are treated comprehensively in James F Nagle, *Federal Procurement Regulations: Policy, Practice and Procedures* (Chicago: American Bar Association Section of Public Contract Law, 1987); *The FAR System: Its Critical Formative Years* (Chicago: American Bar Association Section of Public Contract Law, 1988).

9. John F Lehman, Jr., *Command of the Seas* (New York: Scribners, 1989), p. 191.

10. See Andrew Mayer, "Military Procurement: Basic Principles and Recent Developments," *George Washington Journal of International Law and Economics* 21 (1987): 165; Richard R. Kaeser, "Major Defense Acquisition Programs: A Study of Congressional Control over DOD Acquisitions," *Federal Bar News and Journal* 34 (December 1987): 430; The MAC Group, *The Impact on Defense Industrial Capability of Changes in Procurement and Tax Policy 1984–1987* (Washington, D.C.: The MAC Group, February 1988), pp. 6–11.

11. See Department of Defense Authorization Act for Fiscal Year 1989, Public Law 100-456 (September 29, 1988); Department of Defense Appropriations Act for Fiscal Year 1989, Public Law 100-463 (October 1, 1988); The Office of Federal

Procurement Policy Act Amendments of 1988, Public Law 100-679 (November 11, 1988); Major Fraud Act of 1988, Public Law 100-700 (November 19, 1988); Drug-Free Workplace Act of 1988, Public Law 100-690 (November 18, 1988); Business Opportunity Development Reform Act of 1988, Public Law 100-656 (November 15, 1988); Prompt Payments Act Amendments of 1988, Public Law 100-496 (October 17, 1988); and Omnibus Trade and Competitiveness Act of 1988, Public Law 100-418 (August 23, 1988).

12. The Ill Wind inquiry is described in Caryle Murphy and Ruth Marcus, "Convictions, Guilty Pleas Rise As Pentagon Probe Continues," *Washington Post,* May 10, 1989, p. A1; "The Defense Scandal," *Business Week,* July 4, 1988, p. 28; David E. Rosenbaum, "Pentagon Fraud Inquiry: What Is Known to Date," *New York Times* (National Edition), July 7, 1988, p. A1.

13. Prominent among new legislative reform proposals are measures that would impose limits on the use of consultants, establish broader certification and reporting requirements for contractors, create a new weapons acquisition corps independent of the individual armed services, and increase criminal penalties for violations of federal procurement regulations. See David C. Morrison, "Tinkering with Defense," *National Journal,* September 3, 1988, p. 2178; Sandra Sugawara, "Legislators Draft Military Procurement Reforms," *Washington Post,* January 17, 1989, p. C1; "The Outlook for Legislative Activity Affecting Defense, Space, and Procurement Policy," *Bureau of National Affairs Federal Contracts Report* 51 (January 23, 1989): 156.

14. For representative assessments, see J. Ronald Fox, *The Defense Management Challenge: Weapons Acquisition* (Boston: Harvard Business School Press, 1988); Gansler, *Affording Defense;* Norman R. Augustine and Robert F. Trimble, "Competition and the Defense Procurement Process," *Yale Journal on Regulation* 6 (Summer 1989): 333–47.

15. See Gansler, *Affording Defense,* pp. 150–54; Thomas L. McNaugher, *New Weapons, Old Politics: America's Military Procurement Muddle* (Washington, D.C.: Brookings Institution, 1989); Steven Kelman, "Defense Bureaucracy's Corrupting Influence," *Wall Street Journal,* July 6, 1988, p. 22; Murray Weidenbaum, "Whether It's Bombers or Cookies, Filling Pentagon Orders Is a Drag," *Christian Science Monitor,* November 15, 1988, p. 12.

16. President's Blue Ribbon Commission on Defense Management, *A Formula for Action: A Report to the President on Defense Acquisition* (Washington, D.C.: U.S. Government Printing Office, April 1986), p. 18.

17. Ibid.

18. Ibid.

19. Fox, *Defense Management Challenge,* p. 5.

20. See William W. Kaufmann and Lawrence J. Korb, *The 1990 Defense Budget* (Washington, D.C.: Brookings Institution, 1989), pp. 2–12.

21. See Michael Weisskopf, "Defense Report's Tone Divides Panel," *Washington Post,* February 19, 1986, p. A1.

22. See Benjamin F. Cooling, *Gray Steel and Blue Water Navy: The Formative Years of America's Military Industrial Complex, 1881–1917* (Hamden, Conn.: Archon, 1979).

23. See Robert Higgs, *Crisis and Leviathan* (New York: Oxford University Press, 1987), pp. 211–15, 230–33.

24. Leonard D. White, *The Republican Era: A Study in Administrative History, 1869–1901* (New York: Free Press, 1958), p. 159.

25. Samuel P. Hayes, *The Response to Industrialism, 1885–1914* (Chicago: University of Chicago Press, 1957), p. 165.

26. Cooling, *Gray Steel and Blue Water Navy,* pp. 120–37, 167–212; Alfred D.

Chandler, Jr., and Stephen Salsbury, *Pierre S. DuPont and the Making of the Modern Corporation* (New York: Harper & Row, 1971), pp. 259–300; W. H. S. Stevens, "The Powder Trust, 1872–1912," *Quarterly Journal of Economics* 26 (1912): 444; Melvin Urofsky, "Josephus Daniels and the Armor Trust," *North Carolina Historical Review* 45 (1968): 237.

27. Cooling, *Gray Steel and Blue Water Navy*, p. 181.

28. Ibid., pp. 203–12.

29. Robert Higgs, "Private Profit, Public Risk: Institutional Antecedents of the Modern Military Procurement System in the Rearmament Program of 1940–41," in *The Sinews of War: Essays on the Economic History of World War II*, ed. Geofrey Mills and Hugh Rockoff (Ames: Iowa State University Press) (forthcoming).

30. Higgs, *Crisis and Leviathan*, pp. 214–15, 230–33; J. S. Dupre and W. E. Gufstafson, "Contracting for Defense: Private Firms and the Public Interest," *Political Science Quarterly* 77 (1962): 161.

31. Dwight D. Eisenhower, "Farewell Radio and Television Address to the American People, January 17, 1961," in *Public Papers of the Presidents of the United States: Dwight D. Eisenhower, 1960–61* (Washington, D.C.: U.S. Government Printing Office, 1961), pp. 1035, 1038.

32. Ibid., p. 1038.

33. Ibid.

34. Merton J. Peck and Frederic M. Scherer, *The Weapons Acquisition Process: An Economic Analysis* (Boston: Division of Research, Graduate School of Business Administration, Harvard University, 1962), pp. 17–54.

35. In the postwar era, foreign governments became major purchasers of some American-built weapon systems. *See* Andrew J. Pierre, *The Global Politics of Arms Sales* (Princeton: Princeton University Press, 1982); Anthony Sampson, *The Arms Bazaar* (New York: The Viking Press). Foreign military sales transactions take place pursuant to the extensive supervision and control of the United States government, including DOD and the Department of State. See G. Gregory Letterman, "United States Regulation of High-Technology Exports," *International Lawyer* 20 (Fall 1986): 1147.

36. For example, DOD presently is funding a consortium of firms to seek advances in semiconductor technology. See Andrew Pollack, "Sematech's Weary Hunt for a Chief," *New York Times,* April 1, 1988, p. D1.

37. Perhaps the most recent and dramatic example of this phenomenon is the B-2 bomber, which encompasses dramatic state-of-the-art advances in propulsion, materials, and avionics. Owing to its exotic technology, the B-2 now has an estimated Cost of $516 Million per aircraft. See Molly Moore, "Stealth Bomber to Cost $516 Million: Most Expensive Military Plane Ever," *Washington Post,* December 17, 1988, p. A2.

38. See William B. Burnett, "Competition in the Weapons Acquisition Process: The Case of U.S. Warplanes," *Journal of Policy Analysis and Management* 7 (Fall 1987): 17, 20–21.

39. See Peck and Scherer, *The Weapons Acquisition Process: An Economic Analysis,* pp. 55–64; Jacques S. Gansler, *The Defense Industry* (Cambridge, Mass.: MIT Press, 1980), pp. 29–96; J. Ronald Fox, *Arming America: How the U.S. Buys Weapons* (Boston: Harvard University Press, 1974), pp. 26–40.

40. For example, Tenneco's Newport News shipyard is the sole supplier of the Navy's nuclear-powered aircraft carriers.

41. For discussion of a particularly egregious and costly example, see Robert Higgs, "Hard Coals Make Bad Law: Congressional Parochialism versus National Defense," *Cato Journal* 8 (Spring/Summer 1988): 79.

42. These programs are described in John Cibinic, Jr., and Ralph C. Nash,

Jr., *Formation of Government Contracts,* 2d ed. (Washington, D.C.: George Washington University Government Contracts Program, 1986), pp. 944–68.

43. Ibid., pp. 968–80. Regulatory limitations on the use of foreign suppliers (for example, the Buy American Act) at times serve the legitimate goal of ensuring that DOD does not become dangerously dependent on unreliable sources of supply for critical weapons systems and components. See Tim Carrington, "Military's Dependence on Foreign Suppliers Causes Rising Concern," *Wall Street Journal,* March 24, 1988, p. 1. However, Congressional opposition to purchasing from offshore sources frequently arises chiefly from the fear that domestic firms will suffer a decline in revenues if DOD awards contracts to foreign companies. See David D. Morrison, "Made in America," *National Journal,* November 28, 1988, p. 3036.

44. The discussion in this section is derived from William E. Kovacic, "Blue Ribbon Defense Commissions: The Acquisition of Major Weapon Systems," also in this volume.

45. See, e.g., Helen Dewar and George C. Wilson, "Hill Leaders Demand Swift Justice," *Washington Post,* June 18, 1988, p. A1 (reporting Congressional reaction to the initial disclosure of the existence of the Justice Department's Ill Wind investigation).

46. See, e.g., Fox, *The Defense Management Challenge,* pp. 177–245; Gansler, *Affording Defense,* pp. 207–14, 331–32; President's Blue Ribbon Commission on Defense Management, *A Quest for Excellence: Final Report to the President* (Washington, D.C.: U.S. Government Printing Office, June 1986), p. 66.

47. See Packard Commission, *A Quest for Excellence,* pp. 49–51.

48. Modern scholarship concerning defense procurement has drawn increasingly upon the new "institutional" economics and has applied its insights concerning the strengths and weaknesses of alternative governance approaches to weapons acquisition. See Robert J. MacKay, "The Theory of Contracts: An Application to Defense Procurement" (1986) (mimeo). The contributions of the new institutional economics to analyzing various modes of regulation are discussed in Crew and Kleindorfer, *The Economics of Public Utility Regulation,* pp. 146–65.

49. These aims can be characterized as efficiency-related. As suggested above, they are not the sole nominal or real aims of the defense acquisition regulatory process. The discussion in this part of the article focuses on the efficient attainment of military capability goals rather than addressing specific regulatory approaches for achieving Congressional patronage and distributional ends.

50. The following discussion of governance strategies for defense procurement is derived in part from William B. Burnett and William E. Kovacic, "Reform of United States Weapons Acquisition Policy: Competition, Teaming Agreements, and Dual-Sourcing," *Yale Journal on Regulation* 6 (Summer 1989): 249.

51. The parallels between traditional public utility regulation and defense procurement regulation are treated in George R. Hall, *Defense Procurement and Public Utility Regulation* (Santa Monica: Rand Corporation, 1967); D. N. Jones, "Extension of the Social Control of Utilities," *Land Economics* 41 (1965): 297; Murray L. Weidenbaum, "Arms and the American Economy: A Domestic Convergence Hypothesis," *American Economic Review* 58 (1968): 428.

52. The history and aims of the 1947 statute are discussed in J. P. Miller, *Pricing of Military Procurements* (New Haven: Yale University Press, 1949).

53. This trend is analyzed in Burnett and Kovacic, "Reform of United States Weapons Acquisition Policy"; William B. Burnett and William E. Kovacic, "Armed Services Using Competition Strategy to Reduce Expenses," *Legal Times,* July 13, 1987, p. 14.

54. Public Law 98–369, 10 United States Code Sec. 2301(a)(5).

55. The armed services procurement statutes use the term "major defense acquisition program" to denote projects whose cost exceeds substantial dollar thresholds. The term includes weapons programs whose costs in Fiscal Year 1980 dollars are estimated to exceed $200 million in research, development, test, and evaluation outlays or $1 billion in total procurement expenditures. 10 United States Code Sec. 2430.

56. Public Law 99–145, 10 United States Code Sec. 2438(b)(1).

57. Public Law 99-591, 10 United States Code Sec. 2365(a). In Section 802 of the Department of Defense Authorization Act for Fiscal Year 1989, Congress enacted a sunset provision that terminates the competitive prototyping requirement on September 30, 1991. Public Law 100–456 (September 29, 1988).

58. Acceptable grounds for departing from the competition requirements include a showing that the mandated competition technique will raise total program costs without offsetting benefits.

59. This requirement was established by the Competition in Contracting Act. See 10 United States Code Sec. 2318(b).

60. The GAO's bid protest jurisdiction is discussed in Cibinic and Nash, *Formation of Government Contracts*, pp. 1005–46. See also Joel R. Feidelman, "Knowing and Using the Rules: Maximizing Your Likelihood of Success at the GAO and the Agency," in *Getting the Contract . . . and Keeping It* (Chicago: American Bar Association Section of Public Contract Law, 1989), Section I.

61. The impact of the "Carlucci Initiatives" is discussed in Donald L. Pilling, *Competition in Defense Procurement* (Washington, D.C.: Brookings Institution, 1989).

62. Executive Order 12,352 (March 17, 1982), reprinted in *Weekly Compilation of Presidential Documents* 18 (Washington, D.C.: U.S. Government Printing Office, March 22, 1982): 332.

63. Packard Commission, *Quest for Excellence*, p. xxvi.

64. See, e.g., Lehman, *Command of the Seas*, pp. 242–44.

65. The United States used dual-sourcing extensively during World War II to produce fighter and bomber aircraft. See Frederic M. Scherer, *The Weapons Acquisition Process: Economic Incentives* (Boston, Division of Research, Graduate School of Business Administration, Harvard University, 1964), pp. 119–26.

66. See, e.g., Robert W. Drewes, *The Air Force and the Great Engine War* (Washington, D.C.: National Defense University Press, 1987); Lehman, *Command of the Seas*, pp. 196–265; Michael Isikoff, "Bidding Battle Puts Ax to Tomahawk Missile's Price," *Washington Post*, April 12, 1987, p. H1.

67. See Clarence T. Kipps, Jr., and John L. Rice, *Living with TINA: A Practice Guide to the Truth in Negotiations Act* (Washington, D.C.: Washington Legal Foundation, 1989).

68. The requirements of the 1962 statute are discussed in Cibinic and Nash, *Formation of Government Contracts*, pp. 895–97.

69. The role of cost observation in setting prices in public procurement contracts is analyzed in Jean Laffont and Jean Tirole, "Using Cost Observation to Regulate Firms," *Journal of Political Economy* 94 (1986): 614.

70. See American Bar Association Section of Public Contract Law, *DCAA's Access to Records* (Chicago: American Bar Association, 1989); American Bar Association Section of Public Contract Law, *Audits and Costs: A Pot of Problems at the End of the Rainbow* (Chicago: American Bar Association, 1988).

71. Frank M. Alston, Margaret M. Worthington, and Louis P. Goldsman, *Contracting with the Federal Government*, 2d ed. (New York: Wiley, 1988), p. 22.

72. American Bar Association Section of Public Contract Law, *DCAA's Access to Records*, p. 30.

73. John G. DeGooyer, "Government Access to Records and People: Con-

tractor Rights vs. Auditor Demands," in American Bar Association Section of Public Contract Law, *Audits and Costs,* Section D.

74. Ibid.

75. The operation of these profit ceilings and DOD profit policy is discussed in Cibinic and Nash, *Formation of Government Contracts,* pp. 909–1036; Alston, Worthington, and Goldsman, *Contracting with the Federal Government,* pp. 68–73. For a comparison between profit policies applied, respectively, in defense procurement and traditional public utility settings, see Arthur E. Burns, "Profit Limitation: Regulated Industries and the Defense-Space Industries," *Bell Journal of Economics* 3 (1972): 3.

76. The role of DOD profit policy in eliciting desired levels of contractor innovation is discussed in William P. Rogerson, "Profit Regulation of Defense Contractors and Prizes for Innovation: Theory and Evidence" (Evanston: Northwestern University Center for Mathematical Studies in Economics and Management Science, January 1988).

77. Gansler, *Affording Defense,* p. 253.

78. See, e.g., The MAC Group, *Impact on Defense Industry Capability,* pp. 41–44. The profitability of DOD's suppliers is also affected by other policies, including the setting of rates for progress payments.

79. See Murray Weidenbaum, "The Military/Space Market: The Intersection of the Public and Private Sectors," in U.S. Congress, Senate, Committee on the Judiciary, *Competition in Defense Procurement: Hearings Before the Subcommittee on Antitrust and Monopoly of the Senate Committee on the Judiciary,* 90th Cong., 2d sess., 1968: 883, 898–99.

80. See Fox, *Arming America,* pp. 240–43; Scherer, *The Weapons Acquisition Process: Economic Incentives,* pp. 134–37, 153–270; Ralph C. Nash, Jr., "Pricing Policies in Government Contracts," *Law and Contemporary Problems* 29 (1964): 361, 365–74.

81. See Ingemar Doerfer, *Arms Deal: The Selling of the F-16* (New York: Praeger, 1983), p. 32 (discussing Grumman's overruns on the F-14); Sampson, *The Arms Bazaar,* pp. 218–19 (discussing Lockheed's overruns on the C-5A).

82. Cibinic and Nash, *Formation of Government Contracts,* pp. 775–90.

83. Tim Carrington, "McDonnell, Dynamics Get $4.38 Billion Job," *Wall Street Journal,* January 14, 1988, p. 10.

84. The fixed price contract in DOD procurement is roughly similar to the use of price caps in setting rates for public utilities. The fixed price motivates the contractor to improve productivity and cut costs, as each dollar of costs saved below the fixed price is retained as earnings.

85. The Federal Acquisition Regulations require that a contractor's costs satisfy three criteria before they may be charged to a government contract. The cost must be related to the government contract, it must be reasonable in amount, and it must be "allowable." To conform to the allowability requirement, the contractor must abide by a collection of FAR "cost principles" that specify discrete categories of expense that may not be charged to the government. See W. Noel Keyes, *Government Contracts Under the Federal Acquisition Regulation* (St. Paul: West Publishing, 1986), pp. 400–422.

86. For the should-cost concept, see Cibinic and Nash, *Formation of Government Contracts,* p. 907; for design-to-cost, see M. G. Sovereign, "Application of the Conceptual Model for Setting Design-to-Cost Goals: The FFG-7," in *Auctions, Bidding, and Contracting: Uses and Theory,* ed. R. Engelbrecht-Wiggans, M. Shubik, and R. Stark (New York: New York University Press, 1983).

87. On the importance of greater funding stability to achieving weapon system cost reductions, see Fox, *The Defense Management Challenge,* pp. 304–6.

88. Unlike the situation in most public utility regulatory systems, the customer in weapons procurement (DOD) is also the regulator. DOD uses compliance with its regulatory commands as a criterion for deciding which suppliers will obtain future contracts.

89. See Steven D. Overly, "Government Contractors Beware: Civil and Criminal Penalties Abound for Defective Pricing," *Loyola of Los Angeles Law Review* 20 (1987): 597; W. Bruce Shirk and Bennett D. Greenberg, "An Analysis of the Web of Civil and Criminal Liability for Defective Pricing of Government Contracts," *Catholic University Law Review* 33 (1984): 319; Note, "Regulating Fraud in Military Procurement: A Legal Process Model," *Yale Law Journal* 95 (1985): 390.

90. The content and administrative application of the debarment and suspension remedies are discussed in Paul D'Aloisio, "Accusations of Criminal Conduct by Government Contractors: The Remedies, Problems, and Solutions," *Public Contract Law Journal* 17 (1987): 265; Comment, "Moving Toward a Better-Defined Standard of Public Interest in Administrative Decisions to Suspend Government Contractors," *American University Law Review* 36 (1987): 693.

91. Howard W. Cox, "DOD Suspension and Debarment Policy," in *Out in the Cold: The Worldwide Consequences of Government Contract Suspension and Debarment* (Chicago: American Bar Association Section of Public Contract Law, 1988), Section F.

92. See Murphy and Marcus, "Convictions, Guilty Pleas Rise As Pentagon Probe Progresses," p. A8.

93. See Howard W. Cox, "Agency Investigations of Anticompetitive Conduct: Techniques and Focus," *Antitrust Law Journal* 57 (1988): 579. By one estimate, the total number of DOD auditors, inspectors, and investigators has grown from 17,000 in 1982 to 22,000 in 1989. Milton L. Lohr, Principal Deputy Under Secretary of Defense for Acquisition, "Perspective on Defense Procurement and Its Impact on Industry" (Washington, D.C.: May 10, 1989) (Presentation at the Brookings Institution Leadership Seminar for Corporate and Government Executives on "Restructuring the Defense Industry: By Design or Chance?").

94. See Fred Strasser, "When the Big Whistle Blows . . .," *National Law Journal,* May 8, 1989, p.1.

95. False Claims Act Amendments of 1986, Public Law 99–562 (1986). If the government intervenes in the lawsuit and prosecutes the qui tam action, the individual who originally files the lawsuit is entitled to a bounty of between 15 and 25 percent of all funds recovered. If the government declines to participate, the qui tam plaintiff is entitled to between 25 and 30 percent of the funds recovered on the government's behalf.

96. See Strasser, "When the Big Whistle Blows . . .," p. 42.

97. See Laurie P. Cohen, "U.S. Joins Lawsuit Against Singer Co. Over Job Claims," *Wall Street Journal,* March 15, 1989, p. B8; Gregory Stricharchuk, "GE Agrees to Pay $3.5 Million to Settle Four Suits Brought by Whistle-Blowers," *Wall Street Journal,* February 24, 1989, p. B8.

98. See, e.g., Howard L. Berman and Charles E. Grassley, "Defense Procurement: Exposing Crime Pays," *Wall Street Journal,* September 6, 1988, p. 30.

99. See, e.g., Michael Wines, "Ex-Unisys Official Admits Paying Bribes to Get Pentagon Contracts," *New York Times,* March 10, 1989, p. A1.

100. Among other consequences, submission of a false certification can be prosecuted as a false statement (18 United States Code Section 1001) or a false claim (18 United States Code Section 287).

101. The 1986 False Claims Act Amendments permit the court to require the qui tam plaintiff to pay the defendant's reasonable attorney's fees and expenses if the defendant can show that the qui tam action was "clearly frivolous, clearly vexatious,

or brought primarily for purposes of harassment." 31 United States Code Sec. 3730(d)(3).

102. Packard Commission, *A Quest for Excellence*, pp. 77–78.

103. Ongoing reassessment of regulatory initiatives is an essential ingredient of a successful transition from one regulatory regime to another. See Stephen Breyer, "Antitrust, Deregulation, and the Newly Liberated Marketplace," *California Law Review* 75 (1987): 1005.

104. On the work of blue ribbon defense commissions since World War II and its impact on the weapons acquisitions process, see Kovacic, "Blue Ribbon Defense Commissions," in this volume.

105. Within DOD, observes one prominent commentator, "much activity is directed toward launching public relations campaigns to prove implementation instead of monitoring implementation efforts and following up to ensure that lasting change occurs." Fox, *The Defense Management Challenge*, p. 321.

106. DOD organizations such as DCAA and the Office of the Inspector General have resisted the efforts of the purchasing agencies to relax data disclosure requirements from contractors facing competition.

107. See Kovacic, "Blue Ribbon Defense Commissions."

108. See Michael A. Crew and Charles K. Rowley, "Toward a Public Choice Theory of Monopoly Regulation," *Public Choice* 57 (1988): 49 (describing how rent-seekers within a system of regulation prefer that their rent-seeking conduct be shielded from the view of observers who otherwise might act to prevent the rent-seeking).

6

Models of Arms Transfer in American Foreign Policy: Carter's Restraint and Reagan's Promotion, 1977–1987

ILAN PELEG

In the postwar era, arms transfers to foreign countries have been an important component—and in some periods, regions, and contexts even a central component—in the foreign policy of the United States. While among the military dimensions of the American Policy we can easily identify more important elements, such as the deterrence posture vis-à-vis the Soviet Union and the establishment of military bases abroad, the supply of weapons to allies, friends, and clients proved to be (especially over the last decade) a more volatile, controversial, and politically sensitive component of U.S. defense policy than the policies in those areas.

The supply of weapons to foreign nations, both U.S. formal allies and countries in the Third World, has changed dramatically. In 1950 the United States supplied all countries in the Third World weapons valued at $29,281,000; by 1985 the figure had risen to $6,946,269,000, a remarkable increase.[1] Moreover, the sophistication of weapons supplied to other nations also increased dramatically, particularly insofar as the Third World was concerned. In the 1950s and in almost all instances during the 1960s, second-hand, obsolete, or surplus equipment was routinely supplied to less developed countries; in the 1970s and 1980s there was a pronounced shift toward the supply of the most technologically advanced weapons, "hot off the design table," particularly to countries that could afford such weapons.[2]

Since the late 1960s, and even more so since the mid-1970s, arms

The author wishes to thank Ted Galen Carpenter for comments made on a previous version of this paper.

supply to foreign countries has emerged as a hotly debated political issue within American society. The Vietnam War, which broke the foreign policy consensus in many areas of U.S. foreign policy, convinced many Americans that the United States ought not to fight another major war anywhere in the Third World. Nevertheless, public opinion remained loyal to the notion that the U.S. ought to defend the countries of the free world against future "Communist aggression" through military and other means. To resolve a seemingly contradictory set of demands, President Nixon suggested that to defend its allies in the Third World the United States ought to supply them generously with military equipment and training. The solution was embodied in what became known as the Nixon Doctrine, which has been accepted, at least in principle, by all U.S. administrations since the early 1970s.

Nevertheless, when the supply of U.S. weapons to Third World nations intensified in the mid-1970s in what seemed to some "a policy run amok," a controversy over the issue erupted in Washington. Growing criticism of the U.S. policy and practice of supplying weapons to others was expressed particularly during the brief presidency of Gerald Ford. The controversy came to a head during the presidential campaign of 1976.

When Jimmy Carter became President, he immediately initiated a well publicized change of policy, calling for an American policy of restraint in the supply of weapons to other countries, particularly those in the Third World.[3] The newly installed president hoped that through an American unilateral initiative to reduce the supply of weapons to other nations, an international regime based on restraint in this area would emerge. His policy, however, was not without its own critics, especially when it became evident that it was inconsistently applied. In 1981, shortly after his inauguration, Ronald Reagan shifted the policy on arms transfer once again, returning to the promotion model (see below, pp. 136–40) practiced by Nixon, Ford, and Kissinger.[4] Thus, in the late 1970s and early 1980s, arms transfers, traditionally a rather peripheral matter in American foreign policy, became a critical, publicly debated issue.

In this paper I offer an analysis of U.S. arms transfers over the decade 1977–87. The analytical focus is on a comparison between the arms transfer policies of Presidents Carter and Reagan. The paper describes the policies in some detail and explores the objectives behind them and their results.

In both cases the chief executive seems to have adopted a strong ideological position toward the issue of arms transfer, a position that can be understood only as a component of a more general ideological stance. Both presidents arrived at the White House with a clear preconceived notion of what they wanted to achieve in the field of foreign policy and what role arms transfers ought to play in achieving the overall objective.

Yet even a brief look reveals that the environment within which each President had to operate was not always supportive of what the president

wanted to do regarding arms transfer. In fact, the environment often resisted the policy, even when defined by the president as essential. The
failure, or at least the limited success, of both Carter and Reagan to implement their arms transfer policies was in effect a reflection of the environmental resistance to an ideologically inspired policy at the White House
level. In the collision between the visionary policy and the reluctant (if not
outright hostile) environment, the latter survived more often than the
former. This generalization suggests that what is needed is a theoretical
framework that would enable us to deal analytically with situations in
which a specific, well-defined policy in the field of foreign affairs interacts
with its domestic and international environment.

Accordingly, an analytical framework is offered here for dealing with
the interaction between a declared policy in the field of foreign affairs and
the domestic and international environments within which the policy is
carried out; the framework is accompanied by predictions of the success of a
policy in different environments, and by some historical examples.

Following this analytical framework, two diametrically opposed, conflicting perspectives on arms supply as a foreign policy instrument are
presented. One is called the *Restraint Perspective* and the other the *Promotion
Perspective;* these two theoretical, ideal-type models are followed by a description of the Restraint Perspective as practiced by Jimmy Carter and the
Promotion Perspective as practiced by Ronald Reagan.

Finally, Carter's and Reagan's policies are analyzed in terms of success
or failure. Since the focus of the initial analytical framework is the interaction between the policy and the environment, the analysis of the two
presidents' policies is, in effect, an empirical examination of the general
propositions presented at the outset.

THE ANALYTICAL FRAMEWORK

In comparing the arms transfer policies of Carter and Reagan, one
focus must be on the president himself as the chief foreign-policy decision-
maker. If one tries to determine the extent to which the two presidents were
successful in carrying out their policies, one must first determine what
exactly they wished to achieve.

Within the theoretical framework of this paper, I will refer to the
presidential objectives in promoting a policy as *ideological commitment.* This,
in the area of arms supply, could take various forms: it could be a commitment to promote weapons supply or to restrain it; it could be intense or
weak; it could be central to the president's overall foreign policy or peripheral. What is clear is that ideological commitment, as an important
variable potentially determining the fate of arms transfer, is composite and

complex; it reflects the president's personality and style as well as the priorities of his administration.

The fate of any arms transfer policy is likely to be determined by the interaction between what I term the ideological commitment of the President to such a policy, on the one hand, and the support or opposition of the environment of the policy, on the other hand. The nature of arms supply is such that it is unlikely to end up first on any president's foreign-policy agenda. Arms transfers, after all, rarely determine the very survival of the United States. Yet arms supply as a policy issue is unlikely to rank very low on the national agenda. It is a public issue that signals international commitment on the part of the supplier, and it is sufficiently controversial to receive the attention of the chief executive and his close advisers.

In discussing arms transfers in terms of ideological commitment, the important question is how central the issue is in the eyes of the president, either in itself or as a part of a larger context (such as the competition with the USSR or relations with the Third World). Presidential commitment is essential for policy success. Yet, the success of a policy is obviously not merely a function of its centrality in the eyes of the president. It is also a function of other factors, which, within my theoretical framework, are referred to as the support of the "domestic environment" and the "international environment." Those environments may be supportive of the presidential commitment (whether it is to promote or restrain arms supply), indifferent to the policy proposed by the president, or hostile to it. The intensity of these conditions may also vary significantly.

What I term "domestic" and "international" environments are obviously complicated entities composed of many ingredients. The *domestic environment* relevant for arms supply includes such factors as economic interests supportive of arms production (e.g., arms companies, labor unions) or export (Treasury officials concerned with the trade deficit), internal public opinion (which may oppose arms sales on moral grounds or support them on political grounds), culturally held belief-systems within a society (e.g., the belief that the human rights situation in a would-be recipient country is relevant for a decision on whether arms should be delivered to it). The *international environment,* whose support is relevant for the fate of presidential arms transfer initiatives, is also highly complicated. It includes such components as the international demand for weapons systems, U.S.-USSR regional competition (where arms supply may play a role), the necessity of satisfying clients lest they "go nuclear," and so forth.

In the analytical framework on which this paper is based, then, the dependent variable—the phenomenon we strive to explain—is the success or failure of a particular presidential policy in the field of arms transfer. This success is, hypothetically, determined by the interaction between three independent (or explanatory) variables: (1) the ideological commitment of the president to a policy; (2) the support of the domestic environment; and (3) the support of the international environment.

The key to the strength of this analytical schema is that it takes into account factors related to the personality (and here "commitment" is merely a short-hand term for other personality factors such as style and persuasive powers), elements of the domestic environment, and ingredients of the international system. Attention is given then to at least three significantly different "levels of analysis."[5] Moreover, the analytical framework is based on the assumption that the *interaction* of the three independent variables (the "determinants" of success or failure of a particular arms supply policy) is critical. Thus, the analytical framework leads to the prediction that when the ideological commitment of the president (to whatever policy) is high, the support of the domestic environment is assured but the international environment resists the policy—a case that I call Internationally Opposed Decision-Making—one may expect only mixed results (in terms of success) for the policy. In a case of a presidential commitment running against the opposition of both environments, on the other hand, one can quite safely predict a failure for the presidential policy.

Table 6.1 identifies all possible combinations of the three independent variables, thus creating eight patterns of foreign-policy decision-making.[6] Each pattern has a likely result—in terms of success or failure—also specified in the table. Finally, three kinds of examples are specified for illustrative purposes: (a) examples relating to U.S. arms supply policies, including those on which this paper dwells; (b) examples from U.S. foreign-policy in general; (c) examples from the foreign policies of other nations.

CONFLICTING PERSPECTIVES ON ARMS SUPPLY

On the whole, American policy on arms supply to foreign countries was not a hotly debated issue in the first generation following World War II.[7] As on most issues of foreign policy, consensus tended to prevail. The Vietnam debacle, shattering the overall consensus on American foreign policy, led, albeit not immediately, to the emergence of conflicting perspectives on weapons supply as well.

Fully understanding the implications of Vietnam, the highest echelon of the political leadership in the United States tried to reestablish a measure of agreement on American foreign policy, but with limited success. Both the Nixon and the Ford administrations wanted to create consensus around the policy of Soviet-American détente. Although temporarily successful, détente ran into serious problems by the mid-1970s. During the presidential campaign of 1976, President Ford himself decided to throw off the term détente as "unnecessary, excessive baggage that he could ill afford to carry into the struggle to gain the presidential nomination of his own party."[8]

Jimmy Carter's efforts to recreate foreign-policy unity by deemphasizing the Soviet-American conflict, focusing on human rights, and repairing relations with Third World countries (in such regions as Central America, Africa, and the Middle East) also proved only a short-term, ineffective medicine for healing the breakdown in foreign-policy consensus. Carter was quickly criticized as indecisive and weak on Communism. His human rights campaign was condemned as "a weapon aimed primarily at allies, [a weapon which] tends to weaken their domestic structures."[9] While Carter was quite successful at the beginning—as indicated by movement toward conflict resolution in Central America (Panama) and the Middle East (Egyptian-Israeli relations)—his well-intentioned efforts did not prevail on central issues such as the ratification of the SALT II Treaty and movement toward

Table 6.1. Classification of Foreign Policy
Decision-Making Patterns

DECISION-MAKING DETERMINANTS	DECISION-MAKING PATTERN CONSENSUS DECISION-MAKING (I)	DOMESTICALLY OPPOSED DECISION-MAKING (II)	LEADERSHIP CRUSADE DECISION-MAKING (III)	INTERNATIONALLY OPPOSED DECISION-MAKING (IV)
Leadership Commitment	+	+	+	+
Domestic Support	+	−	−	+
International Support	+	+	−	−
Policy Result (for leadership)	Success	Failure (High Probability)	Failure (High Probability)	Partial Success Possible
Examples				
1. Arms Supply Policy	Nixon-Ford	U.S. to Latin America (1970s)	Carter	Reagan
2. U.S. Foreign Policy	Marshall Plan	U.S. Join League (1919)	Continue Vietnam War	Grenada Invasion
3. Other Countries' Foreign Policy	Germany's Close Relations with U.S.	Shah's Close Relations with U.S.	Israel's Lebanon War	Begin's Foreign Policy

an Israeli-Palestinian reconciliation. Even the human-rights campaign proved useful mainly as a highly publicized assertion of a principle, not as a set of policy guidelines. Moreover, this idealistic campaign, rather than serving as a foreign-policy unifier, further exposed the existing cleavages within American society.

The fate of arms transfer, a well-defined issue on the agenda of American foreign policy, was similar. The publicity given to it by the Carter administration did not foster unity but rather emphasized fundamental differences. In fact, one may look at the issue of arms transfer as reflecting two sharply divided, diametrically opposed perspectives within the American foreign-policy community.

Table 6.2 presents two alternative outlooks on the policy of arms supply as a component of the overall American foreign policy. One outlook is called the *Restraint Perspective,* and it tended to dominate the thinking of most people in the Carter White House. The other outlook is called the *Promotion Perspective,* and it characterized the ideological commitment of Ronald Reagan and his aides.

On the whole, while Restraint tends to reflect a retrenching, dovish foreign policy, Promotion is usually associated with an expansive, hawkish mood. Those who endorse the enlargement of America's obligations abroad, including expanded arms supply to allies and clients, tend to think in terms of the bipolar competition between the superpowers; weapons transfer is perceived merely as one more instrument in a global struggle. Those who recommend restraint in arms supply tend to see moderation in the supply of arms either in purely moralistic terms or, instrumentally, as a means for maintaining stability in Third World regions. While both schools of thought declare stability their goal, for the hawks it is to be achieved through the supply of weapons (helping allies to defend themselves or to deter aggression), while for the doves is to be achieved by refusing to supply weapons (or by reducing their numbers and quality), thus denying adversaries the necessary warmaking capabilities.

The restraint perspective is clearly dominated by the moral impetus of preventing violent conflict: weapons, as instruments of war, are simply considered wrong, if sometimes necessary. Therefore, if anyone, supplier and recipient alike, wants to transfer them, the burden of proof for the necessity of the proposed deal is on him. For the Promotion people arms supply is a normal, even common component of the international scene: it goes along with the business of international politics. Moreover, arms transfers are perceived as a political (and maybe even a moral) obligation of a superpower toward its allies. Although never quite stated in this fashion, the promotion perspective is based on the assumption that the burden of proof is on those who want to block a proposed arms deal.

On the whole, for those who preach restraint, arms supply ought to be practiced as an exceptional act of foreign policy. For those who preach

Table 6.2. Two Alternative Perspectives on Arms Transfer Policy

Trait of Approach	Restraint Perspective	Promotion Perspective
General foreign-policy posture	dovish-isolationist	hawkish-interventionist
Main goal of arms transfer	maintain regional stability in Third World regions	deal with Soviet threat
Focus of foreign-policy	North-South relations	East-West relations
Centrality of arms transfer (within foreign policy)	an exceptional foreign-policy instrument	an essential, indispensable foreign-policy instrument
Approach to arms supply	comprehensive	case-by-case
Burden of proof for a deal	on promoters of the deal	on opponents of the deal
Functions of arms export in promoting economy	nonexistent or peripheral	central (weapons for oil, balance of payment, production efficiency)
Promotion of sales by U.S. agents	unacceptable	acceptable
Unilateral initiatives for control	should be attempted	shouldn't be attempted
Arms transfer talks with allies and adversaries	promoted	not promoted
Supply of sophisticated weapons to Third World nations	unacceptable	acceptable
Third World retransfer of arms	unacceptable	acceptable
Coproductions agreements with Third World nations	unacceptable	acceptable
Development of export weapons	unacceptable	acceptable
Procedures for weapons export	difficult	easy

promotion, however, arms supply is an essential and indispensable instrument of American foreign policy, particularly in the post-Vietnam era: it is perceived as, altogether, a flexible, effective tool that a superpower cannot afford to give up.

The "restrainers" tend to look at the arms supply picture comprehensively. Since their goal is overall reduction in the weapons trade, they highlight the growth of the arms market and the potential dangers to peace it entails. The "promoters," on the other hand, tend to look at each arms supply situation individually, emphasizing its usefulness in solving concrete problems.

The restraint and the promotion perspectives differ also in their approach to the solution of the arms sales dilemma. For the restrainers a unilateral good-will gesture of reducing arms sales is an acceptable U.S. policy, sometimes even a preferred tactic in bringing about a reduction in the international flow of weapons. The promoters see unilateralism as unwise and ineffective. While the restrainers believe that, in some circumstances, allies could be persuaded to join an American initiative for arms supply reduction and even adversaries might be lured (especially the USSR), the promoters tend to doubt that either U.S. allies or adversaries have any interest whatsoever in limiting the international arms traffic.

Similarly, while the party of restraint argues for the imposition of severe limitations on weapons coproduction agreements with allies, the party of promotion emphasizes the advantages of coproduction. While the restrainers tend to limit retransfer of major weapons systems (when American components allow the U.S. to impose such limitations), the promoters tend to relax existing limitations on retransfer. Moreover, while those who support restraint want to ban U.S. representatives abroad from assisting American arms manufacturers in promoting their products, those who support the increase of arms sales do not see any reason for U.S. representatives to refrain from helping American arms companies. On the whole, in the eyes of the promoters the role of the U.S. government is to aid the transfer of weapons as much as possible; this position is rejected, often vehemently, by the restrainers.

Although the restraint and promotion perspectives as described here are merely ideal types—representation of pure forms of what they may or may not be in reality—by and large the Carter administration adopted a policy of restraint, especially at the outset (say, 1977–78), while the Reagan administration adopted a policy of promotion. This is not to say that either policy was in fact successful, but that the highest echelon of the U.S. government, and particularly the president himself, was publicly committed to a well-defined, announced policy. To this policy we now turn.

Carter's Perspective: Restraint Applied[10]

Soon after moving into the White House, Carter issued a directive for a new policy on the transfer of weapons.[11] At the heart of the new policy—a dramatic deviation from past practice—was the position that in the future conventional arms transfer ought to be regarded as an exceptional instrument of foreign policy: arms should be delivered only when it could be demonstrated that the delivery contributed to the national interest of the United States, and the burden of proof in each case ought to be on those who favored the transfer.

Carter's initiative fulfilled his 1976 campaign pledge to curb arms sales. During the campaign Carter asserted that the weapons supply policy of the Nixon and Ford administrations was irresponsible, unwise, and even immoral. Carter accused his predecessors of conducting a policy of indiscriminate arms transfer.

Following the inauguration, Carter quickly issued a directive for a comprehensive review of arms supply policy. The study, known within the government as PRM-12, concluded that security assistance should be linked to the human-rights performance of the receiving government. This conclusion reflected the feeling of many in Congress who questioned the arms supply policy on moral grounds.[12]

Carter's emphasis on restraint ran counter to the Nixon-Ford policy, executed so brilliantly by Henry Kissinger. The new president was trying to redirect U.S. supply policy. By the time Carter was elected, the volume of international arms shipments was increasing by about 20 percent a year, and the level of weapon sophistication even more dramatically. By the mid-1970s, the United States was clearly the leading member of the arms export club. The new president was determined to reverse this trend.

Carter assumed that the blame for what he saw as an uncontrolled system rested with American weapons producers: they were perceived as artificially whetting the appetites of Third World leaders, who would then purchase sophisticated American arms in great quantities. To deal with this problem, at least in part, Carter ordered U.S. representatives abroad to refrain from assisting arms salesmen on visits to foreign countries.[13] This policy complemented the imposition of a series of concrete controls on arms supply: a commitment to limit the total volume of shipments from 1977 to 1978 and, in later years, refusal to initiate advanced weapons supply to any Third World region; a ban on coproduction arrangements and retransfer practices.

The policy of restraint, however, had an Achilles' heel: while it rejected Nixon's (and Ford's) arms transfer policy, it was not implemented within a framework negating the Nixon Doctrine itself.[14] In fact, while accepting the Nixon Doctrine, Carter rejected its natural outgrowth in the area of arms transfer and military assistance.

The Nixon Doctrine provided a way to manage what Henry Brandon characterized as "the retreat of American power,"[15] the reduction of American commitment abroad without the loss of confidence in the U.S. by its allies or the misperception of U.S. intentions by its enemies. The transfer of

Table 6.3. U.S. Arms Transfers, 1965–85: Data From Four Sources*

	SIPRI data: major weapons exports; constant 1975 prices, U.S. $ million	U.S. arms deliveries to the Third World, IRRC calculations, 1985 prices, U.S. $ million	U.S. arms transfers, ACDA data, constant 1983 prices, U.S. $ million		Foreign military sales deliveries, DOD data, U.S. $ million
1965	540	3,710			
1966	514	4,828			
1967	481	4,478			
1968	754	7,074			
1969	1,244	7,275			
1970	1,258	9,003			
1971	1,179	9,859			
1972	1,166	10,752			
1973	1,061	13,843			
1974	1,404	9,278		% Total Exports	
1975	2,343	8,883	18,770	4.5	
1976	3,892	9,819	18,850	5.1	5,313
1977	4,826	11,520	18,690	5.5	6,551
1978	4,727	11,679	20,500	4.5	6,367
1979	2,036	10,381	24,030	3.4	6,538
1980	3,029	7,486	26,720	2.9	5,766
1981	2,585	7,868	26,170	3.7	7,705
1982	2,971	8,891	22,200	4.4	8,815
1983	2,682	11,830	20,050	5.9	11,004
1984	2,069	8,104	21,060	4.7	8,341
1985		6,946	19,940	4.4	8,645

SOURCES: SIPRI Yearbook 1985, *World Armaments and Disarmament* (London, Philadelphia: Taylor and Francis, 1985), table 11A.1, pp. 372–3 (1985); Paul L. Ferrari, Jeffrey W. Knopf, and Raúl L. Madrid, *U.S. Arms Exports: Policies and Contractors* (Washington, D.C.: Investor Responsibility Research Center, 1987), p. 6; United States Arms Control and Disarmament Agency, *World Military Expenditure and Arms Transfer 1986* (Washington, D.C.: U.S. Government Printing Office, 1987), p. 139; DOD, Security and Assistance Agency, *Foreign Military Sales, Foreign Military Construction Sales and Military Assistance Facts* (Washington, D.C.: Data Management Division, Comptroller, DSAA, 1985), pp. 10–11.
*The reason for different estimates is that different studies take different approaches to data collection regarding arms transfer (see Michael Brzoska and Thomas Ohlson, "The Future of Arms Transfer: The Changing Pattern," *Bulletin of Peace Proposal* 16, no. 2 [1985]).

conventional weapons to America's allies and friends served as an instrument for the achievement of Nixon's objective: withdrawal of formal presence in foreign countries while still assuring allies and friends that America would continue to provide for their defense. In short, U.S. conventional weapons were perceived as a substitute for an American physical presence abroad.

Trends in American military assistance reflected the role of arms transfer in the thinking of the Nixon (and later the Ford) administration. The dollar volume of U.S. arms transfers to Third World countries rose dramatically in the early 1970s, reaching almost $14 billion in 1974 alone; by 1976, U.S. arms exports exceeded, for the first time ever, 5 percent of America's total annual exports. Table 6.3 contains quantitative evidence of the trend.

During the Nixon-Ford years (1969–76) the United States not only increased the total volume of its supply but changed the overall character of its military assistance. First, a growing emphasis on military sales rather than grant assistance became evident. During the period 1967–76 the Military Assistance Program (grant aid) amounted to about $800 million per year; it dropped to $200 million in 1976. Sales, on the other hand, multiplied eightfold over a ten-year period (1967–76), from just over $1 billion in 1967 to more than $8 billion in 1976. The dramatic growth in sales began in 1971 and peaked in 1974 with large orders from Israel, Iran, Saudi Arabia, and the NATO countries amounting to $10.6 billion.[16]

Second, the proliferation of extremely sophisticated weapons became common. The obsolete equipment that characterized arms transfers in the 1950s and 1960s was replaced in the 1970s and 1980s by state-of-the-art technology.[17]

The increase in dollar volume of arms shipments, the trend toward sales and away from grants, and the ever-increasing sophistication of the equipment transferred enabled the United States to decouple the direct linkage with allies and friends. The new pattern of arms transfers, in its totality, added to the overall capability of the recipients to defend themselves without direct American assistance or intervention; thus it strongly supported the Nixon Doctrine.

The Carter administration never rejected the overall objective of the Nixon Doctrine, namely, defending U.S. allies by means other than direct intervention. In fact, Carter was even less interventionist in his overall approach than either Nixon or Ford. Nevertheless, the arms transfer policy was perceived by the new president as excessive, dangerous, and immoral. Carter, reflecting an idealistic tilt in his approach to foreign policy in general, saw the existing arms supply policy as fundamentally un-American.

Carter's moralistic attitude toward arms supply was based on four assumptions. First, the president believed that the United States had a special, unique responsibility to restrain the world trade in conventional arms, if necessary even by adopting a unilateralist approach. Like many other Americans, Carter believed that America was fundamentally different from the rest of the world because of the uniqueness of its historical and political experience. American exceptionalism, to him, meant special responsibilities in the field of arms supply as elsewhere.

A second assumption (more implicit than the first one) on the part of President Carter was that the United States had an obligation, a mission of sorts, to educate the rest of the world in its different, better ways. The president believed that if other nations understood what the United States was trying to accomplish in its policy of weapons restraint, they would surely follow its example. As in the human-rights campaign, Carter's initiative in the area of arms supply had a pronounced missionary zeal.

Thirdly, the Carter policy reflected the assumption that every problem has a solution, if only good will and rationality are applied to it in large doses. In short, Carter's policy reflected traditional American optimism. What it lacked in historical realism it possessed, in abundance, in zestful hope.

A final assumption of the Carter initiative was that conventional weapons transfers were necessarily destabilizing, at least in most of the world's regions. This assumption was not based on a carefully conducted empirical study of world realities; it was, primarily, culturally based. The assumption was that arms and conflict are linked—the accumulation of the former leads to the latter—and that, in general, force and diplomacy are mutually exclusive instruments of foreign policy. If one supplies weapons, one is preparing for war rather than seeking diplomatic solutions for world problems.

The outgrowth of this set of unexamined assumptions was that the U.S. should deliver weapons only as an exceptional act and that, in any event, it must pursue diplomacy rather than arms sales as a means for the achievement of its foreign policy goals.

The ultimate failure of the Carter initiative reflected in a painful manner the problematical nature of its assumptions. The unilateral willingness of the United States to restrict its arms shipments to other nations failed to impress not only America's adversaries but even its friends. The missionary zeal and the zestful hope for a better world remained, by and large, unanswered. The President himself found out that arms supply could supplement diplomacy rather than contradict it,[18] and that often it could guarantee stability rather than undermine it.

Reagan's Perspective: Promotion Applied

As in many other areas of both domestic and foreign policy, in the field of arms transfers Ronald Reagan adopted a position that "has been nearly a polar opposite to that of the Carter White House."[19] Although the shipment of weapons was not a major issue in the 1980 presidential election, Reagan's position toward the use of weapons transfer as a major foreign policy tool was known to be affirmative.

The change of policy, from Carter's to Reagan's, became apparent in the earliest days of the new administration.[20] Within a few months Reagan terminated most of Carter's reforms, so carefully designed to curb arms transfers. First, Reagan declared that arms supply ought to be looked at not only as a legitimate foreign-policy instrument but even as "an indispensable component" of U.S. foreign policy. Second, the annual arms transfer ceiling (publicly declared by President Carter in 1977) was eliminated, in effect opening the gate to unlimited supply (which, as will be shortly explained, never materialized). Third, the Reagan administration declared that proposals for the development of intermediate-capability weapons solely for export, which Carter defined as unacceptable, deserved "careful consideration." Fourth, it was announced that overseas governmental officials "will be expected to provide the same courtesies and assistance to firms that have obtained licenses to market items on the United States Munitions List as they would to those marketing other American products."

Reagan's arrival at the White House changed the armament supply picture overnight, although the liberalization of Carter's initially stiff controls had begun even before the departure of the Democratic president. The Reagan administration let it be known that human-rights violations had been dropped as an impediment to arms transfers. The deviation from the existing policy was so sharp that *Aviation Week and Space Technology* editorialized: "The Reagan guidelines are more a repeal of Carter human-rights doctrinairism than the adoption of a new policy."[21]

Although this interpretation could and should be challenged, there can be no question that Reagan's position rested on negating all that Carter had been trying to do in the area of arms transfer. In contrast with Carter, who looked for means for reducing the flow of U.S. weapons abroad, Reagan was committed to allow this flow unabated. One Reagan administration official expressed the new position succinctly and colloquially: "We can't sign treaties any more, we can't deploy forces abroad—so how the hell else do you do it?"[22] The "it" was, in Reagan's mind, the defense of U.S. allies against the Russians, and the answer to the question was obvious: you do "it" by massive arms shipments.

The promotion perspective led the new administration not only to drop all of Carter's controls but also to create incentives for the generation of more arms shipments. The administration sought to ease the credit terms to some foreign countries, especially in view of the debt crisis faced by many in the Third World. The financial procedures regulating foreign military sales were revised, enabling more countries to purchase weapons with FMS credits at below-market interest rates. Moreover, the list of nations eligible for "concessional" repayment arrangements was expanded: in addition to

Israel, it now included Egypt, Greece, Somalia, Sudan and Turkey. According to the terms of this arrangement, these countries became entitled to a
10-year grace period on loans for financing their arms purchases, followed
by a 20-year repayment period.

The Reagan administration also reversed the trend toward complete
elimination of grant aid as a means for facilitating arms purchases, In fact, in
its first four years (1981–85), the administration increased military assistance
grants from $250 million to $700 million.[23] In his first appearance before
Congress, Secretary ,of State Haig said that the administration would request a 30-percent increase in the grant military assistance for fiscal year
1981.

To ease further the supply of weapons, the administration also created a
Special Defense Acquisition Fund. The Fund was designed to enable the
Pentagon "to purchase military equipment in anticipation of future arms
sales agreements,"[24] and thus reduce the time-lags between orders of weapons and their deliveries.

The underlying rationale behind the new policy on arms supply was
twofold: (a) it reflected a new policy of global interventionism on the part of
an invigorated imperial presidency, led by a president fully subscribing to
the assumptions of the Cold War era;[25] (b) it also reflected a new determination to engage in a vigorous global competition with the USSR, a determination that formed the ideological center of Reagan's foreign policy.
While the Carter administration viewed arms transfer mainly within a
North-South context, emphasizing the instability that unrestrained arms
supply may bring, the Reagan administration looked at it in an East-West
context, attempting to strengthen U.S. allies in the Third World against
their Soviet-supported rivals.

Paul Hammond and his associates wrote in *The Reluctant Supplier:*

> It is quite clear that the assumptions of President Reagan and his key advisors
> about the contribution of military power to the maintenance of peace are
> different from the assumptions held by President Carter and those who initially
> guided the foreign policy of his administration. Principally, the Reagan admin-
> istration appears to be committed to the military containment of the Soviet
> Union as a major foreign-policy objective and the President has often expressed
> a determination to strengthen America's allies militarily and to increase U.S.
> military presence throughout the world.[26]

The Reagan administration was convinced that Carter's restraint policy
had undermined U.S. political influence and the credibility of its international commitments. Former Senator James Buckley, who was put in charge
of Reagan's new arms supply policy as under secretary of state for security
assistance, science, and technology, argued that the Carter position undercut "the capabilities of strategically located nations in whose ability to
defend themselves we have the most immediate and urgent self-interest."[27]

Of course, the Reagan policy attracted critics. Some of these "likened it to throwing open the doors of a candy store to children who can buy as many sweets as they want as long as they pay."[28] Reagan's detractors worried about the instability that an unrestrained policy would produce.

Nevertheless, as early as 1981, some analysts suspected that "in practice, the Reagan arms transfer policy may prove to be less distinct from the Carter policy than the two policy statements [of the two presidents] would indicate."[29] As the discussion of the results of the policies indicates (see below, pp. 148–52, this judgment proved, on the whole, quite correct. Although starting from a very different assumption about the world, and with different intentions regarding arms supply policy, Carter's and Reagan's policies were much closer than their ideologically expressed formulas would have indicated. The ideals of restraint and promotion, in their pure forms, proved in reality too dangerous to pursue. The distance separating intentions and reality, ideology and policy, was too great to bridge in both cases.

After the election of Ronald Reagan, especially in the first few years of his presidency, there was a new enthusiasm for arms supply, something of a return to the policy of the years 1973–76. This enthusiasm was evident in both the administration's top echelon and throughout Washington's "political class" (even beyond the administration). A genuine effort was made to offer attractive financial arrangements to potential buyers, and even the oversight of the legislative branch over the arms supply policy began to loosen up. At the urging of the new administration, Congress relaxed the requirements for administration reports regarding arms sales to members of NATO and ANZUS and to Japan. The objective was to "eliminate all opportunities for Congressional review and veto of weapons sales to close allies."[30] Reflecting similar thinking, the required pre-sale notification period was reduced from thirty to fifteen days, making the chances of effective Congressional opposition to any proposed arms deal even lower than before. In 1981 Congress also agreed to raise the threshold for required notification for major defense packages from $25 million to $50 million, while the notification for major weapons systems was raised from $7 million to $14 million.[31]

On January 1, 1985, the International Traffic in Arms Regulations (ITAR) were revised by the Department of State.[32] The new regulations called for "a relaxation and partial elimination"[33] of the duty of Americans to obtain State Department approval prior to making an arms sale proposal abroad, an approval that was clearly required under Carter's ITAR regulations.

In general, during his first four years in office Reagan was able to get surprising support from Congress for his arms transfer policy. Although Congress declined to approve sales to countries such as Argentina and Chile because of human-rights violations, the Clark Amendment, barring aid to antigovernment forces in Angola, was repealed in 1985. In general, Congress followed Reagan's lead in approving aid to anti-Communist forces (Afghanistan, Cambodia, Nicaragua).

Nevertheless, it seems that Congress's willingness to go along with the arms supply policy of the President may have come to an abrupt end with the 1987 revelations about the administration's involvement in clandestine weapons shipments to Iran, linked to the supply of funds and weapons to the contra rebels in Nicaragua. As a result of the complicated Iran/contra affair, the administration's arms export policy came under intense scrutiny and attack.

Although the president's involvement in some sensitive aspects of the affair (such as the diversion of funds to the contras) has not been and probably never will be established, it is clear that the arms-for-hostages deal with the Iranians and the clandestine assistance to the Nicaraguan rebels were masterminded at the highest echelons of the Central Intelligence Agency and executed by personnel within the National Security Council.

POLICY RESULTS

An examination of the results of Carter's and Reagan's arms supply policies reveals the limits of any President's effectiveness in promoting his policy objectives in an unfriendly environment. Carter's policy had, at best, mixed results, despite his overwhelming personal commitment to the reduction of American and global arms transfers. Reagan fared only somewhat better.

To be sure, an examination of Carter's policy at the outset of his administration reveals impressive activity. An elaborate machinery of control was put in place, and in the first fifteen months of the newly announced policy of restraint as many as 614 requests for weapons, submitted by ninety-two countries for a total of more than $1 billion, were turned down in a determined effort to turn the arms export tide.[34]

Nevertheless, the overall arms transfer policy of the Carter administration failed. During its last year (1980), the administration approved the transfer of equipment estimated at close to $27 billion, a record. In the fiscal years 1978–81, for which the administration bore responsibility, the United States supplied foreign countries with equipment valued at the staggering figure of more than $97 billion.[35]

Ferrari and his associates concluded that "the announced ceiling on arms transfer turned out in practice to be relatively ineffective."[36] Although Carter reduced sales to countries subject to his controls, namely the nations of the Third World, the overall arms exports of the United States did not drop. In 1977 arms sales to nonexempt countries amounted to $9.3 billion. They fell to $8.55 billion in 1978 and $8.43 billion in 1979, maintaining the 8 percent lower level for two consecutive years. Yet sales to the eighteen nations exempt from the controls (members of NATO and ANZUS, and Japan), and sales of services and construction to all nations (not included in the ceiling imposed by the President) offset the decline in arms transfers to nonexempt nations. In fact, according to some calculations, arms transfers climbed from $12.8 billion (in 1977) to $17.1 billion (in 1980) during Carter's tenure in the White House.

A more detailed analysis could easily reveal some of the reasons for the poor results. The failure did not stem from lack of presidential commitment but from the conditions of the international system and from the reluctance of the environment to support the president's efforts.

Most importantly, within a short period after the inauguration, the Carter White House found out that its policies ran against other demands of the international system, demands judged more important than "transfer control" by the administration itself. For example, in 1978 Carter agreed to sell three Middle Eastern states two hundred aircraft valued at $4.8 billion; about the same time, the U.S. committed itself to the supply of no less than seven AWACS (Airborne Warning and Control Systems) to Iran. The requirements of diplomacy in the Middle East took priority over the overall presidential commitment to reduce arms supply to foreign countries.

The problem of actually implementing the restraint perspective was highlighted particularly in the context of Carter's commitment to human rights, an ideologically based commitment similar to the one he had toward arms supply. Though the Carter administration announced its intention to refuse weapons to human-rights violators, its policy was never applied systematically. Stohl, Carleton, and Johnson concluded that "the Carter administration did not implement a policy of human rights which actually guided the disposition of military and economic assistance."[37] Human-rights violators that were strategically important (Iran, the Philippines, South Korea, Zaire) received weapons in abundance, while human rights violators that were strategically less important did not. In short, the strategic environment overcame the presidential commitment in determining the flow of American weapons.

Carter's inclination to link arms sales and human-rights performance backfired both domestically and internationally, demonstrating the reluctance of both internal and external environments to accept such a link. First, the inconsistency of the application of the policy antagonized many members of Congress. Second, some countries saw the human-rights emphasis as a new interventionist policy on the part of the United States. They then refused to accept any U.S. military assistance (Argentina, Brazil, El Salvador, Guatemala, Uruguay), causing long-term damage to U.S. interests.

Above all, the environment taught Jimmy Carter, who arrived at the White House with an almost religious zeal to curb arms supply, that the transfer of weapons was politically "too useful for too many purposes to be extensively curtailed."[38] Resistance to any significant change from practically any important producer/supplier on the international scene was evident. Quiet discussions with America's European allies, increasingly relying on arms exports, revealed that the big suppliers—Britain, France, Italy and others—were uninterested in pursuing the control initiative announced by the Americans.

Meetings with representatives of the Soviet Union were, surprisingly, more encouraging. Between December 1977 and December 1978 American and Soviet delegations convened on four different occasions to deal with arms supply under the umbrella of what became known as CATT, the Conventional Arms Transfer Talks. Yet the last and decisive discussion, the meeting in Mexico City in late 1978, ended in failure. First, the increasing mistrust among the superpowers in the late 1970s had a chilling effect on the talks. Second, internal disagreement within the Carter administration itself was harmful. The State Department adopted a conciliatory position, the NSC did not, and the line of the latter finally prevailed. Third, by making unilateral moves on conventional arms control, Carter undermined his own effort to produce a more conciliatory Soviet approach. Some analysts felt that the Russians had already got what they wanted, namely, American restraint.

Thus, Carter failed in his attempt to produce an arms transfer control system in which all large producers/suppliers would take part, something akin to the nuclear nonproliferation regime. The American initiative to elicit an international response simply did not work. As the unilateral effort became weaker (due to inconsistent application and demonstration of the damage it caused to U.S. interests) the efforts of the United States to convince others to join it in conventional arms control became increasingly less credible. The collapse of CATT signaled the beginning of the end of an effective policy of global restraint.

The results of the arms supply policy pursued by Ronald Reagan have also been mixed, although Reagan arrived at the White House determined to reverse the Carter initiative. Reagan's position on arms transfers initially caused concern among many who believed that the President would open the gates for a totally unrestrained flow of arms. But an examination of the results of Reagan's policy reveals more similarity to the results of Carter's policy than one would have expected.

At the onset the new administration seemed poised to release a flood of U.S. military equipment, shipped without discrimination to all who wanted it. In his first three months in office, Reagan promised foreign buyers military equipment and services valued at $15 billion.[39] A number of weapons requests that had been either delayed or disapproved by the Carter administration were quickly approved. Some of these were truly controversial: a sale of F-16s to Pakistan, despite its well-publicized effort to gain nuclear capability; a promise of F-16s to Venezuela, reversing a longstand ing, pre-Carter American policy not to sell supersonic aircraft to Latin American countries; an approval of the export of the Israeli Kfir jet, equipped with an American engine, to other countries; shipments of weapons to Jordan and Morocco; and others. According to Ferrari and associates, a dramatic increase in arms supply occurred in 1981 and 1982.[40]

Nevertheless, in its totality, Reagan's policy has not been so different from the Carter policy as might be expected from listening to the rhetoric of the two presidents. While the Carter administration did not really cut U.S. military supplies drastically, the Reagan administration did not really increase them drastically. In fact, after 1982 the arms supply of the United States declined quite consistently.

A number of factors explain the mixed results of Reagan's arms supply policy. First, to a large extent, by the early 1980s the weapons market had become saturated following the purchasing "extravaganza" of the 1970s. Second, many countries, particularly in the Third World, ran into growing economic difficulties in financing their purchasing plans: the economic recession of the early 1980s, the scarcity of hard currency funds and credits, indebtedness, high interest rates, negative balance of trade, and the strong position of the U.S. dollar made the acquisition of American weapons nearly impossible for some nations. Third, the growing indigenous military production in Third World countries cut into the market share of external suppliers, including the United States.[41] Fourth, the decreasing revenues of oil exporters eliminated from the market the single most important determinant of recipient purchasing capability. Those who could afford, in the 1970s, any weapon system, regardless of sophistication and price, now became much more conscious of cost. Fifth, the increasingly aggressive sales policy of some West European suppliers also cut into the market share of the U.S. (and, incidentally, that of the USSR). Sixth, continuing Congressional opposition to a "wild" transfer policy also helped to restrain the initial Reagan reversal of policy, and this opposition was assisted by other domestic forces worried about uncontrolled military assistance. Some industrialists opposed coproduction arrangements; Treasury officials felt uneasy about the growing cost of foreign aid for military purposes (a feeling shared by many in Congress); the armed forces opposed the exportation of top-line military equipment; the human-rights lobby continued to press for a moral stance.[42] On some occasions, Reagan administration officials declined requests because of their potential political damage—for example, Taiwan was refused the Northrop F-20s, Honduras the F-5s.

On the whole, it is evident that the decline in U.S. arms supply did not result from a decision by the president to pursue his promotion policy less vigorously. Rather, the environmental, systemic conditions enumerated above caused the decline. In effect, the international system forced moderation on Reagan's weapons promotion instincts, just as it forced severe limitations on Carter's restraint initiative.

According to Brzoska and Ohlson, the annual growth in the volume of deliveries of major conventional weapons in the 1970s amounted to about 15 percent, "largely due to the increased purchasing power of many countries in the Third World (especially oil producers) and to conflicts in the Middle East."[43] In other words, this growth was not a function of personal commitment to promote weapons, nor was it curtailed by personal commitment to restrain weapons supply. Only in the early 1980s did the weapons market diminish, again despite the effort of an American president to reverse the trend. The decline of U.S. sales was even more dramatic than that of the market as a whole.

While the weapons market of the 1960s tended to be hegemonic and sometimes oligopolistic, in the 1970s a more commercial market developed, characterized by an increasing number of suppliers and fierce competition. By the 1980s the market had become truly polypolistic,[44] controlled by economic rather than political interests and peopled by a larger number of suppliers and recipients. The growing number of producers/suppliers made the market increasingly competitive; yet due to the economic factors mentioned above, in the mid-1980s the world weapons market shrank.

In a market affected by global reduction in demand and, simultaneously, growing competition between producers—a buyer's market—no leader of a producer/supplier nation could hope to exercise control. Hence, in coming years, we are unlikely to see a reversal of the phenomenon described in this paper, a situation in which the personal commitment of the president could prevail over environmental preferences.

This study demonstrates the power of reality when it collides with vision, and the power of the environment when it clashes with ideology. Although no one may doubt Carter's commitment to weapons restraint, nor his dogged effort to implement such restraint, weapons supply remained an essential instrument of American foreign policy during and after his tenure in office as it had been before. Although Reagan's determination to promote American arms abroad as a barrier to Soviet expansion also cannot be denied, his promotion perspective had only short-lived success. Both presidents' policies were defeated by unfriendly environments, which in the first case dictated promotion and in the second restraint.

NOTES

1. Paul L. Ferrari, Jeffrey W. Knopf, and Raúl L. Madrid, *U.S. Arms Exports: Policies and Contractors* (Washington, D.C.: Investor Responsibility Research Center, 1987), p. 6. The figures quoted are in 1985 constant prices and are based on the data published annually by the Department of Defense's Defense Security Assistance Agency.

2. Anne H. Cahn, "Have Arms, Will Sell," *Arms Control Today* 4, no. 10, (October 1974): 1–3.

3. The restraint policy of President Carter was, in principle, a general and global policy. In practice, however, it was not applied to countries belonging to NATO and ANZUS, nor to Japan, nations that were exempt from practically all the policy's restraints.

4. For Reagan's policy, see "U.S. Arms Sales, Administration Outlook Policy," *Facts on File*, 41, July 10, 1981, p. 472.

5. J. David Singer, "The Level-of-Analysis Problem in International Relations," in *The International System: Theoretical Essays,* ed. Klaus Knorr and Sidney Verba (Princeton: Princeton University Press, 1961), pp. 77–92.

6. For a somewhat similar methodology, see Charles Hermann, "International Crisis as a Situational Variable," in *International Politics and Foreign Policy: A Reader in Research and Theory,* ed. James N. Rosenau (New York: Free Press, 1969), pp. 409–21.

7. Interestingly enough, there was a serious debate, with significant moralistic overtones, over this issue during the 1930s.

8. Ole R. Holsti, "The Three-Headed Eagle: The United States and System Change," *International Studies Quarterly* 23, no. 3 (September 1979): 382.

9. Henry Kissinger, "Straight Talk from Henry Kissinger," *Newsweek,* Dec. 11, 1978.

10. Parts of this section are based on Linda P. Brady and Ilan Peleg, "Carter's Policy on the Supply of Conventional Weapons: Cultural Designs and Diplomatic Consequences," *Crossroads* 5 (Winter 1980): 41–68.

11. Office of the Federal Register, *Weekly Compilation of Presidential Documents, Administration of Jimmy Carter* 13, May 19, 1977.

12. David J. Loucher and Michael D. Salomon, "Conflicting Trends for Arms Transfer Restraint," *Naval War College Review* 33, no. 6 (1980): 82–88.

13. United States House of Representatives, Committee on International Relations, *Conventional Arms Transfer Policy,* 95th Congress, 2nd session, Feb. 1, 1978, p. 43.

14. See Robert Jefferson Wood, "Military Assistance and Doctrine," *Orbis* 15 (Spring 1971): 247–74.

15. Henry Brandon, *The Retreat of American Power* (New York: Dell, 1972).

16. NSC-202, p. 6.

17. Anne H. Cahn and Joseph J. Kruzel, "Arms Trade in the 1980s," in *Controlling Future Arms Trade,* ed. Anne H. Kahn, et al. (New York: McGraw-Hill, 1977), p. 31.

18. As in the generous arms deal with both Israel and Egypt following, and as part of, the Camp David peace conference.

19. Ferrari, *U.S. Arms Exports,* p. 29.

20. The most authoritative declaration of Reagan's new policy was the president's statement of July 8, 1981. See the source cited in note 4.

21. H. Gregory, "Controlling Military Sales," *Aviation Week and Space Technology,* June 29, 1981, p. 11.

22. "Arming America's Friends," *Newsweek,* March 23, 1981, p. 33.

23. Ferrari et al., *U.S. Arms Exports,* p. 33, quoting data from the Defense Security Assistance Agency, *FMS and MAP Facts 1985.*

24. Ibid.

25. See Ted Galen Carpenter, "Global Interventionism and a New Imperial Presidency," Cato Institute *Policy Analysis* 71, May 16, 1986.

26. Paul Hammond et al., *The Reluctant Supplier: U.S. Decision-Making for Arms Sales* (Cambridge, Mass.: Oelgeschlager, Gunn, and Hain, 1983), p. 54.

27. An address before the meeting of the Board of Governors, Aerospace Industries Associations, Williamsburg, Va., May 21, 1981.

28. Michael Moodie, "Arms Transfer Policy: A National Dilemma," *Washington Quarterly* (Spring 1982): 109.

29. Congressional Research Service, *Changing Perspectives on U.S. Arms Transfer Policy* (Washington, D.C.: U.S. Government Printing Office, 1981), pp. 95–99.

30. Ferrari, *U.S. Arms Exports,* p. 34.

31. Arms Export Control Act, Section 47, 22 U.S.C., 2794, note.

32. See Joseph P. Smaldone, "U.S. Commercial Arms Exports: Policy, Process, and Patterns," in *Marketing Security Assistance: New Perspectives on Arms Sales,* ed. David Loucher and Michael Solomone (Lexington, Ky.: Lexington Books, 1987), pp. 185–208, and Eric L. Hirshhorn, "The Revised Arms Export Control Regulations," *International Lawyer* 19, no. 2 (Spring 1985): 675–87.

33. Smaldone, "U.S. Commercial Arms Exports," p. 197.

34. See Andrew Pierre, *The Global Politics of Arms Sales* (Princeton, N.J.: Princeton University Press, 1982), p. 55; also Congressional Research Service, *Changing Perspectives,* p. 30.

35. See Table 3.

36. Ferrari, *U.S. Arms Exports,* p. 26.

37. Michael S. Stohl, David C. Carleton, and Steven E. Johnson, "Human Rights and U.S. Foreign Asssistance from Nixon to Carter," *Journal of Peace Research* 21, no. 3 (1984): 1.

38. Hammond et al., *The Reluctant Supplier,* p. 194.

39. Pierre, *The Global Politics of Arms Sales,* p. 65.

40. Ferrari, *U.S. Arms Exports,* p. 31. Table 3 does not reflect this increase.

41. See Ilan Peleg, "Military Production in Third World Countries: A Political Study," in *Threats, Weapons, and Foreign Policy,* ed. Pat McGowan and Charles W. Kegley, Jr., Sage International Yearbook 5, 1980 (Beverly Hills, Calif.: 1980), pp. 209–30.

42. See Hammond et al., *The Reluctant Supplier,* p. 54.

43. Michael Brzoska and Thomas Ohlson, "The Future of Arms Transfer: The Changing Pattern," *Bulletin of Peace Proposal* 16, no. 2 (1985): 129.

44. Ibid., p. 132.

7

Contributions to Federal Election Campaigns by Government Contractors

FRANK R. LICHTENBERG

INTRODUCTION

In the pure neoclassical theory of the firm, product demand and production cost schedules are assumed to be strictly exogenous to the firm. Economists recognize, however, that in the real world firms may be able to influence demand and cost conditions by making certain types of expenditures. Two categories of expenditure often hypothesized to influence demand and/or cost are advertising expenditure and research and development (R&D) expenditure. Many models of advertising expenditure determination are predicated on the assumption that the quantity of a firm's product demanded at a given price is an increasing function of the firm's (current and perhaps past) advertising expenditure. At least part of firms' expenditure on product-oriented R&D investment (which accounts for about three-fourths of total R&D investment) may also be aimed at stimulating consumer demand. Process-oriented R&D, on the other hand, is presumably undertaken in order to reduce costs of production at given factor prices.

In this paper, I investigate the hypothesis that corporate expenditures to sponsor political action committees (PACs) constitute an additional category of expenditure undertaken to increase product demand and/or reduce production costs. It is widely recognized that the cost and/or demand conditions faced by the typical modern American corporation are affected in a large number of ways by federal government policies. Environmental, minimum wage, and health and safety regulations clearly influence firms' costs of production. Certain types of industry regulation may erect or

I am grateful to the MacArthur Foundation Faculty Research Program at Columbia University for financial support. Donald Siegel provided capable research assistance. I am responsible for any errors.

maintain barriers to entry to an industry, thus increasing demand for incumbent firms' products; deregulation may have the opposite effect. Antitrust and international trade policies may also influence the firm's economic environment in crucial respects. Another Federal policy that affects product demand (and whose impact on specific firms our data enable us to measure) is procurement. Defense contracts account for over three-fourths of the total value of government procurement (Federal Procurement Data Center [1987, p. 2]).

Because firms' cost and demand schedules are affected by government policies, benefits may potentially be realized from influencing government policies. We hypothesize that sponsorship of a political action committee is a means for influencing these policies. The primary purpose of a corporate PAC is to accumulate funds that will be used to make contributions to, or expenditures on behalf of, candidates in federal election campaigns. The Federal Elections Campaign Act (FECA) prohibits the contribution of a corporation's own treasury funds to a PAC. Corporate funds and resources may be used, however, to establish and operate the PAC, and to solicit contributions from certain corporate employees and shareholders.[1]

The objective of this paper is to develop and estimate a model that accounts for whether or not a firm is a PAC sponsor and, if it is, for how much revenue its PAC will raise and distribute to candidates. The model is based on the assumption that firms can influence government policies that affect their costs and/or demand (hence profits) by making contributions to candidates. There are, in principle, several ways in which contributing could influence policy. First, it could influence which candidates are elected. This could happen, for example, if there were two candidates for an office holding opposite and immutable positions on an issue of concern to the firm, and their relative probabilities of being elected were a function of their relative amounts of contributions received. A second possibility is that candidates' positions on issues are not immutable, and in fact can be shifted in a direction favorable to the firm by the firm's contributions. In other words, candidates are willing to change their positions if it will increase their chances of being elected, which a higher level of contributions will do. A third possibility is that contributions purchase what Fiorina and Noll (1978) call "facilitation services." As those authors note, many policy decisions that affect the welfare of firms (and consumers) are made in administrative agencies (such as the Department of Defense) rather than in the legislature. In order to effectively influence "bureaucratic" decision-making in these agencies, firms may need to secure the assistance of (incumbent) congressmen, which the latter are willing to provide in exchange for campaign contributions.

While it is plausible (and perhaps popularly accepted) that contributions can influence policy in one or more of the ways described, we must acknowledge that available evidence does not provide much support for any of these potential channels of influence of contributions on policy outcomes. Most contributions are to incumbents, and econometric studies by Jacobson (1978) suggest that campaign expenditures by incumbents have little if any effect on their probability of reelection. Moreover, even if total expenditure by a candidate did affect his election probability, the contribution by a single firm to the candidate would be unlikely to be large enough materially to affect the outcome. Due to this free rider problem, the probability of changing the electoral outcome is unlikely to motivate firms to contribute.

With regard to the hypothesis that contributions cause candidates to alter their positions, Chappell (1982) has shown that although legislators receiving contributions from an interest group tend to vote on key bills in the way the group would prefer, their voting behavior is *not* caused by having received contributions. Rather, interest groups are inclined to contribute to legislators having ideologies with which they agree; it is the legislator's ideology that "causes" both his voting behavior and the amount of contributions he receives from interest groups.[2]

As to the third possible means by which contributions might affect policy—via the purchase of facilitation services—Fox (1974) provides anecdotal evidence that congressmen attempt to intervene on behalf of defense contractors (who, however, are not necessarily contributors to these congressmen) in decision-making by DOD procurement officials about the award and cancellation of defense contracts. He concludes, however, that these attempts to intervene generally have a negligible impact on these decisions.

Despite the paucity of convincing evidence that firms can influence government policy by making contributions to candidates in federal elections, in the next section we formulate a simple theoretical model of PAC formation and activity based on this assumption. This model provides a framework for understanding why some, but not all, firms sponsor PACs, and for explaining the effect of various firm characteristics on PAC size. The construction of a data base suitable for estimating the equations implied by the theory is then documented. The data base contains information about a sample of 226 firms which had some government contracts and were observed during both the 1979–80 and 1981–82 federal election cycles. Empirical results are then presented, followed by a summary and concluding remarks.

A THEORETICAL MODEL OF PAC SPONSORSHIP AND SIZE

In this section we specify a model that determines whether or not a firm will sponsor a PAC and, if so, how large (measured in terms of total receipts) the PAC will be. Because the principal objective of PACs is to contribute funds to candidates in federal elections, the decision to sponsor a

PAC may be regarded as a decision to "produce" contributions to the PAC. Sponsoring the PAC enables the firm to enter the "campaign-contributions industry." The problem facing the firm is, does it want to enter this industry and, if so, how much "output" (what level of PAC receipts) does it want to produce? We postulate that there are both cost and demand (average revenue) schedules for PAC receipts. The firm will choose to enter the campaign-contributions industry only if there is some level of receipts at which total expected revenue exceeds total cost. If this condition is satisfied, the firm will set receipts such that marginal revenue equals marginal cost. We develop the model as follows. First, we specify and discuss a PAC-receipts cost function. Next, we do the same for the demand function. We then derive the conditions for equilibrium PAC formation and size. Finally, we perform comparative-statics analysis, which indicates the effect of variation in cost and demand parameters (hypothesized to be due to variation in firm characteristics) on PAC formation and size.

We assume that the long-run PAC-receipts cost function is quadratic:

$$(7.1) \qquad C(R) = c_0 + c_1 R + \tfrac{1}{2} c_2 R^2 \qquad c_0, c_1, c_2 > 0$$

The above specification embodies two substantive assumptions: that there are costs of sponsoring a PAC (c_0) that are independent of the level of receipts collected, and that the marginal cost of acquiring receipts is increasing. Included in c_0 are the costs of registering and filing periodic financial statements with the Federal Elections Commission and holding meetings of PAC committee members to determine PAC policies (e.g., to which candidates funds will be contributed). The hypothesis that an activity is subject to increasing marginal costs is usually due to the presence of a fixed factor. In this case, the fixed factor is the size (or income) of the group of individuals that the PAC is permitted to solicit. Data presented by Handler and Mulkern (1982) about PAC solicitation strategies are consistent with the increasing marginal costs hypothesis. They note that the majority of PACs do not solicit contributions from all of their sponsor's exempt (from collective bargaining agreement) employees: 14 percent of PACs solicit only their highest company officers, and an additional 47 percent also solicit middle-management employees (but not other exempts). Their data indicate that as the group that is solicited expands to include employees lower in the corporate hierarchy, both the fraction of those solicited contributing and the average contribution per contributor decline. Thus, even if the marginal cost of soliciting an employee is constant or slightly declining with respect to number of employees solicited, these data suggest that the marginal cost of acquiring receipts is increasing.

We consider next the "demand" for, or average revenue generated by, receipts. The collection of receipts enables the PAC to contribute to, or make expenditures on behalf of, candidates in federal elections. We assume that making such contributions increases the firm's expected profits (or reduces its expected losses) by increasing the probability that federal policies that increase the demand for or reduce the cost of producing the firm's conventional output will be adopted. We assume that the average increase in expected profits produced by making contributions declines with successive increases in PAC receipts (or contributions). It is convenient to postulate that the "demand" for receipts is linear:

$$(7.2) \qquad D(R) = d_1 - \tfrac{1}{2}d_2 R \qquad d_1, d_2 > 0, d_1 > c_1$$

This, of course, implies that the total and marginal revenue functions are quadratic and linear, respectively:[3]

$$T(R) = R \cdot D(R) = d_1 R - \tfrac{1}{2}d_2 R^2$$
$$T'(R) = d_1 - d_2 R$$

We assume that the firm determines the level of receipts R★, which maximizes the difference between the total returns and total costs of receipts, i.e., the level at which marginal revenue equals marginal costs. If the difference ("net returns") is positive at R★, it produces R★; otherwise it produces nothing, i.e., it does not sponsor a PAC. Define net returns as

$$\pi(R) \equiv T(R) - C(R)$$
$$= d_1 R - \tfrac{1}{2}d_2 R^2 - (c_0 + c_1 R + \tfrac{1}{2}c_2 R^2)$$

Hence

$$\pi'(R) = (d_1 - c_1) - (d_2 + c_2)R$$

R★ is determined implicitly by

$$\pi'(R^*) = 0 \Rightarrow R^* = \frac{(d_1 - c_1)}{(d_2 + c_2)}$$

Net returns at R★ are

$$\pi(R^*) = -c_0 + \frac{(d_1 - c_1)^2}{2(d_2 + c_2)}$$

Hence, the firm's decision rule is to set

$$(7.3) \qquad R = \frac{(d_1 - c_1)}{(d_2 + c_2)} \quad \text{if} \quad \frac{(d_1 - c_1)^2}{2(d_2 + c_2)} > c_0$$

$$= 0 \text{ otherwise.}$$

The equilibrium value of R for a given firm depends on the values of all of the parameters of the cost and demand functions. We seek to develop a theory that provides a parsimonious explanation of interfirm variation in R. We therefore postulate that c_0 and the sum $(d_2 + c_2)$ are constant across firms, but that the logarithm of the difference $(d_1 - c_1)$, which we denote by $y^\star$, varies across firms as a regression function of a vector of firm characteristics X_i:

(7.4) $$y_i^* \equiv (\ln(d_1 - c_1))_i = X_i \beta + u_i$$

where u_i is a normally distributed disturbance term with mean zero and variance σ^2.

We enumerate below the firm characteristics hypothesized to shift the supply or demand for receipts schedules, and hence determine $y_i^\star$. Before doing so, we show that the foregoing assumptions lead to two related estimating equations: an equation determining whether or not a firm sponsors a PAC, and an equation determining (the logarithm of) equilibrium receipts, given that a firm sponsors a PAC. To derive the first equation, we begin by defining a dummy variable PAC_i equal to one if firm i sponsors a PAC, and equal to zero otherwise. Since $\ln(d_1 - c_1)$ is considered as varying randomly across firms, we can reinterpret the first part of equation (7.3) as follows:

$$\text{Prob}(PAC = 1) = \text{Prob}\left(\frac{(d_1 - c_1)^2{}_i}{2(d_2 + c_2)} > c_0\right)$$

$$= \text{Prob}(\ln(d_1 - c_1)_i > \tfrac{1}{2}\ln(2c_0(d_2 + c_2)))$$

$$= \text{Prob}(X_i\beta + u_i > K_0)$$

(7.5, 7.6) $$= \text{Prob}\left(\frac{u_i}{\sigma} > \frac{K_0 - \beta x_i}{\sigma}\right) = \Phi\left(\frac{\beta X_i - K_0}{\sigma}\right) \equiv \Phi_i$$

where $K_0 \equiv \tfrac{1}{2}\ln(2c_0(d_2 + c_2))$ is invariant across firms and $\phi(\ )$ is the cumulative normal distribution function. Given observations on PAC_i and X_i for a sample of firms, we can obtain consistent estimates of $\frac{\beta}{\sigma}$ by estimating the profit equation (7.6). Thus, we can determine the sign and significance, but not the magnitude, of the effect of the various X's on $y^\star$, since β itself is not identified in this equation. For those firms with PACs, however, we have additional information about the random variable $\ln(d_1 - c_1)_i$. For those firms

(7.7) $$\ln R_i = \ln(d_1 - c_1)_i - \ln(d_2 + c_2) = K_1 + X_i\beta + u_i$$

where $K_1 \equiv -\ln(d_2 + c_2)$. While β is identified in eq. (7.7), least-squares estimation of that equation will not, in general, yield a consistent estimate of β, since, as eq. (5) indicates, u_i is not independent of X_i.

There are two alternative possible approaches to the problem of consistently estimating β in this context. The first is to directly estimate the likelihood function for the full sample, including both firms with PACs and firms without PACs. This approach is potentially attractive because we could test and impose the restriction implied by the model that the vector of probit coefficients in (7.6) is proportional to the vector of regression coefficients in (7.7). Unfortunately, direct maximization of the likelihood function is often computationally burdensome, and when we attempted to estimate the model in this way the procedure did not converge.

The second approach is the two-stage approach proposed by Heckman (1979). In the first stage we estimate the probit eq. (7.6), obtain maximum likelihood estimates of the vector $\frac{\beta}{\sigma}$, and use these estimates to compute predicted values of $\Phi_i, \hat{\Phi}_i \equiv \Phi\left(\frac{\beta X_i}{\sigma}\right)$, and of its derivative $\hat{\Phi}_i'$. The ratio $\hat{\Phi}_i'/$ $\hat{\Phi}_i$ (the "Mills ratio") is an estimate of the expected value of the disturbance in (7.7). In the second stage we estimate (7.7) by OLS on the subset of observations corresponding to firms with PACs, including as a regressor the computed Mills ratio; in principle, the coefficient on the latter is the parameter σ, so this coefficient is expected to be positive. While including the Mills ratio potentially corrects for "sample selection bias" and therefore enables consistent estimation of β, unless there are variables which determine the probability of being in the sample (i.e., which determine PAC_i) which do not determine $\ln R_1$—which isn't the case in our model—this ratio is merely a nonlinear function of variables already included in the model. Consequently, it would not be surprising if the Mills ratio were not significant and if its inclusion increased the standard errors of the coefficients of the other variables.

We conclude this section with a discussion of the characteristics of firms hypothesized to determine y^*, whose effects are analyzed empirically below. They are: (1) firm size; (2) the fraction of firm revenue derived from sales to the federal government; and (3) the firm's market share. Here we briefly discuss the reasoning underlying each of these postulated effects.

Firm Size. The cost of acquiring any given level of revenue should be lower, *ceteris paribus,* the larger the firm. It is also possible that the absolute benefit resulting from a given level of disbursements might be higher for larger firms. If a given PAC contribution results in a certain percentage increase in a firm's sales (or percentage reduction in its costs), then a large firm will benefit more from a specified level of contributions.

While we hypothesize that both the probability that a firm sponsors a PAC and (conditional on its doing so) the size of the PAC increases with firm size, we are agnostic as to whether the elasticity of PAC size with respect to firm size is greater than, equal to, or less than one. In our empirical analysis we consider whether the ratio of PAC size to firm size is increasing, constant, or decreasing with respect to firm size.

Government Share in Firm Sales. A \$1 million increase in firm size (measured by sales) due to an increase in government sales is hypothesized to increase equilibrium PAC disbursements by more than a corresponding increase due to nongovernment sales. In other words, the marginal propensity to contribute out of government sales is higher, since government-contractor divisions (or lines of business) are more likely to realize benefits produced by campaign contributions than commercial divisions. Because we are interested in both estimating the elasticity of disbursements with respect to total sales and testing for different effects of government and nongovernment sales, we specify our model of y^* as follows:

$$(7.7a) \qquad y^* = \beta_0 + \beta_1 \ln(NON + (1+\theta)GOV) + u$$

where NON = nongovernment sales
and GOV = government sales.

θ represents the percentage difference between the marginal effects of GOV and NON on Y^* (hence the logarithm of disbursements), and β_1 represents the elasticity of disbursements with respect to total "effective" sales $(NON + (1+\theta) GOV)$. This expression is nonlinear in the parameters, but it can be approximated by the linear function

$$(7.7b) \qquad y^* = \beta_0 + \beta_1 \ln SALES + \beta_1 \theta\, GOV\% + u$$

where $SALES \equiv GOV + NON$ denotes total sales and $GOV\% \equiv GOV/SALES$ denotes the share of government sales in total sales. The statistical significance of the coefficient on GOV% may be interpreted as indicating the significance of the difference between the effects of GOV and NON on disbursements; the ratio of the GOV% to ln SALES coefficients indicates the magnitude of this differential.

Market Share. A government action that benefits a given firm may either benefit, harm, or not affect other firms in the same industry. In previous analyses[4] it has often been implicitly assumed that the government actions that firms seek to promote by contributing are "industry public goods," i.e., they are actions that would benefit all firms in the industry. When government action confers industry public goods (or bads), one would expect the free rider problem to emerge. The propensity of the firm to make contributions would be expected to be strongly positively correlated with its market share (or share of industry output), because the contributor's share of the benefits (output increase or cost reduction) is assumed to be roughly equal to its share in industry output (or costs).

But firms may seek to promote government actions about which other firms in their industry are either indifferent or to which they are opposed. An example of an action about which other firms might be essentially indifferent is an "add-on" to a procurement program affecting only a single firm in an appropriations bill. Source-selection decisions, on the other hand, are decisions that benefit one firm at the expense of other potential suppliers. As noted above, source-selection decisions are made in the bureaucracy (e.g., the Defense Department) rather than in the legislature, but there is some evidence that legislators seek to influence these decisions on behalf of contractors.

One would expect the benefits of contributing (and hence the propensity to contribute) to depend upon the firm's market share only to the extent that the government actions sought by the firm are industry public goods. If other firms in the industry do not benefit from (are indifferent to or harmed by) these actions, no free rider problem exists, and market share would not be expected to play an important role. Pittman (1977) found that hypothesized determinants of the "social" (industry) returns to contributing had a significant positive effect on total contributions by firms in the industry only in "concentrated" industries, i.e., industries in which most of the returns could be appropriated by a small number of relatively large firms.

Because the government actions sought by government contractors need not be industry public goods, one would not necessarily expect market share to have a significant positive influence on a firm's propensity to contribute. Indeed, the magnitude and significance of market share may yield insight into the extent to which benefits sought by firms are industry public goods. The measure of market share used in our empirical analysis is the firm's (weighted-average) share in federal markets, defined as follows:

$$(7.7c) \qquad \mathrm{MKTSHARE}_i = \sum_j \frac{X_{ij}}{X_{i.}} \frac{X_{ij}}{X_{.j}}$$

where X_{ij} = sales to government by firm i of (4-digit Federal Supply Code) product j

$X_{i.}$ = total sales to government by firm i (of all products)

$X_{.j}$ = total sales to government of product j (by all firms)

An alternative approach by which we attempt to measure the industrial structure of the markets linking the firm to the government is by classifying the firm's government contracts by extent of competition in negotiation (competitive versus noncompetitive). In a recent study (Lichtenberg [1988]), we demonstrate that the propensity of firms to conduct R&D in anticipation of government contract opportunities depends importantly on the method of government procurement. Similarly, we can test whether a firm's PAC activities vary according to the fraction of its contracts awarded on a competitive rather than a noncompetitive basis. The benefits from contributing may be more appropriable, and the free rider problem less severe, in the case of noncompetitive procurement.

DATA BASE CONSTRUCTION

The data base for our econometric analysis was constructed by merging data from three different sources: the Compustat General Annual

Industrial File, the Federal Procurement Data System, and the Final Reports of Financial Activities of PACs issued by the Federal Elections Commission.

Data on company sales were obtained from the Compustat file, which is based on 10-K Reports filed with the Securities and Exchange Commission by over two thousand publicly traded companies.

Data on the value of federal procurement contracts, total and by method of procurement, were derived from a Special Report prepared for the author by the Federal Procurement Data Center (FPDC).[5] This Center was established by the Office of Federal Procurement Policy, Office of Management and Budget, and began operation of the Federal Procurement Data System in Fiscal Year 1979. The Special Report contained a putatively complete enumeration of all federal contract actions (obligations) of the top thousand federal contractors (ranked by value of contracts). The FPDC data on federal contracts (government sales) were matched to the Compustat data on total sales. Although the absence of a firm from the FPDC file could perhaps be interpreted as indicating that the firm had negligible government sales, it could also reflect reporting error or misidentification of a firm. Rather than imputing zero values of government sales to firms missing from the FPDC file, we excluded from the sample firms not represented in both the Compustat and FPDC files. Many of the remaining firms had extremely low values of GOV%, the ratio of government to total sales.

Data on the financial activities of corporate-sponsored political action committees were obtained from the Federal Elections Commission (FEC). Since the mid-1970s, upon the conclusion of every two-year "election cycle" the FEC has prepared a Final Report on the Financial Activity of PACs during the cycle. The report contains both summary financial data (e.g., data on total PAC receipts) and detailed information about the value of contributions to specific candidates. As noted, the final report provides data on the campaign contributions of PACs, not of firms. There is, however, essentially a one-to-one correspondence between PACs and corporate sponsors, and the linkage between the two can be made using the Sponsor-Committee Index, which was also obtained from the FEC. When a given firm sponsored more than one PAC, the financial data for these PACs were added together.[6] Because the FEC Final Report contains information on the entire universe of corporate PACs, we can be confident that the failure of a company to be reported as a PAC sponsor in the report indicates that the firm is not a PAC sponsor.

We obtained the final reports for two election cycles: 1979–80 and 1981–82. We matched data on total PAC disbursements (which is generally very close to total PAC receipts) during each of these cycles to contemporaneous data on total sales and government sales contained in the linked Compustat-FPDC data set. The sequence of data-matching procedures described above resulted in a data set containing observations on 226 companies in each of two election cycles, for a total of 452 observations. The firm was a PAC sponsor in 274 (60.6 percent) of these cases.[7] The PACs sponsored by these firms disbursed a total of $15.7 million during both election cycles. As a benchmark, the entire universe of 1,557 corporate PACs disbursed a total of $43.4 million during the 1981–82 cycle alone. Average disbursements made by PACs included in our sample are about two to three times as large as average disbursements of corporate PACs in general.

EMPIRICAL RESULTS

Mean values of selected variables for sponsors versus non-sponsors of PACs are shown in Table 7.1. Mean total sales of PAC firms were $5.8 billion, about 3.7 times that of non-PAC firms. Mean government sales was 6.6 times as large, and the ratio of mean government sales to mean total sales was 5.6 percent for PAC firms versus 3.2 percent for non-PAC firms. The mean of the ratio of government to total sales, however, was higher for non-PAC firms: 9.6 percent as opposed to 8.4 percent. Noncompetitive contracts account for a slightly larger fraction of the total government sales of sponsors (218/329 = 66%) than of nonsponsors (62%) of PACs. Sponsors also tended to have higher federal market shares; this is not surprising, in view of the greater size of these firms.

Estimates of eq. (7.6), the probit equation determining whether or not a firm sponsors a PAC, are reported in Table 7.2. As hypothesized, the coefficients on ln(SALES) and GOV% are positive and significantly different from zero. The ratio of the second to the first coefficient is about 2, suggesting that government sales have an effect on the unobserved $y^\star$ about

Table 7.1. Mean Values of Selected Variables:
Sponsors Versus Nonsponsors of PACS

	Sponsors of PACS (N = 274)	*Nonsponsors of PACS (N = 178)*
SALES	$5845 million	$1585 million
GOV	$329 million	$50 million
GOV / SALES	8.36%	9.59%
GOV. COMP	$111 million	$19 million
GOV. COMP / SALES	3.08%	4.11%
GOV.NCOMP	$218 million	$31 million
GOV.NCOMP / SALES	5.28%	5.48%
MKTSHARE	16.81%	9.93%

Table 7.2. Maximum Likelihood Estimates of Probit Equation (7.6)
Determining PAC Sponsorship
(Standard errors in parentheses)

	(1)	(2)	(3)
ln (SALES)	.538	.537	.515
	(.053)	(.054)	(.056)
$\frac{GOV}{SALES}$	1.073		.979
	(.477)		(.486)
$\frac{GOV.\ COMP}{SALES}$		.987	
		(1.25)	
$\frac{GOV.\ NCOMP}{SALES}$		1.115	
		(.745)	
MKTSHARE			.705
			(.538)
CONSTANT	−3.663	−3.658	−3.585
	(.398)	(.403)	(4.03)
−2 times log likelihood ratio	135.398	135.404	137.124

three times as large as nongovernment sales. As noted above, the fact that the coefficient on ln(SALES) is significantly less than one does not necessarily imply that β_1 is less than one, since this coefficient is an estimate of $\frac{\beta_1}{\sigma}$, not of β_1. The estimates in the second column indicate that we cannot reject the hypothesis that the ratios of competitive and noncompetitive contracts to sales have equal effects on the probability of sponsoring a PAC. MKTSHARE has a positive effect on this probability, but this effect is only marginally significant.[8]

Estimates of variants of eq. (7.7), where R_i is defined as PAC disbursements of firm i, are presented in Table 7.3. The first column of the table displays the regression of the logarithm of disbursements on ln(SALES) and GOV%, without the correction for sample-selection bias. As in the probit equation, both coefficients are positive and significantly different from zero, and the first coefficient is also significantly less than one, indicating that the ratio of PAC size (disbursements) to firm size (sales) declines with firm size. This model shows that the effect on y* of government sales is about 4.6 times that of nongovernment sales, somewhat larger than the estimate implied by the probit estimates.

In the second column of Table 7.3 we report the same regression including the Mills ratio. Including this ratio reduces the magnitude of the coefficients on the other variables and increases their standard errors. Nevertheless, it confirms the findings that firm size and government-sales-intensity have a significant positive effect on PAC disbursements, and indicates that the difference between the elasticity with respect to sales and unity is greater when we correct for selectivity bias. The coefficient of the Mills ratio, although similar in magnitude to $\hat{\sigma}$ (the root mean squared error of the equation, 1.066) has the "wrong" (negative) sign, but this coefficient is not significantly different from zero at the 10 percent level. Because of both this anomaly and the fact that the correction for selectivity bias does not have a substantial effect on our estimates, we ignore the selectivity issue in the remainder of this study.

Several factors could account for our finding an elasticity of disbursements with respect to sales significantly less than unity. The first is a purely econometric consideration: sales may be a poor (error-ridden) measure of firm size, and standard errors-in-variables analysis implies that this mismeasurement would result in an underestimate of the true elasticity. It is unlikely, though, that measurement error could account for the entire discrepancy between the estimated coefficient and unity.

Two other potential explanations for this result are substantive (behavioral) rather than purely statistical. As firm size increases, the number of executives and managerial employees (the principal donors to corporate

Table 7.3. OLS Estimates of Variants of Disbursements Equation (7.7)
(Standard errors in parentheses)

	(1)	(2)	(3)	(4)
ln (SALES)	.714	.430	.706	.713
	(.058)	(.207)	(.059)	(.061)
$\dfrac{\text{GOV}}{\text{SALES}}$	2.597	2.080		2.587
	(.411)	(.546)		(.431)
MILLS RATIO		−1.221		
		(.852)		
$\dfrac{\text{GOV. COMP}}{\text{SALES}}$			1.245	
			(1.211)	
$\dfrac{\text{GOV. NCOMP}}{\text{SALES}}$			3.289	
			(.713)	
MKTSHARE				.044
				(.539)
CONSTANT	3.961	6.825	4.033	3.966
	(.472)	(2.055)	(4.75)	(.477)
ROOT MSE	1.068	1.066	1.067	1.070
R^2	.4068	.4115	.4101	.4068

PACs) increases, and the free rider problem within the firm intensifies. Although the firm as a whole might benefit from higher PAC receipts, it becomes increasingly difficult for the PAC to monitor potential individual contributors to prevent their shirking their financial "responsibilities." Finally, the legislated limit on contributions of $5,000 per PAC per election per candidate could depress the sales-elasticity of disbursements by imposing a (flexible) ceiling on desired total PAC receipts. Because we have data on contributions by each PAC to individual candidates, we can investigate empirically the question of how binding this limit actually is.

Before doing so, we consider estimates of the disbursements equation including as regressors the firm's market share or the fraction of its sales accounted for by competitive versus noncompetitive government contracts. In the regression shown in the third column of Table 7.3, the ratio of government to total sales is disaggregated into two components, the ratios of competitive and noncompetitive government contracts to total sales, to test the hypothesis that these two methods of procurement have different effects on the propensity to disburse PAC funds. The estimates imply that the marginal propensity to disburse funds out of competitive contracts is the same as the propensity to disburse out of nongovernment sales, but the firms that are noncompetitive-contract-intensive are likely to disburse more funds than their counterparts of equal size. Evidently, the returns to contributing to election campaigns are highest for firms doing business with the government on a sole-source basis. The MKTSHARE variable is included in the regression shown in the fourth column of Table 7.3. Its coefficient is positive, suggesting that the PACs of firms with higher government-market shares tend to disburse more funds, perhaps because they can appropriate a greater fraction of industry-public-good benefits from contributing, but the coefficient is far from significant.

We conclude our empirical analysis by examining evidence concerning the size distribution of contributions by PACs to individual candidates, which may yield insight into the role and effectiveness of statutory limits on such contributions. Percentage distributions of corporate PAC contributions to individual candidates by $500 intervals for the 1979–80 and 1981–82 election cycles are shown in Table 7.4. The largest number of contributions is in the $0–$500 range, and the number declines monotonically until the $4,501–5,000 interval. The fact that the number of contributions in this and the highest, open-ended (over $5,000) interval exceeds the number in each of the three intervals between $3,000 and $4,500 suggests that there is some truncation of the distribution at $5,000 and therefore that the limit is somewhat binding. But only slightly more than one percent of corporate PAC contributions exceed $4,500—these account for about 10 percent of dollars contributed—so that the statutory limit does not appear to be very binding in practice, nor could it account for the less than unitary elasticity of disbursements with respect to sales.

The regressions reported in Table 7.3 tell us about the effects of firm characteristics on (the logarithm of) total PAC disbursements (TOTDISB); the latter may be interpreted as the product of the number of candidates to which the PAC contributed (NCAND) and the average contribution per candidate (AVCONTRIB = TOTDISB/NCAND). Hence ln(TOTDISB) = ln(NCAND) + ln(AVCONTRIB), and it is of interest to ask to what extent the effect of SALES, for example, on TOTDISB is due to its effect on NCAND as opposed to AVCONTRIB. Regressions of ln(NCAND) and of ln(AVCONTRIB) on ln(SALES), GOV% and MKTSHARE are presented in Table 7.5. The coefficients in the ln(TOTDISB) equation are the sums of the corresponding coefficients in these two equations. The estimates reveal that an increase in sales increases TOTDISB mostly via an increase in

Table 7.4. Statistics Characterizing Distribution of Corporate PAC Contributions to Individual Candidates, 1979–80 and 1981–82 Election Cycles

	Election Cycle	
	1979–80	1981–82
Percentage Distribution of Contributions, By Amount		
$ 0–500	70.9	65.1
501–1000	17.6	20.7
1001–1500	4.4	5.8
1501–2000	2.8	3.6
2001–2500	1.4	1.4
2501–3000	0.8	1.0
3001–3500	0.3	0.4
3501–4000	0.4	0.4
4001–4500	0.1	0.2
4501–5000	0.7	0.5
over 5000	0.5	0.7
Percentage of total value of contributions accounted for by contributions over $4500	10.5	10.1
Average contribution per candidate	$608	$655
Median contribution per candidate	$524	$562
Average number of candidates per PAC	84	89
Median number of candidates per PAC	66	73

Table 7.5. Regressions of ln(NCAND) and ln(AVCONTRIB)
on Selected Firm-Characteristics[a]
(Standard errors in parentheses)

	Dependent Variable: ln (NCAND)	Dependent Variable: ln (AVCONTRIB)
ln (SALES)	.588	.081
	(.074)	(.039)
GOV / SALES	1.627	1.180
	(.531)	(.284)
MKTSHARE	.112	−.380
	(.154)	(.387)
CONSTANT	−.851	5.661
	(.572)	(.306)
ROOT MSE	.944	.504
R^2	.3780	.1310

[a] These regressions were estimated using data for the 1981–82 election cycle only (N = 125).

NCAND rather than by an increase in AVCONTRIB. Most of the increase in disbursements associated with an increase in firm size is accounted for by an increase in the number of candidates supported, not by an increase in average contribution. On the other hand, holding firm size constant, an increase in government sales intensity increases AVCONTRIB by nearly as much as it increases NCAND: more government-oriented firms contribute more per candidate as well as to more candidates.

SUMMARY AND CONCLUSIONS

In this paper we have developed a theoretical model that determines whether or not a firm will sponsor a PAC and, if it does, the quantity of funds that the PAC will receive and disburse. The model is based on the assumption that the firm faces supply and demand schedules for PAC receipts and that it maximizes the difference between total returns and total costs of receipts. If the maximized value of this difference is negative (due to fixed costs of sponsoring a PAC), the firm does not sponsor a PAC. Several firm characteristics—in particular, firm size, government sales intensity, and market structure—are hypothesized to shift the supply and demand schedules.

Two related estimating equations were derived from the theoretical model: a probit equation for PAC sponsorship, and a disbursements equation. In principle, the second equation should be estimated with a correction for sample selection bias. Both equations were estimated using pooled data on 226 companies during the 1979–80 and 1981–82 election cycles.

The following are the major conclusions of the empirical analysis.

(1) The elasticity of disbursements with respect to total sales is positive and significantly less than one, indicating that the ratio of PAC disbursements to firm size is a declining function of firm size. Most of the increase in disbursements associated with an increase in firm size is accounted for by an increase in the number of candidates supported, not by an increase in average contribution.

(2) The marginal propensity to disburse PAC funds out of government sales is much greater than—about three to six times as high as—the propensity to disburse out of nongovernment sales, presumably due to the greater benefits realized by government contractors. Apparently, the returns to contributing to election campaigns are highest for firms doing business with the government on a sole-source basis. We are unable to reject the hypothesis that market share has no influence on PAC disbursements. Both the number of candidates supported by a PAC and the average contribution per candidate are substantially higher, the more government-oriented the PAC sponsor is.

(3) Statutory limits on PAC contributions evidently exert only a minor influence on the contributions of corporate PACs. The number of contributions at or near the per-candidate ceiling is quite small.

NOTES

1. In practice, very few PACs solicit contributions from shareholders. The original FECA prohibited organizations which received federal funds from establishing PACs. Some major unions receive federal job-training funds and wanted to establish PACs. They therefore successfully lobbied Congress to amend the FECA to permit PAC sponsorship by government contractors. Epstein (1979) notes that the elimination of this prohibition probably benefited corporations much more than it benefited the labor movement and that this regulatory reform partially accounts for the much greater growth in corporate PACs.

2. Chappell's evidence, we should note, refers to roll-call voting on bills reported to the floors of the House and Senate. The fact that roll-call voting is evidently not significantly influenced by contributions does not necessarily mean that legislator behavior is entirely unresponsive to contributions. In their capacity as members of Congressional committees and subcommittees, legislators determine both the provisions of bills and whether or not they will be reported out of committee. For example, members of defense appropriations subcommittees vote on whether or not to include an "add-on" to a specific defense procurement program in the defense appropriations bill. Contributions might influence legislator voting at the committee level (which is probably less visible to the general public than roll-call voting).

Moreover, Johnson (1985) found that corporate PAC contributions had a significant effect on legislators' votes on four of nine bills affecting the real estate industry.

3. There is, however, a potential problem with assuming that the marginal revenue (or benefit) of receipts declines at a constant rate (d_2), independent of R. This problem arises due to the existence of legislated limits on contributions. Under the Federal Election Campaign Act (FECA), a PAC is prohibited from contributing more than $5000 per election to any candidate during any two-year election cycle. Notice that the limit is on contributions to a given candidate, not on total contributions. Suppose, however, for the sake of argument, that there were a limit equal to $\bar{R}$ on total contributions. In that case, the marginal revenue function $T'(R)$ would be discontinuous at the value $\bar{R}$, with $T'(R) = 0$ for $R > \bar{R}$: although the PAC is free to raise as much money as it likes, there is no point in raising more money than it can contribute to candidates. Because the ceiling on contributions is a per candidate ceiling (and there is a large number of candidates), we do not expect there to be a fixed threshold value $\bar{R}$ beyond which the marginal benefit of total receipts is zero. But due to the possibly highly imperfect substitutability of contributions to one candidate for contributions to another in the production of political influence, we expect that once a PAC has contributed the limit to the candidates it regards as crucial, the returns to additional contributions decline very rapidly. One might allow for this by specifying the marginal revenue function to be concave, at least for large values of R. Unfortunately, allowing for a concave (e.g., quadratic, or piecewise linear) marginal revenue function renders derivation of equilibrium conditions difficult. We therefore retain the linear specification, but reconsider the issue of contribution-ceiling-induced concavity when interpreting our empirical results.

4. See, for example, Epstein (1980), Esty and Caves (1983), Mann and McCormick (1980), and Pittman (1977).

5. Estimates of MKTSHARE were also computed from this source.

6. The Federal Election Campaign Act places limits on the joint contributions of all of a firm's PACs.

7. In a handful of cases, the firm sponsored a PAC that had zero disbursements; these cases were treated as if the firm did not sponsor a PAC.

8. This insignificance may also be a result partially of errors in measuring MKTSHARE.

REFERENCES

Brock, William A., and Stephen P. Magee (1978). "The Economics of Special Interest Politics: The Case of the Tariff." *American Economic Association Papers and Proceedings,* May, pp. 246–50.

Chappel, Henry W., Jr. (1982). "Campaign Contributions and Congressional Voting: A Simultaneous Probit-Tobit Model," *Review of Economics and Statistics* 64. February, pp. 77–83.

Constantini, Edmond, and Joel King (1982). "Checkbook Democrats and their Copartisans." *American Politics Quarterly* 10, no. 1, January, pp. 65–92.

Epstein, Edwin M. (1979). "An Irony of Electoral Reform," *Regulation,* May/June, pp. 35–41.

———— (1980). "Firm Size, Market Structure, and Business Political Influence." In *The Economics of Firm Size, Market Structure, and Social Performance,* ed. John Siegfried (Washington: Government Printing Office).

———— (1984). "PACs and the Modern Political Process," In *The Impact of the Modern Corporation,* ed. Eli Noam (New York: Columbia University Press).

Esty, Daniel C., and Richard E. Caves (1983). "Market Structure and Political Influence: New Data on Political Expenditures, Activity, and Success," *Economic Inquiry* 21 January, pp. 24–38.

Federal Procurement Data Center (1987). Standard Report, Fiscal Year 1987 through Second Quarter.

Fiorina, Morris P., and Roger Noll (1978a). "Voters, Bureaucrats, and Legislators." *Journal of Public Economics* 9, pp. 239–54.

——— (1978b). "Voters, Legislators and Bureaucracy: Institutional Design in the Public Sector." *American Economic Association Papers and Proceedings,* May, pp. 256–300.

Fox, Ronald (1974). *Arming America: How the U.S. Buys Weapons* (Boston: Harvard Business School Division of Research).

Handler, Edward, and John Mulkern (1982). *Business in Politics* (Lexington: Heath).

Heckman, J. (1979), "Sample Selection Bias as a Specification Error." *Econometrica* 47 January, pp. 153–61.

Jacobson, Gary C. (1978). "The Effects of Campaign Spending in Congressional Elections," *American Political Science Review* 72, June, pp. 469–91.

Johnson, Linda (1985). "The Effectiveness of Savings and Loan Political Action Committees." *Public Choice* 46, pp. 289–304.

Kau, James, Donald Keenan, and Paul Rubin (1982), "A General Equilibrium Model of Congressional Voting." *Quarterly Journal of Economics* 92, May, pp. 271–93.

Lichtenberg, Frank (1988). "The Private R&D Investment Response to Federal Design and Technical Competitions." *American Economic Review* 78, June, 550–59.

Malbin, Michael J. (1979). "Neither a Mountain nor a Molehill." *Regulation,* May/June, pp. 41–43.

Mann, H. Michael, and Karen McCormick (1980), "Firm Attributes and the Propensity to Influence the Political System." In Siegfried, *The Economics of Firm Size,* pp. 300–313.

Pittman, Russell (1977). "Market Structure and Campaign Contributions." *Public Choice,* Fall, pp. 37–52.

8

Congress and the Defense Budget: Parochialism or Policy?

JAMES M. LINDSAY

> That's not a way to choose a multi-billion-dollar weapons system. . . . To think a member of Congress would be that parochial to spend money on a faulted weapon because it might produce jobs in his district is awful. Ye gods, that's no way to do it.
> —Rep. Charles E. Bennett (D-Fla.)[1]

Rep. Bennett to the contrary, many if not most people believe that members of Congress support unnecessary defense spending because it employs their constituents. In contrast, the implicit assumption in Bennett's remarks—that legislators grapple with the substantive questions surrounding defense issues—attracts far fewer supporters. Yet it is one thing to hold a belief about how the world works; it is another to subject that belief to scrutiny. To what extent do parochial interests rather than policy views shape how members of Congress evaluate the defense budget?

Previous work on this question has produced some surprising results. Despite its popularity, political scientists have labored long and hard without producing definitive evidence for the parochial explanation. Indeed, many studies have concluded that ideology and not economics plays the major role in determining how members of Congress vote on defense issues.

How can one square these findings with the powerful intuitive and theoretical appeal of parochialism? To some extent these results can be blamed on methodological and data problems that hamper any inquiry into how Congress handles defense policy. Yet the main problem is theoretical.

The talk of parochialism grossly oversimplifies the variety of programs in the Department of Defense (DOD) budget. The apparent contradiction between intuition and evidence dissolves when the theory is adapted to recognize that members of Congress view different parts of the defense budget from different perspectives. Some programs lend themselves to parochially oriented behavior while others tend to elicit ideologically based behavior.

In general, the crucial fault line in the defense budget cuts between military bases on the one hand and weapons programs on the other. Members of Congress face tremendous electoral pressures to protect military installations in their constituencies. Base closings can devastate local economies and thereby alienate entire blocs of voters. In contrast, opposition to a weapons system often poses lower electoral costs, particularly for liberal members. At times, it even provides electoral benefits. Also, norms shape how members assess electoral costs. Because weapons systems quite clearly influence national security, legislators may be more inclined to evaluate these programs from a national perspective than they are with military bases.

Although there are no firm figures on how much needless defense spending Congressional parochialism produces—that depends upon one's definition of "needless"—it undoubtedly costs the American taxpayer billions of dollars. Yet there is no easy remedy for Congress's penchant to protect obsolete military installations. Congress zealously guards its prerogative to oversee base closings and it fears ceding that authority to the executive branch. The only solution—provided Congress is willing to accept the idea that base realignment is needed—lies with bipartisan commissions that have a mandate to elaborate objective criteria for closing bases.

PAROCHIALISM VERSUS POLICY

It is widely believed that "pork barreling" or "parochialism" shapes the way Congress handles the defense budget.[2] The national news media, members of Congress, and political scientists frequently claim that a "parochial imperative" guides Congressional decision making on defense matters. In comparison, few TV broadcasts or textbooks contend that Congress wrestles with the substantive issues in defense policy. Despite the popularity of the parochial hypothesis, political scientists have failed to produce systematic evidence to support the argument. Indeed, the evidence produced thus far suggests that legislators' policy views play a more significant role in Congressional decision making than is commonly acknowledged.

The national media are fascinated with parochialism. Political magazines such as the *National Journal* and the *Washington Monthly* often carry articles alleging (or implying) that particular legislators have used their influence to steer defense dollars into their districts. When the House and then the Senate allowed television to cover their proceedings, the broadcast media took up the parochialism theme. For example, in 1986 the three major networks covered Sen. Alfonse D'Amato's (R-N.Y.) effort to save the T-46 jet trainer, which was built in his state. Even though the T-46 was a drop in the bucket in terms of dollars, it was irresistible news because Sen. Barry Goldwater (R-Ariz.), chairman of the Senate Armed Services Committee (SASC), and the Air Force adamantly opposed production of the plane.

Members of Congress also frequently credit the parochial imperative as an important influence on decision making. Rep. Les Aspin (D-Wis.) writes, "Because of the nature of the information a congressman gets, the Armed Services Committee is typically less concerned about the question of how much we are buying in defense than the question of where we are buying it."[3] Likewise, Rep. Thomas Downey (D-N.Y.) observes, "When the A-6 [airplane] was going to be killed, I'm the congressman from that district and I'm on the Armed Services Committee. It's my job, whether I think the A-6 is good or not, to support it. . . . You wind up feeling that you're helping them and they're helping the district and it's all very wholesome."[4]

Political scientists have been quick to take up the parochial imperative theme. After all, if the hypothesis is true, it corroborates the belief that the primary motivation for Congressional behavior is the desire to be re-elected.[5] Much of the defense budget involves distributive policies. Many defense programs can be subdivided into many parts, each of which can be implemented in different areas of the country, and legislators have some influence over whether and where these funds will be spent. Constituents often notice new defense spending for a base or a firm in their district or state (especially if they work for the base or firm in question), and they are likely to credit their representative or senator for securing it (something the legislator invariably will do his best to broadcast). Consequently, legislators who represent districts or states with major defense bases or contractors have an incentive to support defense spending.

Despite the popularity of the parochial imperative as an explanation, there are some dissenters. Alton Frye, a former Senate staff member, writes, "I believe that policy concerns are far more important to members' judgments on defense issues than the often-cited pork-barrel considerations."[6] Administration officials occasionally testify to the need to argue the merits of their proposals before Congress. Donald C. Latham, an assistant secretary of defense, comments, "It turns out that, even with guys like Rep. Joseph Addabbo and others who are not at all that much in love with defense at times, I have succeeded in convincing some of them of the merits of our programs."[7] Still, arguments that legislators care about the substance of policy have drawn little close analysis, let alone support, even in the political science community.[8]

Not surprisingly, the parochial imperative and not the policy explanation has drawn the most empirical study. One tactic has been to assess the motivations legislators have had for seeking seats on the defense committees—the armed services committees and defense appropriations subcommittees in each house. These studies have shown that parochial interests and policy concerns both constitute important motivations for members. A study of House freshmen during the Ninety-second Congress (1971–73) found that of those who sought seats on HASC, five did so for constituency reasons and three for policy motives.[9] A study of House and Senate freshmen in the Ninety-seventh Congress (1981–83) reported similar findings.[10] Of those freshmen who sought a seat on HASC, constituency motivations were mentioned eleven times and policy motivations were mentioned seven times. In the case of SASC, constituency motives and policy motives were both mentioned four times.

Interviews with members of HASC and the House Appropriations Defense Subcommittee (HADS) during the Hundredth Congress (1987–89) paint a similar picture.[11] Of the nineteen members of HASC interviewed, thirteen said that they sought a seat on HASC because the committee dealt with issues important to the economic well-being of their districts. Policy concerns were mentioned eight times. (The two figures sum to more than nineteen because some representatives listed more than one reason for seeking the seat.) In the case of HADS, of the three members interviewed, one mentioned constituency motives, one mentioned policy concerns, and one mentioned both.

The parochial imperative hypothesis has also attracted statistical analysis. One approach has been to test the proposition that districts and states represented by members of the defense committees benefit disproportionately when compared to other districts and states.[12] In general, these studies have found that members of the defense committees tend to come from districts with greater levels of DOD civilian and military employment than nonmembers. Yet with one important exception these studies have failed to produce statistical evidence that members of the defense committees are able to use their positions to benefit their constituents, regardless of whether the observed variable was gross DOD spending, military employment, or expenditures for prime military contracts.

A second line of quantitative research has tested the proposition that defense spending influences how members of Congress vote on defense issues.[13] A few of these studies have discovered a small correlation between DOD payrolls in a state and the "hawkishness" of Senate voting, but none has found a similar correlation in the case of the House. Moreover, none of these studies has found evidence that prime military contracts are correlated with voting in either the House or the Senate. Instead, these studies have generally concluded that a legislator's party affiliation and general ideological disposition provide better predictors of congressional voting.

In short, then, the parochial imperative hypothesis makes a great deal of sense in explaining how Congress handles the defense budget. There certainly is much anecdotal evidence to support it. Yet attempts to validate the hypothesis have been discouraging at best. No clear relationships have emerged between parochial interests and defense spending. Conversely, the literature has produced evidence that ideology shapes how legislators vote.

RETHINKING CONGRESS AND THE DEFENSE BUDGET

Why have repeated studies failed to substantiate the parochial imperative? Methodological and data problems provide one possible explanation. But beyond these difficulties lies a more fundamental problem. Scholars have treated the defense budget in a simplistic fashion. They have persistently assumed that legislators view the defense budget as one undifferentiated lump of programs. Yet in practice members of Congress distinguish among defense programs and treat different types of spending differently. Once the diversity inherent in defense spending is taken into account, a more accurate picture of Congressional decision making emerges.

There are several possible explanations for why repeated studies have failed to substantiate the major predictions of the parochial imperative hypothesis. First, the theory may be wrong.[14] It may be the case that all legislators seek defense-related benefits for their districts and that membership on one of the defense committees does not give a legislator influence. Then-Senator Dan Quayle quoted an anonymous federal official saying, "We've got to hand out something to all 435 congressmen."[15] In the case of prime military contracts, it may be that often only a few firms can build a weapon system. As a result, legislators may be at best limited to attempts to influence the distribution of subcontracts.[16] Likewise, ideology may be a more important influence on how representatives and senators vote than parochial interests.

Second, these negative findings may be the result of the data used. DOD publishes data on its total expenditures and prime military contracts, but only for individual counties and cities. This has forced analysts looking at voting behavior in the House, the subject of most studies, to estimate district outlays. This is easy to do for rural areas because each district usually encompasses several counties. It is much harder to do for urban areas, because each Congressional district typically covers only part of a county. Since there is no obvious way to determine the district's share of county expenditures, the resulting estimate of district outlays is of dubious value. Moreover, researchers have used data on prime military contracts because the data for subcontracts are unavailable, not because prime military contracts are the theoretically appropriate data. Either of these attempts to circumvent data problems may have produced incorrect results.

Third, almost every study of Congressional voting has taken as its dependent variable a mixture of votes on defense and foreign policy.[17] Yet it is an error in logic (the so-called "universalistic fallacy") to conclude that a correlation for a set of phenomena entails the same association for each and every subset of these phenomena.[18] Indeed, one should be particularly wary of the universalistic fallacy when discussing something as broad as the combination of votes on defense policy and foreign policy. A study that examined a more restricted set of issues, say, votes on defense issues only, might produce very different results than those already reported in the literature.

Finally, scholars may have failed to find evidence that members of the defense committees benefit disproportionately relative to nonmembers because they have tested the proposition incorrectly. R. Douglas Arnold argues that the decision and not the constituency is the proper unit of analysis to employ.[19] At best, the focus on the constituency can establish a correlation between membership on the defense committees and a district's or state's receipt of defense spending (however defined). Employing the decision as the unit of analysis, Arnold found for the period from 1952 to 1974 that members of the House defense committees used their influence to prevent base closings in their districts.

One should be wary, however, in extrapolating from Arnold's results. A key part of his argument is that Congressional influence over the allocation of federal expenditures varies with the substance of the decision under consideration. Indeed, Arnold himself suggests that the nature of the allocational process varies widely within the defense budget. Although he argues that parochialism motivates Congressional actions on basing questions, at the same time he writes, "Congressmen see defense issues primarily in ideological terms; their support for the defense establishment has very little to do with how their districts benefit from defense spending."[20]

Arnold's observation highlights a fundamental problem hampering investigations of Congress and the defense budget. Most studies assume, either explicitly or implicitly, that legislators view all defense spending alike; every DOD program presents an opportunity to provide benefits to constituents. Yet the defense budget contains a vast array of programs, ranging from food research laboratories to advanced stealth bombers. Given this diversity, it is worthwhile to entertain the hypothesis that legislators differentiate among defense programs. Some types of programs may attract more parochially oriented behavior than other programs.

The suggestion that members of Congress do not view the world with tunnel vision is not novel. Richard Fenno pointed out over a decade ago that members of Congress pursue a mix of different objectives.[21] Moreover, each legislator places a different priority on each of these goals, and the rank ordering may change over time. In a similar vein, a recent analysis of the House Committee on Education and Labor found that "different interests incite participation on different issues and that motivational effects vary in predictable ways across legislative contexts."[22] In other words, members of the Education and Labor Committee did not view issues as interchangeable, and they often viewed the same issue differently.

Although it is easy to suggest that an analysis of how Congress handles the defense budget should consider that members view different types of programs differently, it is more difficult to specify in the abstract how they discriminate among programs. After all, legislators may disagree among themselves in how they perceive a particular issue. Some members may see the program in question in parochial terms while others see it in policy terms.

This point notwithstanding, I shall argue in the remainder of this paper that members of Congress distinguish between spending on military facilities and spending on weapons systems. Decisions about military bases generally elicit parochially motivated behavior on the part of members of Congress. In contrast, members generally rely on their policy views rather than constituent interests in determining how to vote on weapons acquisition issues.

The remaining discussion will not touch upon programs in the personnel and operations and maintenance (O&M) accounts, which together account for approximately 50 percent of the defense budget. These two areas of the defense budget have not been adequately studied. Most treatments of Congress and defense spending mention manpower policies in passing if at all. As for O&M, it is widely recognized that Congress cuts requests in this account to the extent needed to bring defense spending under the Congressionally mandated budget cap. This tends to suggest that legislators do not view O&M from a parochial perspective. On the other hand, within the O&M account there are major items that are the direct product of the parochial imperative.[23] In the absence of detailed knowledge of how Congress handles personnel and O&M issues, these two areas of the defense budget are omitted.

MILITARY BASES

Military bases constitute one area of the defense budget where the parochial imperative clearly motivates Congressional behavior. Put simply, members of Congress, be they Democrats or Republicans, hawks or doves, junior or veteran legislators, fight for military installations in their districts and states. Over the past twenty years members have effectively suppressed the ability of the executive branch to close military bases, regardless of military necessity or efficiency. Moreover, many legislators devote considerable time and effort to seeing that DOD invests new monies in the facilities in their districts.

The importance of military bases to members of Congress can be seen clearly in the case of members of HASC. Of the eleven freshmen members of the Ninety-seventh Congress who sought a seat on HASC for a parochial reason, eight said that their interest in the committee rested in its jurisdiction over military installations in their districts. In contrast, only three of the eleven mentioned defense plants in their districts as a reason for seeking to join HASC.[24] Likewise with members of HASC at the start of the Hundredth Congress: of the thirteen members who stated that parochial concerns played a role in their decision to seek a seat on HASC, ten mentioned the committee's jurisdiction over military installations and only four listed defense firms in their district.[25] This finding is notable since these members were selected for interviews because they sat on either the Procurement or Research and Development subcommittees. Only four of the thirteen also sat on the Military Installations Subcommittee, which presumably would have the greatest influence over defense facilities.

Military bases are important to senators and nonmembers of the defense committees as well. The truth of this claim is most evident with respect to the realignment of military facilities. Most legislators automatically oppose administration plans to close or reduce military bases in their district or state. Moreover, although most members agree that some bases are no longer needed, there is a tacit agreement not to question bases in other states. For example, in 1983 Sen. John Tower (R-Tex.), then chairman of the Senate Armed Services Committee (SASC), invited each of his ninety-nine colleagues to list the military installations and programs in his or her state that could be trimmed because they were not needed for national defense. Only six senators responded. "Their combined proposals for savings in their own states totaled less than $200 million, of which not one penny involved a military facility from their own state or that of any other member."[26] The result of this attitude is that, in the words of Rep. Richard Armey (R-Tex.) and former Sen. Goldwater, "in Congress . . . trying to close down bases is not just a job, it's an adventure."[27]

The ability of Congress to block DOD decisions to restructure military facilities is a recent development.[28] Three decades ago there were few legal constraints on the authority of the executive branch to order bases closed or to realign men and materiel. However, when the Johnson and Nixon administrations moved aggressively to close down unneeded military installations, Congress reacted by passing several pieces of legislation that increased its say over base closings and retrenchments. The end result was that the executive branch essentially lost the authority to close military bases, regardless of the merits of the case. To quote Secretary of Defense Caspar Weinberger, "the restrictions that are presently on the books for closing bases mean that practically speaking we cannot close any facility, no matter how much we want to or how little need there is for it."[29]

Efforts to block plans to close military installations are only the most visible way in which legislators protect parochial interests. Almost as important is obtaining funds to upgrade existing bases. Rep. G. William Whitehurst (R-Va.), in his remarkably candid diary, admits that he and other members fought strenuously to add funds to finance projects at bases in their district.[30] Rep. Roy Dyson (D-Md.) defended his efforts to add funds to the 1985 defense budget for a base in his district because "I was sent here to do that."[31] Similarly, a member of HASC recently displayed a mock bazooka in his office to highlight his success in convincing the Army to store bazookas in an arsenal in his district, thereby providing jobs for his constituents.[32]

Many of these add-ons represent relatively mundane projects with small price tags. Rep. Dyson's efforts, for example, were aimed at funding new family housing, a chapel, and a day care center. Other efforts, however, entail substantially larger costs. In 1987, for instance, Rep. Samuel S. Stratton (D-N.Y.), the third ranking Democrat on HASC, wrote to his constituents that he would "continue to be in a crucial position to supply Defense Department funds" for such projects as the "near-billion-dollar" renovation of Fort Drum.[33]

Legislators may also seek large investments in local installations to make it financially imprudent for the military to close the facility. For example, in 1970, 1974, and 1979 DOD reduced the size of the staff at Loring Air Force Base (AFB) in Maine. These reductions were widely seen as a prelude to a decision to close the base. To avert this, Sen. William Cohen (R-Maine) used his position on SASC to press for improvements at the base. Between 1980 and 1983 more than $135 million was appropriated for new construction and maintenance at Loring. Similarly, in 1979 DOD announced that it would seek to close Goodfellow AFB in Texas. Congressional opposition forced DOD to drop this proposal, and between 1981 and 1984 Goodfellow received over $25 million in new funds, even though it is a small single-mission base.[34]

Members of Congress also often seek to influence the basing of planes and ships. Such basing decisions ensure the flow of money and jobs into the district. For instance, Rep. Mickey Edwards (R-Okla.) was credited with convincing the Navy to base E-6A communication aircraft at Tinker AFB in Oklahoma City, even though Tinker had not been on the original list of bases considered.[35] Also, legislators often haggle over the provision of new equipment to their state's National Guards. One Congressional staff member comments: "Members worry a lot about the Air National Guard and Air Reserve. They all fight to make sure that the outfit in their state gets a new allotment of fighter planes. There is a rotation system going on. You got taken care of last year; we should get taken care of this year. All in all, it's a nice political plum to hand out."[36]

None of this is to say that members of Congress always support spending on military facilities. In 1989, Congress accepted the recommendation of the nonpartisan Commission on Base Realignment and Closure that 91 bases be closed or partially closed. Moreover, on occasion, members have opposed proposals for new base construction. Legislators from Nevada and Utah lobbied furiously against the Carter administration's proposal to base MX missiles in the Great Basin. This ultimately helped to kill the proposal. The Michigan and Wisconsin Congressional delegations fought, with some success, to kill a Navy plan to construct a sprawling ELF (extremely low frequency) antenna for the purpose of communicating with submarines at sea. Both these proposed projects, however, threatened massive environmental destruction and imposed substantial socioeconomic costs on the local populations. Seen in this light, these cases, and others like them, do not refute the contention that Congressional actions on military bases are motivated by parochial concerns.

WEAPONS SYSTEMS

The parochial imperative is less important in Congressional decision making on weapons acquisition issues than on military installations. The quantitative analyses that have been conducted thus far all suggest that ideology offers a better explanation of Congressional voting on weapons programs than does any measure of constituency interest. This is not to say that parochialism is never involved in weapons acquisition issues. It undoubtedly is. Still, most legislators do not appear to make their decisions on the basis of parochial concerns.

Several studies have demonstrated the importance of individual policy views in shaping Congressional decisions on weapons acquisition issues. One example is the controversy over the Sentinel/Safeguard ABM proposal. An analysis of Senate votes on this issue between 1968 and 1970 came to three conclusions.[37] First, a senator's position on a general liberal-conservative scale—measured by interest-group ratings of ideology—provided the best predictor of the ultimate vote. Second, none of several measures of state economic benefit from the ABM program produced statistically significant results. Third, virtually all of the senators who changed their stance on ABM between 1968 and 1970 moved from a position that was out of accord with their basic ideological position to one that was closer to it.

An analysis of the controversy over the B-1 manned strategic bomber in the mid-1970s produced similar results. Using different methods, one author found that a senator's position on a general liberal-conservative scale provided the best predictor of how he or she voted.[38] In contrast, there was little evidence that a state's economic interest in the program influenced how the senators from that state voted. Conservative senators from low-benefit states voted in ways indistinguishable from conservative senators from high-benefit states. Likewise, liberal senators from high-benefit states generally displayed no statistically significant differences in their voting patterns when compared to liberal senators from low-benefit states.

These results are striking because the B-1 is one weapon system where parochialism should be evident. To begin with, the Air Force deliberately maximized the geographical spread of contracts and subcontracts for the B-1 in order to produce the most votes in Congress.[39] As a result, every state but Montana and North Dakota received a contract or subcontract for the B-1. Second, for two decades Congress had tried to force successive administrations to build a new bomber, and the Air Force considered construction of a successor to the B-52 its highest priority. Any liberal legislator representing a high-benefit state had ample justification to vote in favor of the B-1. Third, in 1977 Congress rebuffed Carter's plan to kill eighteen water projects, demonstrating that it was willing to rebuff a president to protect local interests.[40] Moreover, spending on the water projects amounted to less than one-fifth of the spending on the B-1. Nonetheless, Congress sustained Carter's decision to cancel the bomber.

The parochial imperative does not appear to have been important in the battle over the MX. The six states which received the largest share of MX funds were California, Massachusetts, Utah, Colorado, New York, and Florida. Taken together, over 85 percent of the MX jobs were created in these six states.[41] If the parochial imperative correctly describes Congressional voting on weapons systems, then most if not all the senators from these states should have voted in favor of the missile. Yet an analysis of Senate votes cast in 1983 and 1984 shows that six senators from these states generally voted for and six generally voted against MX.[42] In contrast, if one examines the general ideology of these senators, all six senators with an Americans for Democratic Action (ADA) rating above 50 (i.e., more liberal) voted against MX and the six senators with an ADA rating below 50 (i.e., more conservative) voted for MX.[43] Thus even senators from states with the largest economic stake in the MX program tended to vote along ideological rather than parochial lines.

Senate voting on the Strategic Defense Initiative (SDI) looks much the same. California, New Mexico, Massachusetts, Alabama, and Washington have received the five largest shares of SDI contracts. Taken together, they have absorbed over 75 percent of SDI expenditures.[44] In 1985 and 1986 seven senators from these states generally voted in favor of SDI and three generally voted to cut SDI funding.[45] Clearly, a state's economic benefit does not predict how senators will vote. In contrast, a general measure of ideology offers a nearly perfect voting predictor: six of the seven pro-SDI senators had ADA ratings less than 50 (Sen. Bingaman was the lone exception), and all three anti-SDI senators had ADA ratings greater than 50.[46]

No one has undertaken a quantitative analysis of Congressional voting on a conventional weapons system. Nonetheless, the available evidence suggests that the parochial imperative is not a major factor in why the U.S. acquires the conventional weapons it does. The MBT-70 tank, a program initiated in the 1960s to build a new main battle tank, is a case in point. After several years of controversy, the MBT-70 was canceled. A study of the program concluded that "the involvement of a member's district in MBT-70 contracting worked *against* rather than *for* the system."[47] Several key House members, whose districts stood to benefit from production of the tank, opposed the program because they believed it was an inferior weapon. Surprisingly, the strongest support for the program came from senators whose states did not stand to benefit from the production of the tank.

The more recent case of the Sergeant York Division Air Defense (DIVAD) gun also suggests that parochialism is less important in acquisition decisions than commonly thought. Many legislators criticized the DIVAD because it repeatedly flunked development tests. After the Army failed to solve the problems plaguing the gun, Congress imposed several restrictions on the program. When it became clear that DIVAD would never meet the requirements set by Congress, Secretary Weinberger canceled the program. Significantly, this move was applauded on Capitol Hill, even though over $2 billion would have been spent to procure the Sergeant York.

An objection that may be raised is that these findings apply for the most part to the Senate alone. One might argue that representatives are more constituency-oriented than senators because they tend to represent smaller and more homogeneous constituencies.[48] Also, until recently the House, unlike the Senate, rarely challenged weapons systems. Representatives may have been drawn into passivity because of the parochial benefits of defense contracts.

A thorough rebuttal of these objections is impossible because no statistical analyses have been published on this point. Still, it is likely that parochialism is a relatively unimportant factor explaining how representatives vote. The most cursory review shows that virtually every vote on a weapon system in the House splits along ideological lines. Although before the mid-1970s the House generally refrained from questioning DOD programs, this passivity reflected more the House's greater attachment to the norm of deference to committee specialization than any difference in the strength of the parochial imperative.[49] Until the late 1970s the House ratified the decisions made by HASC and HADS even though both were significantly more conservative on defense issues than the chamber as a whole.[50] In the 1980s, after the power of the House defense committees was diminished, the House and not the Senate took the lead in scrutinizing proposed new weapons systems.

A second objection that might be raised is that the acquisition decisions just discussed are atypical. After all, most weapons systems, nuclear or conventional, never become the subject of debate in committee or on the floor. Parochialism may operate by persuading members of Congress not to challenge defense programs. There is some merit to this argument. Legislators generally do not sift through the programs important to their district looking for ones to kill. As former Rep. Robert Leggett (D-Calif.) puts it: "I've got to be picky and choosy about what I try to terminate, because if I've got a large submarine with 8,000 people working on it in my district, I'm not about to terminate the contract and put 8,000 people out of work."[51]

At the same time, legislators probably heed the parochial imperative on conventional weapons more readily than they do with nuclear weapons. Rep. Nicholas Mavroules (D-Mass.) helped lead the anti-MX fight even though the program provided jobs in his district. Simultaneously he fought for other defense contractors in his district. When asked about the discrepancy Mavroules argued:

> I don't have any trouble at all when it comes to contracts for the district, because ninety-five percent of it has been for conventional weapons. Avco has a little nuclear work, but otherwise it is F-18, Patriot [an antiaircraft missile], and other Raytheon missiles, which are conventional. The argument I put forth is that we have all the nuclear deterrent we require; modernization of conventional weapons is what we need today. That argument sells pretty well.[52]

Likewise, Rep. Tom Downey (D-N.Y.) opposed the B-1 bomber and Trident II missile, two programs that brought jobs to his district. When it came to the A-6 and T-46 (conventional) planes, however, Rep. Downey was "eager to promote the programs of Long Island's aircraft manufacturers."[53]

Although possible differences between conventional and nuclear weapons should be kept in mind, two other factors play a far more important role in determining why Congress does not debate more weapons systems, particularly conventional ones. First, with the exception of chemical, biological, and nuclear (CBN) weapons, there is little opposition, either in Congress or outside it, to most of the weapons DOD requests. Nearly everyone agrees that the Pentagon should buy rifles, grenades, troop transports, and the like. As a result, one would expect most weapons to sail through Congress.

Second, time and available resources constrain the number of issues Congress can place on its agenda. Even the defense committees face this problem. Former Sen. Thomas McIntyre (D-N.H.), who earned a reputation as an aggressive overseer of Pentagon budget requests during his tenure as chair of SASC's Subcommittee on Research and Development, lamented that "We spend an awful lot of time, but we are lucky if we can take a look at or have a briefing or hearing on, say, 15 percent of those [R&D] projects."[54] Although the defense committees have increased the size of their staffs substantially over the past two decades, these are dwarfed by DOD's staff resources.[55] As a result, the defense committees face a daunting task in discharging their responsibility to oversee DOD.

The foregoing comments do not imply that no parochialism is involved in acquisition decisions. Some members do try to advance parochial interests. Deliberations on the 1986 defense budget provide two examples. As noted earlier, Sen. D'Amato (with help from Rep. Downey and others) fought to save the T-46 fighter trainer. The contractor for the plane, Fairchild Republic, was a major employer on Long Island. Rep. Sam Gejdenson (D-Conn.) offered an amendment to the defense authorization bill to add funds for the construction of an additional Trident submarine, which was built in his district. As House Republicans were quick to point out, only days earlier Gejdenson had voted not to procure the missiles that the Trident would carry. What academics and the media often lose sight of, however, is that both of these parochially motivated efforts (and many others like them) were easily defeated.

Many legislators also act as agents for firms back in the home district. They inform local companies of contract opportunities and help steer them through the Pentagon's contracting maze. They also seek to arrange meetings between constituents and DOD officials, and to discover why a local firm's contract bid lost.[56] In addition to helping firms on an individual basis, members also pass legislation that alters the decision-making process to negate the market advantages some firms might have. DOD's acquisition regulations include provisions for minority businesses, small businesses, and firms in economically depressed regions, not to mention "Buy American" requirements. These rules contribute to higher defense costs, but they do not affect the composition of the force structure.

Finally, even if parochialism on weapons systems is limited, it may still influence program decisions. If Congress is split on the wisdom of a program, the fact that a handful of legislators bow to the parochial imperative—assuming that it conflicts with their policy preference—may be enough to save the program. Similarly, it is frequently alleged that on controversial issues some legislators will trade their votes for concessions from the executive branch in other areas. For instance, Rep. Tommy Robinson (D-Ark.) said after he voted for the MX missile in 1985, "I'm always asking [the White House] for something. They didn't have to trade with me because I was committed to the MX. But be honest. One has to look out for one's self and one's district. That's just the way the game is played."[57]

In sum, parochialism does affect acquisition decisions. No doubt at times senior members use their positions to persuade DOD to continue programs important to their constituents. Some legislators swallow their policy objections and vote for programs important to their constituents. And some members do sacrifice their policy views on defense issues to gain commitments from the administration to favored programs in other domains. Overall, however, parochialism appears to be a relatively minor factor in decisions to acquire or not acquire weapons systems. Instead, those decisions hinge more on the policy views of legislators.

EXPLANATIONS

What explains the difference in how members of Congress treat military construction and weapons systems? The answer lies in the different electoral costs associated with each issue. Legislators who fail to work to protect military installations in their districts run tremendous electoral risks. Base closings can devastate local economies and thereby alienate substantial numbers of voters. In contrast, opposition to a weapons program often poses lower electoral costs, particularly for liberal legislators, and, in certain situations, it may even be an electoral plus. At the same time, norms shape how members assess electoral costs. Because weapons have a direct link to national security, legislators may be more inclined to evaluate these programs from a national perspective than they otherwise would be.

Most observers concur that reelection is the primary objective of all legislators. Yet members have other goals as well, including a desire to advance their conceptions of good public policy.[58] Such "policy work" runs the gamut from voting one's views to mobilizing others to support a favored bill. Members engage in policy work because, contrary to the claims of their critics, they are not content to be "errand-boy ombudsmen" for their constituents.[59] They want to contribute, to matter. "Men and women want to count for something. . . . The need for meaning prods legislators to be something more than freeloading hypocrites."[60] Of course, the importance of policy work as an objective varies among members of Congress. Some members see it as their guiding purpose while others merely pay lip service to it.

Policy work may do one of three things for a legislator's reelection hopes. The first possibility, and the one that has drawn the most comment, is that it may hurt them. Policy work poses opportunity costs; it diverts efforts from more electorally rewarding tasks. Former Rep. Charles A. Vanik (D-Ohio) argues: "Now under the unique American process, the legislator can be deliberate and thoughtful, but these are *privileges* which must be compressed out of the legislator's time."[61] Also, constituents may disagree with a member's position on an issue, which may affect their vote in the next election. And, if constituents do have an economic interest in a program, they are likely to be displeased (to say the least) if their legislators vote to cancel or curtail that program.

The second possibility is that policy work may have no effect on a member's electoral prospects. One congressman notes, "My experience is that people don't care how I vote on foreign aid, federal aid to education, and all those big issues, but they are very much interested in whether I answer their letters.[62] Finally, policy work might increase a member's reelection chances. Given that time and resources are limited, and numerous issues come before Congress each year, legislators may use policy work on salient (or potentially salient) problems to improve both policy and their visibility with constituents. Also, individuals and organizations, including those outside the district or state, frequently contribute to reelection campaigns on the basis of a legislator's stand on particular issues.

Members of Congress undoubtedly prefer to make their goals of reelection and good policy complement one another. Yet they often find themselves in situations where a vote in accord with their policy preferences will cost them support at the polls. How they assess these trade-offs varies among legislators. Some members are election maximizers. They regularly vote against their policy preferences to enhance their reelection chances. At the other extreme, some legislators are "saints" who would rather risk defeat at the polls than tailor their issue positions to appease their constituents.[63] No doubt most members of Congress fall somewhere in between. They will risk offending some constituents to pursue their policy preferences but they stop short of committing the political equivalent of seppuku.

Although individual legislators differ in their willingness to alienate voters, generally speaking, the greater the electoral costs associated with a particular policy position, the more likely members of Congress are to abandon it. The point is crucial because, more often than not, members who oppose military installations place themselves in greater electoral jeopardy than those who oppose weapons programs that bring jobs to the district. The greater electoral costs associated with the closure of military installations are the result of at least three factors.

First, the closure of a military base generally imposes greater hardships on districts than does the loss of a weapons contract. Frequently, several towns will depend on the well-being of the military base. A decision to close a base could literally turn the surrounding communities into ghost towns as base personnel leave, related businesses collapse, and the tax base dries up. As a result, even when legislators recognize that a military facility is obsolete, they know that political reality demands that they defend it. Any other course of action would be electoral suicide. Entire regions of the district or state could quickly throw their support to a political opponent.

Decisions to cancel or scale back defense contracts generally have a less devastating impact. Most districts are not dependent on defense contracts to the extent that many districts are on military bases. As a result, the loss of a weapons contract does not cause so much economic dislocation. One legislator comments, "Defense contracts in my district are spread across the board. It's not like an army or air force base."[64] The economic pain caused by the loss of a weapons contract will also be eased if the firms in question have other defense contracts or substantial commercial interests. As result, legislators who vote against their district's economic interests on weapons matters do not expose themselves to the same electoral risks they would face if they voted against the district's economic interests on basing matters.

Of course, districts that host prime contractors typically depend as much on that weapon as other districts do on military bases. Members who represent these districts may have little electoral choice but to support the program. This would explain why Sens. Alan Cranston (D–Calif.) and John Tunney (D–Calif.) both supported production of the B-1 bomber even though most other liberals opposed the plane: California received nearly three times as much money from the B-1 program as any other state.[65] In the case of the T-46 trainer, it was well known that Fairchild Republic's ability to remain in business as an aircraft manufacturer depended upon the contract to build the jet trainer. The potential loss of thousands of jobs gave the members of the Long Island Congressional delegation a strong incentive to fight to save the T-46.[66] For Electric Boat (EB), the subsidiary of General Dynamics which builds the Trident, submarine construction is its sole business. Since EB is a major employer in both Connecticut and Rhode Island, members of these Congressional delegations have always been solicitous of its needs.[67]

The second factor behind the greater cost of base closing is that these usually elicit different constituency reactions than do efforts to cancel weapons systems. When DOD threatens to close a military installation, most of the affected constituents rally to save the base. At the same time, generally no group arises to defend fiscal integrity and military efficiency. The absence of groups lobbying for base closings means that members who vote against their district's interests on basing issues run tremendous electoral risks. They cannot expect offsetting electoral support from other quarters. Consequently, only brave (or foolhardy) legislators resist the parochial imperative on basing matters.

In contrast, controversial weapons often trigger the emergence of public-interest groups that lobby against the proposed program. This is especially true for nuclear weapons programs. For example, the anti-MX missile coalition brought together a diverse assortment of lobbying groups.

> The lobbying effort on behalf of the anti-MX amendment was some of the best and most professional ever. A group of Washington-based lobbyists representing arms control, religious and environmental groups inundated the Hill with arguments, personal visits, and MX materials. There were daily meetings of the American Baptist Churches, Americans for Democratic Action, Coalition for New Foreign and Military Policy, Common Cause, Council for a Livable World, Friends Committee on National Legislation, Friends of the Earth, National Association of Social Workers, Network, Physicians for Social Reponsibility, Sane, United Church of Christ, Union of Concerned Scientists, and others.[68]

Likewise, President Reagan's decision to accelerate research on ballistic missile defenses sparked a boom in public-interest groups both for and against space weapons.[69]

The existence of these groups means that members representing districts that benefit from the production of a weapon will offend some constituents no matter how they vote. This is important because members care about which voters they disappoint. They much prefer to offend voters who do not belong to their reelection constituency than those who do.[70] While this holds true for all legislators, conservatives and liberals occupy unequal positions on defense issues. Since conservative members typically support greater defense spending, and presumably their supporters do as well, they can satisfy both the parochial imperative and the ideological leanings of their reelection constituency with the same vote. The only voters conservatives are likely to alienate are those outside their reelection constituency.

Liberal members, however, face conflicting pressures. If they defend their constituency's parochial interests and vote for the weapon in question, they may alienate like-minded voters who belong to their reelection coalitions and open themselves up to politically damaging charges that they are inconsistent.[71] If they vote against the weapon, however, they probably will anger those employed by the program. Yet some of these offended voters may not be a part of their electoral coalition. As a result, doves who oppose systems that employ their constituents do not run the large risks that the parochial imperative suggests.[72] Indeed, if individuals in the reelection coalition feel strongly about the issue, opposition may help a legislator.[73]

At the same time, the existence of different lobbying pressures would explain any differences in the degree of parochialism that motivates Congressional decision making on nuclear versus conventional weapons. Arms control and pro-defense organizations care deeply about CBN weapons. They do not display the same passion for conventional weapons. Moreover, few public-interest groups have sprung up to lobby for or against conventional weapons. Thus liberal legislators may believe that even if they vote for a disputed conventional weapon system, members of their reelection constituency will not defect because they do not have intense preferences on the issue.

Third, the incentive to logroll is greater with military installations than with weapons systems. All states, and almost 60 percent of the Congressional districts, contain or are near some military installation.[74] Also, members of Congress know that DOD would like to close or realign a large number of bases. These two factors create a natural basis for logrolling. Members recognize that if they vote to close a facility in another district today, they will lose potential allies in tomorrow's fight to preserve the base in their district. As a result, even though legislators may know of military installations in other parts of the country that should be closed, they refuse to support the closures in return for tacit agreement not to close bases in their districts. The response (or lack thereof) to Sen. Tower's inquiry about bases that might be candidates for closure underscores the power of this norm.

In contrast to military installations, DOD rarely lobbies Congress to discontinue a weapons system. Since the cancellation of one weapon does not herald the cancellation of others, members have less of an incentive to logroll. They know that they can vote against the MX without fearing that they are jeopardizing the F-16. Of course, DOD might punish members it sees as hostile by steering contracts to other constituencies (which is often hard to do) or by manipulating basing matters. For example, the Air Force reportedly declined to base the B-1B at Wurtsmith AFB in Michigan because, as one general put it, "We have legislators in Michigan who have not defended the B-1 program—and those states with B-1 opponents will be the first to be cut."[75] Still, members of Congress contend that DOD rarely acts in this manner.[76]

The diminished incentive legislators have to logroll on acquisition decisions is important because most spending on weapons is concentrated in a small number of states. This was noted with regard to MX and SDI, and it holds true for the B-1 as well. When Congress ratified President Carter's decision to cancel the bomber it was estimated that five states would have absorbed more than 70 percent of all the funds spent on the plane.[77] B-1, MX, and SDI are, of course, among the largest defense programs; most weapons programs involve far smaller sums of money. Thus not only do legislators have a smaller incentive to logroll, they also typically have either a very small constituency interest in the weapon in question or none at all.

In addition to assessments of electoral costs and benefits, norms also help to explain why members of Congress handle basing and weapons matters differently. Put simply, norms shape how legislators assess costs. Decisions to acquire weapons systems have obvious implications for national security and legislators may be more likely to look at these from a national rather than local perspective. Carol Goss has written:

> Decisions about weapons acquisition are closely related to matters that affect the perceptions of foreign governments—especially potential enemies. While it is immaterial to potential enemies whether the Texas airfield site is chosen over the California site (the same Air Force commands them both) it *is* important that our technological capabilities be viewed with the utmost respect. . . . It is all well and good to boost one's district, but if it is true, as the Defense Department may claim, that the contractor in the other fellow's district makes a better missile, it is best to try again on another slice of the defense pie.[78]

In contrast, it has long been considered legitimate in Congress to discuss military installations as local issues. Consequently, legislators feel no compunction about discussing basing decisions as domestic issues. (Whether it is proper to view bases from a perspective other than military need is a separate question.) As a result, members may be more willing to bear electoral costs when dealing with weapons rather than basing issues.

The structure of the Congressional budget process provides the best evidence that legislators view basing and weapons issues differently. Military construction is considered separately from the rest of the defense budget. Also, the appropriations committees in both the House and Senate have subcommittees just for military construction. The differences in how members of Congress debate bases and weapons provide additional evidence that different norms govern the two issues. Appeals to parochial interests are relatively uncommon during debates over weapons systems. Thus it was a departure from practice when Rep. Stratton urged his colleagues in 1985 to vote for the MX missile because it would "put some of the unemployed back to work."[79] However, efforts to prevent base closings and reductions are commonly justified in terms of their local impact. To take but one example among many, the FY 1980 military construction bill blocked a DOD proposal to reduce personnel at five bases until DOD had redone the required impact statements to "place special emphasis on socioeconomic factors in the affected areas."[80]

To recognize the importance of norms is not to argue that most or even many members of Congress are saints. Legislators who doubt the need for a particular weapon learn to live with their qualms when the program employs many of their constituents. Rep. Matthew G. Martinez (D-Calif.), who opposed production of the MX missile, nevertheless noted that "If there were 10,000 jobs for my district from MX contracts, or even 5,000 jobs, I would regard that as positive enough to swing my vote. Unemployment in my district is over 10 percent, and when you have that kind of unemployment rate, 5,000 jobs becomes a very attractive number."[81] Still, norms do matter. Members often shoulder more electoral costs than they otherwise would, simply because they believe it is the right thing to do.

REFORM

Parochially oriented defense spending inflicts substantial costs on the American taxpayer. Yet it is far easier to denounce parochialism than it is to change the way Congress allocates funds. Parochialism results from the political incentives that confront members of Congress and not from flaws in the budget process. Put simply, it is rational for individual legislators to protect their constituents' economic interests, particularly in the area of military facilities. However wasteful parochialism may be, legislators are not likely to change their behavior out of altruism for the taxpayer.

There is no consensus on how much parochialism costs the American taxpayer annually. Rep. Armey and Sen. Goldwater believe the U.S. would save up to $2.5 billion each year if obsolete military bases were closed. The Grace Commission on Government Waste suggested that the figure may be as high as $5 billion annually.[82] In 1985 Assistant Secretary of Defense Lawrence J. Korb estimated the price tag was "at least $10 billion a year."[83]

These estimates should be kept in perspective. Given that the defense budget today is about $300 billion, in relative terms parochialism is a minor annoyance. Still, $10 billion is a considerable sum of money. This is especially true when all, Democrats and Republicans alike, are looking for ways to reduce the federal budget deficit. What then, if anything, can be done to reduce parochialism in the defense budget?

Any discussion of reform must begin by recognizing that existing political forces do not favor major changes in how Congress handles the defense budget. Parochialism exists because there are powerful political incentives for members to give in to parochial pressures. It is all well and good to insist that legislators display political courage, but they know that "bringing home the bacon" enhances their reelection chances. Members may agree that a military installation in their district has outlived its usefulness, but they also know that if they do not fight for the base, they probably will face stiff competition in the next primary or general election.

At the same time, what constitutes necessary defense spending is often subjective. For base closings, such decisions are important not only in purely military terms. They also have a tremendous impact on the lives of entire communities. Local concerns are real and the defense establishment can ignore these concerns. Moreover, the decisions that emerge from the Pentagon do not always reflect solely rational-technical calculations. As the historian Walter Millis observed nearly four decades ago:

> Military programs are not engineering blueprints adjusting means to ends; rather . . . they are growths, reflecting so many, such complex, such contradictory, and such frequently unscientific factors as to have an appearance of organic development. No doubt a very large amount of technical knowledge and scientific study enters into them. But so do public fears or apathy, political pressures, service traditions, vested interests, personal abilities or ambitions, the accidental distribution of stupidity at one point or imaginative iconoclasm at another in the vast military-bureaucratic machine.[84]

Subsequent analyses of DOD have only confirmed Millis' observation. Thus what at first looks like blatant Congressional parochialism may turn out on closer inspection to be service parochialism.

Of course, it is easy to envision a decision-making process that would limit the ability of members of Congress to act parochially. But what may be easy in theory is usually hard in practice. After all, there is no "supra-Congress" to impose rules on the House and Senate. Only Congress can dictate what rules it will follow. Not surprisingly, Congress generally does not adopt rules that curb the freedom of its members to act in what they perceive to be their best interests. Altruism may be the mark of a hallowed life but it is not a characteristic of Congressional behavior.[85]

So, what can be said of the major reform proposals? The two most popular proposals, both of which the Bush administration advocates, would grant the President authority to order base closings and to veto budget line items. Thus far Congress has shown no inclination to adopt either measure. Even if they were politically realistic, neither reform is desirable. Once enacted, these proposals would create a different set of problems, namely, that a president could use them as political weapons. As Rep. Armey and Sen. Goldwater point out, "It's conceivable that a president facing a close vote, could tell a member of Congress, 'If you don't vote with me on this legislation, I'll close down that Air Force Base in your district.' "[86] Only the president's personal ethics would limit the use of such threats.

The possibility that the executive branch would manipulate military bases for political ends is not farfetched. In February 1986 Secretary Weinberger announced that DOD would seek to close three military facilities. All three were located in the districts of leading Democratic critics of high defense spending.[87] Some legislators representing districts with no military installations believe they have greater freedom to vote their consciences on other defense issues. One House Democrat goes as far as to thank President Nixon for shutting down many of the bases in his state: "He did us a favor. He gave us freedom. As Janis Joplin sang, 'Freedom's just another word for nothing left to lose.' We don't have to grovel any more."[88] Thus the benefits gained by consolidating power in the executive branch might be outweighed by the potential it creates for political manipulation.

A third reform proposal calls for the creation of special nonpartisan commissions to make the budgetary decisions that members of Congress find too costly to address. In recent years Congress has resorted to such a procedure on several controversial issues, including the imbroglio over how to base the MX missile and the issue of obsolete military bases. From a legislator's perspective blue-ribbon panels have three virtues: they generally will make a decision, they provide political cover for members, and, unlike the line-item veto, they do not give the President a political weapon with which to badger members of Congress.

Although the idea of using nonpartisan commissions to solve politically difficult issues is appealing, the record of such endeavors is mixed. The Scowcroft Commission's MX package collapsed after only two years. As for the work of the Commission on Base Realignment and Closure, its recommendations will save only $700 million annually, far less than the $2.5 billion originally envisioned. Moreover, now that Congress has ordered some military bases closed, it is unlikely that it will close other bases any time soon. To quote Rep. Aspin, "the issue is dead for a decade or better, and bases . . . will be safe from the axe for a long time."[89]

In sum, it is illusory to believe that all congressionally inspired waste in the defense budget can be eliminated. Reforms may blunt some of the more egregious examples of parochial behavior. Still, congressional parochialism is rooted in the very nature of the American political system, and it is inevitable that some obsolete or unnecessary military programs will continue to escape the budget cutters' knives through the deft application of political pressure. As such, wasteful spending is an inherent cost of democratic politics.

NOTES

1. Quoted in Hedrick Smith, "MX and the New Guns-and-Butter Argument," *New York Times*, March 19, 1985, p. A20.

2. The terms "parochialism" and "parochial imperative" are used here because of the overwhelmingly negative connotation associated with the term "pork barrel." The term "parochial imperative" is taken from Randall Fitzgerald and Gerald Lipson, *Porkbarrel: The Unexpurgated Grace Commission Story of Congressional Profligacy* (Washington, D.C.: Cato Institute, 1984).

3. Les Aspin, "Games the Pentagon Plays," *Foreign Policy* 11 (Summer 1973): 91.

4. Quoted in Richard A. Stubbing with Richard A. Mendel, *The Defense Game: An Insider Explores the Astonishing Realities of America's Defense Establishment* (New York: Harper and Row, 1986), p. 91.

5. The seminal work in this vein is David Mayhew, *Congress: The Electoral Connection* (New Haven: Yale University Press, 1974).

6. Alton Frye, *A Responsible Congress: The Politics of National Security* (New York: McGraw-Hill, 1975), p. 12.

7. Quoted in Deborah G. Adams and Benjamin F Schemmer, "An Exclusive *AFJ* Interview with: Donald C. Latham, Assistant Secretary of Defense for Command, Control, Communications, and Intelligence," *Armed Forces Journal International* 122 (February 1985): 58.

8. In 1970 John Manley observed, "Political scientists have not given sufficient emphasis to substantive considerations of policy questions as a variable that helps explain the actions of policy makers. Political necessities and advantages, group pressures, institutional rivalries, and electoral considerations all do their part in accounting for public policy. But so too does scrutiny of problems and solutions." Twenty years later little has changed. Quoted in Joseph M. Bessette, "Deliberation in Congress." Paper presented to the 1979 Annual Meeting of the American Political Science Association, Washington, D.C., p. i.

9. Charles S. Bullock III, "Motivations for U.S. Congressional Committee Preferences: Freshmen of the 92nd Congress." *Legislative Studies Quarterly* 1 (May 1976): 201–12.

10. Steven S. Smith and Christopher J. Deering, "Changing Motives for Committee Preferences of New Members of the U.S. House," *Legislative Studies Quarterly* 8 (May 1983): 271–81, and Smith and Deering, *Committees in Congress* (Washington, D.C.: CQ Press, 1984), p. 90.

11. These interviews were conducted by the author in conjunction with a related study on the role Congress plays in the nuclear force acquisition process. The interview sample reported here differs from earlier studies in two respects. First, interviews were not limited to freshmen committee members. Second, these findings were based on interviews with members themselves and not with their staff.

12. Carol F Goss, "Military Committee Membership and Defense-Related Benefits in the House of Representatives," *Western Political Quarterly* 25 (June 1972): 215–33; Bruce A. Ray, "Congressional Losers in the U.S. Federal Spending Process," *Legislative Studies Quarterly* 5 (August 1980): 359–72; Ray, "Congressional Promotion of District Interests: Does Power on the Hill Really Make a Difference?" in *Political Benefits: Empirical Studies of American Public Programs,* ed. Barry S. Rundquist (Lexington, Mass.: Lexington Books, 1980), pp. 1–35; Bruce A. Ray, "Military Committee Membership in the House of Representatives and the Allocation of Defense Department Outlays," *Western Political Quarterly* 34 (June 1981): 222–34; Leonard G. Ritt, "Committee Position, Seniority, and the Distribution of Government Expenditures," *Public Policy* 24 (Fall 1976): 463–89; Barry S. Rundquist, "On

Testing a Military Industrial Complex Theory," *American Politics Quarterly* 6 (January 1978): 29–53; Rundquist and David E. Griffith, "An Interrupted Time-Series Test of the Distributive Theory of Military Policy-Making," *Western Political Quarterly* 29 (December 1976): 620–26; and Rundquist and John A. Ferejohn, "Observations on a Distributive Theory of Policy-Making: Two American Expenditure Programs Compared," in *Comparative Public Policy,* ed. Craig Liske, William Loehr, and John McCamant (New York: Wiley, 1975), pp. 87–108.

13. See Robert A. Bernstein and William W. Anthony, "The ABM Issue in the Senate, 1968–1970: The Importance of Ideology," *American Political Science Review* 68 (September 1974): 1198–1206; Barry Bozeman and Thomas E. James, "Toward a Comprehensive Model of Foreign Policy Voting in the U.S. Senate," *Western Political Quarterly* 28 (September 1975): 477–95; James Clotfelter, "Senate Voting and Constituency Stake in Defense Spending," *Journal of Politics* 32 (November 1970): 979–83; Stephen A. Cobb, "Defense Spending and Foreign Policy in the House of Representatives," *Journal of Conflict Resolution* 13 (September 1969): 358–69; Cobb, "The Impact of Defense Spending on Senatorial Voting Behavior: A Study of Foreign Policy Feedback," in *Sage International Yearbook of Foreign Policy Studies,* ed. Patrick J. McGowan (Beverly Hills, Calif.: Sage, 1973), pp. 135–60; Cobb, "The United States Senate and the Impact of Defense Spending Concentrations," in *Testing the Theory of the Military Industrial Complex,* ed. Steven Rosen (Lexington, Mass.: D.C. Heath, 1973), pp. 197–223; Cobb, "Defense Spending and Defense Voting in the House: An Empirical Study of an Aspect of the Military-Industrial Complex Thesis," *American Journal of Sociology* 82 (July 1976): 163–82; Charles Gray and Glenn W. Gregory, "Military Spending and Senate Voting," *Journal of Peace Research* 5 (1968): 44–54; Neil Heighberger, "Representative's Constituency and National Security," *Western Political Quarterly* 26 (June 1973): 224–35; Wayne Moyer, "House Voting on Defense: An Ideological Explanation," in *Military Force and American Security,* ed. Bruce Russett and Alfred Stepan (New York: Harper and Row, 1973), pp. 106–42; Peter Navarro, *The Policy Game: How Special Interests and Ideologues Are Stealing America* (New York: Wiley, 1984); Bruce A. Ray, "Defense Department Spending and 'Hawkish' Voting in the House of Representatives," *Western Political Quarterly* 34 (September 1981): 438–46; Bruce Russett, *What Price Vigilance? The Burdens of National Defense* (New Haven: Yale University Press, 1970), pp. 72–79; and Frank Whelon Wayman, "Arms Control and Strategic Voting in the U.S. Senate," *Journal of Conflict Resolution* 29 (June 1985): 225–51.

14. Some proponents of the theory have been reluctant to recognize this. Ray, for example, admits there is a possibility that members of the defense committees cannot dictate outcomes but argues "this contradicts the overwhelming mass of congressional literature and, therefore, appears to be unlikely." Ray, "Congressional Promotion of District Interests," p. 30.

15. Quoted in Theodore J. Crackel, "Pentagon Management Problems: Congress Shares the Blame," Heritage Foundation *Backgrounder,* no. 405, January 22, 1985, p. 7.

16. See Ken Mayer's contribution in this volume.

17. One exception is Bernstein and Anthony, "The ABM Issue in the Senate," pp. 1198–1206.

18. For a discussion of the universalistic fallacy, see Hayward Alker, "A Typology of Ecological Fallacies," in *Quantitative Ecological Analysis in the Social Sciences,* ed. Stein Rokkan and M. Doggan (Cambridge, Mass.: The MIT Press, 1969).

19. Arnold, *Congress and the Bureaucracy,* pp. 85–87, 222–23.

20. Ibid., p. 17.

21. Richard F. Fenno, Jr., *Congressmen in Committees* (Boston: Little Brown, 1973), p. 1.

22. Richard L. Hall, "Participation and Purpose in Committee Decision-Making," *American Political Science Review* 81 (March 1987): 105.

23. For discussion of one particularly egregious example, see Robert Higgs, "Hard Coals Make Bad Law: Congressional Parochialism versus National Defense," *Cato Journal* 8 (Spring/Summer 1988): 79–106.

24. Smith and Deering, *Committees in Congress,* p. 106.

25. The numbers sum to more than thirteen because two representatives mentioned both military bases and defense plants.

26. Fitzgerald and Lipson, *Porkbarrel,* p. 13.

27. Dick Armey and Barry Goldwater, "Close the Obsolete Military Bases," *Washington Post,* May 7, 1987, p. A27.

28. The rise of the Congressional veto over military base restructuring is the subject of Charlotte Twight's contribution in this volume.

29. U.S. Congress, Senate, Committee on Armed Services, *Organization, Structure and Decisionmaking Procedures of the Department of Defense, Part 1,* 98th Cong., 1st sess., 1983, p. 9.

30. Whitehurst reports that in 1973 he succeeded in having a $3.4 million authorization to the military construction budget earmarked for bases in his district. This required a compensatory cut elsewhere in the budget, and this turned out to be for a pollution abatement project at Mare Island, California. Whitehurst writes, "I could stand the smell from California a lot better than the noise I would get from Norfolk." G. William Whitehurst, *Diary of a Congressman* (Norfolk, Va.: The Donning Co., 1983), p. 43. See also Whitehurst, *Diary of a Congressman: ABSCAM and Beyond* (Norfolk, Va.: The Donning Co., 1985).

31. Quoted by Howard Kurtz, "On Hill, Legislators Erect Home-District Defenses," *Washington Post,* April 7, 1985, p. A10.

32. Interview.

33. Quoted in *National Journal,* February 21, 1987, p. 407.

34. These and other examples are presented in Fitzgerald and Lipson, *Porkbarrel,* pp. 25–26.

35. See Charles Peters, "Tilting at Windmills," *Washington Monthly* 19 (May 1987): 6.

36. Interview.

37. Bernstein and Anthony, "The ABM Issue in the Senate," pp. 1198–1206.

38. Richard Fleisher, "Economic Benefit, Ideology, and Senate Voting on the B-1 Bomber," *American Politics Quarterly* 13 (April 1985): 200–211.

39. Craig Liske and Barry Rundquist, "The Politics of Weapons Procurement: The Role of Congress," *Monograph Series in World Affairs,* vol. 12, no. 1 (Denver: The Social Science Foundation and Graduate School of International Studies, University of Denver, 1974), p. 82.

40. For a discussion of this legislative battle see Fitzgerald and Lipson, *Porkbarrel,* pp. 1–12.

41. The breakdown is as follows: California (45 percent), Massachusetts (13), Utah (9), Colorado (8), New York (4), and Florida (4). *Congressional Record,* March 7, 1985, p. H1189.

42. The six senators who generally voted for MX were Armstrong (R-Colo.), D'Amato (R-N.Y.), Garn (R-Utah), Hatch (R-Utah), Hawkins (R-Fla.), and Wilson (R-Calif.). The six senators who generally voted against MX were Chiles (D-Mass.), Cranston (D-Fla.), Hart (D-Colo.), Kennedy (D-Mass.), Moynihan (D-N.Y.) and Tsongas (D-MA). This pure party line split does not hold for the Senate as a whole. Moreover, it should be noted that for the first several decades after World War II, the ideological split in U.S. foreign policy cut across party lines. Thus Democrats and Republicans fell on both sides of the ABM debate in the late 1960s and even of the

B-1 debate in the mid-1970s. In contrast, since the Vietnam war, the ideological cleavage in U.S. foreign policy has increasingly mirrored party lines, largely because of the death of the liberal wing of the Republican Party and the weakening of the conservative wing of the Democratic Party. For statistical documentation of this, see Peter Trubowitz, *Ideology, Party, and U.S. Foreign and Defense Policy: An Analysis of Senate Voting, 1947–1984* (Ph.D. diss., Massachusetts Institute of Technology, 1986).

43. These results are not altered if the ratings compiled by Americans for the Constitutional Action Research Institute or the American Security Council are used.

44. The breakdown is as follows: California (45 percent), New Mexico (12), Massachusetts (8), Alabama (6), and Washington (5). "SDI Contractor Study," *F.A.S. Public Interest Report* 40 (April 1987): 4.

45. The seven pro-SDI senators were Denton (R-Ala.), Domenici (R-N.M.), Evans (R-Wash.), Gorton (R-Wash.), Wilson (R-Calif.), Heflin (D–Ala.), and Bingaman (D-N.M.). The three anti-SDI senators were Cranston (D-Calif.), Kennedy (D-Mass.), and Kerry (D-Mass.). See the qualification in footnote 42.

46. These results are not altered if the ratings compiled by Americans for Constitutional Action Research Institute or the American Security Council are used.

47. Liske and Rundquist, "Politics," p. 63.

48. Bernstein and Anthony, "The ABM Issue in the Senate," p. 1199.

49. See James M. Lindsay, "Congress and Defense Policy: 1961 to 1986," *Armed Forces and Society* 13 (Spring 1987): 371–401.

50. See Bruce A. Ray, "The Responsiveness of the U.S. Congressional Armed Services Committees to their Parent Bodies," *Legislative Studies Quarterly* 5 (November 1980): 505–15.

51. Quoted in Liske and Rundquist, "Politics," p. 85.

52. Quoted in Gregg Easterbrook, "When Is a Nuclear Weapon Not a Nuclear Weapon?" *New England Monthly* 4 (July 1987): 40. Avco's "little nuclear work" consisted of building the warhead for the MX missile.

53. Michael Barone and Grant Ujifusa, *The Almanac of American Politics 1988* (Washington, D.C.: National Journal, 1987), p. 798.

54. Quoted in Louis Fisher, "Senate Procedures for Authorizing Military Research and Development," in U.S. Congress, Joint Economic Committee, *Priorities and Efficiency in Federal R&D*, 94th Cong., 2nd sess., 1976, p. 26.

55. In 1968, HASC had ten professional staff members while SASC had eleven. By 1987 the respective figures were 48 and 45. *Congressional Staff Directory* (Mount Vernon, Va.: Congressional Staff Directory, Ltd., 1968 and 1987).

56. See Ken Mayer's contribution in this volume.

57. Quoted in Andy Plattner, "House Freshmen Play a Minor Role . . . But Have Their Say on a Major Issue," *Congressional Quarterly Weekly Report*, March 30, 1985, p. 569. For an example of how vote trading has the potential to shape the outcome of an issue, see Pat Towell with Steven Pressman, "House Gives President the Go-Ahead on MX," *Congressional Quarterly Weekly Report*, March 30, 1983, p. 563.

58. Fenno writes that "of all the goals espoused by members of the House, three are basic. They are: *re-election, influence within the House, and good public policy.*" Fenno, *Congressmen in Committees*, p. 1 (emphasis in the original). John Kingdon contends that members of Congress engage in agenda-setting activities "to achieve the member's conception of good policy." John W. Kingdon, *Agendas, Alternatives, and Public Policies* (Boston: Little, Brown, 1984), p. 42.

59. The phrase is from Morris P. Fiorina, *Congress: Keystone of the Washington Establishment* (New Haven: Yale University Press, 1977), p. 47.

60. William K. Muir, Jr., *Legislature: California's School for Politics* (Chicago: University of Chicago Press, 1982), p. 186.

61. Charles A. Vanik, "Congress Is Deliberative: Compared to What?" in *The United States Congress*, ed. Dennis Hale (New Brunswick, N.J.: Transaction Books, 1983), p. 16. Emphasis supplied.

62. Quoted in Mark J. Green, James M. Fallows, and David R. Zwick, *Who Runs Congress?* (New York: Grossman, 1972), p. 199.

63. Former Sen. Paul Douglas (D-Ill.) called Sen. Frank Graham (D-N.C.) a "saint" because the latter refused to cater to constituent opinion and was defeated in a 1950 primary. See Paul H. Douglas, *In the Fullness of Time* (New York: Harcourt Brace Jovanovich, 1972), pp. 238–41, and Mayhew, *Electoral Connection*, pp. 15–16.

64. Interview.

65. Fleisher notes that aside from Cranston and Tunney, "all other liberals from high benefit states can be considered as not crossing the minimum threshold. That is, the amount of benefits that the state received was not so great as to reduce Senators' options." Fleisher, "Senate Voting on the B-1 Bomber," p. 209.

66. In March 1987, Fairchild Republic announced that it would close its plant on Long Island. This decision eliminated 2,500 jobs immediately, and it was estimated that Long Island would lose an additional 7,500 jobs because of the ripple effects of the plant closing. Clifford D. May, "2,500 to Lose Jobs in L.I. Plant as U.S. Ends Jet Contract," *New York Times*, March 14, 1987, pp. 1, 39, and Philip S. Gutis, "Layoffs Disrupt Stable Lives of L.I. Families," ibid., March 20, 1987, pp. B1, B5.

67. For example, in 1971 Sen. Claiborne Pell (D-R.I.) favored legislation to limit MIRVed missiles. He feared, however, that the bill would hurt EB's contract to convert Polaris submarines to carry MIRVed Poseidon missiles. When the bill's supporters could not allay his fears, Pell voted no. *Congressional Record*, September 24, 1971, pp. 33296–315.

68. John D. Isaacs, "The Lobbyist and the MX," *Bulletin of the Atomic Scientists* 39 (February 1983): 56.

69. See David C. Morrison, "'Star Wars': A Thriving Cottage Industry," *National Journal*, May 23, 1987, pp. 1368–69.

70. Fenno argues that members see their constituencies as a nest of four concentric circles: the geographical constituency; the reelection constituency; the primary constituency; and the personal constituency. See Richard F. Fenno, Jr., *Home Style: House Members in Their Districts* (Boston: Little, Brown, 1978), pp. 1–30.

71. John Kingdon's work suggests that representatives believe inconsistency hurts them with the electorate. John W. Kingdon, *Congressmen's Voting Decisions* (New York: Harper and Row, 1973), p. 256. Senators probably are the same in this regard.

72. See Fleisher, "Senate Voting on the B-1 Bomber," p. 208.

73. When legislators draw electoral support both from those employed by a program and from those opposed to it, then they must assess the relative importance of the two groups. This assessment will depend not only on the number of people in each group, but also the intensity with which they support the legislator. For instance, Fenno tells of one congressman who relied heavily on support from people in the peace movement, even though the number of peace activists was small. "But 100 activists can do a lot. On Moratorium Day, they had 15,000 people marching up Riverside Boulevard." Fenno, *Home Style*, p. 201.

74. Fitzgerald and Lipson, *Porkbarrel*, p. 13.

75. Nick Kotz, *Wild Blue Yonder: Money, Politics, and the B-1 Bomber* (New York: Pantheon Books, 1988), p. 11.

76. Interviews.

77. These states were California (30.9 percent), Ohio (18.7), Washington (9.6), New York (8.6), and New Jersey (4.1). Moreover, California and Ohio alone accounted for more than 75 percent of the prime contract and subcontract dollars

spent on the B-1 program between 1970 and 1975. *Congressional Record,* May 17, 1976, pp. 14142, 14144. See Ken Mayer's contribution to this volume for the complete breakdown of B-1 expenditures by state.

78. Goss, "Military Committee Membership," p. 232.

79. *Congressional Record,* March 7, 1985, p. H1189.

80. U.S. Congress, House, Committee of Conference, *Military Construction Authorization Act, 1980,* 96th Cong., 1st sess., H Rept. 595, 1979, pp. 22–23.

81. Quoted in Smith, "Guns-and-Butter," p. A20.

82. Armey and Goldwater, "Obsolete Military Bases," p. A27.

83. Quoted in Stubbing, *The Defense Game,* p. 101. See also, "Audit of 7 Defense Contractors Announced," *Washington Post,* April 1, 1985, p. A7.

84. Walter Millis, "Our Defense Program: Master Plan or Makeshift?" *Yale Review* 39 (March 1950): 391.

85. This point is discussed in greater detail in James M. Lindsay, "Congress and the Defense Budget," *Washington Quarterly* 11 (Winter 1988): 57–74.

86. Armey and Goldwater, "Obsolete Military Bases," p. A27.

87. See Fred Kaplan, "Weinberger Lists 3 Facilities to Shut," *Boston Globe,* February 13, 1986, p. 3. See Charlotte Twight's contribution to this volume for additional evidence that the executive branch has used base closings to further its political ends.

88. Interview.

89. *HASC Tasks,* November 1988, p. 1.

9

Patterns of Congressional Influence in Defense Contracting

KENNETH R. MAYER

A popular impression of defense contracting is that most, if not all, contracts are awarded for political reasons. Defense contracts, it is supposed, are funneled to wavering legislators to secure their votes on defense budgets, and large contracts parceled out to districts represented by the "friends" of the Department of Defense (DOD). Yet all careful studies of the subject have found rumors of rampant political infestation to be exaggerated. This apparent discrepancy arises largely because much of the political activity that pretends to influence DOD source selection is, ultimately, for show: congressmen and senators take credit for awards, when in all likelihood they had no influence whatsoever on the final decision; they seek to mitigate the consequences of "losing" large contracts by criticizing DOD decisions, and by demanding publicly that the department account for its contract actions.

The fact is that there is little an individual legislator can do to determine where defense prime contracts go.

This is not to suggest, though, that "politics," more broadly construed, plays no role in the weapons acquisition process. Some contracts are indeed awarded for political reasons—a notable recent example is the award of a small business set-aside contract to Wedtech Corporation, given to the company after White House intervention—and Congressional politics definitely intrude on parts of the process. But politically motivated awards are too rare to allow generalizations.

The structure of the prime contract award process precludes routine political meddling by congressmen and senators who want to channel contracts to their constituents. The scope of the source selection process immunizes it against the kinds of political pressures legislators can bring to bear. Contractor proposals are evaluated, and winners selected, in a highly formalized setting; DOD contracting activities are governed by a large body of law and departmental regulation; and losers have a variety of administrative and judicial remedies available to them if they suspect unfair treatment. Most important, though, is the fact that defense contracting is a "negative sum" game, in that for each winner, there can be many losers. It would be nearly impossible for the process to systematically respond to Congressional pressure to target prime contracts.

This structure does not provide total insulation from Congressional influence. But when it intrudes, it does not affect prime contractor source selection. Rather, pressure seeps in at other points. The two phases of the procurement process that are most susceptible to pressure are (1) the Congressional phase, where legislators determine which programs are funded, and how DOD conducts its business; and (2) the subcontracting phase, where prime contractors become political targeters, allocating subcontracts to maximize economic and political effects.

This chapter focuses on these Congressional and prime contractor activities. The emphasis is on source selection, which forms only a part of the weapons acquisition process. The major question is how much influence legislators have over DOD procedures to select particular contractors for a specific program. This truly must be the basis of any discussion of strategic contract targeting. Peripheral issues that may affect Department activities— employment by contractors of former officers or DOD officials, kickbacks and other types of fraud, and contractor campaign contributions—are excluded from the analysis.

The following discussion of the existing literature on the political aspects of defense contracting shows that bureaucratic decision-making is not as politicized as is often suggested, and that the search for DOD-centered conspiracies is likely to prove fruitless. The analysis then turns to aspects of the process that are more political—floor and committee activity in Congress, and subcontract targeting. The results will show that even though "traditional" avenues of influence are narrower than supposed, there are still enough other paths to make the contracting process highly politicized.

CONGRESSIONAL INFLUENCE IN SOURCE SELECTION

A major problem with studying the politics of contracting is that it is extremely difficult, even impossible, to prove that a particular contract award was made on political grounds. The 1962 award of the TFX contract (the development program that led to the F-111 fighter-bomber) illustrates this problem.

On November 24, 1962, the Defense Department announced that

General Dynamics had won, over Boeing, the competition to develop a new generation of combat aircraft, one that could fulfill a number of different military missions. The TFX was likely to be the only large aircraft program of the 1960s and was worth $5.8 billion in 1962 dollars (about $20 billion in 1987 dollars, or roughly two-thirds the size of the B-1 program). Secretary of Defense Robert McNamara awarded the contract to General Dynamics despite the unanimous recommendation of the Air Force Source Selection Board, which evaluated the proposals through four separate rounds of competition, that Boeing be declared the winner.

The announcement unleashed furious criticism. The claim was that General Dynamics had won the contract because (1) the plane would be built in Texas, home of Vice President Lyndon Johnson; (2) Boeing would have built the plane in solidly Republican Kansas; and (3) several high-ranking DOD officials, including Deputy Secretary of Defense Roswell Gilpatric, had had professional ties to General Dynamics prior to taking their current jobs. The contention that General Dynamics had not been awarded the contract on merit was reinforced when the aircraft ran into serious cost and technical problems.

Two weeks after the announcement, Senator Henry Jackson (D-Wash.), in whose state Boeing's headquarters was located, called for a Congressional investigation. The resulting McClellan Hearings, convened under the auspices of the Senate Committee on Government Operations, were held in two sessions in 1963 and 1970. The hearings looked into every conceivable aspect of the contract award. Yet despite what committee chairman John L. McClellan (D-AR) called "one of the longest and most extensive congressional investigations ever undertaken,"[1] the committee was unable to show that the award was politically motivated. The main conclusion was merely that the decision was a bad one. There was simply no hard evidence that politics had played a role in the final decision.[2] Yet there are many government officials who felt at the time, and who remain convinced, that McNamara was looking after the political interests of the president.[3]

Similar charges were made about the C-5A program, where critics claimed that the contract was awarded to Lockheed (with Boeing again the loser) to win the support of Senate Armed Services Chairman Richard Russell (D-Ga.). As with the TFX, the Air Force Source Selection Board favored Boeing, but this recommendation was reversed at the secretarial level.[4] By giving the contract to Lockheed, who would produce the aircraft in Marietta, Georgia, Senator Russell was given a large economic stake in the program. This, according to some, was enough to overcome his initial opposition.[5] But, as with the TFX, there is no conclusive evidence of political influence.

In the 1970s, the award of the M-1 tank contract to Chrysler raised a different set of issues. Once again, a service decision (in this case, the Army's) was reversed by a civilian secretary. The Army declared that

General Motors was the preferred producer, but Secretary of the Army Donald Rumsfeld rejected this recommendation, opting instead for Chrysler. The decision was justified on NATO standardization grounds, but according to a former Office of Management and Budget official, this was a smokescreen for a "hidden agenda," namely:

(1) that President Ford, a native of Michigan, had to be sensitive to the needs of a depressed automobile industry, particularly since the presidential election was approaching.

(2) that a defense contract was preferred to other forms of government aid to Chrysler, such as a "bail-out" guaranteed loan.[6]

This explanation is less than compelling, considering that Chrysler received a government loan anyway, and that the contract award was announced a week after the election, on November 12, 1976.

Perhaps as a result of examples like these, many people involved in weapons acquisition believe that congressmen can effectively lobby on behalf of specific companies and that political considerations can dictate which company will win contracts:

[One] congressman stated that many of his colleagues had an attitude of "the next big contract will not go to the state which won the last big one." An executive of a major contractor reported that "many of us believe that the Pentagon and the politicians merely say 'whose turn is it this time?'" And a former executive of Aerojet General expressed a similar view: "During the 1960's, it was generally felt by our people that major contracts were awarded on a rotation basis. We would get our contract after the others had each won one."[7]

Despite the prevalence of such beliefs, careful case studies of a large number of acquisition programs have uniformly concluded that Congressional politics plays, at most, an extremely limited role in source selection.

One set of studies, done at the Harvard Business School, examined a number of large programs through the 1950s and early 1960s.[8] It concluded that "the direct effects of politics in the weapon acquisition processes tend to be exaggerated."[9] The authors recognized that their conclusion was at odds with prevailing opinion, and left open the possibility that they had not dug deep enough into the decision-making processes to uncover political effects. But, they added, "we can only report what we have seen: that politics counts for less in selecting weapons contractors than many people think."[10]

Later work covering the 1960s and 1970s, also done at Harvard, reached an identical conclusion.[11] The author of that study found, through interviews and research, only one example—out of several hundred programs—where it could be said that Congressional influence determined the outcome.[12]

This conclusion is confirmed by political scientists working with aggregate level data. Research in this area has focused on detecting particular patterns of contract awards that should arise if the source selection process were politicized. Most work begins with the observation that bureaucracies devise budgetary and programmatic strategies in order to maximize Congressional appropriations.[13]

One way agencies can improve Congressional budget support is by giving congressmen stakes in agency programs. Most federal expenditures, including defense spending, produce some sort of economic benefit—jobs, mass transit subsidies, and the like—and congressmen whose districts receive these benefits are more likely to support the programs that produce them,[14] since happy constituents tend to discourage challengers.

But budgets are always too small to provide benefits to everyone, so agencies must determine which areas (and congressmen) will benefit, and which will not. One possible method is to focus benefits on members of the relevant appropriating and authorizing committees. Since these members have more influence over agency budgets than nonmembers, it would pay to keep them satisfied. Satisfied committee members should, the thinking goes, view department budgets more favorably. This idea derives from the "distributive theory" of policy-making propounded by Rundquist, Arnold, and others.[15]

When applied to defense policy, the distributive theory predicts that members who sit on either the armed services committees or the defense appropriations subcommittees will receive more defense-related benefits (defense contracts and military bases) than nonmembers. Testing the theory involves comparing contract levels between member and nonmember districts or states.

The empirical results are surprising. Setting aside military bases for the moment, no link has ever been found between committee membership and contract award levels. Contract awards to particular districts or states did not change when members from those areas gained or lost seats on the military committees,[16] and committee members fared no better than nonmembers in obtaining contracts for their districts—in fact, they often did worse. Rundquist, in the most comprehensive work to date, summarized his findings for the House of Representatives:

> There is no type of contracting in which the 44 districts represented on the two military committees combined averaged significantly greater ratios of prime contracts to manufacturing capability than the 281 districts not represented on those committees. In fact, nonmembers' districts actually average *more* than committee members' districts in 9 of the 15 types of contracting, and in three of these—chemicals, rubber, and aircraft and missiles—the difference is statistically significant.[17]

Some research uses misleading analytical methods to make the connection between committee membership and contract levels. The Council on

Economic Priorities, for example, notes that 92 percent of the prime contracts for Strategic Defense Initiative research awarded in Fiscal Year 1985 went to states represented on Senate military committees.[18] However, that statistic by itself says little. Of the $4.3 billion in FY 1985 SDI contracts awarded to those states, $3.7 billion, or 86 percent, went to only four states: California, New Mexico, Massachusetts and Alabama. California and Massachusetts top the list of states doing defense work, so their presence here is not surprising. Los Alamos National Laboratory, one of the largest recipients of SDI contracts, is a major high-energy physics research center located in New Mexico. And Alabama is home to the Army Ballistic Missile Defense Command, which oversees many SDI contracts. Clearly the location of contractors and research facilities able to perform SDI work, and not committee memberships, is the main reason these contracts are distributed as they are.[19]

The distributive theory's failure to explain the distribution of defense contracts rests with its assumptions about the sources of Congressional behavior, and the nature of defense benefits. Not all congressmen seek committee membership solely for the purpose of obtaining defense benefits. Some members may wish to have some substantive influence on defense policy—this explains the Armed Services Committee membership of congressmen like John Spratt (D-S.C.) and chairman Les Aspin (D-Wis.), whose districts contain few defense contractors.

In addition, not all benefits take the form of contracts—military bases play a major role. Unlike contracts, bases are definitely tied to committee membership. Committee members are more likely to come from districts with large installations,[20] and bases in members' districts are less likely to be closed than bases in nonmembers' districts.[21] The dominance of Southerners on the defense committee through the 1970s is easily understood in this light. South Carolina, Mississippi, and Georgia have produced many of the more prominent military committee members; they are also the sites of many major defense bases. Mendel Rivers (D-S.C.), chairman of the House Armed Services Committee during 1965–1971, was legendary for his ability to obtain military installations for his district. It was said, only half jokingly, that if one more defense base was located there, the district would sink into the Atlantic.

At an analytic level, we can see why defense contracts cannot, as a general rule, be a form of political currency. A key property of defense contracts is that they are "negative-sum": for each company (and Congressional district) that wins a particular competition, there are usually many losers. If defense contracts were routinely used to promote political ends, the Pentagon, in making one congressman happy, would incur the wrath of multiple losers, each of whom would press harder for the next award. This phenomenon would be aggravated by expectations that defense contracts would be used as a form of political reward or incentive. Because of the negative-sum property of contracts, losers would accumulate faster than winners. It would therefore be extremely difficult for the Pentagon to keep abreast of competing demands, and it simply could not satisfy everybody. If contracts were awarded on the basis of political expediency rather than merit, the contracting process would collapse into chaos as congressmen tried to cut deals in order to obtain them. This holds less for military bases, which are not allocated as part of an ongoing process. The "negative sum" property is in fact seen when new bases are established, as during the Navy's controversial homeporting plan.

At the very least, as Peck and Scherer point out, we can expect these competing Congressional demands to cancel each other.[22]

There is thus very little evidence to support the argument that defense contracts are doled out for political reasons. Both individual and aggregate level analyses show that source selection is not systematically affected by Congressional politics. Why this interpretation should be accepted will become clear when the structure of the contracting process is examined in detail.

THE SOURCE SELECTION AND CONTRACT AWARD PROCESSES

The processes by which contractors are selected and contracts awarded are structured, intentionally or not, so that Congressional influence cannot play a major role. Because of the statutory authority involved in the contracting process, and the tremendous attention generated by defense contract awards, the system is, as it must be, set up to maximize objectivity and minimize political influences.

All contracts awarded by the federal government (covering the activities of all agencies, not just the Defense Department) must adhere to the Federal Acquisition Regulation, or FAR (48 CFR Chap. 1, Parts 1–51), which was implemented in September 1983.[23] DOD activities are under the additional authority of the Department of Defense FAR Supplement (48 CFR Chap. 2), and the regulations promulgated by the individual services.

These laws spell out precisely the manner in which defense contracting is to be conducted. The regulations specifically cover source selection in competitive negotiated contracts (the kind involved in many large programs, including the TFX) and attempt to insure objectivity in department procedures.

Contractors who feel that the law has not been followed have the option of protesting the final award. Contractors may appeal decisions to the contracting officer or to higher levels within the Defense Department, the General Accounting Office, or the General Services Board of Contract Appeals.[24] They may also seek remedy through the courts, although this action usually closes off administrative protest channels. While protests do not prevent the Defense Department from allowing political considerations to prejudice contract awards—since it is often easy to come up with a nonpolitical justification for an award—blatant favoritism or bias in source selection, to the point where it is clear that department regulations or federal law have been broken, will likely not stand up to the scrutiny of protest procedures.[25] Many companies that lost contracts to firms tied to the Ill Wind procurement fraud investigation have protested to the GAO, asking that the awards be rescinded.[26]

Furthermore, internal department procedures governing source selection would appear to preclude routine political meddling. Contractor proposal and technical evaluations can involve many months of work and hundreds of people. Simply analyzing proposals (as opposed to cost negotiation, which occurs later) is a monumental task. The amount of data contractors submit in their proposals can be staggering. On the C-5A program, for example, six companies submitted proposals totalling 240,000 pages; with multiple copies, the entire set weighed some thirty-five tons.[27] One survey of six programs found that proposal evaluation for large programs required an average of 267 analysts and 35,000 man-hours of work.[28]

To the groups evaluating the specific aspects of a contractor proposal (cost, technical risk, maintainability, etc.), the political ramifications of their decisions are of little concern. The engineer responsible for assuring that a plane's wings will not fall off does not care which congressmen his conclusions may annoy. At this point in the acquisition cycle, decision-making responsibility is divided into too many separate parts to allow broad political factors to be considered. According to one study,

> Department of Defense respondents were not concerned about which city won a major contract, or the economic consequences to a given area if it won or lost a specific contract. Instead, they projected an image of professionals administering the contract award process, and being above the political battles and lobbying that existed in many major weapons system contract awards.[29]

Overturning the recommendations produced by the source selection process, as in the TFX case, is likely to arouse considerable suspicion. Such rejections do occur, but they are rare.[30]

Nearly all participants in the procurement process, from congressmen to defense officials to contractors, agree that once the acquisition cycle reaches the source selection phase, it is nearly impossible for congressmen and senators to influence decisions; too much bureaucratic machinery is in motion, and entrenched advocates have already formed around particular proposals or contractors for reasons that have little to do with politics. Liske and Rundquist report that "virtually never, at this stage, can any congressmen or group influence a decision on which firm will get the contract. . . . Even for someone with 'clout,' like a committee chairman, it is difficult to determine where a procurement contract will finally go."[31]

At the early stages in the acquisition cycle, responsibility is too fragmented and dispersed to permit political contamination. At the later stages, most decisions have been cast in stone. Neither phase is amenable to Congressional meddling.

CONGRESSIONAL POLITICS AND DEFENSE CONTRACTS

How can this picture of apolitical source selection be reconciled with the unwavering impression that defense contracting is governed by politics? Several alternatives suggest themselves.

First, there certainly is a great deal of political activity surrounding defense contracting, and legislators like to give the impression that they hold sway with the Pentagon—a myth reinforced by the practice (since discontinued) of having legislators announce contract awards to local companies. Moreover, constituents involved in defense business can often obtain valuable assistance from their representatives. Congressmen can extract from DOD information on contracting activities, otherwise unavailable, that can improve a local firm's chances of receiving an award.

Second, it is easy to confuse the many aspects of defense policy and defense spending, some of which manifestly have political roots. It is a short leap, then, to concluding that politics controls all defense policy, including contracting and source selection. In particular, contracts are often confused with miltiary bases. While the former, as indicated above, are distributed largely apolitically, the latter are a classic example of political pork. And there is some circumstantial evidence that the political objectives of the executive branch may affect the distribution of contract dollars.

Third, prime contractors regularly distribute subcontracts to generate political advantages. By awarding program subcontracts to firms in a large number of Congressional districts, primes increase the number of members whose districts depend on the program's survival. This improves Congressional support, along the lines suggested by the distributive theory.

CONGRESSIONAL ACTIVITY

Although congressmen and senators do not, as a rule, have a great deal of influence over DOD source selection, they often behave as though they do. If members can convince constituents that they really can determine the outcome of contract competitions, they can then claim credit for local awards. Some are blunt in their claims to influence. Said one: "Every time I go to the Pentagon to obtain a contract for one of my constituents, I run into hundreds of retired officers."[32] This credit claiming is important, as it provides members with many benefits: reelection funds, votes, campaign workers and the like.[33]

Credit claiming was, until 1970, institutionalized in contract award announcement procedures. Some legislators—usually those most sympathetic to the Defense Department—were given the option of publicly announcing contract awards to firms in their district or state, prior to release of the news to the general public. This certainly fostered the impression that the member's efforts had a hand in the award, particularly since the information was selectively provided. The practice was stopped by language in the FY 1971 DOD Authorization Act, partially because of criticism like that raised by Senator John Williams (R-Del.), who argued that "political influence in the awarding of Government contracts should not be encouraged, nor should either the Congress or the Administration condone a policy which gives the appearance of influence peddling."[34]

Because of this kind of credit claiming, constituents have come to expect help from their representatives on contract matters. Congressmen and senators are often contacted by local defense contractors who are unhappy with DOD decisions; usually these contacts occur after a firm has lost a contract. These matters are treated with the utmost seriousness by both members and Pentagon officials.

Usually, however, the member's function is simply to find out why a constituent lost a contract. One Armed Services Committee member explained:

> We owe it to any constituent to investigate their complaint. I'd call upon the Pentagon and ask, 'what happened?' And they would respond. Usually, since the process is open to public scrutiny, they follow the rules—it's the contractor [who is at fault].
> We'd get back to the contractor and say 'The Pentagon abided by the rules, and here's what you didn't do right.' We give them information they might otherwise not have, since the contractor usually hears nothing other than 'you didn't win.'[35]

Members can also arrange meetings between department officials and local firms that want to start doing defense business, and otherwise see to it that constituents are treated fairly. Efforts to obtain information and facilitate contacts are usually effective. Attempts to influence contract decisions are not; they are made more for domestic consumption, to convince voters that the member is looking after their interests.[36] In the words of one congressman, "to be very candid about it, the effort has to be made because the public expects it."[37] Another study concluded that

> . . . much of this political activity has a ritualistic flavor. A congressman will inquire about a selection at the request of an influential constituent, even when he doubts that it will make any difference. The service responds to the congressional inquiry with cordiality, but such inquiries have little impact at the

operating levels where the source selection decision is usually made. The constituent, however, leaves Washington convinced that dealing with the government is all a matter of politics.[38]

At the source selection stage, members often engage in public lobbying for local companies, even though these efforts almost never have any impact on the outcome. If a local firm does win the contract, though, members can point to their lobbying as instrumental in the decision.

The congressman's goal is to convince constituents that he is working on their behalf and assuring the district its fair share of defense business. Failure to do so can result in serious electoral problems. In the 1970 California Senate race, successful challenger John Tunney charged that incumbent George Murphy had not worked hard enough to bring contracts to the state. In particular, Tunney claimed that the $8 billion F-15 contract had not gone to Southern California–based North American Rockwell because "Murphy did practically nothing in California's behalf."[39] Even though there is no substance to claims of influence, appearances do matter, and legislators work hard to maintain the illusion.

AUTHORIZATION LANGUAGE

One way that members can exercise some real, albeit indirect, influence over the award of defense contracts is through their control over the purse strings. By funding or cutting particular programs or altering more general aspects of defense procurement policy, congressmen can affect where defense money goes.

The objective is to compel or prohibit specific DOD actions through language in the defense authorization or appropriations bills. These efforts have the advantage of being both effective (if the language finds its way in) and highly visible to constituents. Two recent examples are the M-1 tank engine and the T-46 trainer aircraft.

The M-1 Tank

Section 107 of the Department of Defense Authorization Act of 1984 consisted of the following sentence: "The Secretary of the Army may not make a contract for the purpose of establishing a second source for production of the engine for the M-1 tank." The clause gave Connecticut-based AVCO Corporation a legally binding lock on M-1 turbine engine production, despite serious reliability problems and large cost increases. The language was severely criticized by defense officials:

> . . . the Congress must accept its fair share of the blame for inefficient defense policies. Too often, Members of Congress emphasize the public works

aspects of the defense budget. A second production source of the M-1 tank engine is a recent example. The Army, after much congressional criticism over its failure to use competitive procurement, proposed a second source for the M-1's engine when the AVCO Corporation proved an unreliable supplier.

Instead of rewarding the Army for this endeavor, Congress explicitly prohibited a second supplier. The message sent to the Pentagon was clear: Congress is not serious about reforming DOD spending practices.[40]

The provision clearly had its roots in members' desires to look after local interests. This objective was made explicit in the floor debate on the question, when several members from Connecticut (where much of the work was performed) appealed on behalf of the 12,000 residents who worked on the program. Congressman William Ratchford (D-Conn.) warned: "So I say to the Members, 'Don't think it couldn't be you, and don't think it couldn't be your state.' "[41]

The provision is still in effect. Local jobs have been protected, and the congressmen and congresswomen responsible are regarded as local heroes.

The T-46

The T-46 was a trainer aircraft designed by Fairchild Republic Company to replace the Air Force's aging fleet of T-37 trainers. But the plane ran into problems. Costs rose, schedules slipped, and the Air Force took disciplinary action against the manufacturer, including increasing supervision and withholding progress payments.[42]

When it became clear that the program was in serious trouble, a large Congressional battle developed between the New York delegation (which represented the areas where the plane was built), and the Air Force and the Kansas delegation (which represented T-37 manufacturer Cessna Aircraft Company). The New York delegation, in September 1985, asked the Air Force to grant Fairchild additional time to resolve the program's shortcomings.[43] Shortly thereafter, Senator Robert Dole (R-Kan.) publicly urged the Air Force to drop the plane from the 1987 defense budget. When the problems proved intractable, the Air Force decided in March 1986 to scrap the program.

The Senate accepted the Air Force recommendation and voted no funds for the T-46.[44] The House, though, approved the House Armed Services Committee provision to restore funding.[45] In a major victory for the New York members, a T-46 vs. T-37 fly-off competition was mandated in the House-Senate conference bill.

Again, as in the M-1 engine debate, local jobs were a significant factor in the outcome. Congressional activity and voting were predictable, with the entire New York delegation voting to keep the program alive and lobbying hard for the support of other members. William Dickinson, the ranking Republican on the House Armed Services Committee, had no patience with the struggle:

> . . . many of the very people who voted to cut the defense budget Friday led the fight to stuff the T-46 into the budget Monday. The T-46 is a $3 billion program of airborne pork . . . a program that wasn't even included in the $320 billion budget request that some people called bloated.[46]

There are innumerable examples of this kind of constituency-interest language creeping into the defense budget, as members try to protect and promote local programs. Congress bought both A-7 and A-10 attack aircraft after the Air Force no longer wanted them;[47] there are even allegations that the Reagan Administration offered to buy additional A-10s in exchange for votes on the Omnibus Tax Bill.[48] Laws have been enacted to impede competition on major Navy programs. In one instance the Navy was prohibited from using any funds to provide Xeroxed Trident submarine blueprints to a potential second source.[49]

Sometimes these provisions reach absurd levels. The Pentagon, for example, was forced for decades to buy U.S. coal to heat German bases (and was prohibited from converting those bases to more economical fuels), prevented from recycling aluminum, and forced to buy small transport planes it neither wants nor needs.[50] This strategy is used even more widely in military construction appropriations, where Congress almost always includes funds for projects not requested by the Pentagon ($300 million worth in 1982, according to one estimate).[51]

It is not hard to see why congressmen and senators resort to these activities. It is one way they can force the Pentagon to act; there is no fussing with compromise or logrolling. Congress simply uses its legal authority to coerce. Second, it is highly visible, with activity getting lots of home-town coverage. Even if efforts are unsuccessful, members can still get credit for trying. It is a simple strategy, one that bypasses all of the complicated procurement rules and regulations. As with subcontract targeting (see below), it is a form of influence that is "allowable" and effective. It is, not surprisingly, used often.

MILITARY BASES

Evidence that military base benefits are handled in a more political fashion than contracts has already been presented. Committee members are less likely than nonmembers to lose bases in their districts,[52] and base protection is a primary incentive for members to seek membership on the military committees. There are clear examples, moreover, that bases are used as an incentive or punishment.[53] In a February 1986 response to a letter from Senate Armed Services Committee Chairman Barry Goldwater (R-Ariz.) requesting a list of military facilities that could be closed to save money, Secretary of Defense Weinberger named three installations. All were in districts represented by liberal Democratic opponents of President Reagan's defense budgets—House Speaker Thomas P. (Tip) O'Neill (D-Mass.), William H. Gray, III (D-Pa.), and Patricia Schroeder (D-Colo.).[54] No one expected that the bases would be closed on the secretary's recommendation. On the contrary, it is likely that Weinberger was using this fact to make a point: that critics of large defense budgets are hypocrites in that they protect spending in their own districts. Nevertheless, it is unlikely that a similar maneuver would be attempted with weapons systems.[55]

Contracts and bases are treated differently because the rules governing the two are different. The Defense Department has, more or less, free reign in determining where bases are located (and until 1976, when Congressional legislation made it all but impossible to close any installation, which bases to close). There is no FAR counterpart for bases. Simply put, the rules do not prohibit DOD discretion or allow protests. So the Pentagon can use bases for political purposes.

During 1988, the political struggle to close obsolete military bases entered a new phase when Congress voted to create an independent, bipartisan Commission on Base Realignment and Closure. The Commission was charged with selecting bases that could be closed, consolidated, or cut back. Unlike previous efforts to shut obsolete facilities, the process was set up to be as apolitical as possible. When the Commission announced its list of target bases, Congress would have to accept or reject the decision in toto; adding to or deleting from the list was specifically prohibited. Unless Congress rejected the Commission's decision, an unlikely outcome given the public's sensitivity to issues of waste and fat in the defense budget, the cuts would automatically take effect.

Not surprisingly, when the Commission made public its proposed list of 86 facilities to shut (a larger number than anyone expected), including several major installations, members from the affected districts and states howled in protest. They vowed to fight the closure; some, like Senator Pete Wilson (R-Cal.), who wanted to protect the 17,000 jobs California would lose, threatened to derail the entire process by withholding the appropriations needed to fund the closures.[56] Others made high-profile efforts to attack the Commission's data and methods or convince colleagues to reject the list. Their antics, clearly seen as a face-saving measure, fooled no one. About one half of those legislators who attacked the Commission, in fact, had voted to establish it in the first place,[57] and none of the opponents really expected to prevail. (By a vote of 381 to 43, the House ultimately rejected a resolution to prevent the closings from taking place.) Yet the effort was considered necessary to show constituents that members were fighting for them. Said one Congressional aide, "What representative up here, when confronted with two major bases closing in his or her district, wouldn't fight for it? Are we to be blamed for this?"[58]

Once members of Congress tried to remove base closings from the political arena, they gave themselves much the same kinds of influence over the process as they have over prime contract source selection. Members who stood to lose bases began acting like members fighting for contracts: mostly bluster and little substance.

EXECUTIVE POLITICS

It should be clear that when the Defense Department makes source selection decisions, it is unconcerned with Congressional politics. Yet the examples given above raise the possibility, at least, that executive politics might have more of an impact. The civilian Pentagon leadership, after all, is beholden to the president, and may look after his needs.

Consider the 1980 election, when Ronald Reagan swept incumbent Carter out and ushered in a period of unprecedented peacetime military spending. The period 1978–1981 saw major shifts in the distribution of contract awards which make sense when placed in a political-electoral context.

The Carter campaign, in mid-1980, had divided the fifty states into five categories, ranked by the probability that Carter would carry them in the election.[59] If the economic benefits that accrue from defense contracts are real, it would have made sense for the Carter Administration to channel contracts away from states already ensconced in Reagan's camp, and toward the marginal states, where economic benefits could pull them decisively in Carter's direction.

Table 9.1 lists the five categories of states, along with the average percentage change in contract awards (in 1972 dollars) for all states in each category for three periods: 1978–79, 1979–80, and 1980–81. Several clear patterns are discernible. From 1979 to 1980, when Carter officials were still in the Defense Department, strong Reagan states experienced a stark decline in contract awards—from a 16-percent increase to a 1.2-percent decrease. Safe Carter and swing states had the largest increases, with the safe Carter states averaging a 46-percent increase, up from a 10-percent decrease in the preceding period. These shifts could represent a political insurance policy, one designed to maximize potential electoral votes. One observer noted that, during the fall campaign,

> Vice President Mondale sailed into a Philadelphia navy yard aboard the U.S.S. *Saratoga,* where the aircraft carrier began a $526 million overhaul that brought thousands of jobs and millions of dollars in contracts to Pennsylvania (27 electoral votes), Delaware (3), and New Jersey (17). (At the time, Carter was

running neck-and-neck with Reagan in Pennsylvania; Virginia, which lost the contract, seemed safely in Reagan's column).[60]

These patterns were markedly reversed once Reagan assumed control of the White House and DOD. From 1980 to 1981, contract awards to the safe and marginal Carter states went down, and they were the only categories to do so. Swing states had the highest average increases, 39 percent. Safe Reagan states were not far behind with a 30.6-percent average increase.

The shifts hold up even when a few outlying states—Wyoming, Hawaii, and Louisiana—which do not do much defense business but had large increases or decreases in contract awards, are removed (table 9.2). In every category of states, movement is still in the expected direction. In the safe Carter states, gains during the election year (46-percent increase) were stopped during the first year of the Reagan Administration (−1.1). The

Table 9.1. Percentage Changes in Contract Awards for States
by Carter Campaign Classification 1978–1981

	1978–1979	*1979–1980*	*1980–1981*
Safe Carter	−10.2	46.0	10.4
Marginal Carter	6.2	13.3	11.8
Swing	−2.5	17.5	39.0
Marginal Reagan	5.4	12.6	24.0
Safe Reagan	16.0	−1.2	30.6

SOURCES: State categories from Caddell, "Memorandum I," in Drew, *Portrait of An Election*, p. 392 (note 59). Contract data from author's calculations using Department of Defense, *Military Prime Contract Awards by State, Fiscal Years 1953 to 1983* (1984).

Table 9.2. Percentage Changes in Contract Awards for States
by Carter Campaign Classification 1978–1981
(Outliers Removed)

	1978–1979	*1979–1980*	*1980–1981*
Safe Carter	−10.2	46.0	−1.1[1]
Marginal Carter	6.2	13.3	11.8
Swing	−2.5	17.5	10.8[2]
Marginal Reagan	5.4	12.6	24.0
Safe Reagan	6.5[3]	4.8[4]	30.6

[1] Excluding Hawaii (67.8-percent increase).
[2] Excluding Louisiana (292.7-percent increase).
[3] Excluding Wyoming (82.9-percent increase).
[4] Excluding Wyoming (43.2-percent decrease).

SOURCES: State categories from Caddell, "Memorandum I," in Drew, *Portrait of An Election*, p. 392 (note 59). Contract data from author's calculations using Department of Defense, *Military Prime Contract Awards by State, Fiscal Years 1953 to 1983* (1984).

pattern is quite clear: Reagan states suffered under Carter and were rewarded under Reagan. The exact reverse holds for Carter states.

There are a number of nonpolitical explanations for this pattern. Reagan brought in a number of defense officials from geographic areas (primarily the West) which included those states most strongly pro-Reagan. Defense industry officials from those same areas thus had a built-in network of DOD contacts, which was undoubtedly valuable in improving information flow and thus contract chances. Furthermore, many projects that went to pro-Reagan states (notably the B-1, which went to California) were already in process before Reagan became president. Nevertheless, the figures display some interesting patterns, which are more in line with the popular view of a politicized defense contracting process:[61]

> The political party in control of the executive branch also exerts a powerful influence on source selection, as evidenced by the current administration with its sizable California contingent—including the President, the Secretary of Defense, and several key White House advisors. In their first three years in office a number of major programs were launched by the Reagan Administration which favored California contractors, including the $30 billion B-1 program, the Trident II missile, and the advanced air-launched cruise missile.[62]

SUBCONTRACT TARGETING

In many respects, the distribution of subcontracts is the most political phase of the actual contract award process. Scholars and procurement analysts have long suspected that prime contractors distribute subcontracts (which include orders for raw materials, equipment, and parts not manufactured by the prime) so as to maximize the geographic spread of acquisition programs. The existence of this strategy is confirmed by some in the defense industry: "It happens. But you'll never get anyone to admit it. . . . There'll be a situation where someone will say we're getting 'X' from New York and 'Y' from Connecticut. We'd better get 'Z' in California or Seattle."[63] One high-ranking DOD procurement official indicated flatly that this sort of targeting occurs routinely.[64]

Subcontractor targeting occurs for the same reason that many believe prime contracts are targeted. By giving more congressmen and senators an economic stake in a weapons program, chances of full funding go up and the probability of cancellation drops.

> When contracts include widely distributed subcontracts, the services feel their job is much easier, for such patterns provide ready and calculated answers to the questions of uncommitted congressmen. . . . The services have a vested interest in assuring as many congressmen as possible a piece of the action for their district.[65]

It is a cheap strategy. Apart from perhaps some production control or quality assurance problems—the kind that might require periodic visits from the prime—it makes very little difference to a prime contractor in Connecticut whether a standard part is produced in New York, Texas, or California. Managing a distant sub is no more difficult than managing a local one. And since many smaller parts involved in military programs are standard, costs will not vary much. Subcontract targeting is an effective, low-cost, and low-risk strategy for insuring a weapon system's political health.

While legislators have little say in where prime contracts go, they can insure that subcontractors in their districts are awarded their share of work:

> The efforts of legislators to keep their home-state or home-district [subcontract] suppliers in the defense business make it difficult for a new supplier to replace one that has such high level support. Congressmen will often argue that it is in the interest of national security to keep a particular supplier in business, even when he may not have been the low bidder. *Such arguments, passed down to a prime contractor through the DOD from Congress, have considerable weight.*[66]

As with bases, the reason why congressmen have more influence over subcontracts than prime contracts—and subcontract targeting is much more common than prime contract targeting—is because the rules, both formal and informal, that govern the two are different. Subcontracting is not subject to the same FAR constraints as prime contracting, and companies passed over for subcontracts have no government protest rights. Since primes typically have a free hand in selecting subcontractors, the Defense Department is insulated from criticism.[67] Subcontracts are, finally, much less visible than prime contracts, so they generate less attention and controversy.

As a political strategy, subcontract targeting is in most cases superior to prime targeting. There are only so many choice primes to go around. But one large prime contract must be divided into thousands of subcontracts, each of which can be used as an incentive or reward for program support. There is little doubt that the Defense Department encourages this type of activity by its primes.

Despite the apparent ease and prevalence of subcontract targeting, it has been difficult to show it occurs. The problem can be traced to the lack of appropriate data: information on subcontracts is difficult to obtain, and it is impossible to assemble complete and accurate records based on prime contract information or even the subcontract announcements published in industry trade periodicals like *Aerospace Daily*. Most companies consider subcontract information to be proprietary or commercially sensitive and are reluctant to release it.

Furthermore, the Defense Department does not keep detailed subcontract records. The rationale is that the effort is not worth the considerable cost. Typically, 50 percent of the dollar value of prime contracts is subcontracted. The percentage varies from one contract to the next but has remained relatively stable over the past twenty-five years.[68] For large programs, billions of dollars in subcontracts may be issued to tens of thousands of individual subcontractors: forty-thousand companies were involved in the Minuteman missile program.[69] Keeping track of this much information would be an enormous task and, according to some DOD officials, one with little payoff.[70]

An attempt was made in 1977 to establish a subcontract database, when the FY 1978 DOD Appropriations Act directed the Secretary of Defense to collect subcontract data for all firms receiving more than $500,000 in prime contracts. DOD opposed the requirement, and industry compliance was poor.[71] A few preliminary reports were issued with incomplete data, and the requirement was formally canceled in 1981.

About the only time detailed subcontracting data appears is when a program is in trouble in Congress. Then the Pentagon, working with the prime contractor, often assembles a list of subcontracts by Congressional district. These data are circulated on the Hill to impress upon members their economic stake in the program. In March 1987, such a report for two controversial aircraft carriers circulated.[72]

Using this kind of data, it is possible to analyze subcontract targeting. One way of showing that subcontracts are distributed for political effect is to examine subcontracts for comparable commercial and military programs. Commercial programs, it is safe to assume, will not be affected by political calculations. To a civilian aerospace manufacturer, the main considerations in selecting suppliers will be price, quality, and delivery schedule; there is no reason to expect subcontract distribution to reflect anything but economic efficiency. Commercial programs, then, form a control group against which military programs can be measured. Substantially different distributions would support the hypothesis that political considerations affect the placing of military subcontracts.

The B-1

One of the best programs to examine for evidence of strategic subcontract distribution is the B-1 bomber. The B-1 has had a long and labored history, surviving one cancellation, cost overruns, and technical snags. Allegations have been made from the program's inception that subcontracts have been spread over as wide an area as possible.[73] An Air Force officer involved with the B-1 stated that "one major goal of the program was to distribute subcontracts throughout the country in a manner designed to produce the most votes in Congress."[74] The charge is often heard that B-1 business is spread over three hundred Congressional districts and forty-eight states.

Data on subcontract distribution are available for the B-1, although it is dated. In the mid-1970s, the Council on Economic Priorities prepared a report on the economic impact of the B-1. The report included B-1 development and total program expenditures, listed by state, which were released by prime contractor Rockwell International in response to a request by Senator George McGovern (D-S.D.).[75]

Table 9.3 lists the percentage distribution, by state, for the B-1, along with supplier distribution data for two large commercial aircraft programs.[76] The B-1 data are adjusted to reflect only production expenditures, since the commercial data are for mature production programs. B-1 production expenditures for states with less than $1 million in subcontracts were estimated by the author using B-1 development expenditures.[77]

By any measure, the B-1 program is far more dispersed than either of the commercial programs: 44.3 and 56.6 percent of the commercial subcontractors are in the same state as the final manufacturer, but only 28.5 percent of the B-1 work is done in Rockwell's home state, California. Commercial suppliers are located in twenty-two and twenty-three states, respectively, as opposed to forty-eight for the B-1. Ninety percent of the commercial work is performed in four and seven states; the corresponding number for the B-1 is eleven.

If we consider each state to be one "firm," and the percentage of subcontracts in a state to be analytically equivalent to that firm's market share, there are several measures of industrial concentration that can be used to examine the differences between the B-1 and commercial programs. The concentration ratio (C_n) is the percentage of work done (here the equivalent to market share) in the n largest states (firms); n can be any number, but the most common values are four, eight and ten.[78] Larger values indicate more concentration. C_4, or the ratio for the four largest states, is .662 for the B-1, and .799 and .890 for commercial programs A and B, respectively.

For measuring geographic dispersion, though, the concentration ratio is an imperfect measure, as it ignores size differences among firms and is insensitive to the total number of firms in an industry.[79] Other indicators, such as the Herfindahl index *(H)*, attempt to correct for this. H is simply the sum of squares of the market share of every firm in an industry—it varies between 1 (monopoly) and $1/n$ (n firms with identical market shares), with higher values again indicating more concentration. This index shows more clearly the dispersion of B-1 subcontracts. H for the B-1 program is .143, significantly smaller than the commercial-program H's—.240 for program A, and .358 for program B.[80]

These differences take on additional importance when we consider that the commercial data reflect only subcontracts; final assembly and any other

Table 9.3. Dispersion of Subcontracts for the B-1 Bomber and Commercial Aircraft

	B-1 Bomber			Commercial Program A			Commercial Program B	
State	Percentage of Total	Cumulative Percentage	State	Percentage of Total	Cumulative Percentage	State	Percentage of Total	Cumulative Percentage
CA	28.5	28.5	1	43.5	43.5	1	56.6	56.6
OH	18.5	47.0	2	13.8	57.3	2	13.4	70.0
WA	10.1	57.1	3	11.9	69.2	3	9.9	79.9
NY	9.1	66.2	4	10.7	79.9	4	9.1	89.0
NJ	4.3	70.5	5	5.8	85.7	5	3.6	92.6
OK	3.7	74.2	6	3.7	89.4	6	1.0	93.6
MD	3.5	74.7	7	2.0	91.4	7	0.9	94.5
KA	3.4	81.1	8	1.8	93.2	8	0.8	95.3
TN	2.8	83.9	9	1.3	94.5	9	0.6	95.9
TX	2.6	86.5	10	1.0	95.5	10	0.5	96.4
GA	2.2	88.7	11	0.8	96.3	11	0.5	96.9
MA	2.0	90.7	12	0.7	97.0	12	0.5	97.4
IL	1.5	92.2	13	0.5	97.5	13	0.5	97.9
FL	1.4	93.6	14	0.5	98.0	14	0.4	98.3
CT	1.1	94.7	15	0.5	98.5	15	0.4	98.7
MI	0.9	95.6	16	0.4	98.9	16	0.4	99.1
AZ	0.9	96.5	17	0.3	99.2	17	0.2	99.3
PA	0.6	97.1	18	0.3	99.5	18	0.2	99.5
IN	0.4	97.5	19	0.2	99.7	19	0.2	99.7
VT	0.4	97.9	20	0.1	99.8	20	0.1	99.8
UT	0.3	98.2	21	0.1	99.9	21	0.1	99.9
WI	0.3	98.5	22	0.1	100.0	22	0.1	100.0
OR	0.2	98.7	23	0.1	100.1[1]			
CO	0.2	98.9						
IA	0.2	99.1						
NH	0.2	99.3						
WV	0.1	99.4						
MI	0.1	99.5						
NM	0.1	99.6						
VA	0.1	99.7						
MN	0.1	99.8						
MO	0.1	99.9						
SD		100.0						
LA								
NC								
KY								
NE								

Table 9.3 *(continued)*

	B-1 Bomber			Commercial Program A			Commercial Program B	
State	*Percentage of Total*	*Cumulative Percentage*	*State*	*Percentage of Total*	*Cumulative Percentage*	*State*	*Percentage of Total*	*Cumulative Percentage*
ID								
AL								
HA								
RI	Less than 0.1%							
NV								
DE								
MT								
AR								
SC								
ME								
ND								

Herfindahl H
$$H = 0.143 \qquad\qquad H = 0.240 \qquad\qquad H = 0.358$$

SOURCE: See notes 75 and 76.
[1] Totals may not sum to 100 due to rounding.

work performed by the prime contractor is not included. For the B-1, though, production expenditure data include work done by Rockwell in California—which, according to the industry rule of thumb, should be about 50% of the program's value. If data were available just for subcontracts, they would show even wider geographic dispersion, as the significant chunk of work done in California would be excluded.

An alternative way of viewing the data is shown in figure 9.1, which displays graphically the cumulative percentage of subcontracts, from the largest to smallest value states, for the three programs in table 9.3. Steeper slopes toward the left of the graph indicate more geographic concentration. Lines that are closer to the diagonal show a wider geographic spread.[81] Such graphs are sometimes called concentration curves.[82]

The extent of the B-1's dispersion is apparent. The B-1 line's slope is not as steep as the lines for the commercial programs, it flattens out much later, and it is much closer to the diagonal. By the twenty-fifth state, both commercial programs have exhausted their subcontracts, but there is still a residual amount to go around for the B-1.

Obviously, the B-1 is a more complicated system than any commercial aircraft. It requires costly and sophisticated equipment that has no commercial analogue, such as fire-control computers, radar jamming systems, and specialized avionics. The B-1's unit price is also substantially higher (around

Figure 9.1. Expenditure Distribution by State

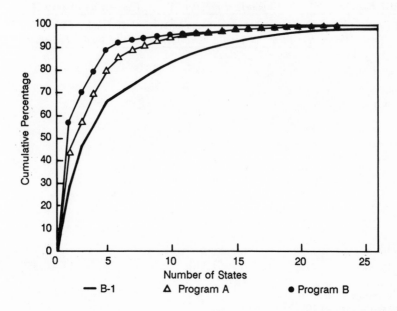

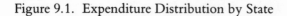

$300 million) than those of even the largest commercial planes, which sell for approximately $50–80 million.

However, more complexity and higher unit costs do not imply, a priori, a wider geographic distribution of suppliers. Subcontracts for the Apache attack helicopter, which has a unit price of $10 million (less than most commercial planes), are spread out over nearly as many states (forty-five) and Congressional districts (273) as subcontracts for the B-1 (see table 9.4). Furthermore, commercial program B, the more concentrated of the two commercial programs, has a military variant that includes some of the same kinds of avionics and communication equipment found on the B-1. These military components are included in that program's distribution data. In short, while comparisons are inexact, the types of programs can be considered at least roughly equivalent.

Although these circumstantial comparisons do not prove that the B-1 has been strategically targeted, they do highlight some of the significant differences between commercial and defense programs. Combined with statements about the extent of B-1 targeting, they provide persuasive evidence that some sort of noncommercial phenomenon is occurring. Part may be due to the increased complexity of military systems. But most of it stems from political considerations: the desire to give as many congressmen as possible an economic stake in the program.

The Apache

Because of contractor lobbying, extremely detailed subcontract data are available for the AH-64A Apache attack helicopter. A report published by McDonnell Douglas Helicopter Company (the prime contractor) lists every subcontract—including some worth only $2,000—awarded under the program, broken down by amount, location, and type of work performed.[83]

The state-by-state distribution for the complete system and for subcontracts only (representing all work except that done by prime contractor McDonnell Douglas and Rockwell International, builder of the Apache's Hellfire missile) are given in table 9.4. The total system distribution shows an exceptionally high level of dispersion: the two largest states (California and Arizona) receive approximately equal percentages (25.4 percent and 24.7 percent respectively), while the third largest (Georgia) is only slightly behind at 18.97 percent. This bunching occurs for two reasons. First, prime contractor work was performed in two separate locations: Southern California and Arizona, sites of Hughes Helicopter (now a subsidiary of McDonnell Douglas). Second, the dollar totals include subcontracts for the Hellfire missile, the Apache's main armament, which is produced in Georgia by Rockwell International, even though the Hellfire is a separate program. Hence the significant boosts in the percentages of the aircraft work performed in the second and third largest states.

The distribution for subcontracts only shows, as expected, that removing prime contractor work significantly increases the dispersion of the program. Although the percentage of subcontracts awarded to the largest state, California, increases (to 34.7 percent), the remaining money is much more evenly spread to the other forty-four states. The Herfindahl index for the entire program is 0.171; it is 0.158 for subcontracts only. Note that these values are close to the Herfindahl index for the B-1 (0.143).

Figure 9.2 shows the distributions graphically. As in figure 9.1, the graph displays the cumulative percentage of work done, by state. Except for the first data point (California), the subcontract line is always below the total program line, indicating wider distribution. This lends additional support to the argument that the B-1 state percentages are biased toward enhanced concentration, since they include prime work done in California.

Other interesting findings can be gleaned from the Apache data. One clear result is that geographic dispersion is independent of unit cost and complexity. Another involves the curious saga of a company called Martin Marietta Subtier Suppliers (MMSS). Martin Marietta (Orlando Aerospace) builds the Apache's target detection and infrared vision system (called TADS/PNVS, for Target Acquisition Display Sight/Pilot Night Vision Sensor). The company, according to the data, orders components and parts from MMSS, a loose organization of private firms unconnected with Martin Marietta located throughout the country.

Figure 9.2. Apache Helicopter: State Distribution

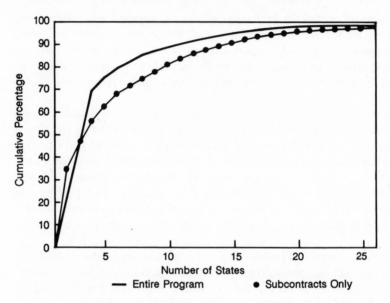

The geographic spread of these orders is astonishing. Martin Marietta awarded second-tier subcontracts to MMSS offices in 176 different Congressional districts in 34 states. In fifty-five of those districts no other Apache subcontracts were issued.

The TADS/PNVS distribution positively erases any connection between program size and distribution scope: the TADS/PNVS system has a unit price of about $1.5 million dollars, yet is spread out over nearly as wide an area as the entire Apache program, which is over ten times as large. The second-tier TADS/PNVS subcontracts total $336 million; the average contract is thus about $1.9 million. Judging from the size of the awards to MMSS, which ranged from $2,000 to $77 million, one suspects that most of the work did not involve highly complex equipment. There would appear to be little reason why the subcontracts would have to go to a specific location or be spread over so wide an area. In fact, the awards to the districts where the MMSS subcontract is the only work done are, on average, smaller than the awards to the remaining areas ($1.2 million as opposed to $2.2 million).

Table 9.5 divides MMSS subcontracts, in both single and multiple subcontract districts, into three categories: under $10,000, under $100,000, and under $1 million. In every category the subcontracts given to districts that receive no other Apache business are far more likely to be small than subcontracts in districts receiving other work. The percentage of MMSS subcontracts under $10,000 is twice as large (15 percent) for these districts as

Table 9.4. Dispersion of Total Program and Subcontracts for the AH-64 Apache Attack Helicopter

	Total Program				Subcontracts Only		
	Dollars (thousands)	Percentage of Total	Cumulative Percentage		Dollars (thousands)	Percentage of Total	Cumulative Percentage
CA	1,914,960	25.42	25.42	CA	1,304,860	34.74	34.74
AZ	1,862,557	24.73	50.15	FL	463,563	12.39	47.13
GA	1,428,558	18.97	69.12	MA	330,014	8.82	55.95
FL	463,563	6.15	75.27	CT	230,000	6.15	62.10
MA	330,014	4.39	79.65	NJ	222,686	5.95	68.05
CT	230,000	3.05	82.71	IL	140,298	3.75	71.80
NJ	222,686	2.96	85.66	OH	119,721	3.20	75.01
IL	140,298	1.86	87.53	MN	113,997	3.05	78.05
OH	119,721	1.59	89.11	IN	111,167	2.97	81.02
MN	113,997	1.51	90.63	NY	105,414	2.82	83.84
IN	111,167	1.48	92.10	NM	83,695	2.24	86.08
NY	105,414	1.40	93.50	PA	68,206	1.82	87.90
NM	83,695	1.11	94.61	AZ	60,112	1.61	89.51
PA	68,206	0.91	95.52	GA	54,955	1.47	90.98
IA	48,140	0.64	96.16	IA	48,140	1.29	92.27
WI	42,678	0.57	96.73	WI	42,678	1.14	93.41
MI	36,874	0.49	97.22	MI	36,874	0.99	94.39
OR	36,221	0.48	97.70	OR	36,221	0.97	95.36
TX	26,388	0.35	98.05	TX	26,388	0.71	96.07
UT	22,946	0.30	98.35	UT	22,946	0.61	96.68
AR	18,522	0.25	98.60	AR	18,522	0.50	97.17
KY	12,927	0.17	98.77	KY	12,927	0.35	97.52
VA	11,965	0.16	98.93	VA	11,965	0.32	97.84
NH	11,758	0.16	99.08	NH	11,758	0.31	98.15
AL	9,382	0.12	99.21	AL	9,382	0.25	98.41
WA	9,329	0.12	99.33	WA	9,329	0.25	98.65
TN	7,836	0.10	99.44	TN	7,836	0.21	98.86
MD	6,953	0.09	99.53	MD	6,953	0.19	99.05
RI	6,309	0.08	99.61	RI	6,309	0.17	99.22
MS	5,462	0.07	99.68	MS	5,462	0.15	99.36
DE	4,071	0.05	99.74	DE	4,071	0.11	99.47
NC	3,677	0.05	99.79	NC	3,697	0.10	99.57
VT	3,540	0.05	99.83	VT	3,540	0.09	99.67
WV	3,391	0.05	99.88	WV	3,391	0.09	99.76
OK	2,702	0.04	99.92	OK	2,702	0.07	99.83
KS	1,675	0.02	99.94	KS	1,675	0.04	99.87
MO	1,514	0.02	99.96	MO	1,514	0.04	99.92
CO	1,249	0.02	99.97	CO	1,249	0.03	99.95
NE	977	0.01	99.99	NE	977	0.03	99.97
SC	431	0.01	100.00	SC	431	0.01	99.99
SD	336		100.00	SD	336	0.01	99.99

Table 9.4 *(continued)*

	Total Program				Subcontracts Only		
	Dollars (thousands)	*Percentage of Total*	*Cumulative Percentage*		*Dollars (thousands)*	*Percentage of Total*	*Cumulative Percentage*
ME	161	<0.01	100.00	ME	161	<0.01	100.00
NV	12		100.00	NV	12		100.00
Total	7,532,262				3,740,717		
Herfindahl H			H = 0.171				H = 0.158

SOURCE: See note 83.

for districts receiving other work (7 percent). The percentage of subcontracts over $1 million is about half as large (16 percent) as that for the multiple award districts (30 percent).

This difference indicates that the single award districts get the less complicated subcontracts—those involving routine work that is more easily spread out, since it requires no particular expertise. These districts make up almost one-quarter of the districts involved in building the Apache. There is thus good reason to believe that Martin Marietta made a conscious, explicit decision to use these simple subcontracts to spread the work over as many districts as possible.

Some of the MMSS subcontract spreading is probably due to the FAR requirement that a certain percentage of subcontracts for defense programs—often less than 1 percent—be awarded to "small and disadvantaged" businesses. Most of these companies are, because of their size, able to perform only simple work, and contractors are required to seek them out. Martin Marietta has an "aggressive" small/disadvantaged subcontracting program,[84] and undoubtedly attempted to disperse its subcontracts to these firms. Geographic dispersion, then, is in fact an integral part of the federal government's overall procurement policy.

DIVAD

Table 9.6 lists the state distribution of work for another system, the Sergeant York Division Air Defense Gun (DIVAD)—a weapon that was ultimately canceled. Although there is no comparable commercial program for DIVAD, the data are still instructive. Work was performed in 38 states, and the ones excluded were among the least populous in the U.S.: Montana, Wyoming, North Dakota, etc. There was a particularly wide spread, considering the relatively small amount of money involved—less than $2 billion, or one-fifth the size of the Apache program and one-fifteenth the size of the B-1—and the fact that key components of the DIVAD program either

Table 9.5 Distribution of MMSS Second-Tier Subcontracts

	Percentage of Contracts in	
Contract Value	Districts Receiving No Other Subcontracts	All Others
Under $10,000	14.5	6.6
Under $100,000	56.4	43.8
Under $1 million	83.6	70.2

SOURCE: See note 83.

Table 9.6. Sergeant York Division Air Defense Gun (DIVAD) Program Distribution

State	Dollars (thousands)	Percentage of Total	Cumulative Percentage
CA	$918,400	50.9	50.9
MD	292,400	16.2	67.1
IN	116,600	6.5	73.5
MA	115,400	6.4	79.9
NY	53,900	3.0	82.9
MI	45,700	2.5	85.4
TX	30,000	1.7	87.1
WI	25,600	1.4	88.5
NJ	23,100	1.3	89.8
MN	22,400	1.2	91.0
MO	21,800	1.2	92.2
AZ	21,600	1.2	93.4
PA	21,300	1.2	94.6
FL	16,000	0.9	95.5
IL	13,300	0.7	96.2
VA	11,000	0.6	96.8
OH	10,000	0.6	97.4
CT	9,500	0.5	97.9
AL	7,600	0.4	98.3
UT	7,000	0.4	98.7
RI	5,400	0.3	99.0
KY	3,000	0.2	99.2
TN	2,400	0.1	99.3
VT	1,700	0.1	99.4
GA	1,500	0.1	99.5
SC	1,300	0.1	99.6
IA	1,300	0.1	99.6
KA	1,200	0.1	99.7
AR	1,000	0.1	99.8

Table 9.5 *(continued)*

	Contract Value	Percentage of Contracts in Districts Receiving No Other Subcontracts	All Others
OR	900		99.8
CO	800		99.9
MS	600		99.9
DE	500		99.9
NH	400	<0.1	99.9
NC	300		100.0
WA	300		100.0
OK	200		100.0
NV	200		100.0

SOURCE: Unpublished map prepared by Westinghouse.

already existed (and therefore were not constructed under DIVAD contracts) or were built outside the U.S.

The DIVAD used an M48A5 tank chassis, which was provided to prime contractor Ford by the government and modified by a subcontractor. The system's 40mm cannon and ammunition were built by Bofors, a Swedish firm (there were plans to eventually license a U.S. firm to produce this item).[85] If these components had been built domestically under the DIVAD contract, the program would have been even more widely distributed. DIVAD work was thus concentrated in California (where Ford's facility is located): since an abnormally low percentage of the program was subcontracted to U.S. firms, Ford's percentage share of the work, as prime contractor, was higher than normal, raising California's participation to over 50 percent. This fact cannot explain, though, the wide spread of subcontracts.

The three different defense systems examined here, of different size, scope, and type, all show a high level of geographic distribution of subcontracts to forty-eight, forty-five, and thirty-eight states. Two large commercial programs show levels roughly half as large, to twenty-two and twenty-three states. The geographic spread of the defense program was not affected by either the size of the weapons program or the complexity of the final product. For each defense program, there are indications that the work was spread over a wider area than required by the scope of the program, and there is evidence that subcontracts were purposely spread over the entire U.S. Martin Marietta's activity on the Apache is an especially clear case.

The data presented here relate only to outcomes; there is no explicit evidence concerning the decision-making processes of the officials involved. But better evidence of subcontract targeting probably does not exist. There will be no damning memoranda or smoking guns. It is apparent, though, that in this phase of the procurement cycle, political concerns dictate to some degree how defense money is spread.

CONCLUSION

That politics affects the weapons acquisition process is undeniable. Influence patterns, however, are subtle. The structure of the procurement process makes some political strategies easier and some more difficult. Small wonder, then, that political strategies take the path of least resistance. This means that politics affects the spending of Pentagon funds above all in the following ways.

> Congressmen cannot, as a rule, influence DOD source selection decisions. Yet they can use the authorization process to force the Pentagon to purchase specific systems, and otherwise tinker with procurement policy to protect constituent interests.
> Since prime contracts cannot be readily targeted, efforts focus on subcontract targeting. The latter is the preferred way to maximize geographic and economic impact.
> Military bases are handled separately, and differently, from contracts. Their distribution and disposition are much more political.

It should be clear that, of all the phases in the acquisition cycle, the subcontracting process is most consistent with a political model of defense contract distribution. To some degree, the veneer of objectivity that the FAR gives to the contracting process may, in fact, serve as a politically serviceable cover for subcontract targeting. That cover gives the impression that political manipulations have been excluded from the prime contract award process, when in fact they have only been shifted over to the subcontract business necessarily contained in every prime award.

The rules of the procurement process dictate how easily political strategies are carried out. In many respects, the contracting process is politicized to a degree consistent with the popular view. The paths of influence may differ, but the goals and outcomes are the same. It is not possible to isolate contract awards entirely from political effects. Since the defense budget is the product of a political process, it would be astonishing if the money so allocated were spent solely on the basis of military effectiveness criteria. In the system as currently configured, though, every player in the game wins: The Pentagon can "spread the wealth" and protect its programs without crossing the boundary of the law, legislators can make exaggerated claims about the extent of their influence, and constituents can keep their jobs. But the process effectively eliminates egregious political manipulation of defense prime contracts.

NOTES

1. United States Congress, Committee on Government Operations, Report of the Permanent Subcommittee on Investigations, *TFX Contract Investigation* (Washington, D.C.: U.S. Government Printing Office, 1970).

2. One study argued that McNamara's decision reflected his desire to force the services (here the Air Force and the Navy) to procure a single aircraft. See Robert J. Art, *The TFX Decision: McNamara and the Military* (Boston: Little, Brown, 1968).

3. Interviews conducted by the author. Also, Terry J. Miller, "The Interaction Between the Private, Public, and Third Sector in the Defense Contract Award Process: Lobbying for Defense Contracts in Los Angeles County 1951–1972" (Ph.D. Dissertation, University of Southern California, 1980), p. 180.

4. William Proxmire, *Report from Wasteland: America's Military-Industrial Complex* (New York: Praeger, 1970), p. 100.

5. Interviews conducted by the author.

6. Richard Stubbing, *The Defense Game* (New York: Harper and Row, 1986), p. 169.

7. Miller, "Lobbying for Defense Contracts," pp. 105–6.

8. Merton J. Peck and Frederick M. Scherer, *The Weapons Acquisition Process: An Economic Analysis* (Boston: Division of Research, Graduate School of Business Administration, Harvard University, 1962), and Frederick M. Scherer, *The Weapons Acquisition Process: Economic Incentives* (Boston: Division of Research, Graduate School of Business Administration, Harvard University, 1964).

9. Peck and Scherer, *Weapons Acquisition Process,* p. 114.

10. Ibid., p. 382.

11. J. Ronald Fox, *Arming America: How the U.S. Buys Weapons* (Boston: Division of Research, Graduate School of Business Administration, Harvard University, 1974).

12. Ibid., p. 281.

13. Still the best works are Aaron Wildavsky, *The Politics of the Budgetary Process* (Boston: Little, Brown, 1960), and Richard Fenno, *The Power of the Purse* (Boston: Little, Brown, 1966).

14. R. Douglas Arnold, *Congress and the Bureaucracy* (New Haven: Yale University Press, 1979), Chapter 2.

15. Barry S. Rundquist, "Congressional Influence on the Distribution of Prime Military Contracts" (Ph.D. Dissertation, Stanford University, 1973); Barry S. Rundquist and David Griffith, "An Interrupted Time-Series Test of the Distributive Theory of Military Policy-Making," *Western Political Quarterly* 29 (December 1976); Arnold, *Congress and the Bureaucracy;* Carolyn F Goss, "Military Committee Membership and Defense-Related Benefits in the House of Representatives," *Western Political Quarterly* 25 (June 1972); Bruce Ray, "Military Committee Membership in the House of Representatives and the Allocation of Defense Department Outlays," ibid. 34 (June 1981).

16. Rundquist and Griffith, "Time-Series Test."

17. Barry S. Rundquist, "On Testing a Military Industrial Complex Theory," *American Politics Quarterly* 6 (1978): 38.

18. Rosy Nimroody, *Star Wars: The Economic Fallout* (Cambridge: Ballinger, 1988), p. 97.

19. This in no way diminishes the council's conclusion that the Strategic Defense Contracting Office has used contracts to create constituencies in academia, nor the fact that SDI contractors have given large campaign contributions to House

and Senate military committee members. See Nimroody, *Star Wars*, pp. 77–91, 100–103.

20. Goss, "Military Committee Membership."

21. Arnold, *Congress and the Bureaucracy*, p. 108.

22. Peck and Scherer, *Weapons Acquisition Process*, p. 21.

23. Prior to that time, the contracting activities of the Defense Department were governed by the Armed Services Procurement Regulation (ASPR), which was created by the Armed Services Procurement Act of 1947. The ASPR was superseded in the 1970s by the Defense Acquisition Regulation (32 CFR Chap. 1, Parts 1–39). Civilian agencies were under the authority of the Federal Procurement Regulations System (41 CFR Subtitle A, Chapters 1–49).

24. The General Accounting Office publishes a guide on how to protest contract awards. See U.S. General Accounting Office, *Bid Protests at GAO: A Descriptive Guide*, 2nd ed. (Washington, D.C.: U.S. GAO, 1985).

25. Contractors do avail themselves of their protest rights. The GAO reported that in fiscal year 1987, 1,783 protests were lodged with the GAO bid protest office by contractors doing business with DOD. Of these, 1,276 were either withdrawn or dismissed prior to adjudication. Of the remaining 487 cases, fifty-seven were sustained in favor of the contractor (U.S. General Accounting Office, *Bid Protest Report*, OGC/B-158766, January 31, 1987).

26. Sandra Sugawara, "Losing Bidders Challenging U.S. Contracts," *Washington Post*, Dec. 20, 1988, p. C-1.

27. Fox, *Arming America*, p. 266.

28. Ibid., p. 269.

29. Miller, "Lobbying for Defense Contracts," p. 149.

30. Peck and Scherer report that during one twenty-year stretch in the Navy Bureau of Aeronautics (now the Naval Air Systems Command), "only once in 38 new system competitions . . . did the Bureau chief overturn recommendations submitted by Bureau evaluation groups." Peck and Scherer, *Weapons Acquisition Process*, p. 383.

31. Craig Liske and Barry Rundquist, *The Politics of Weapons Procurement: The Role of Congress* (Denver: University of Denver Social Science Foundation and Graduate School of International Studies, Monograph Series in World Affairs, vol. 12, no. 1, 1974–75), p. 83.

32. Peck and Scherer, *Weapons Acquisition Process*, p. 113.

33. Arnold, *Congress and the Bureaucracy*, p. 29.

34. *Congressional Record*, August 3, 1970, p. 26960.

35. Interview conducted by the author.

36. Interviews conducted by the author. Also, Fox, *Arming America*, p. 282.

37. Clarence Danhof, *Government Contracting and Technological Change* (Washington, D.C.: The Brookings Institution, 1968), p. 216.

38. Peck and Scherer, *Weapons Acquisition Process*, p. 381.

39. Miller, "Lobbying for Defense Contracts," p. 141.

40. Statement of Richard Stubbing, Office of Management and Budget, in United States Congress, Committee on the Budget, *Review of Defense Acquisition and Management* (98th Congress, 1st Session, 1983), p. 564.

41. *Congressional Record*, July 20, 1983, p. H-5302.

42. "Fairchild Tightens Procedures Following Air Force Review," *Aviation Week and Space Technology*, September 9, 1985, p. 18.

43. "New York Legislators Ask for Fairchild Reprieve," ibid., September 9, 1985, p. 18.

44. "Senate Votes to Scrap T-46," *New York Times*, May 19, 1986, p. D5.

45. John R. Cushman, Jr., "Panel Acts to Revive Air Force Jet Produced on

L.I.," ibid., June 26, 1986, p. A24; Jonathan Fuerbringer, "House Moves to Retain Trainer Jet Made on L.I.," ibid., August 12, 1986, p. A21.

46. David C. Morrison, "Chaos on Capitol Hill," *National Journal,* September 27, 1986, p. 2305.

47. Rone Tempest, "U.S. Defense Establishment Wields a Pervasive Power," *Los Angeles Times,* July 10, 1983, Part IV, p. 1; Walter S. Mossberg, "Pork Barrel Politics: Some Congressmen Treat Military Budget as a Source for Patronage," *Wall Street Journal,* April 15, 1983, p. 1.

48. Mark Rovner, *Defense Dollars and Sense: A Common Cause Guide to the Defense Budget Process* (Washington, D.C.: Common Cause, 1983), p. 60.

49. Interview conducted by the author.

50. Mossberg, "Pork Barrel Politics," p. 22.

51. Ibid., p. 22.

52. Even for nonmembers, base closing matters are handled gingerly. For example, when the Defense Department closed nine major installations in 1964, it was surely no coincidence that the announcement was made on November 19, several weeks after election day (which also gave voters a complete election cycle to forget the loss). I would like to thank R. Douglas Arnold for making this information available to me.

53. Numerous additional examples can be found in Charlotte Twight, "DOD Attempts to Close Military Bases: The Political Economy of Congressional Resistance," in this volume.

54. Fred Kaplan, "Weinberger Lists Three Facilities to Shut," *Boston Globe,* February 13, 1986, p. 3.

55. A favorite tactic of hawks is to pressure critics of high defense spending to name programs in their own districts that can be cut. Not surprisingly, few such programs are offered up for sacrifice.

56. "Panel Proposes Closing 86 Bases," *Los Angeles Times,* December 30, 1988, p. 1; Mike Mills, "Base Closings: The Political Pain Is Limited," *Congressional Quarterly,* December 31, 1988, p. 3626.

57. Molly Moore, "Base Closings: This Means War!" *Washington Post,* March 14, 1989, p. 25.

58. Mike Mills, "Base Closings: A Dogged, if Futile, Trench War Is Planned by Some on Hill," *Congressional Quarterly,* March 25, 1989, p. 661.

59. Patrick Caddell, "Memorandum I: General Election Strategy," June 25, 1980, reprinted in Elizabeth Drew, *Portrait of an Election: The 1980 Presidential Election Campaign* (New York: Simon and Schuster, 1981), pp. 388–409.

60. Steven J. Rosenstone, *Forecasting Presidential Elections* (New Haven: Yale University Press, 1983), p. 61.

61. If Carter and Reagan resorted to this sort of electoral targeting, they would not have been the first. Wright found that New Deal spending was directly targeted to maximize political and electoral effects in the 1930s. See Gavin Wright, "The Political Economy of New Deal Spending: An Econometric Analysis," *Review of Economics and Statistics* 56, no. 1 (February 1974).

62. Stubbing, *The Defense Game,* p. 186. In all fairness, it must be noted that there is no direct evidence of political manipulation; California has long been the largest recipient of contract dollars (by a wide margin).

63. Michael R. Gordon, "Are Military Contractors part of the Problem or Part of the Solution?" *National Journal,* July 11, 1981, p. 1234. Also interviews conducted by the author.

64. Interview conducted by the author.

65. Liske and Rundquist, *Politics of Weapons Procurement,* p. 82.

66. Jacques Gansler, *The Defense Industry* (Cambridge: MIT Press, 1980), p. 150. Emphasis added.

67. This is not always true. On many sole-source programs, the government will insist on certain subcontracting requirements; a certain level of competitively awarded or dual-sourced subcontract dollars, for example. And prime contractors are responsible for assuring subcontractor compliance with various federal laws (equal opportunity, child labor, etc.).

68. Gansler, *Defense Industry*, p. 43, and Eric Greenberg, "Some Aspects of the Distribution of Military Prime Contract Awards," *Review of Economics and Statistics* 49 (May 1966): 205.

69. Gansler, *Defense Industry*, p. 43.

70. Ibid., p. 129.

71. U.S. General Accounting Office, *Defense Department Subcontract-Level Reporting System* (GAO/ID-83-30), Report B-208826, January 21, 1983, pp. 1–3.

72. George C. Wilson, "Navy Lobbies to Add Two Carriers," *Washington Post*, March 29, 1987, p. A5.

73. Bill Keller, "In Bull Market for Arms, Weapons Industry Lobbyists Push Products, Not Policy," *Congressional Quarterly*, October 25, 1980, p. 3206.

74. Liske and Rundquist, *Politics of Weapons Procurement*, p. 82.

75. The report is reprinted in *Congressional Record*, May 17, 1976, pp. 14141–44.

76. Data for the commercial programs were provided on the condition that neither the manufacturers nor the programs be identified. State names are coded to prevent identification of the manufacturer's main plant location.

77. For these smaller states, the dollar total was calculated by (1) regressing total expenditures on development expenditures (which were provided for all states), and (2) multiplying development expenditures by the resulting regression coefficient for the small dollar states. This calculation did not appreciably change the overall distribution percentages.

78. See M. A. Utton, *Industrial Concentration* (Harmondsworth: Penguin, 1970), p. 43.

79. See Stephen Davies, "Choosing Between Concentration Indices: the Iso-Concentration Curve," *Economica* 46 (February 1979): 67.

80. The Herfindahl index is not without its detractors, and there is a lively debate about how best to measure industrial concentration. For present purposes, however, even approximate indices will suffice. See Davies, "Choosing between Concentration Indices," and "Measuring Industrial Concentration: An Alternative Approach," *Review of Economics and Statistics* 62, no. 2 (May 1980): 306–9.

81. A program with the widest possible distribution will have 2 percent of its subcontracts let in each of the fifty states; this line will have a slope of 2 and will pass through the origin. A program with the narrowest possible distribution will have 100 percent of the program built in one state; graphically, a line from the origin with slope 100, turning into a line of slope 0. So, as lines deviate from the diagonal, the subcontract distribution becomes more narrow.

82. Utton, *Industrial Concentration*, p. 43.

83. McDonnell Douglas Helicopter Company, *Demographic Overview: AH-64A Production Program, as of January 1987*.

84. Interview conducted by the author.

85. See J. Philip Geddes, "The U.S. Army's Division Air Defense Gun," *International Defense Review* 7 (1981): 879–87, and *Jane's Weapon Systems 1984–85* (London: Jane's Publishing Company, 1984), pp. 121–22.

10

Department of Defense Attempts to Close Military Bases: The Political Economy of Congressional Resistance

CHARLOTTE TWIGHT

INTRODUCTION

"I contend that much of our inefficiency and waste is mandated by Congress. We have the Maybank Amendment, Davis-Bacon, limitation on contracting, sole sourcing, restraints on base closings and a thousand and one hurdles that the Congress puts in the way of the Defense Department in trying to operate efficiently."[1]

—Senator Phil Gramm

Enormous waste plagues defense operations as a result of parochial efforts by members of Congress to retain inefficient domestic bases that the Department of Defense wants to close. Yet during the 1970s some five hundred military bases or activities were closed at DOD's request. Of 105 base closures requested by DOD in 1976, ninety-four were implemented. Of 235 base closures requested by DOD during 1978 and 1979, 215 were implemented.[2]

How are these statistics consistent with the reality of Congressional resistance to base closures? The answer lies in the fact that the bases successfully closed have been predominantly small installations whose beneficiaries lacked the political clout to inspire diligent effort by senators and representatives. In stark contrast, large military installations have been the bread and butter of many influential congressmen. As we will see, their successful efforts effected political and statutory changes that resulted in utter frustration of all DOD attempts to close major military facilities between 1977 and 1987.

Why the Congressional resistance to major base closures? A person unencumbered by the jargon of academia would probably answer with a knowing laugh and be on his way: it does not require an advanced degree to understand political pork. But if it were only pork, I would not have much to add to other writers' observations about what goes on at the trough.

Writers on this subject are tempted to tell a story that reflects well-defined ideological or economic interests. Either DOD is always on the side of the angels, resisted at every turn by unprincipled congressmen trading patronage for reelection, or Congress occupies that angelic role, sparring endlessly with a Defense Department bent on playing politics with base closures. In truth, as public choice theory would predict, neither one of these stories alone conveys the complex reality of the base closure struggle.

This paper will explore major military base closures and realignments as a case study in the economics of defense. Of particular interest will be statutory changes enacted in 1985 and in 1988[3] that altered the institutional ground rules governing the battle over military base closures. What emerges is fundamentally an application of public choice theory to a particular subset of interrelationships between the legislative and executive branches of government.

BASE CLOSURES: TOWARD A PUBLIC CHOICE PERSPECTIVE

> "I have yet to see the evidence that Members of Congress are prepared to withdraw from a primary posture of being sales agents for Defense bases and military-industry firms and the like."[4]
>
> —Prof. Seymour Melman

Certain applications of public choice theory to political dogfights over military base closures are immediately apparent. Retaining an obsolete or inefficient military base presents a classic example of concentrated benefits and dispersed costs. Whereas the benefits from sustaining an unneeded or inefficient facility fall squarely upon a narrowly defined segment of the population in the affected geographic region, the costs in terms of reduced military readiness and wasted resources are borne by all citizens. The residents of Limestone, Maine, have no trouble understanding that closure of Loring Air Force Base would mean a direct loss of income to them, but people in Boise, Idaho, have much less incentive to understand or act on the understanding that keeping Loring AFB open would slightly reduce the military effectiveness of the United States. Even in the absence of logrolling

incentives, one would predict greater political viability for the special interests representing the affected region than for the more widely dispersed
opposition.

From the politician's perspective, it is cheap to applaud efficiency and
the closure of unnecessary domestic bases provided that the bases proposed
for closure are not in the politician's own district. Thus in hearings on
military base closures and realignments, congressmen representing districts
targeted for base closures usually begin by genuflecting toward efficiency
and end by saying that neither efficiency nor national security would be
served by closing bases in their districts. Representative Edwin Forsythe of
New Jersey typified this response when he opined regarding the proposed
closure of Fort Dix, New Jersey, that "As responsible Members of Congress,
we must support any legitimate move to increase efficiency and save dollars
in our defense establishments but in this instance [Fort Dix] we firmly
believe that the Army has not established a good case in terms of its own
strategic or management priorities."[5] In 1976 Senator Symington remarked
concerning the need for improved DOD management of base closures that
"The Congress itself has been partly to blame because, on the one hand we
have been attempting to reduce Defense expenditures, yet on the other
delegations affected by Defense cutbacks in their districts or States have
worked to stave off those cutbacks."[6]

Also relevant from a public choice perspective is the timing of marginal
costs and benefits associated with base closures. Major base closures or
realignments usually require cash outlays in the short run—for relocation
expenses, enhancements for other facilities intended to assume the mission
of the closed base, and the like. The benefits come later in the form of costs
avoided as a result of not operating the inefficient facility. Economists have
no problem making the appropriate present-value computation and recognizing that if net present value from closing the base is positive, then closing
is a good thing to do despite the differing time lines of the costs and
benefits. With shorter time horizons imposed by the constraint of reelection, however, even politicians whose districts escape being targeted for
closures are less willing to accommodate such present-value mandates. The
reality is that the voting public has not internalized the normative implications of present value, so it comes as no surprise that politicians experience
pressure to respond in ways inconsistent with its dictates.

Public choice theory also suggests that logrolling will thrive in this
environment. The legislative history discussed in subsequent sections is
consistent with this prediction. In most instances, however, these trades
cannot be documented via the printed record, because votes to perpetuate
obsolete bases are almost invariably submerged in huge defense authorization or appropriation bills which are adopted with near unanimity. Even
when the yeas and nays are recorded, these votes merely signal approval of
all the trades that have been made off the record prior to the final vote on

passage of the omnibus legislation. As one senator commented in floor debate on the 1985 changes to the base closure legislation, "Log-rolling takes place in a general way. Sure. Am I saying anybody here has done it? I am not prepared to quote chapter and verse on that. . . . But we all know that it has happened."[7]

Moreover, it is apparent that the trades are not exclusively of the "you support my base and I'll support yours" variety: support for one congressman's base may be bought with reciprocal support on a nondefense issue. For example, describing his efforts to obtain a House hearing on proposed base closures affecting his district, Representative St. Germain (Rhode Island) stated, "My plea was that we and our delegations have consistently in the matter of floods, hurricanes, tornadoes, come to the assistance of our fellow Members of Congress to assist their constituents."[8]

Inherently high transaction costs coupled with transaction-cost augmentation by elected and appointed officials characterize the political milieu in which base closure issues are decided.[9] If a member of Congress or a DOD official argues that a particular military facility must be retained for national defense reasons, it is extraordinarily difficult to counter that assertion. Since every military facility was ostensibly created for the purpose of defense, it is easy to assert that any existing installation serves some defense function. Of course, from an opportunity cost perspective, retaining an inefficient or redundant military facility entails forgoing the additional military readiness that could be purchased by expending those resources on a more efficient facility or on more productive avenues to military preparedness, not to mention the forgone civilian uses of those resources.[10] However, given pervasive lack of public comprehension of opportuntiy cost and net present value, politicians and other interested parties can readily stigmatize base closure proposals as antidefense.

As we will see more concretely in the next sections, information costs to the public and to legislators are extreme in defense matters in general and base closure cases in particular. Not only is it difficult to oppose defense politically; it is often nearly impossible for an unbiased observer to determine what really is in the interest of national defense. Representative Latta (Ohio), though hardly an impartial observer in the case at hand, alluded to this problem in hearings on DOD's case for inactivation of his state's Rossford Arsenal, commenting that "I have absolutely no information, as you well know, to refute the facts and figures that have been presented in this case. We have no way of knowing whether these figures are correct, but we have to assume that they are such."[11] We have already seen how misleading statistics can be where base closures are involved. Moreover, information costs to the public regarding base closures are surely an exponential function of information costs to congressmen, a problem exacerbated by the tendency of every warm-blooded politician to wave the flag of "defense" when the purpose at hand is unadulterated parochialism.

In the following sections many aspects of Congressional and constituent rent-seeking behavior will be examined. That behavior is perhaps most prominent when congressmen from two contending states each battle to have the other state's base closed and its mission relocated to a base in the congressman's home state.[12] As public choice theory would predict, the legislators scrape and claw just as businesses do in the analogous competition for government-granted licenses in an entry-restricted market. In both situations the contenders are willing to expend resources up to the amount of the nonmarket gains derivable from winning the competition.

Other implications of public choice theory regarding Congressional resistance to base closures are perhaps less obvious. We will see below that in the three major legislative upheavals regarding base closures between 1961 and 1985, the House of Representatives was consistently more resistant to base closures and hence more supportive of restrictions on DOD base closure flexibility than was the Senate. This is consonant with public choice theory in that representatives, with their more narrowly drawn constituencies, have incentives to be more vociferous proponents of the parochial perspective. Although parochial motivation is strong in the Senate also, there it is moderated somewhat by each senator's larger and more diverse constituency.

Another motivation of legislators in both houses is a desire not to be undercut politically by the executive branch. I call it the "political double-cross," and its reverberations can be felt across the ground where base closure battles are fought. Nothing arouses Congressional ire more than to authorize and appropriate funds at DOD's request for military bases that DOD shortly thereafter deems inefficient, obsolete, or redundant. Representative Arends commented that he sometimes wondered whether DOD personnel could understand why members of Congress raised questions about certain base closings. His explanation was that

> just going back a few months we sat in the Armed Services Committee and heard the eloquent pleas [of DOD] and we obligingly go [sic] along, not because we wanted to go along but because we thought it was the thing to do. We authorized. We later appropriated. And then find on the very first effort on the cutback on things, the very essential and basic things which many of us basically believed were necessary and vital to the welfare of the serviceman, we find the first thing, off goes its head.[13]

We will see below that the use or avoidance of the political double-cross partially explains how legislators define their self-interest regarding proposed base closures. The potential for political double-cross thus also figures importantly in designing institutional reforms for implementing necessary base closures.

CONGRESSIONAL ATTEMPTS TO CURTAIL BASE CLOSURES, 1961–88

> "Now, that is fine if the Congress in its wisdom
> decides that bases should be kept open for economic
> reasons or for the benefit of a local community. . . .
> But then don't turn around and say that we are ineffi-
> cient and open us up to charges that we don't know
> what we are doing, that we have a bunch of bumblers
> over here wasting the taxpayers' money. You can't
> have it both ways."[14]
>
> —Dr. Lawrence Korb,
> Department of Defense

Between 1961 and 1988, major upheavals in the institutional mechanisms for handling major base closures and realignments occurred. To
integrate events it will be useful to view these twenty-eight years as four
relatively cohesive periods: 1961–65, culminating in President Johnson's
initial veto and subsequent approval of legislation in 1965; 1966–76, ending
with President Ford's initial veto and later approval of a 1976 base closure
statute; 1977–85, terminating in enactment of new legislation in 1985; and
1986–88, resulting in passage of the Base Closure and Realignment Act of
1988.

Several constants emerge from the flux of time and circumstance. First,
the election cycle often dictates the timing of base closure announcements.
Second, in the predictable outcry over proposed base closures by affected
legislators, members of the House of Representatives are regularly more
vehement in the aggregate than their senatorial counterparts, for reasons
discussed above. Finally, cycles of base closure announcements handled
administratively in ways anathema to Congress historically have given rise
to cycles of restrictive legislation curtailing DOD's flexibility to implement
major military base closures or realignments.

1961–65

With the inauguration of President Kennedy in 1961, momentum for
base closures began to develop. In his State of the Union message Kennedy
announced that he was instructing Secretary of Defense McNamara to study
possible base closures, mentioning the importance of the base closure program again in his budget message on March 28, 1961. Then on March 30,
1961, McNamara announced the first major round of base closures: seventy-
three military installations were slated for closure, thirty-seven of them in
the United States.

Congress was furious. Hearings were held by a subcommittee of the House Armed Services Committee in July, and the subcommittee sided with the irate congressmen. Although DOD spokesmen protested that this was not a new policy, DOD directive 4165.20 having instructed military departments to identify "excess" properties since August 29, 1958, the subcommittee nonetheless opposed closure in specific cases contested by affected legislators.[15]

Undaunted, McNamara announced additional closures and realignments over the next few years: thirty-three military installations on December 12, 1963; sixty-three military installations on April 24, 1964; and ninety-five additional bases and installations on November 19, 1964. The November announcement was the final straw, coming as it did a scant two weeks after the presidential election. As was to be typical in later years, impetus for major restrictions on DOD's flexibility to implement such base closures centered in the House. In May 1965 the House Armed Services Committee amended the military construction authorization bill to give the House and Senate armed services committees power to block base closures proposed by DOD. The original House bill would have given the committees a thirty-day review period during which either committee could introduce a resolution rejecting a proposed base closure. If such a resolution were introduced, the bill provided an additional forty days during which the full house whose committee had acted could approve of the resolution. If such approval were forthcoming—in effect a one-house veto—the closure could not be implemented.[16]

The Senate Armed Services Committee voted to remove this provision from the military construction authorization bill (H.R. 8439), citing concern that it would allow blockage of closures by one house acting alone rather than by passage of formal legislation. After a House-Senate conference on H.R. 8439, a compromise provision was approved by both houses. The new provision prevented the Secretary of Defense from implementing base closures until 120 days after he provided a detailed report and justification of his proposals to the armed services committees. Moreover, base closures could be proposed only between January 1 and April 30 of each year. As the conference report stated, this provision would give the armed services committees "an opportunity to hear the matter of any particular base closure at a time when it is considering the military construction authorization bill and to write restrictive language in such legislation in the case it disapproved such a base closure."[17]

President Johnson vetoed H.R. 8439 on August 21, 1965, resting his disapproval primarily on his contention that the bill violated the separation of powers between the legislative and executive branches of government. In his veto message he stated that

The President is the Commander in Chief of the armed forces. The President cannot sign into law a bill which substantially inhibits him from performing his duty. He cannot sign into law a measure which deprives him of power for eight months of the year even to propose a reduction of mission or the closing of any military installation, and which prohibits him from closing, abandoning or substantially reducing in mission any military facility in the country for what could be a year or more and must be 120 days. The times do not permit it. The Constitution prohibits it.[18]

Congress did not attempt to override the veto, instead adopting a watered-down provision that merely required the Secretary of Defense to delay implementation until thirty days after giving the armed services committees a full report and justification for proposed closures affecting bases with a total of more than 250 military and civilian personnel. Upon signing the bill into law, President Johnson commented that it "refreshed my faith in our institutions of government."[19]

1966-76

The new law was mild. By and large DOD continued to prevail in base closure matters, despite much Congressional sound and fury. A succession of base closure and realignment packages emerged, although noticeably absent in election years. A hundred and forty-nine closures or realignments were proposed on December 8, 1965, 126 of which were in the United States; 39 realignment or closure actions were announced on January 19, 1967; then after an election-year hiatus 40 realignment or closure proposals on April 24, 1969, followed by 280 more on October 29, 1969, and an additional 341 on March 6, 1970. The tide was turning, however, and Fitzgerald and Lipson report that on January 21, 1971, Secretary of Defense Melvin Laird "let it be known that the White House had scrapped its plan for nationwide realignment."[20]

Nonetheless, the real furor was yet to come. Major base closure announcements in 1973 and 1976 that were part of a general scaledown in forces due to termination of the Vietnam War triggered intense Congressional resistance. On April 17, 1973, Defense Secretary Elliot Richardson announced a base closure package that entailed 274 separate realignment or closure actions. This 1973 package led to extensive hearings by several Congressional committees: the printed record of hearings chaired by Senator Symington on base closures in Massachusetts and California alone required three volumes.[21] Some very powerful senators' webs had been disturbed, and the general hostility to the closures and the manner in which they were handled was extreme. Senator Claiborne Pell of Rhode Island reflected the intensity of Congressional resistance in his proposal for a "Military Installation Closing Commission" to review DOD's justification for base closure proposals, a bill that would have prevented DOD from acting for 180 days following notification of Congress.[22]

When in March and April of 1976 DOD announced 147 more bases and installations as candidates for closure or realignment, Congress was ready to act. Legislation again was passed by both houses of Congress that would have imposed severe constraints on DOD. In section 612 of the military construction bill (H.R. 12384), Congress required notification when bases were "candidates" for closure or major realignment, followed by a mandatory waiting period of nine months during which DOD was to comply with the National Environmental Policy Act (NEPA) and respond to reasonable Congressional requests for information. After the nine-month delay, DOD had to notify the armed services committees and provide a detailed justification of any final decision to proceed with a base closure or major realignment. Thereupon an additional ninety-day delay commenced in order to enable Congress to enact legislation to block DOD's action if it so desired. In essence H.R. 12384 imposed a mandatory one-year delay prior to implementation of any base closure or major realignment desired by DOD.[23]

President Ford vetoed H.R. 12384, citing section 612 as the objectionable provision that prompted his veto. Surprisingly, Ford's veto message focused primarily on the "arbitrary time limit" and "budgetary drain on the defense dollar" that the bill augured, not making any reference to Lyndon Johnson's earlier veto of similar legislation. Indeed, Ford's only reference to the separation of powers issue was the oblique comment that "section 612 raises serious questions by its attempt to limit my powers over military bases. The President must be able, if the need arises, to change or reduce the mission at any military installation if and when that becomes necessary."[24] That was it.

Many members of Congress took the veto message to mean that there was no problem with the constitutionality of the bill. In any event the sentiment for the bill was strong: the House voted by a two-thirds majority to override Ford's veto, while the Senate override attempt failed despite 51 votes favoring it.[25]

Despite the failure to override President Ford's veto, Congress's will prevailed. Congress quickly changed the offending provision in the Military Construction Authorization Act and sent the revised bill (H.R. 14846) to Ford for his signature. Practically nothing of substance was altered. The one-year forced delay on base closure implementation was shortened to sixty days, but the change was meaningless because the mandated NEPA procedures would take at least a year anyway. As Representative Ichord stated during consideration of the revised measure by the House, "The original bill required a waiting period of 12 months. This bill requires only 60 days, but I would point out in most cases I would expect by the time they comply with the National Environmental Policy Act and they provide the information to the Congress, that a year would be required."[26]

Congress also held fast in its insistence that DOD provide extremely detailed justification of proposed closures or realignments. Congress first required notification that a base was a "candidate" for action, then mandated compliance with NEPA, and last demanded a "detailed justification" of any final decision reached by the Secretary of Defense, including "the estimated fiscal, local economic, budgetary, environmental, strategic, and operational consequences of the proposed closure or reduction."[27] The sixty-day waiting period before DOD could take irrevocable action to implement a closure or realignment commenced after compliance with NEPA, upon the submission of the detailed justification to the armed services committees. When on the floor of the House Representative Cohen asked, "[I]s it not true under the amendment passed by the Senate, that in essence the Defense Department would have to supply the very information we sought to have given us in section 612 adopted by the House, giving complete justification from the military point of view and the economic point of view?", Representative Ichord responded that "the gentleman is correct."[28]

President Ford signed this bill into law on September 30, 1976. In what can only have been a face-saving remark intended for those not apprised of the details of the two bills, Ford remarked that "The bill which I am signing today represents a substantial compromise on behalf of the Congress and refreshes my faith in the system of checks and balances established by our Constitution."[29]

The die thus was cast for the ensuing years. As originally enacted, the base closure provision applied only to military installations authorized to employ five hundred or more civilians. It applied to all closures of such installations and to any reduction in civilian personnel by 50 percent or by one thousand or more employees. Its mandates also applied to any "construction, conversion, or rehabilitation" at another military facility occasioned as a result of closures or reductions in personnel controlled by the new law. This statute, codified as 10 U.S.C. section 2687, was the prototype of legislation which was to throttle all DOD attempts to close or realign major military bases between 1977 and 1988.

1977–85

The legislation enacted in 1976 was made permanent in 1977, as the original statute had been adopted for one year only. On August 1, 1977, President Carter signed into law the fiscal year 1978 Military Construction Authorization Act, which contained a new section 612 essentially identical to the earlier provision, slightly modifying its wording and making it a permanent feature of U.S. law.[30] It was amended a year later to apply to military installations authorized to employ three hundred or more civilians, thus broadening its scope. As a DOD spokesman would later describe it, the 1977 legislation was "the functional equivalent of giving Congress a veto" over base closure and realignment proposals.[31]

DOD took a brief stab at implementing base closures under the new institutional arrangement. Defense Secretary Harold Brown released a list of eighty-five proposed base closures and realignments on April 26, 1978, followed by proposals for 157 realignment actions on March 29, 1979. Congress had a field day contesting these proposals as well as fighting realignments first announced in the spring of 1976 which were retroactively covered by the 1977 legislation.[32] Congress now had a profusion of tools with which to undercut proposed base closures: NEPA court challenges, Congressional hearings on the candidate bases and on the detailed justifications DOD submitted, Congressional demands for environmental studies during the authorization and appropriation process even when not otherwise required by law, denial of design funds for base consolidation, disapproval of construction funds to effect closures or realignments, imposition of requirements for alternate use studies or one-year delays prior to implementation, and "remedial" legislation to block entirely DOD's decision to close or realign a military base.

These tools were employed with zeal. The result was that no major base closures—none—were implemented between 1977 and 1985. As it became clear that none of the major realignments proposed in 1978 would be implemented, DOD gave up even proposing realignments, submitting no new base-closure packages between April 1979 and 1985. In 1985 a DOD spokesman testified that "With major bases now, it is almost impossible to close them, based upon my experience over the last 4 years."[33]

Certain senators were very upset about the waste of taxpayers' money that this situation implied, and the Senate Armed Services Committee held hearings in February 1985. Defense Secretary Caspar Weinberger there testified that "At the moment it takes about 22 months before a base can be closed [after a decision is made to close it] due to the number of hurdles that are in the statutes that must be cleared before a single base closure can take effect," and he promised recommendations for statutory changes to alleviate this problem.

The recommendations were cast as "emergency" measures, a budget deficit serving as the purported emergency that would trigger their application. The political sleight of hand was widely recognized, given a political environment in which most congressmen and their constituents expected budget deficits to be the norm rather than the exception for the foreseeable future. DOD sought authority to implement military base closures or realignments during the twenty-four months following submission of a budget reflecting a deficit without regard to other provisions of law that would prevent or delay such action, including appropriation act restrictions on expenditures to close bases, NEPA, and 10 U.S.C. section 2687, the 1977 base closure statute. DOD also sought freedom to use funds appropriated for military construction to design and build facilities required to implement desired closures and realignments.[34]

As 1985 proceeded, several proposals emerged to give DOD more flexibility in implementing base closures, the most prominent among them proffered by Senator Phil Gramm. Senator Gramm's proposal included many of the features on Weinberger's wish list, and it was adopted by a narrow margin in the Department of Defense Authorization Act reported by the Senate Armed Services Committee (S. 1160). During rancorous debate on the Senate floor, the opposition charged that the provision had been included without adequate hearings. A DOD-supplied "illustrative" list of twenty-two bases that might be evaluated for closure or realignment if S. 1160 were enacted poured fuel on the flames. Nevertheless, the Senate twice defeated attempts to delete or gut the Gramm amendment and then passed the Defense Authorization Act with the "emergency" base closure amendment intact.

Reflecting its traditionally more intense opposition to base closures, the House of Representatives had no such provision in its version of the act, making necessary a House-Senate conference. The base closure provision that emerged from that conference changed the 1977 law in two important ways. First, it eliminated the old two-step process in which DOD initially announced a base as a "candidate" for realignment and only later, after the intervening NEPA process, conveyed the "final decision" for closure or realignment to Congress in conjunction with submission of its detailed justification. Instead, only one announcement was to be made: DOD's final decision to close or realign the facility. Second, the new provision required DOD to submit its base closure decisions in conjunction with its annual request for authorization of appropriations.

Another change stimulated much debate but ultimately was of no consequence: the explicit requirement that DOD comply with the provisions of NEPA was removed, but only on the understanding that NEPA nonetheless would continue to apply, since DOD was not explicitly exempted from that statute. In addition the conference report deleted the "deficit emergency" hocus-pocus from S. 1160. The waiting period of sixty days under the 1977 law was changed to thirty legislative days or sixty calendar days to avoid the possibility of losing the waiting period due to adjournment of Congress. Finally, the reporting requirement retained as its criteria the fiscal, local economic, budgetary, environmental, strategic, and operational consequences of the proposed realignment, but it changed the mandatory level of information from a "detailed justification" to an "evaluation."

Both houses of Congress agreed to the conference report, and President Reagan signed the bill into law on November 8, 1985 without a whimper.[35] That in itself was astounding: no veto; no mention of questionable constitutionality, despite the fact that the executive branch now could submit base closure proposals only during a set time period, the very substance of the provision Johnson vetoed in 1965 (requiring submission of base closure proposals between January and April).

One important question is, what made it politically feasible to implement changes in 1985 and not at some other time? Why did effective sentiment to loosen constraints on DOD materialize in 1985, given the magnitude of Congressional resistance to base closures in the 1970s? Several factors appear to have been conducive to this outcome. As we will see below, Congress had come to recognize that the 1977 law made it politically impossible not to resist base closures, a role that some legislators viewed with increasing discomfiture. The Reagan administration was strongly pro-defense, as was the mood of the country, suggesting greater tolerance of DOD autonomy. The defense budget in the early 1980s was growing in real terms beyond anything ever before experienced in peacetime,[36] which reduced the likelihood of extensive base closures not offset by additional spending elsewhere. No major base closures had occurred for over seven years, making the reality of their economic impact less tangible to voters. Moreover, the federal budget deficit loomed larger than at any previous time in the history of the United States, increasing the political attractiveness of savings wherever they might be found. The confluence of these circumstances created a political environment more supportive of base closure policy reform than at any time in more than a decade.

Nonetheless, for reasons discussed in the next section, the 1985 statutory changes ultimately failed to break the deadlock regarding base closures.

1986–88

In practice, the 1985 reforms proved totally ineffective. NEPA procedures as well as Congress's enhanced ability under the 1985 provisions to embed blocking provisions in mammoth, almost veto-proof omnibus military construction authorization acts sustained the institutional invitation to Congressional resistance. Equally important, the 1985 provisions still required DOD to beseech Congress for funding of specific construction projects needed to carry out base closures or consolidations.

DOD first tried to use the new statutory mechanism in its base closure requests for FY 1988. Each service offered one base for possible closure or realignment. Action on the Army's candidate—the Army Materials Technology Laboratory at Watertown, Massachusetts—was stopped cold after the Army withdrew its request, citing data inaccuracies. However, a DOD official stated in a telephone interview that the real reason for the withdrawal was political pressure exerted on the Army by key legislators from Massachusetts. Perhaps most alarming was Congressional response to the Air Force's candidate, Mather Air Force Base in California. When Mather was identified in DOD's request, Congress immediately adopted defense bill language to prevent expenditures even to study closure of Mather. Hence, despite DOD's efforts, the 1985 statutory changes brought forth no major base closures or realignments.

To remedy the situation, Representative Dick Armey (Texas), Senator William Roth (Delaware) and others sponsored bills in 1987 and 1988 to empower the Defense Secretary to expedite implementation of changes in the military base structure. In October 1988, after more than two years of political maneuvering, Congress approved a modified version of Armey's proposal, which subsequently was signed into law by the President.[37] Its centerpiece is a newly established Commission on Base Realignment and Closure.[38]

The legislation required the Commission on Base Realignment and Closure, by December 31, 1988, to transmit to the Defense Secretary and to Congress its conclusions and recommendations regarding which U.S. military bases should be closed or realigned. Contingent upon his approval of all the Commission's recommendations by January 16, 1989, the Defense Secretary was empowered to implement the recommended changes without regard to both 10 U.S.C. section 2687 (the 1977 rules) and statutory restrictions on base closure or realignment expenditures included in appropriation or authorization acts. The new law also made specific provision for a "DOD Base Closure Account" designed to reduce the appropriations barrier to implementation of base closures. Receipts from disposal of surplus real property and facilities located at military bases closed or realigned under the act are to be placed in the account, making such funds available to enhance facilities intended to accommodate relocated missions without the necessity for specific Congressional appropriations.

Earlier versions of the bill elaborately specified the composition of the Commission, reflecting Congressional fears that particular partisan views otherwise would dominate the Commission. Much political horse-trading surrounded the statutory language that actually emerged. The Senate came to accept appointment of the Commission's members by the Defense Secretary in conjunction with preappointment of most Commission members[39] and insertion of another provision that made the recommendations of the Commission an "all-or-nothing" proposition from the Secretary's perspective. To assuage some historically well-grounded fears that base closures might be used to whip recalcitrant members of Congress into shape,[40] the bill provided that the Secretary of Defense had to accept all of the Commission's realignment and closure recommendations or none of them: the Secretary was not allowed to pick and choose. Congress explicitly reserved its right via expedited joint resolution to disapprove the Commission's plan within a period of 45 session days commencing March 1, 1989, but it too contemplated an up-or-down vote on the entire package.

As of this writing, the Commission has made its recommendations,[41] the Secretary of Defense has approved them, and the 45-day clock has expired. There were some local outcries, and Congressional hearings allowed affected members their predictable fulminations. Joint resolutions of disapproval were introduced in both houses. Nonetheless, for political reasons explained more fully below, Congress failed to enact a joint resolution of disapproval,[42] despite the fact that the Commission's plan targets 86 bases for complete closure.

Again one can ask, why now? Despite strong efforts by opponents to scuttle the bill, Armey was able to overcome most of them by hard work, compromise, and a systematic media campaign. His bold last-minute move to substitute the original language of the bill for the amendment-gutted shell on the House floor proved strategically decisive.[43] Politically, many viewed 1988 as a window of opportunity for such contentious issues, allowing the political heat to be directed toward the outgoing Reagan administration. Moreover, as the final section of this chapter will demonstrate, the statutory language that emerged from the House-Senate conference incorporated key changes to Armey's original bill that—from Congress's perspective—left the door to parochial base closure opposition comfortably ajar.[44]

The power of the new law's approach lies in its attempt to put the entire base closure package rather than individual bases on the margin in the political decision-making process—for Congress as well as for the Secretary of Defense. It is an effort to prevent the process from unraveling in the parochialism and interbranch suspicion that historically have attended Congressional and executive branch decisions on individual bases. The final section of this paper analyzes to what extent the statutory language accomplishes this goal and whether it provides a viable long-term solution to the base closure problem. In the next two sections, we examine how these conflicting motives—the parochial and the non-parochial—have stymied previous Congressional attempts to close bases that DOD labeled as obsolete and inefficient.

CONGRESSIONAL RESISTANCE: THE PAROCHIAL RATIONALE

> "[I]f there is one thing in this whole town that keeps this body from cutting expenses it is the word 'parochialism.' "[45]
>
> —Senator Barry Goldwater

It is the perceived duty of every senator and representative to block military base closures or reductions in his or her state or district within the bounds of existing law. Constituents demand it; reelection requires it.

Throughout U.S. history, and particularly when the 1977 legislation was in place, legislators have used all manner of openly parochial maneuvers to keep "their" bases open. There is both a cynical and a sincere side to this. Apart from the desire for reelection, members of Congress often feel that, even if they abhor waste associated with inefficient bases, they owe it to their constituents to defend home district military bases as part of the general obligation to represent their interests. During hearings in 1973, for example, Representative Waldie (California) asked with apparent sincerity, "How can a member of Congress from Rhode Island give up his advocacy of employment for his constituents, no matter what the source of that employment is, when they are out of work? . . . With Rhode Island being shut down . . . what does that congressman do? Does he say, well, that is okay, because it was a mistake to have operated Rhode Island as a defense installation over the years . . . ?"[46] Particularly in conjunction with the DOD incentives and behavior described in the following section, it is difficult to dismiss such pleas as purely self-interested maneuvering for reelection.

There is, however, enough self-interested maneuvering for reelection to be found without scratching so hard. It was hardly subtle when Senator John Glenn of Ohio testified in 1979 that "I am here today also on a very parochial basis, because I feel that the State of Ohio is being asked to bear a disproportionately large share of the Defense Department's cutbacks. . . . This disproportion is unfair because Ohio already gets less than its fair share of military spending."[47] Nor is there reason to ignore DOD's assessment of Congressional resistance to base closures during the late 1970s and early 1980s. DOD's Lawrence Korb stated in 1985 that during the previous ten years, of 601 major bases in the continental U.S., twenty-four had been studied as primary candidates for closure, eight of which were closed. He reported that "Of the remaining sixteen, most were deterred from closure as a result of Congressional action or the threat thereof. . . . It is political pressure, at times subtle and indirect, that usually precipitates a Department decision not to pursue an announced closure plan." His explanation of this subtle and indirect pressure suggested that perhaps "undocumentable" would be a better label. Dr. Korb stated that "Lots of times as soon as people overhear we will even do the minor things the phone is picked up and it is if you want my vote on this, don't do that. . . . I can tell you that on at least 10 occasions, that has happened to me."[48]

The resistance that *can* be documented is impressive. Congress has not hesitated to write specific measures into military construction authorization and appropriation statutes prohibiting base closures desired by DOD. For example, in 1971 Congress ordered that "Notwithstanding any other provision of law, none of the lands constituting Camp Pendleton, California, may be sold, leased, transferred, or otherwise disposed of by the Department of Defense unless hereafter authorized by law."[49] In 1986 Congress ordered that the correctional facilities at Fort Riley, Kansas, cannot be "closed, transferred, or relocated" unless the Secretary of Defense notifies Congress and a 180-day period elapses after Congress receives that notice.[50]

Congress's resistance to closing the Naval Academy Dairy Station provides a particularly intriguing glimpse of parochialism in the trenches. Although this Maryland dairy was established in 1911 "to provide the midshipmen with a source of pure milk following an outbreak of typhoid fever attributed to the unprocessed milk purchased for the midshipmen's mess," by the mid-1960s commercial dairies could satisfy the Navy's needs for pure milk products at lower cost. Based on a GAO report showing potential savings of $83,803 per year if this facility were closed, the Navy in 1965 initiated plans to phase out the dairy farm. In response Congress enacted legislation in 1967 that specifically prohibited the Navy from closing, transferring, or phasing out the farm.[51]

What is unusual is that a representative from Maryland opposed the preservation of the dairy farm. During House debate of the bill, Representative Mathias stated that while he had "a high regard for cows, whether they are found at the Naval Academy dairy farm or elsewhere," that he "made it a matter of high principle to treat all cows with a fine degree of impartiality." He strongly dissented from "the proposition that 600 cows at Gambrills, Md., should be beatified by this bill and be hereafter considered as sacred cows," stating that the bill "would exempt these 600 sacred cows from the laws of economics, and . . . from the disciplines of the free enterprise system." A hold-out from the "parochial imperative"? The good representative from Maryland in fact wanted the Navy to be able to close the dairy farm because the federal land was extremely valuable, and he hoped that more federal jobs would be provided on that turf if it were freed up for another governmental use.[52]

The provision preserving the dairy farm served another purpose also. Although the Senate's version of the bill contained no sacred-cow provision for Maryland, the Senate did insert an altogether different provision to prevent DOD from closing Fort DeRussy, Hawaii. In the House-Senate conference on the bill, the outcome proved consistent with public choice theory: each house accepted the other's pork, and the statute was enacted with both prohibitions.[53]

Parochial objectives have been achieved in ways other than outright Congressional prohibition of base closure, however. For example, the closure of Rickenbacker Air Force Base in Columbus, Ohio, was delayed six years due to local court challenges during the NEPA process. Moreover, in effecting consolidation of basic helicopter training at Fort Rucker, DOD had to prepare five different environmental impact statements. Reacting to the parochial motivations underlying such results, a representative favorable to the 1985 reform idea stated that "There ought to be some point where there is a cutoff . . . so that we in the Congress can continue and a small group can't continually thwart a decision, and I think one impact statement ought to be enough."[54]

Particularly noteworthy examples of Congressional resistance to military base reduction impelled by overt parochialism are Loring Air Force Base in Limestone, Maine, and Fort Dix in New Jersey. Of these two installations, Assistant Defense Secretary Korb stated: "There is no secret that some bases were not closed in the 1970's because of politics. I refer specifically to Fort Dix and Loring Air Force Base."[55]

Loring AFB first appeared in a major DOD realignment package on March 11, 1976, when DOD proposed that base as a candidate for an 83 percent reduction intended to reduce Loring from a main operating base to a forward operating base. The powerful Maine delegation led by Senator Muskie rose to the occasion. Hearings were held on-site in Limestone, and a parade of local residents bolstered by the Save Loring Committee told sad tales about how their own businesses and the Maine economy would suffer if Loring were cut back.[56] While the Maine delegation became prime movers in initiating the restrictive base closure legislation enacted in 1976, their support for Loring AFB did not stop there. When DOD made its decision to reduce Loring AFB final in 1979, the Maine delegation participated vehemently in additional hearings on the realignment, where Senator Muskie averred that the decision to reduce Loring was "unsound, inconsistent with our national interests, and an economic injustice to the people of northern Maine."[57] Undeterred by GAO's independent finding that "the reduction of Loring appears economically justified," they threatened to enact legislation specifically prohibiting the realignment unless DOD relented. In Korb's words, "there was a threat made to pass legislation prohibiting the realignment unless the Department took it off the list."[58]

The ploy worked. The Maine delegation then used the reprieve to make Loring impregnable for the foreseeable future. In the early 1980s they engineered Congressional approval of huge expenditures on the Loring AFB facilities against DOD's wishes. By 1985 DOD's Korb had thrown in the towel, stating that "because of the expenditure of new construction money that was basically *jammed down our throats* by the Congress, it no longer makes any sense to close that installation." It proved to be a long-term victory for parochialism: Loring AFB was not targeted for closure in the Commission's 1988 report. Korb pointed out that in the case of Loring AFB, "we are not just talking about saving money. . . . We actually have endangered national security because you have planes that are in an area where they can be considered to be very close to being shot by submarine launched cruise missiles."[59]

Fort Dix, New Jersey, also proved politically difficult for DOD to dispatch. The Army first examined Fort Dix for possible realignment in 1971 and 1972. As part of its normal review process the Army concluded that it needed only one infantry basic training facility in the region, not two. The issue was which one to close. Consequently in its 1973 realignment package, DOD announced studies of Fort Dix and Fort Jackson, South Carolina, for the purpose of evaluating which to discontinue. This process dragged on until 1979, when on March 29 DOD announced its "final" decision to transfer Army training functions from Fort Dix to four other bases including Fort Jackson.

The New Jersey delegation screamed. They vented their spleens at four separate hearings. They demanded a GAO report. To their dismay, the GAO report concluded that "annual savings should be about $15.8 million and the net one-time cost should be about $72.5 million," interpreted to imply a "payback" period of 4.6 years or less—within DOD's requirements for a worthwhile realignment project.[60]

The New Jersey delegation fought on. They managed to insert in the House-Senate conference report on the military construction bill for fiscal year 1980 a mandate that Fort Dix could not be realigned or closed unless impact statements were created that emphasized the socioeconomic factors in the affected regions. In the early 1980s they fought for huge new expenditures at Fort Dix not requested by the Army.[61]

By 1985 Fort Dix was still in business. For its part DOD was down but not yet out. As part of the "illustrative" list of twenty-two bases that DOD said might be evaluated for realignment or closure if the 1985 reform initiative were successful, DOD listed Fort Dix, New Jersey. Nonetheless, by 1988—seventeen years after the initial investigation of the closure of Fort Dix—parochial pressure still kept it alive. As Senator Bumpers put it, "A lot of bases have been kept open in this country because a Senator had the clout to keep one [sic] open."[62] The Defense Secretary's Commission recommended in 1988 that Fort Dix be reduced to semi-active status and that its entry-level training functions be relocated.

CONGRESSIONAL RESISTANCE: THE NON–PAROCHIAL RATIONALE

> "In instances where the decision is valid . . . I think all of us would like to be as objective as the political situation permits, and in total candor that situation politically is tenable only so long as there is a valid, defensible position which either the Department of Defense may present or may allow us to present to the people we represent."[63]
>
> —Representative Kilgore

Congress is not the only body whose members sometimes allow politics rather than the national weal to influence their actions. As one representative put it, "The history of decisions made exclusively within the executive branch of the Government is one too littered with arbitrariness, parochialism, and caprice." The belief that DOD has played politics with base closures runs deep in Congress. Representative Schroeder, chairwoman of the Task Force on Grace Commission recommendations for the Committee on Armed Services, commented that "The lists which come out of the Pentagon seem to be more based on politics than on military utility."[64]

This assessment has created much impetus for restrictions on DOD flexibility to implement base closures and realignments. For example, during floor debate on the 1985 amendments, numerous senators and representatives spoke of the historical tendency of DOD to play "hardball" with base closures. Senator Bumpers of Arkansas reminded his colleagues that "the reason the [1977 base closure] law is as it is is to keep Secretaries of Defense and Presidents from punishing individual Members who happen to disagree with them." Senator Levin concurred that "these protections against untrammeled executive power to close bases came because Members of this Senate and this Congress felt that the power to close bases had been abused and had been used as a club over Members of Congress."[65]

Members of Congress express much concern about selective use of base closures to secure Congressional acquiescence on the defense budget. As Senator Specter put it, it is "not a matter of mere coincidence that, at the time the Department of Defense issues come before the country and at the time we are considering the budget, there are a series of releases from the Department of Defense about the prospects for reduction in forces, layoffs and base closings." Senator Heinz added that "it is easy for this Senator to imagine how the closing of bases, if skillfully manipulated—there are a lot of dumb ways to do it, and I have seen them, too—but if skillfully manipulated could be used either to influence votes or to exact retribution for votes that did not turn out to be the way the administration in power wanted them to be."[66]

In accord with these views, Seymour Melman notes that the Pentagon "often recommends location of military installations and war-economy facilities in Congressional districts and states that are strategic with respect to key Congressmen in the Senate and in the House." DOD officials are quick to deny all of these charges, claiming that the hypothesis is implausible because base closures often hurt congressmen who are strongly favorable to defense.[67] However, their denials overlook the fact that the stated hypothesis implies DOD support for legislators who are either "on the margin" or in a position to influence those who are, not favoritism toward all strong supporters of defense expenditures.

During May 1985 the *Washington Times* ran a story by Ralph S. Hallow entitled "Back the Budget or Lose Bases, Weinberger Warns Republicans." Although some doubted the story, the fear was real. In Senate debates on the reform proposals, Senator Bumpers remarked that "President Reagan is not a vengeful man. Secretary Weinberger is not a vengeful man. Neither of them would close an air base just to shape up a Senator's conduct. But they are not going to be around forever, and you do not know who the next President might be." Reminding his colleagues of why the 1977 law made it difficult to close a base, Senator Bumpers stated: "It is to make certain that Senators are not disciplined and chastised because they happen to disagree with the Defense Department on a crucial vote." Other Senators noted the "extraordinary correlations" between the jurisdiction of authorization and appropriation committees and the "success rate that members of those committees . . . have in preserving the benefits of Federal largess for their State, for their congressional district. . . ."[68] Similar sentiments were voiced in the hearings, where Senator Levin stated that "The fear of the exercise of untrammeled executive power is what led or what continues to fuel the support for the protections against base closings."[69]

Congress has other complaints as well, many of which pertain to information–cost manipulation. Senators and representatives cite instances in which they have been lied to by DOD, have had information withheld from them, and have not been notified of impending DOD actions. When such situations occur, the legislator is confronted with what amounts to a political double-cross, as he faces constituents with incorrect information later undercut by the reality of DOD action.

Take for instance the case of Representative Frelinghuysen of New Jersey. In McNamara's March 1961 round of base closings, Raritan Arsenal in New Jersey was designated to be closed. Yet in early January of 1961 in response to Frelinghuysen's inquiry, Brigadier General H. A. Gerhardt, Deputy Chief of Legislative Liaison, wrote to Frelinghuysen, "As to the immediate future of Raritan, there are at present no Department of the Army plans to discontinue the arsenal." During hearings on these closures, as information emerged that documents suggesting closure had been produced much earlier, Frelinghuysen asked the Army representative, "I wonder, General, how you could help me justify that statement with the statement you just made, that the survey of Raritan Arsenal had been completed in July 1960, and that your firm determination to close this arsenal entirely was made on the 14th of February? How on the beginning of January could any representative of the Army make a flat statement that there are at present no Department of the Army plans to discontinue the arsenal?" Frelinghuysen went on to label Gerhardt's statement "obviously untrue and I can think of no more charitable way to describe it."[70]

Congressional concern about DOD's withholding information and not giving Congress adequate notice of impending base closures suffuses the hearings and Congressional debates. For example, with regard to the November 19, 1964, base closure announcement, Representative Randall of Missouri stated that a "complete factual blackout" occurred: "No Member of Congress could find out anything that was going to happen, except there had been or would be an announcement about a series of closings or consolidations." Randall went on to state that "Information was first given to the press, then sometime afterward Members of Congress were notified," finding it "intolerable that supposedly irreversible and irrevocable decisions are announced to the press before they are announced to the appropriate committees of the Congress or to the individual members most concerned with these decisions."[71] The printed record indicates that congressmen have no greater affinity than the rest of the human race for being caught with their pants down.

On the Senate side John Pastore was particularly hard hit by the Rhode Island base closure announcement of April 17, 1973. Although other problems discussed below plagued the Rhode Island base closures, one of Senator Pastore's biggest complaints was that he hadn't been notified in advance. He asked DOD officials, "What would have been wrong, while this was developing for you to have discussed this freely with the Members of Congress? . . . You refused to do it. Yet, Mr. Clements [Acting Secretary of Defense] comes here and says we told you. Sure you told us, on April 16, 1973, when it was done."[72]

Representative Flowers of Alabama reported a similar incident in 1976, one that caused him to support the 1976 legislation to constrain DOD. Having heard rumors in January that Craig Air Force Base in his district was targeted for closure, he sought confirmation from the Air Force. His efforts were completely frustrated, as he found it was "impossible" to obtain the information he desired. Yet on March 11, 1976, Craig AFB was indeed announced as intended for closure.[73]

In the case of the New England base closures of April 1973, the withholding of information extended well beyond the date on which they were announced. Representative Heckler of Massachusetts was concerned about the closures, not only those in her state but also the Quonset Point Naval Air Station and the Naval Complex at Newport, Rhode Island, both of which had major employment effects in her district. DOD's official reports to Congress on each of these base closures consisted of a three-page report that in essence stated DOD's conclusions without providing justification for the savings figures claimed. When Heckler tried to obtain the "Case Study and Justification Folder" for each base, the Navy refused, claiming they were "internal documents." Asked by Heckler for statutory justification for withholding these documents from Congress, the Navy replied that "there is no statutory authority but a policy guideline."

Even more disturbing was the Air Force response that the case studies had been "partially destroyed" and that what remained were "internal documents" that would not be released to the congresswoman. Heckler felt that without the justification folders "one is then led to suspicions as to what motivated these decisions, whether political retribution or other factors one does not know, but in the absence of facts the imagination runs wild." By

June 21 DOD and the services still had not turned over the justification folders to the Senate Armed Services Committee, creating what Heckler adjudged "the issue of secrecy, the potential for military coverup . . . an arrogant fiat."[74] Only later were the documents finally given to Congress.

The Rhode Island story offers an unusually well documented example of political machinations behind DOD base closure determinations. As Pastore's comments and Heckler's experience make clear, Congress screamed bloody murder over the way the 1973 Massachusetts and Rhode Island base closures were handled. Congress complained that the Navy had formulated the plan to close the bases two years earlier and yet had repeatedly asserted, right up until April 16, that the bases would not be cut. Some of the bases had even received new missions—Quonset Point Naval Air Station was newly designated as the home of the S-3A Viking antisubmarine weapon on December 20, 1971, only to be deemed unsuited for such functions sixteen months later. Congress complained that new expenditures were made on these bases at DOD's request even when the services knew the bases were targeted for closure. But overriding all was the belief that the closure decisions were politically motivated.

Whose political motivations? John Chafee, Secretary of the Navy from 1969 to 1972, at some point decided to run against Democratic Senator Claiborne Pell in the 1972 senatorial race in Rhode Island, a state that the Nixon administration was very anxious to win. The Nixon camp aggressively fanned the base closure flames in Rhode Island. Two weeks before the election, the Committee to Reelect the President (CREEP) ran a political advertisement in a Rhode Island newspaper threatening that if George McGovern were elected and implemented his intended defense budget, the consequence for Rhode Islanders would be major reductions in employment at their military bases, a blow to the Rhode Island economy that CREEP said would be "staggering." The ad went on to promise that "Fortunately, none of this will come to be if the man who's President right now remains President."[75]

While Secretary of the Navy, Chafee leaned strongly against the military wind to sustain the Rhode Island bases. In fact Admiral Elmo Zumwalt as Chief of Naval Operations and his predecessor Admiral Moorer had both recommended cuts in those bases since at least 1969. Each year the CNO recommended the cuts to Chafee, but when Chafee forwarded his recommendations for closures to the Secretary of Defense, the Rhode Island and Massachusetts bases were omitted from the list.

As Navy Secretary, Chafee acted consistently to bring the bacon home to Rhode Island. He personally assigned the new mission to Quonset Point on December 20, 1971, which the local newspaper labeled "about the best Christmas present that Secretary of the Navy John Chafee could have brought home from Washington for Rhode Island."[76] Then on May 5, 1972,

Chafee resigned as Secretary of the Navy in order to run for election against Pell.[77]

After Chafee's departure, Zumwalt again, as he had since 1970, decided to recommend closure of the Rhode Island bases. Although he reached the decision on October 20, 1972, he waited until after the election to make his report to John Warner, the new Secretary of the Navy. However, Warner testified that it was Defense Secretary Melvin Laird who set the timetable that involved postponing announcement of the base closure decision until after the election.

Warner, determined to move ahead with a base closure package that had in his words "no political implications whatsoever," signed and approved the package in December 1972. The final delay from January to April 1973 ostensibly resulted from the assumption of the Defense Secretary's post in January by Elliot Richardson, who was loathe to recommend closure of the Massachusetts and Rhode Island bases until he personally reviewed the records left by his predecessor, Melvin Laird. In the end Senator Pastore concluded, "it looks rather suspicious to me. During a critical time when it might have affected the election in the State of Rhode Island this was kept under cover."[78]

Congress has also expressed much concern as to whether the expected savings from base closures or realignments reported by DOD are in fact realistic. One major dispute concerned DOD's failure to state nonmilitary governmental costs that would be incurred as a result of a base closure, for DOD was reporting only military costs and benefits.

As early as 1965, senators complained that DOD's savings were often illusory, stating that "The savings announced by the Secretary of Defense reflect only military savings. They in no way reflect governmental savings." Retirement costs, unemployment benefits, and other nonmilitary costs attributable to the realignment were not tallied. Urging his colleagues to support the 1976 base closure legislation, Representative Conte said, "Let us make sure that money will still be saved once unemployment compensation, manpower retraining and relocation expenses, military construction and transfer costs, and the other manifestations of the economic dislocation associated with base closings are taken into consideration."[79] Besides enactment of the 1976 legislation, one result of such complaints was President Carter's issuance on March 27, 1978, of Executive Order 12049, which required DOD to evaluate all federal costs associated with base realignments, not just military costs.

More fundamental questions can be asked about DOD's assessment of the marginal costs and benefits associated with a base closure or realignment. The federal budget in general and military budgets in particular employ cash accounting, implying that treatment of capital assets is completely misguided from a present-value perspective. It is as if the concepts of investment, capital assets, and opportunity cost were foreign to the lexicon of government budgeters. Independent analyses of proposed base closures conducted by the General Accounting Office are often not reported in terms of net present value. Economists can only cringe listening to the following exchange between Representative Schweiker and Paul Ignatius, then Assistant Secretary of Defense, that took place in the 1966 hearings on base closures:

> Mr. SCHWEIKER. Are we figuring here at all in this savings structure any figures relating to the capital assets that we lose by shutting down the base?
> Mr. IGNATIUS. No, sir, we do not; because the Government does not in its accounting system amortize investment costs. We pay for the costs at the time the property is acquired, and we do not amortize or take account of any residual costs. By the same token . . . in our reported savings we did not take credit for what we might gain through selling these facilities.[80]

Absent these crucial considerations, it is hard to envision the expected savings associated with recommended base closures and realignments as anything other than moving the walnut shells around. It is no wonder that members of Congress have labeled existing procedures as "woefully inadequate" and have been appalled that "in far too many cases, such actions now end up costing American taxpayers more than they allegedly 'saved.'" They have had far too many unhappy endings, watching taxpayers foot the bill for base realignment mistakes like the Army's transfer of Aberdeen Proving Ground from Maryland to New Mexico to avoid occasional fog only to find that New Mexico's sandstorms "were so bad that the visibility was not any better than the Maryland fog."[81]

In addition the record yields instances in which studies intended to determine which bases to close allegedly had predetermined outcomes. For example, one of the facilities slated for realignment by the 1973 announcement was the Pacific Missile Range at Pt. Mugu, California. Minutes of a meeting held by top officials of the Naval Air Systems Command two days after the closure announcement indicated the study's results had been dictated before the study began: Senator Cranston called it "a brainstorming session attempting to justify the action announced two days earlier." The person who made the "Shore Establishment Realignment" (SER) study of the Pacific Missile Range allegedly was instructed by his superiors that the Range must be converted to a government-owned, contractor-operated facility by the end of 1974, and that his study had to show a net savings in approximately five years. He purportedly stated that he had never been to the facility and had "no listing" of the workload or the people there, and that he could not ask questions because of a secrecy mandate imposed by his superiors.[82] Perhaps a disgruntled employee, but members of Congress wonder.

Finally there are the base closure decisions that appear to reflect either ineptitude or political gamesmanship. Consider the case of Richards-Gebaur Air Force Base, Missouri, located near the Kansas border and so of immense parochial interest to politicians on both sides of the line. Richards-Gebaur became home to the Air Force Communication Service (AFCS) in 1970 when that facility was moved to Richards-Gebaur from nearby Scott Air Force Base in Illinois, only five hundred miles away. The move was justified at the time as a cost-effective realignment in that the AFCS would be consolidated in a modern facility that more closely matched the requirements of the mission, enabling it to function effectively as a force-wide communications system.

Despite DOD's brief for the efficiency of the move, testimony later revealed that politics also played a role. Representative William Randall of Missouri testified that in 1970 another House member procured appointments for him at the White House "all the way up to the Presidential level." He reminisced that "Everyone in the area worked together to accomplish the objective of reactivation of our base. . . . The Secretary of the Air Force also helped some, but it was the final approval of former President Nixon that led to the establishment of AFCS at Richards-Gebaur."[83]

But the real twist to the story came in 1974. A scant four years after moving AFCS from Scott AFB to Richards-Gebaur, the Air Force decided to move it back to Scott AFB, again citing "efficiency" as its primary rationale. Held up by NEPA challenges in 1975, the proposed move reappeared in the DOD realignment package issued in March 1976. Senator Eagleton commented that "If that move had been made 40 years ago, then one could say it was a long time ago and a different world," but asked "How can a decision in 1970, and an efficient decision made then, be completely reversed and become an efficient decision going back the other way, 6 short years later?"[84]

What of the cost data? Testimony given in hearings chaired by Senator Symington indicated that the Air Force had grossly understated certain housing costs of the relocation to the government by using national average figures rather than data specific to the affected sites.[85] Moreover, the Air Force systematically ignored the impact of the move in the adjacent state of Kansas even though many of the employees at Richards-Gebaur AFB lived in Kansas.

Although Air Force Secretary Thomas Reed insisted that this was merely a "proposal" rather than a final decision and that he was receptive to new information, his protestations did little to soothe affected members of Congress. Representative Bolling cited Speaker Sam Rayburn's advice to new congressmen not to seek military bases in their districts: "His point was that the same kind of arbitrary decision that could bring a defense payroll into an area, could later take it away. Mr. Rayburn believed that people's lives shouldn't be jerked around that way."[86] The next section examines the role of existing institutions in determining the nature and extent of such political manipulation of base closures.

THE INSTITUTIONALIZATION OF PAROCHIALISM

> "[W]e are looking at this from a parochial standpoint. But somebody has to look at it from the standpoint of the whole United States. Somebody has to look at it from the standpoint of the taxpayers."[87]
> —Senator Strom Thurmond

Institutions shape behavior. They define marginal benefits and costs associated with political action. Therefore institutional ground rules governing base closures and realignments figure prominently not only in determining observed behavior but also in guiding efforts at reform. Reform, however, is not always the desideratum of attempts to change institutions. As was evident in 1976, pressures always exist to change institutional ground rules to facilitate rather than constrain rent-seeking behavior. The question is how to design institutions to reduce such institutionalization of parochialism.

The history of the base realignment struggle since 1961 suggests the paramount role of relevant institutional mechanisms. Prior to the 1976 changes, the institutional structure gave members of Congress room to be vocal in resisting base closures requested by DOD but for the most part enabled DOD to act on its judgments. The result? John Lynch reports that between 1960 and 1969, of 954 realignment actions announced by DOD, only two were not implemented. As DOD's Lawrence Korb describes it, "there would be certain concerns expressed by the people most directly affected, and then, by and large, they [the base closures and realignments] would be carried out."[88]

In 1976 the pendulum swung the other way. The new institutional mechanisms so lowered the marginal cost of resisting major base closures and realignments that it became politically untenable for an individual member of Congress not to block realignments. The rules invited such resistance; constituents demanded it. As Senator Thurmond put it, the legislative process established in 1976 "invited interference from the Congress," providing "skillful obstructionists with every conceivable opportunity to delay or totally prevent the closing of nonessential bases." Senator Gramm inquired of Dr. Korb, "Under current law any Congressman or Senator who is ingenious and hard-working can prevent a military base from being closed in his district or his State?" Korb responded, "For all practical purposes, that is correct." Reflecting on the 1977 legislation, Korb felt that the issue was "whether we want to sustain a system that basically compels an elected Representative or Senator to use the law to prevent what his constituents want prevented."[89] In short, under the 1976 rules parochial desires were almost universally guaranteed implementation by the chosen institutional mechanism.

In attempting to nudge the pendulum back in the other direction, the 1985 and 1988 reform efforts offer considerable insight into designing institutional mechanisms more conducive to cost-effective realignments and less vulnerable to political pressures both from Congress and from the executive branch. Collectively they show that, to lessen the institutionalization of parochialism, the law should shape private marginal costs to deflect rather than nurture substantive parochial action, making marginal costs and benefits perceived by individuals more accurately reflect the opportunity costs involved. On the executive side, reform legislation must lower the marginal cost to administration officials and military personnel of implementing cost-effective realignments that are not politically inspired. On the legislative side, base closure reform must raise the marginal cost to the politician of acting on the parochial imperative. It must make the "parochial" less "imperative" to the extent that such behavior is shaped by institutional rules.

Toward that end the statutory framework should leave much room for political demonstration of concern for one's constituents, but it should not allow these parochial concerns to be translated into action without a strong showing that there are nonparochial reasons for doing so. Reform of the base closure process must accommodate the political needs of members of Congress while not blocking base realignments justified on efficiency grounds. Senator Gramm described the political appeal of such reforms:

> The beauty of this proposal is that, if you have a military base in your district . . . under this proposal, I have 60 days. So, I come up here and I say "God have mercy. Don't close this base in Texas. We can get attacked from the south. The Russians are going to go after our leadership and you know they are going to attack Texas. We need this base." Then I can go out and lie down in the street and the bulldozers are coming and I have a trusty aide there just as it gets there to drag me out of the way. All the people in Muleshoe, or wherever this base is, will say, "You know, Phil Gramm got whipped, but it was like the Alamo. He was with us until the last second." The bottom line is the public interest will have been preserved.[90]

Why would Congress ever favor such legislation? Perhaps to avoid the sheer burden of making so many trips to the trough under 1977-style legislation. As Professor Seymour Melman stated in 1973 when testifying on the desirability of adopting institutional mechanisms to facilitate conversion of obsolete military bases to civilian use, "I have the estimate that at some time Members of Congress will favor this change. They will see that . . . it would be a great boon . . . to be relieved of this kind of burden. That burden puts them in a client relation to . . . the Department of Defense, which they are otherwise obliged to regulate and control. Being relieved of that burden improves their position to fulfill the constitutional function for which they take offices in the Congress."[91]

The burden of proof concerning the retention of a military base is crucial to institutional vulnerability to parochialism. Under the 1977 rules, the burden of proof was predominantly on those who wanted to close a military base. As Senator Gramm stated, under the 1976 procedures the system was "totally rigged against closing bases, and it was intended to be rigged against closing bases."[92] Senator Gramm with his 1985 reform proposals rightly desired to shift that burden. To that end it was essential to avoid a two-stage process involving announcement of "candidacy" followed by a "final decision" to close or realign.

Legislators were long forewarned of the institutional consequences of such a two-step process; the 1976 procedures were not naively embraced. Representative Hogan warned in 1973 that if candidates for base closure were made known in advance via a "suspect list," the affected Congressional delegations "would bring unbearable pressure to bear to try to reverse that suspect list to eliminate their own constituencies from that list. . . . It is part of the political system of our democracy." And in 1976, speaking against the legislation initially vetoed by President Ford, Senator McGovern said, "All we are going to accomplish if we override this veto is to provide 1 year for the Chamber of Commerce and the various groups in these affected communities to come here and lobby for special legislation to save these wasteful, surplus facilities that add nothing to the defense interests of the country." To curtail the institutionalization of parochialism, such open statutory invitations to respond to constituent pressure in ways that undermine national security and prosperity must be eliminated.[93]

Another reform essential to insulating institutions from parochialism concerns the appropriation of funds to effectuate base closures or realignments. We have seen that Congress has been very jealous of its power to control expenditures to implement military base realignments. It should be protective of those powers, since they provide an important check on executive branch action. Nonetheless, the manner in which those powers are guarded determines whether parochial concerns dominate the relevant Congressional decisions.

Consider the procedure that has prevailed in the past: In order to implement a base closure or realignment, after complying with all other Congressional requirements, DOD had to seek from Congress the funds to curtail activities at a base being reduced and to upgrade facilities at a base being expanded. That is, appropriations targeted at named bases were prerequisite to effectuating closures and realignments. Once the identity of the base was known, all the familiar logrolling incentives came into play, and the parochial imperative naturally dominated the outcome at the institutional level.

Consider an alternative approach. Knowing that base realignments may be necessary in the ensuing fiscal year, Congress might appropriate money for the purpose of implementing such realignments without knowledge of the specific bases to be affected. Using Buchanan and Tullock's Rawlsian idea that uncertainty regarding one's future state enables one to make political choices not exclusively driven by self-interest too narrowly defined, this procedure would guarantee that legislators focus on the desirable extent of military base realignments without becoming enmeshed in parochial devotion to the narrow economic concerns of a particular constituency. In a sense this would entail imposing a "constitutional" frame of mind on a very particular decision faced by Congress.[94] To the extent that this "constitutional" mindset can be incorporated into the day-to-day institutions of government, we can reduce the dominance of the parochial imperative.

With respect to base closures, this was exactly what Gramm tried to do with his 1985 reform proposals. These included a $1 billion annual fund to implement base closures generally, not tied to named bases. This provision was stripped out of the reform legislation actually enacted by the Congress in 1985, and certain members of Congress openly rejoiced that the base closure purse strings remained in parochial hands. Gramm himself well understood the importance of dissociating the expenditure decision from knowledge of specific bases to be affected. Asked about this provision in his bill, Gramm stated, "If you are going to go to appropriating [funds to be used to close military bases] . . . you have to separate it from the base closings. You have to get people to vote on the principle and not the practice."[95] The extent to which the "DOD Base Closure Account" created by the 1988 legislation may or may not serve a similar purpose is discussed in the next section.

Another reform would lessen the institutionalization of parochialism by dampening community resistance to cost-effective realignments. By enhancing existing efforts to help communities convert from military to civilian employment when military facilities are closed or substantially reduced, one could lower the apparent marginal cost of the realignment to the targeted community, recognizing that the benefits from such realignment are otherwise largely external to that community. Seymour Melman describes the essentials of such economic conversion as follows: "The elemental requirements for conversion of military bases to civilian uses are twofold: advanced planning of a conversion process, and organized responsibility and authority for the planning process and for its implementation in the hands of the local community."[96]

Although some might denounce conversion assistance as a localized subsidy aimed at solving a problem better handled by market adjustments, the political reality is that the benefits of efficient defense realignments are national in scope. A strong equity argument therefore suggests that its costs should likewise be borne more widely by the public in the form of short-term retraining assistance and the like. An even stronger argument grounded in practical politics is that without such conversion assistance, parochial interests will thwart the public's wider interest in efficient defense and economic productivity. In a sense conversion assistance provides a method of actual as opposed to potential compensation to those harmed, a mechanism designed to procure consent to cost-effective realignments. If a proposed move is indeed efficient, the gainers can compensate the losers and yet remain better off themselves.

Economic adjustment programs have existed since 1961, and their success has to some extent blunted parochial resistance to base closures by showing communities that they can emerge from base closure experiences as winners, not losers. In fact, statistics compiled by DOD's Office of Economic Adjustment and the President's Economic Adjustment Committee indicate that "between 1961 and 1981, about 124,000 new jobs were added in 94 localities where less than 90,000 jobs had actually been lost through changes in defense employment."[97]

Between 1964 and 1969, economic conversion efforts were buttressed by a "job-guarantee" program that guaranteed permanent DOD employees whose jobs were eliminated by a base closure the offer of at least one DOD job elsewhere as well as assistance in finding private employment. Although discontinued in 1969, this program offered another institutional mechanism to reduce parochial pressure on Congress by reducing the perceived private marginal cost to constituents of base closures.[98]

Richard Stubbing suggests additional techniques for softening resistance to realignments of major military bases. Besides countering local communities' fear of the closure's negative economic consequences by infusion of federal resources to facilitate conversion, Stubbing suggests spreading the closures out geographically whenever possible in order to minimize any perception of unfairness. One has only to recall the intense opposition to the 1973 base closure package, 47 percent of whose impact was in New England, to appreciate the merit of this idea. Stubbing also suggests mitigating resistance to closures from within the military establishment by rewarding military leaders if they get Congress to endorse base closures, perhaps giving them extra funds to upgrade retained facilities.[99]

Finally, to gain public and Congressional support for military base realignments, it is imperative that DOD and the military services routinely employ accounting procedures that more accurately reflect the marginal costs, marginal benefits, and net present value of alternative base structure proposals. Until DOD and the military services consistently employ cost-accounting procedures appropriate to effective business decision making, properly valuing capital assets and opportunity costs associated with different base configurations, military base realignment will remain the bastard child of parochialism. The extent to which the 1988 base closure statute accomplishes reforms described above is evaluated in the following section.

COMMISSION ON BASE REALIGNMENT AND CLOSURE: A VIABLE REFORM?

If not overwhelmed by political exploitation of loopholes discussed below, important features of the recently enacted base closure legislation[100] satisfy certain reform principles suggested above. With respect to base closures recommended by the Commission, the new law lowers the marginal political cost to legislators of not acting on the parochial imperative, for the affected legislator can truthfully blame the Commission. That is, the measure at least partially removes this particularized benefit from the realm of credit or blame for the legislator and instead puts responsibility for the outcome on the Commission. It moves part way toward making this particularized benefit one for which legislators will be held accountable for their *position* rather than the outcome.[101]

The new law also raises the marginal cost to legislators of acting on the parochial imperative by making certain statutory impediments to base closures inapplicable when bases have been selected for closure or realignment by the Commission. To the extent that Congress is forced to evaluate the entire Commission package rather than individual bases, the new law supports a less parochial appraisal of the recommended closures and realignments.

The 1988 statute potentially raises the marginal cost to executive branch officials of using base closure recommendations for partisan political purposes both (a) by reducing the credibility of recommendations not endorsed by the Commission, and (b) by preventing the Defense Secretary from *selectively* adopting the Commission's recommendations. It simultaneously lowers the marginal cost to DOD officials of implementing cost-effective realignments by removing statutory obstacles to closure of the bases selected by the Commission, by placing relevant executive decision-making authority in the hands of a lame-duck administration, and by providing a partially automatic funding mechanism through the DOD Base Closure Account.

The statute's explicit provision for DOD expenditures on economic adjustment assistance implies continued support for reducing the perceived marginal cost of realignments to adversely affected communities. In addition, facilitating net present value assessments, the new law requires DOD to report not only anticipated expenditures and savings involved in each base closure but also the time period in which such savings are expected to occur. Moreover, while not mandated to do so by this statute, the Commission chose to make its calculations in present value terms, setting what could (and should) be an influential precedent for future base closure evaluations.

Nonetheless, significant loopholes remain. At every step in the legislative process, congressmembers strove to attach emasculating amendments to Armey's bill. To his credit, after four committees effectively recast the "reform" measure into a bill guaranteeing retention of obsolete bases, Armey managed to engineer elimination of the most egregious provisions. Thus committee attempts to require socioeconomic impact statements, retention of historical sites, certification that no retained overseas base is less valuable than a domestic base selected for closure,[102] on-site hearings to receive testimony from affected communities, active Congressional approval of the base closure list, and the like ultimately were defeated.

But Armey had to compromise, and those compromises threaten to undermine the law's original purpose. The major opening wedges for continued parochialism under the new law involve: (1) provision of funds to implement the base closures; (2) applicability of the Federal Property and Administrative Services Act and the Surplus Property Act; and (3) applicability of the National Environmental Policy Act of 1969.

We have seen that Congress's control of funds necessary to implement base closures historically has enabled parochially motivated politicians to block cost-effective changes in base structure. Unfortunately, that pattern is likely to continue. Despite DOD's new statutory power to deposit certain sale proceeds in the Base Closure Account, it is clear from the floor debates that many members of Congress intend to perpetuate "hands-on" funding for closure of named bases. For example, as a gesture of good faith that at least shifted transaction costs to those seeking future changes in the authorization, the Senate bill that went into conference (S.2749) authorized the appropriation of $300 million for *any* fiscal year after 1989.[103] In a disquieting move portending future practice under the 1988 law, the conference committee stripped that authorization from the bill, stating that "since the funding requirements for direct appropriations cannot be determined until the Commission has completed its work, the conferees agree to a provision that would require direct funding of the base closure account to be established each year during the annual authorization and appropriations cycle based upon the Department's budget request."[104] Once again, we face the specter of Congress voting on funds to close named bases. To the extent that DOD must rely on such direct appropriations, the parochial result is likely to follow, and the 1988 law's central effort to decouple base closure funding decisions from logrolling in support of individual named bases could come to naught.

There are other reasons why the Base Closure Account may not fulfill its promise. The new law envisions three sources of funding for base closures: Base Closure Account receipts from DOD sale of surplus or excess properties and facilities; DOD transfers to the Account from funds appropriated for other purposes (reprogramming); and monies specifically authorized and appropriated by Congress. Despite the aforementioned problems with direct appropriations, one therefore might hope that such other receipts and transfers nonetheless would fortify the account. Yet additional obstacles intervene. For example, the law states that the Defense Secretary can make transfers reprogramming funds only "subject to approval in an appropriation Act" after providing "written notice of, and justification for" the transfer to relevant Congressional committees. Thus the appropriations subcommittees again retain explicit statutory power to thwart the process. Moreover, the Defense Secretary's authority to sell property under the act extends only to "excess and surplus real property and facilities located at a military installation closed or realigned under this title." In other words, it is not a broad power to dispose of *other* surplus facilities to generate funds necessary to implement the recommended closures. Finally, as discussed below, procedural requirements under the Federal Property and Administrative Services Act further undercut the Defense Department's ability to transform property disposals into a major funding source obviating direct appropriations.

To facilitate DOD disposal of excess military property, the original reform proposals explicitly waived cumbersome procedural requirements of the Federal Property and Administrative Services Act,[105] permitting sale proceeds to be deposited in the DOD Base Closure Account. The enacted statutory language, by contrast, mandates application of the normal regulations governing disposal of excess property: it simply orders the administrator of General Services to delegate his functions under the relevant statutes to the Defense Secretary to carry out transactions allowable under the new base closure law. Although the statute for the first time allows DOD to realize a direct benefit from certain sales of DOD-owned real property and facilities,[106] protracted procedures under federal property-disposal regulations impair the ability of the Base Closure Account to function as an automatic funding mechanism. Indeed, the hierarchy established by statute for such disposals makes it possible for some transfers of surplus property to be made without remuneration to DOD. With respect to property disposals, the 1988 legislation thus improves upon preexisting statutory law, but falls short of fulfilling the promise of the original bills.

Experience under the 1977 base closure law also attests to the potency of NEPA in blocking closure of major military installations. Accordingly, earlier versions of the Armey and Roth reform proposals waived the National Environmental Policy Act along with other statutory obstacles to base closures. However, the enacted statutory language only partially waives NEPA. While waived with respect to the actions of the Commission and the Defense Secretary in selecting sites for closure or realignment, the NEPA requirements are mandated with respect to *implementation* of base closures or realignments under the act. Implementation of base closures recommended by the Commission is prohibited until 1990 to allow the NEPA evaluation to occur. Still, NEPA's applicability to base closures is narrowed significantly,[107] and it is unlikely to prove as powerful an impediment as it is outside the context of the 1988 act.

Besides the vulnerabilities summarized above, other potential problems exist. For example, the scope and sustainability of a key provision—allowing Commission-recommended closures to proceed despite certain statutory restrictions on base closure expenditures—is debatable. Originally intended to waive statutory restrictions on outlays for specific base closures or realignments contained in *existing* authorization or appropriation acts, its applicability to similar future statutory restrictions is in doubt.[108] Not only would courts likely regard later measures as superseding this provision, but also future restrictions on base closure expenditures could explicitly modify the relevant waiver if that were Congress's desire. The fact that DOD must notify Congress of realignment-related construction projects costing more than the maximum amount for minor construction projects reinforces concerns about such future Congressional prohibition of particular outlays.

Finally, to achieve long-run success the process must become an ongoing one. One of the weakest aspects of the 1988 reform package is its transitory nature, envisioning a single Commission plan to be implemented or rejected within a specified period. No matter how successful on a one-shot basis, it will do little long-term good unless established as a periodic institutional curative.

Beyond the strengths and weaknesses of the new law, certain political aspects of its final enactment merit reflection. Contemporaneous Congressional debates in large measure provided reruns of familiar arguments detailed in earlier sections of this chapter. Of great interest, however, was the posture of legislators on the day of final passage by the House and Senate. On that day practically no one—friend or foe of the bill—even hinted at the avenues to continued parochialism codified in the language being enacted. Supporters congratulated one another on their victory and applauded anticipated efficiencies; long-time, publicly committed opponents decried past Pentagon abuses, DOD's likely influence over a "rubberstamp" Commission, the short time allowed to determine the closure sites, the allegedly inadequate geographic representation on the Commission, etc. Yet hardly a soul mentioned the major loopholes documented above. The closest they came was Representative Armey's subdued acknowledgment that "In the coming years, it is almost certain that some members will attempt to reverse the waste reduction program which we are beginning today," expressing "no doubt" that "some will try to abort the program and break the commitment which we have made."[109]

Of course many in Congress understood full well the unstated implications of the language being enacted. In earlier floor debate on language similar to that ultimately adopted, Representative Kyl (Ariz.) stated that, without authorization of appropriations, the bill would "hold hostage the closing of these bases to the whims of the Armed Services Committee or the Appropriations Committee." Calling it the "fundamental flaw" remaining in the bill, Kyl stated that "because of the need to get the appropriation, it puts that back into the hands of our committee . . . and, therefore, instead of saying 'Are we going to close this group of bases or not?' the question is: 'How can we lobby each other so that we will appropriate X amount of money to close these bases, but no funds shall be appropriated for the purpose of closing Base A, Base B, and Base C?' " In the same debate, Representative AuCoin (Ore.) called it "essential that there be little or no opportunity for Congressional intervention once the bases to be closed have been identified."[110]

From the perspective of public choice and political science, Congressional floor behavior on the day of final enactment presents no mystery. Creating good copy for their constituents and for the press, those who labored more than two years to enact genuine reform legislation naturally sought to highlight their successes rather than their failures. Why not claim credit, when to do otherwise might erode personal political benefits and threaten alliances on which passage of the bill depended? Vocal opponents on record in strong opposition to the bill likewise sought to document for the public the purity of their positions, not wishing to undermine that posture by acknowledging the soft underbelly of the new law. The public display provided gains for legislators on both sides of the issue, supplying yet another example of legislators' augmentation of transaction costs facing the voting public.[111]

Thus we come to analyze the overwhelmingly large margin by which the 1988 Base Closure and Realignment Act was adopted: 370–31 in the House; 82–7 in the Senate. Should we interpret this as an outpouring of support for genuine base closure reform, a fundamental change of heart toward parochialism in these matters? Economics suggests a more plausible explanation. When a "reform" measure is riddled with unpublicized loopholes, it becomes extraordinarily cheap politically for parochially minded legislators to vote in its favor. Extant models of the political process suggest that, from Congress's parochial perspective, that result might be perceived as optimal—a continuation of the tangible benefits of parochialism coupled with credit for fighting it.

CONCLUSION

> "[T]he most telling reason for the retention of many outmoded military facilities has been simple political inertia and pressure."[112]
>
> —John Lynch

Major base closures or realignments directly involve five powerful interest groups: legislators, constituent groups in affected regions, military leadership, DOD, and the public. Each has much to gain or lose from base realignment decisions. To avoid the institutionalization of parochialism as the prime determinant of base closure policy and practice, we must create a statutory superstructure that shapes the perceived marginal cost of parochially inspired actions to reflect more accuately their opportunity cost, channeling those actions in ways that do not undermine either the military security or the economic prosperity of the nation. The perverse incentives of the 1977 base closure legislation must be avoided.

Base closure and realignment decisions are fraught with external costs imposed on others by those who act on the parochial imperative and external benefits not fully experienced by those who act in the larger national interest to effectuate cost-effective changes in the military force structure. To succeed, base closure reform legislation must attempt to make these costs and benefits internal to the decision maker, so that individual action can be more responsive to actual opportunity costs.

To the legislator, we must raise the marginal cost of resisting base realignments on purely parochial grounds. To constituents in the affected regions, we must lower the perceived marginal cost of base closures and raise the marginal cost of resisting closures that are justified on efficiency grounds. To the military leadership and to DOD personnel, we must lower the perceived marginal cost of implementing cost-effective base closures, perhaps creating concomitant marginal benefits that reward efficiency-based closures. To DOD personnel, we must strive to raise the marginal cost of politically motivated base closures or realignments. To the public at large, we must raise the perceived marginal benefit and reduce the perceived marginal cost of base closures necessitated by efficiency, planning and implementing realignments carefully and presenting them in a way that neither stigmatizes base closures as harbingers of reduced defense capability nor encourages speculation that DOD's proposals are politically inspired.

Changes in institutional structure thus represent one potential avenue to reform. As Senator Thurmond once remarked, "Of course, it is natural for a Congressman not to want a base closed. . . . But, after all, if we have somebody who has the courage to do what is best for this Nation, that man being designated as the President, let us not tie his hands so that he cannot act."[113] Still, let us tie his hands just tightly enough so that he also is not encouraged to act on the parochial imperative.

NOTES

1. U.S. Senate, Committee on Armed Services, Hearings, *Department of Defense Authorization for Appropriations for Fiscal Year 1986,* 99th Cong., 1st Sess., S. Hrg. 99–58, Part 1, February 4, 1985, p. 100 [statement by Senator Phil Gramm].

2. U.S. Senate, Committee on Armed Services, Subcommittee on Military Construction, Hearing, *Base Closures,* 99th Cong., 1st Sess., May 2, 1985, p. 2 [testimony of Dr. Lawrence J. Korb, Assistant Secretary of Defense for Manpower, Installations and Logistics]; U.S. House of Representatives, Committee on Armed Services, Subcommittee on Military Installations and Facilities, Hearing, *Base Closures and Realignments,* 99th Cong., 1st Sess., June 12, 1985, pp. 3, 12–13, 51.

3. The sections of this chapter that describe and evaluate the 1988 reforms are adapted with permission from my article entitled "Institutional Underpinnings of Parochialism: The Case of Military Base Closures," *Cato Journal,* Vol. 9, No. 1 (Spring/Summer, 1989).

4. U.S. House of Representatives, Committee on Post Office and Civil Service, Subcommittee on Retirement and Employee Benefits, Hearing, *Federal Employee Assistance in a Reduction in Force,* 93rd Cong., 1st Sess., Serial No. 93–21, June 5, 6, 8, 1973, p. 10 [statement of Seymour Melman, Professor of Industrial Engineering, Columbia University].

5. U.S. House of Representatives, Committee on Appropriations, Subcommittee on Military Construction Appropriations, Hearings, *Base Closures and Realignments Proposed by Department of Defense, Fiscal Year 1979,* 96th Cong., 1st Sess., April 25, 27, 1979, p. 17 [statement by Representative Edwin Forsythe].

6. *Congressional Record* 122, Part 19, 94th Cong., 2d Sess. (July 22, 1976): 23365 [remarks of Senator Stuart Symington].

7. Ibid. 131, No. 69, 99th Cong., 1st Sess. (May 23, 1985): S 6981 [remarks of Senator Heinz].

8. U.S. Senate, Committee on Armed Services, Subcommittee on Military Construction, Hearings, *Base Closures or Realignment Program, Massachusetts,* Part 1, 93d Cong., 1st Sess., June 21, 22, 1973, p. 89 [statement by Representative Fernand J. St. Germain].

9. See Charlotte Twight, "Government Manipulation of Constitutional-Level Transaction Costs: A General Theory of Transaction-Cost Augmentation and the Growth of Government," *Public Choice* Vol. 56, No. 2 (February 1988): 131–52.

10. Murray Weidenbaum explains the opportunity cost of defense spending as follows:

> It is in the sense of alternative opportunities lost that military spending should be considered—the numbers of people employed by the military, the goods and services it purchases from the private sector, the real estate it ties up, and the technology devoted to it. Not only do we lose the opportunity for civilian use of goods and services, but we also lose the potential economic growth that these resources might have brought about. . . . The real cost to society of allocating productive resources to military programs is that these resources are not available for other purposes.

Murray Weidenbaum, *The Economics of Peacetime Defense,* Praeger Special Studies in U.S. Economic, Social, and Political Issues (New York: Praeger, 1974), p. 29.

11. U.S. House of Representatives, Committee on Armed Services, Subcommittee for Special Investigations, Hearings and Report, *Military Base Closures,* 87th Cong., 1st Sess., hearings held July 13–14, 1961, report dated August 1, 1961 (Washington, D.C.: Government Printing Office, 1961), p. 137 [statement by Representative Latta].

12. Two examples are: 1) the debate in 1976 over the relocation of the Air Force Communications Service from Richards-Gebaur Air Force Base, Missouri (on the Kansas-Missouri border) to Scott Air Force Base, Illinois; and 2) the fight in 1965 over the relocation of the small arms research and development mission from Springfield Armory, Massachusetts, to Rock Island, Illinois.

13. U.S. House of Representatives, Committee on Armed Services, Subcommittee No. 4, Hearings, *Base Closures and Reductions,* 89th Cong., 2d Sess., January 25–26, 1966, p. 6537 [statement by Representative Arends].

14. House Committee on Armed Services, Subcommittee on Military Installations and Facilities, Hearings, *Base Closures and Realignments,* 99th Cong., 1st Sess., June 12, 1985, p. 23 [testimony of Dr. Lawrence J. Korb, Assistant Secretary of Defense for Manpower, Installations and Logistics].

15. House Committee on Armed Services, Subcommittee for Special Investigations, *Military Base Closures,* 87th Cong., 1st Sess., hearings held July 13–14, 1961, report dated August 1, 1961.

16. *Congressional Record* 111, Part 10, 89th Cong., 1st Sess. (June 10, 1965): 13228 ff., 13258. The one-house veto language in the original House bill echoed a similar provision in 10 *U.S.C.* section 125 [added Sept. 7, 1962, Pub. L. No. 87-651, Title II, section 201(a), 76 Stat. 515]. Section 125 directed the Secretary of Defense to "take appropriate action (including the transfer, reassignment, consolidation, or abolition of any function, power, or duty) to provide more effective, efficient, and economical administration and operation, and to eliminate duplication, in the Department of Defense." However, "functions, powers, or duties" vested by law in DOD could not be "substantially transferred, reassigned, consolidated, or abolished" unless the Secretary of Defense reported the details of proposed changes to the armed services committees, and either house could reject such changes in a "major combatant function, power, or duty" by adopting a resolution asserting that it would "tend to impair the defense of the United States." When base closures were challenged under this statute, the courts consistently ruled that internal defense management decisions were discretionary, not ministerial, and hence that courts were without jurisdiction to review DOD's determinations. See *Armstrong* v. *United States,* 354 F2d 648 (9th Cir. 1965), *cert. denied* 384 U.S. 946, *affirming* 233 F Supp. 188 (S.D. Calif. 1964); *Local 1106, National Federation of Federal Employees* v. *Laird,* 318 F Supp. 153 (1970); *Disabled American Veterans Department of New York, Inc.* v. *United States,* 365 F Supp. 1190 (E.D.N.Y., 1973); *Perkins* v. *Rumsfeld,* 577 F2d 366 (6th Cir. 1978). The one-house veto technique was held to be unconstitutional in *Immigration and Naturalization Service* v. *Chadha,* 103 S. Ct. 2764 (1983). In accordance with that ruling, the Goldwater-Nichols Department of Defense Reorganization Act of 1986 eliminated the one-house veto provision from 10 *U.S.C.* section 125 [Act of October 1, 1986, Pub. L. No. 99-433, sections 103, 301(b)(1), 514(c)(1), 100 Stat. 992 at 996].

17. *Congressional Record* 111, Part 14, 89th Cong., 1st Sess., H. Rept. No. 713 (August 4, 1965): 19410 ff., at 19421.

18. Lyndon B. Johnson, "Military Authorization Act of 1965, Veto Message from the President of the United States, August 21, 1965," *Weekly Compilation of Presidential Documents* 1 (1965): 132.

19. Military Construction Authorization Act, 1966, Act of Sept. 16, 1965, Pub. L. No. 89-188, Section 611, 79 Stat. 793 at 818; Lyndon B. Johnson, "Military Construction Authorization Act for Fiscal Year 1966, Statement by the President Upon Signing the Bill Into Law, September 16, 1965," *Weekly Compilation of Presidential Documents* 1 (1965): 275. The 250-employee threshold was significant: of 127 military installations in the United States and Puerto Rico affected by the base closure announcement of December 8, 1965, only sixteen came under the provisions of section 611. See House Committee on Armed Services, Subcommittee No. 4, Hearings, *Base Closures and Reductions,* 89th Cong., 2d Sess., Jan. 25–26, 1966, p. 6398.

20. Randall Fitzgerald and Gerald Lipson, *Porkbarrel: The Unexpurgated Grace Commission Story of Congressional Profligacy* (Washington, D.C.: Cato Institute, 1984), p. 17.

21. House Committee on Post Office and Civil Service, Subcommittee on Retirement and Employee Benefits, Hearings, *Federal Employee Assistance in a Reduction in Force,* 93d Cong., 1st Sess., Serial No. 93-21, June 5, 6, 8, 1973; Senate Committee on Armed Services, Subcommittee on Military Construction, Hearings, *Base Closures or Realignment Program, Massachusetts,* 93d Cong., 1st Sess., Part 1, June 21–22, 1973, Part 2, June 22, 1973; U.S. Senate, Committee on Armed Services, Subcommittee on Military Construction, Hearing, *Base Closures or Realignment Program, California,* 93d Cong., 1st Sess., Part 3, June 28, 1973.

22. S. 1548, 93d Cong., 1st Sess. (1973).

23. *Congressional Record* 122, Part 19, 94th Cong., 2d Sess. (July 22, 1976): 23365 ff., 23368.

24. Gerald R. Ford, "Veto of the Military Construction Bill, The President's Message to the House of Representatives Returning H.R. 12384 Without His Approval, July 2, 1976," *Weekly Compilation of Presidential Documents* 12, no. 27, Book 2 (1976): 1113.

25. For the House debate and override vote, see *Congressional Record* 122, Part 19, 94th Cong., 2d Sess. (July 22, 1976): 23421 ff., 23433. The House vote was: yeas—270, nays—131, not voting—31. For the Senate debate and override vote see *Congressional Record* 122, Part 19, 94th Cong., 2d Sess. (July 22, 1976): 23365 ff., 23373. The Senate vote was: yeas—51, nays—42, not voting—7.

26. *Congressional Record* 122, Part 24, 94th Cong., 2d Sess. (Sept. 16, 1976): 30868 [remarks of Representative Ichord].

27. Military Construction Authorization Act, 1977, Act of Sept. 30, 1976 [H.R. 14846], Pub. L. No. 94-431, section 612, 90 Stat. 1349 at 1366.

28. *Congressional Record* 122, Part 24, 94th Cong., 2d Sess. (Sept. 16, 1976): 30868 [remarks of Representative Ichord].

29. Gerald R. Ford, "Military Construction Authorization Bill, Statement by the President on Signing H.R. 14846 into Law, September 30, 1976," *Weekly Compilation of Presidential Documents* 12, no. 40, Book 2 (1976): 1422.

30. Military Construction Authorization Act, 1978, Act of August 1, 1977, Pub. L. No. 95-82, section 612, 91 Stat. 358 at 379.

31. Senate Committee on Armed Services, Subcommittee on Military Construction, Hearing, *Base Closures,* 99th Cong., 1st Sess., May 2, 1985, p. 11 [testimony of Dr. Lawrence J. Korb, Assistant Secretary of Defense for Manpower, Installations and Logistics].

32. The hearings were endless. See, e.g., U.S. Senate, Committee on Armed Services, Subcommittee on Military Construction and Stockpiles, Hearing, *Department of Defense Base Realignment Policy,* 95th Cong., 2d Sess., August 4, 1978; House Committee on Appropriations, Subcommittee on Military Construction, Hearings, *Base Closures and Realignments Proposed by Department of Defense, Fiscal Year 1979,* 96th Cong., 1st Sess., April 25, 27, 1979; U.S. Senate, Committee on Armed Services, Subcommittee on Military Construction and Stockpiles, Hearings, *Department of Defense Base Closures/Alignments,* 96th Cong., 1st Sess., May 1, 16, June 13, 1979; U.S. Senate, Committee on Appropriations, Subcommittee on Military Construction, Special Hearing, *Installation Realignments,* 96th Cong., 1st Sess., May 10, 1979.

33. House Committee on Armed Services, Subcommittee on Military Installations and Facilities, Hearing, *Base Closures and Realignments,* 99th Cong., 1st Sess., June 12, 1985, p. 16 [testimony of Dr. Lawrence J. Korb, Assistant Secretary for Manpower, Installations and Logistics, Department of Defense].

34. Senate Committee on Armed Services, Hearings, *Department of Defense Authorization for Appropriations for Fiscal Year 1986,* 99th Cong., 1st Sess., S. Hrg.

99-58, Part 1, Feb. 4, 1985, pp. 14–15, 101 [testimony and submission for the record of Defense Secretary Weinberger].

35. Department of Defense Authorization Act, 1986, Act of November 8, 1985 [S. 1160], Pub. L. No. 99-145, section 1202, 99 Stat. 583 at 716.

36. Richard A. Stubbing, *The Defense Game: An Insider Explores the Astonishing Realities of America's Defense Establishment* (New York: Harper and Row, 1986), pp. 13–14, 29–30.

37. Defense Authorization Amendments and Base Closure and Realignment Act, Act of October 24, 1988, Pub. L. No. 100-526, Title II, 102 Stat. 2623.

38. Although the 1988 law gave the Commission on Base Realignment and Closure its formal authority, Defense Secretary Frank Carlucci established the Commission and appointed its first nine members earlier in the year under a special "charter" agreement signed May 3, 1988. The Commission held its first hearings on June 8, 1988—a novel political relationship between bureaucratic cart and statutory horse. One rationale for the procedure was to reassure congressmembers of the integrity, expertise, and nonpartisan outlook of the commissioners before Congress faced a vote on the bill. The final bill increased the Commission's membership from nine to twelve, a compromise between those wanting to broaden its geographic representation by increasing membership to fifteen—a number DOD believed unworkable given the statutory time constraints—and those desiring to retain only the original nine members.

39. See note 38 for discussion of the preappointment strategy used to reassure Congress of the nonpartisan nature of the Commission.

40. See the later section of this paper entitled "Congressional Resistance: The Non-Parochial Rationale." See also Dick Armey, "Base Maneuvers," *Policy Review* (1988), pp. 70–75.

41. Affecting 145 installations, these recommendations are predicted to imply a twenty-year savings with a net present value of $5.C billion (using a 10 percent discount rate and 3 percent annual inflation rate). The Commission's report states that "Of this number, 86 are to be closed fully, five are to be closed in part, and 54 will experience a change, either an increase or a decrease, as units and activities are relocated." U.S. Dept. of Defense, December 1988, p. 6.

42. The joint resolution of disapproval (H.J. Res. 165) failed in the House by a vote of 43–381. Therefore the Senate was not required to bring the issue to a vote, since passage by *both* chambers was prerequisite to rejecting the Commission's plan.

43. See *Congressional Record,* July 12, 1988, pp. H5429–H5448.

44. Loopholes in the statute are discussed in the final section of this chapter. Apart from these loopholes a cynic might add that, with Congress never losing under the old rules, individual congressmembers in recent years experienced reduced opportunities for claiming personal credit for saving a local military base. From this perspective, "reform" ironically might expand such credit-claiming opportunities.

45. *Congressional Record* 131, No. 69, 99th Cong., 1st Sess. (May 23, 1985): S6983 [remarks of Senator Barry Goldwater].

46. House Committee on Post Office and Civil Service, Subcommittee on Retirement and Employee Benefits, Hearings, *Federal Employee Assistance in a Reduction in Force,* 93d Cong., 1st Sess., Serial No. 93-21, June 5, 6, 8, 1973, pp. 7–8 [remarks of Representative Jerome Waldie].

47. House Committee on Appropriations, Subcommittee on Military Construction Appropriations, Hearings, *Base Closures and Realignments Proposed by Department of Defense, Fiscal Year 1979,* 96th Cong., 1st Sess., April 25, 27, 1979, p. 109 [testimony of Senator John Glenn].

48. House Committee on Armed Services, Subcommittee on Military Installations and Facilities, Hearing, *Base Closures and Realignments,* 99th Cong., 1st

Sess., June 12, 1985, pp. 53–54 [testimony of Dr. Lawrence J. Korb, Assistant Secretary of Defense for Manpower, Installations and Logistics].

49. Military Construction Authorization Act, 1972, Act of Oct. 27, 1971 [H.R. 9844], Pub. L. No. 92-146, section 709, 85 Stat. 394 at 414.

50. National Defense Authorization Act for Fiscal Year 1987, Act of Nov. 14, 1986, Pub. L. No. 99-661, section 1362, 100 Stat. 3816 at 4001.

51. Military Construction Authorization Act, 1968, Act of Oct. 21, 1967, Pub. L. No. 90-110, section 810, 81 Stat. 279.

52. *Congressional Record* 113, Part 16, 90th Cong., 1st Sess. (August 1, 1967): 20798 ff. [the "sacred cows" remark of Representative Mathias of Maryland appears on p. 20799]. The "parochial imperative" phrase is from Fitzgerald and Lipson, *Porkbarrel*, p. xviii. Fitzgerald and Lipson there define the "parochial imperative" as "an excessive preoccupation with the local impact of spending decisions at the expense of the national interest," which they regard as a "congressional compulsion."

53. Military Construction Authorization Act, 1968, Act of Oct. 21, 1967, Pub. L. No. 90-110, section 809, 81 Stat. 279.

54. House Committee on Armed Services, Subcommittee on Military Installations and Facilities, Hearing, *Base Closures and Realignments,* 99th Cong., 1st Sess., June 12, 1985, pp. 4, 21 [remarks of Representative Dickinson at p. 21].

55. Ibid., p. 3 [testimony of Dr. Lawrence J. Korb].

56. U.S. Senate, Committee on Public Works, Subcommittee on Economic Development, Hearing, *Loring Air Force Base,* 94th Cong., 2d Sess., Serial No. 94-H46, May 10, 1976.

57. Senate Committee on Armed Services, Subcommittee on Military Construction and Stockpiles, Hearings, *Department of Defense Base Closures/Alignments,* 96th Cong., 1st Sess., May 1, 16, June 13, 1979, pp. 111-118 [testimony of Senators Muskie and Cohen; Senator Muskie's statement appears on p. 113].

58. House Committee on Armed Services, Subcommittee on Military Installations and Facilities, Hearing, *Base Closures and Realignments,* 99th Cong., 1st Sess., June 12, 1985, p. 22 [testimony of Dr. Lawrence J. Korb]; General Accounting Office (GAO), *Phased Reduction of Loring Air Force Base,* B-172707, LCD-79-322, 110042 GAO Documents, August 8, 1979 (Washington, D.C.: U.S. Government Printing Office, 1979), p. 1.

59. House Committee on Armed Services, Subcommittee on Military Installations and Facilities, Hearing, *Base Closures and Realignments,* 99th Cong., 1st Sess., June 12, 1985, pp. 8, 60 [testimony of Dr. Lawrence J. Korb].

60. General Accounting Office (GAO), *Review of the Army's Decision to Disestablish the Training Center at Fort Dix, New Jersey,* B-17207, LCD-79-325 (Washington, D.C.: U.S. Government Printing Office, 1979), p. 2. Hearings were held in 1979 by the House Appropriations Committee's Subcommittee on Military Construction Appropriations, by the Senate Armed Services Committee's Subcommittee on Military Construction and Stockpiles, and by the Senate Appropriations Committee's Subcommittee on Military Construction.

61. See, e.g., U.S. House of Representatives, Committee on Armed Services, *Military Construction Authorization Act, 1982,* 97th Cong., 1st Sess., Report No. 97-44, May 15, 1981 (Washington, D.C.: U.S. Government Printing Office, 1981), p. 23 [$18.6 million barracks modernization at Fort Dix not requested by the Army].

62. *Congressional Record* 131, No. 69, 99th Cong., 1st Sess. (May 23, 1985): S 6979 [remarks of Senator Bumpers].

63. House Committee on Armed Services, Subcommittee for Special Investigations, *Military Base Closures,* 87th Cong., 1st Sess., hearings held July 13-14, 1961, report dated August 1, 1961, pp. 86-87 [statement by Representative Kilgore].

64. *Congressional Record* 122, Part 19, 94th Cong., 2d Sess., (July 22, 1976): 23431 [remarks of Representative Dominick V. Daniels]; U.S. House of Representatives, Committee on Armed Services, *House Report No. 99-81,* 99th Cong., 1st Sess., May 10, 1985, p. 452 [views of Representative Patricia Schroeder].

65. *Congressional Record* 131, No. 69, 99th Cong., 1st Sess. (May 23, 1985): S6987 [remark of Senator Levin and "hardball" remark of Senator Specter], S 6988 [remark of Senator Bumpers].

66. Ibid. at S 6980 [remark of Senator Heinz], S 6986 [remark of Senator Specter].

67. Seymour Melman, *The Permanent War Economy: American Capitalism in Decline* (New York: Simon and Schuster, 1974), p. 259; U.S. Senate, Committee on Armed Services, Subcommittee on Military Construction, *Base Closures,* 99th Cong., 1st Sess., May 2, 1985, p. 14.

68. Ibid., S 6979 [remarks of Senator Bumpers], S 6981 [remarks of Senator Heinz on the "extraordinary correlations"], S 6983 [the *Washington Times* story].

69. Senate Committee on Armed Services, Subcommittee on Military Construction, Hearing, *Base Closures,* 99th Cong., 1st Sess., May 2, 1985, p. 14 [remark of Senator Levin]; pp. 25–26 [remarks of Senator Gary Hart].

70. House Committee on Armed Services, Subcommittee for Special Investigations, *Military Base Closures,* 87th Cong., 1st Sess., hearings held July 13–14, 1961, report dated August 1, 1961, pp. 158–59.

71. *Congressional Record* 111, Part 10, 89th Cong., 1st Sess. (June 10, 1965); 13244–45 [remarks of Representative Randall].

72. U.S. Senate, Committee on Armed Services, Subcommittee on Military Construction, Hearing, *Base Closures or Realignment Program, Massachusetts,* Part 2, 93d Cong., 1st Sess., June 22, 1973, p. 255 [statement by Senator Pastore].

73. *Congressional Record* 122, Part 19, 94th Cong., 2d Sess. (July 22, 1976): 23431 [remarks of Representative Flowers].

74. Senate Committee on Armed Services, Subcommittee on Military Construction, Hearing, *Base Closures or Realignment Program, Massachusetts,* Part 1, 93d Cong., 1st Sess., June 21–22, 1973, p. 96 [testimony of Representative Heckler]; House Committee on Post Office and Civil Service, Subcommittee on Retirement and Employee Benefits, Hearings, *Federal Employee Assistance in a Reduction in Force,* 93d Cong., 1st Sess., Serial No. 93–21, June 5, 6, 8, 1973, pp. 78–79.

75. Senate Committee on Armed Services, Subcommittee on Military Construction, Hearing, *Base Closures or Realignment Program, Massachusetts,* Part 1, 93d Cong., 1st Sess., June 21–22, 1973, pp. 5–6. Chafee's election plans were common knowledge at least as early as December 1971.

76. Ibid., p. 13.

77. Although he lost in 1972 against Pell, Chafee was elected to the U.S. Senate in 1976 when John Pastore retired. In 1988, Chafee was reelected for his third term.

78. Senate Committee on Armed Services, Subcommittee on Military Construction, Hearing, *Base Closures or Realignment Program, Massachusetts,* Parts 1 and 2, 93d Cong., 1st Sess., June 21–22, 1973, pp. 13–14, 237–57 [remark of Senator Pastore appears on pp. 256–57].

79. *Congressional Record* 111, Part 11, 89th Cong., 1st Sess. (June 28, 1965): 15006 [remarks of Senator McIntyre]; *Congressional Record* 122, Part 19, 94th Cong., 2d Sess. (July 22, 1976): 23430 [remarks of Representative Conte].

80. House Committee on Armed Services, Subcommittee No. 4, Hearings, *Base Closures and Reductions,* 89th Cong., 2d Sess., Jan. 25–26, 1966, p. 6414.

81. *Congressional Record* 122, Part 19, 94th Cong., 2d Sess. (July 22, 1976):

23429 [remarks of Representative Dodd], 23425 [remarks of Representative Bauman].

82. Senate Committee on Armed Services, Subcommittee on Military Construction, Hearing, *Base Closures or Realignment Program, California,* Part 3, 93d Cong., 1st Sess, June 28, 1973, pp. 35–38, 73–76 [statement by Senator Alan Cranston appears on p. 35].

83. U.S. Senate, Committee on Armed Services, Subcommittee on Military Construction, Hearing, *Proposed Movement of Air Force Communications Service to Scott Air Force Base,* 94th Cong., 2d Sess., Sept. 15, 1976, p. 66 [statement by Representative William J. Randall].

84. Ibid., pp. 78–79.

85. Ibid., pp. 17–33.

86. Ibid., pp. 2 [statement by Representative Richard Bolling], 75–77.

87. *Congressional Record* 131, No. 69, 99th Cong., 1st Sess. (May 23, 1985): S6988 [remarks of Senator Strom Thurmond].

88. John E. Lynch, *Local Economic Development after Military Base Closures* (New York: Praeger, 1970), p. 7; U.S. Senate, Committee on Armed Services, Subcommittee on Military Construction, Hearing, *Base Closures,* 99th Cong., 1st Sess., May 2, 1985, p. 11 [testimony of Dr. Lawrence J. Korb].

89. Senate Committee on Armed Services, Subcommittee on Military Construction, Hearing, *Base Closures,* 99th Cong., 1st Sess., May 2, 1985, p. 1 [statement by Senator Strom Thurmond], p. 11 [statements by Senator Phil Gramm and Dr. Lawrence J. Korb]; *Congressional Record* 131, No. 69, 99th Cong., 1st Sess. (May 23, 1985): S6987 [remarks of Senator Thurmond]; House Committee on Armed Services, Subcommittee on Military Installations and Facilities, Hearing, *Base Closures and Realignments,* 99th Cong., 1st Sess., June 12, 1985, p. 12 [testimony of Dr. Lawrence J. Korb].

90. Senate Committee on Armed Services, Subcommittee on Military Construction, Hearing, *Base Closures,* 99th Cong., 1st Sess., May 2, 1985, p. 17 [statement by Senator Phil Gramm].

91. House Committee on Post Office and Civil Service, Subcommittee on Retirement and Employee Benefits, Hearings, *Federal Employee Assistance in a Reduction in Force,* 93d Cong., 1st Sess., Serial No. 93-21, June 5, 6, 8, 1973, p. 10 [testimony of Professor Seymour Melman].

92. *Congressional Record* 131, No. 69, 99th Cong., 1st Sess. (May 23, 1985): S6981–82 [remarks of Senator Phil Gramm].

93. House Committee on Post Office and Civil Service, Subcommittee on Retirement and Employee Benefits, Hearings, *Federal Employee Assistance in a Reduction in Force,* 93d Cong., 1st Sess., Serial No. 93-21 June 5, 6, 8, 1973, p. 32 [statement by Representative Lawrence Hogan]; *Congressional Record* 122, Part 19, 94th Cong., 2d Sess. (July 22, 1976): 23369 [remarks of Senator George McGovern].

94. James Buchanan and Gordon Tullock, *The Calculus of Consent* (Ann Arbor: University of Michigan Press, 1962), pp. 77–80.

95. Senate Committee on Armed Services, Subcommittee on Military Construction, Hearing, *Base Closures,* 99th Cong., 1st Sess., May 2, 1985, p. 30 [statement by Senator Phil Gramm].

96. Melman, *The Permanent War Economy,* p. 250. For extensive discussion of successful and unsuccessful conversion efforts, see Lynch, *Local Economic Development after Military Base Closures.* See also Seymour Melman, ed., *The Defense Economy: Conversion of Industries and Occupations to Civilian Needs* (New York: Praeger, 1970).

97. Senate Committee on Armed Services, Subcommittee on Military Con-

struction, Hearing, *Base Closures,* 99th Cong., 1st Sess., May 2, 1985, pp. 6–7 [testimony of Dr. Lawrence J. Korb]. See also House Committee on Armed Services, Subcommittee on Military Installations and Facilities, Hearing, *Base Closures and Realignments,* 99th Cong., 1st Sess., June 12, 1985, pp. 25–49 [Office of Economic Adjustment, Report, "Summary of Completed Military Base Economic Adjustment Projects—1961–1981, 20 Years of Civilian Reuse," November 1981]; and Julius Duscha, *Arms, Money, and Politics* (New York: Ives Washburn, 1965), pp.158–74.

98. Lynch, *Local Economic Development after Military Base Closures,* pp. 34–43.

99. Stubbing, *The Defense Game,* pp. 253–55.

100. Defense Authorization Amendments and Base Closure and Realignment Act, Act of October 24, 1988, Pub. L. No. 100-526, Title II, 102 Stat. 2623. See notes 37–40 and accompanying text for discussion of major features of this act.

101. See David R. Mayhew, *Congress: The Electoral Connection* (New Haven and London, Yale University Press, 1974), on position-taking and credit-claiming.

102. However, Congress retained a provision requiring the Defense Secretary to study the overseas base structure for possible efficiencies attainable through closure or realignment and to report the results of that study to the Commission by October 15, 1988. Alan J. Dixon (Ill.), chairman of a seventeen-member Northeast-Midwest Senate Coalition, quickly impugned DOD's report that no overseas bases need be closed. His coalition by letter urged the Commission on Base Realignment and Closure to consider "regional inequities stemming from the location of existing military facilities." (Quoted in *Insight,* November 21, 1988, p. 29.) The same article noted that the Pentagon had cited three installations in northern Illinois for possible closure.

103. Actual appropriations, of course, remained an unresolved question.

104. *Congressional Record* 134, October 11, 1988, p. H9947 (Conference Report on S. 2749, Defense Authorization Amendments and Base Closure and Realignment Act, House Report 100-1071).

105. See Fred Thompson, "Why America's Military Base Structure Cannot Be Reduced," *Public Administration Review* (January/February 1988), pp. 557–563; at pp.559–560 for a discussion of the cumbersome procedures required under Federal Property and Administrative Services Act regulations governing disposal of military property.

106. Thompson reports the previous procedure with respect to land sales: "The military gain nothing from the sale of land; receipts from land sales go not to the military branch holding the asset but to the Land and Water Conservation Fund of the Treasury." See ibid., pp. 557–58.

107. For example, civil suits under NEPA against the Commission or the Defense Secretary must be brought within 60 days of the occurrence of the challenged action.

108. I am indebted to Brian Gunderson, Congressional aide to Representative Armey, for his insights regarding this provision.

109. *Congressional Record,* 100th Cong., 2nd Sess. (October 12, 1988): p. H10035.

110. Ibid. (July 12, 1988): pp. H5440, H5437.

111. See Twight, "Government Manipulation of Constitutional-Level Transaction Costs: A General Theory of Transaction-Cost Augmentation and the Growth of Government," *Public Choice* 56 (1988): 131-152.

112. Lynch, *Local Economic Development after Military Base Closures,* p. 5.

113. *Congressional Record* 122, Part 19, 94th Cong., 2d Sess. (July 22, 1976): 23372 [remarks of Senator Strom Thurmond].

Notes on Contributors

ROBERT HIGGS is the Thomas F. Gleed Professor in the Albers School of Business, Seattle University. He received his Ph.D. in economics from the Johns Hopkins University, has taught at the University of Washington and Lafayette College, and was a visiting scholar at Oxford University and Stanford University. A contributor to many professional journals, popular periodicals, and leading newspapers, and the editor of the volume, *Emergence of the Modern Political Economy*, Professor Higgs is the author of three previous books: *The Transformation of the American Economy, 1865–1914: An Essay in Interpretation; Competition and Coercion: Blacks in the American Economy, 1865–1914;* and *Crisis and Leviathan: Critical Episodes in the Growth of American Government.*

JEFFREY ROGERS HUMMEL is Publications Director for the Independent Institute. He received his M.A. in history from the University of Texas at Austin, and teaches economics at Golden Gate University. He previously prepared audiotape scripts on American history for Knowledge Products. Hummel has also contributed articles to such varied publications as the *Texas Law Review,* the *Encyclopedia of American Business History and Biography,* the *Journal of Libertarian Studies,* and *Reason Papers.*

WILLIAM E. KOVACIC is Assistant Professor of Law at the George Mason University School of Law. A graduate of Columbia University Law School and a member of the New York Bar, Professor Kovacic worked as a *New York Times* reporter, staff member of Congress, attorney at the Federal Trade Commission, and lawyer in private practice, where his clients included a number of firms in the defense industry. He has written extensively for newspapers, law reviews, and other publications.

DON LAVOIE is Associate Professor of Economics at George Mason University and editor of *Market Process,* published by the Center for the Study of Market Processes. He received his Ph.D. from New York University and has authored two books: *Rivalry and Central Planning: The Socialist Calculation Debate Reconsidered* and *National Economic Planning: What Is Left?*

Professor Lavoie is also a co-editor, with A. Klamer, of a book series on interpretative economics.

DWIGHT R. LEE is Professor of Economics and holder of the Ramsey Chair of Free Enterprise at the University of Georgia. He received his Ph.D. from the University of California, San Diego, and previously taught at the University of Colorado, Virginia Polytechnic Institute and State University, and George Mason University. In addition to writing for professional and popular journals, Professor Lee edited *Taxation and the Deficit Economy: Fiscal Policy and Capital Formation in the United States,* and co-authored *Economics in Our Time: Concepts and Issues* (with R. F McNown); *Economics in Our Time: Macro Issues* (with R. F McNown); *Microeconomics: Theory and Applications* (with F Glahe); and *Regulating Government: A Preface to Constitutional Economics* (with R. B. McKenzie).

FRANK R. LICHTENBERG is Associate Professor in the Graduate School of Business at Columbia University, where he has taught since 1983. The holder of a Ph.D. from the University of Pennsylvania, he has written for such leading economics journals as the *Review of Economics and Statistics* and the *American Economic Review.* In 1986, the *Wall Street Journal* featured on its editorial page Professor Lichtenberg's analysis of the relation between military R & D spending and productivity growth rates among major industrial countries.

JAMES M. LINDSAY is Assistant Professor of Political Science at the University of Iowa. Educated at the University of Michigan (B.A.) and Yale University (Ph.D.), he was a researcher in residence at the Brookings Institution during the 1986–1987 academic year. Professor Lindsay's articles have appeared in *Armed Forces & Society* and the *Washington Quarterly.*

KENNETH R. MAYER is Assistant Professor of Political Science at the University of Wisconsin. He has worked as a researcher at the Center for International Affairs at Harvard University, as a researcher in residence at the Brookings Institution, and as a consultant to the Rand Corporation. During 1985–1986, Professor Mayer was a Contract Specialist for the Naval Air Systems Command.

ILAN PELEG is Professor and chairman of the Department of Government and Law at Lafayette College. A native of Israel, he holds degrees from Tel-Aviv University (B.A., M.A.) and Northwestern University (M.A., Ph.D.). He has written numerous articles and reviews on foreign policy, terrorism, and the arms trade. Professor Peleg is also the author of *Begin's Foreign Policy, 1977–1983: Israel's Move to the Right.*

JORDAN A. SCHWARZ is Presidential Research Professor in the Department of History at Northern Illinois University. He received his Ph.D. from Columbia University. He was awarded a Guggenheim Fellowship in 1985–1986. Professor Schwarz is the author of *Liberal: Adolf A. Berle and the Vision of an American Era* and *The Speculator: Bernard M. Baruch in Washington, 1917–1965;* the co-author of *Generations of Americans: A History of the United*

States; and the editor of *The Ordeal of Twentieth-Century America: Interpretative Readings* and *1933 Roosevelt's Decision: The U.S. Leaves the Gold Standard.*

CHARLOTTE TWIGHT is Associate Professor of Economics at Boise State University. Holder of a J.D. from the University of Washington School of Law as well as a Ph.D. in economics from the University of Washington, she is a member of the Washington State Bar. Professor Twight is the author of *America's Emerging Fascist Economy* and several professional articles, and she is currently collaborating with Robert Higgs on a book about Congressional parochialism and the economics of defense.

Index

Aberdeen Proving Ground, transfer of, 260

Abolitionist movement, 48

Acquisition, Under Secretary of Defense for: creation of, 82; first appointment to, 84

Addabbo, Joseph, 176

Advertising expenditure, 155

Agricultural Adjustment Administration (AAA), 11

Aircraft, dispersion of subcontracts for, 222–23t

Air Force Communication Service (AFCS), 261; debate over relocation of, 273n

Altruism, 50, 52

American Bar Association Commission to Study the Federal Trade Commission, 94n

Apache helicopter: dispersion of total program and subcontracts for, 227–28t; state distribution of subcontractors of, 226t; subcontractors on, 225–28; target detection and infrared vision, system of, 225

Arends, Rep., 240

Armed forces, shortage of men and materials in, xvi

Armed Services Board of Contract Appeals, 68–70; unifying operations of, 70

Armed Services Procurement Act, failure to recognize negotiated procurement method, 74

Armed Services Procurement Act of 1947, 65, 113, 223n; 1962 Amendments to, 97n; procurement procedure under, 67

Armed Services Procurement Regulations, 74–75, 233n; expansion of, 69

Armey, Richard, 181, 249; military base closure bill of, 195, 250, 268; on military spending, 193; on waste reduction program, 270

Arms companies, in news, xx–xxiii

Arms contracts, competitive bidding for, xvi. See also Defense contracts

Arms control lobbyists, 191

Arms procurement, unusual aspects of, xxv–xxvii. See also Weapons procurement

Arms transfer: Carter vs. Reagan administration policy on, 132–54; domestic environment for, 135–36; ideological commitment in, 134–35; increase in dollar volume of, 143; international environment for, 135–36; from 1965 to 1985, 142t; perspectives on, 136–48; policy results of, 148–52; political utility of, 149–50; promotion perspective on, 138–40, 144–48; restraint perspective on, 138–44; trends in, 143

Army, personnel strength in interwar years, xvi

Army Ballistic Missile Defense Command, 207

Arnold, R. Douglas, 179